Lecture Notes in Artificial Inte

Subseries of Lecture Notes in Computer Science
Edited by J. G. Carbonell and J. Siekmann

Lecture Notes in Computer Science

Edited by G. Goos, J. Hartmanis and J. van Leeuwen

Springer
Berlin
Heidelberg
New York
Barcelona
Hong Kong
London
Milan
Paris
Singapore
Tokyo

Mathias Bauer   Piotr J. Gmytrasiewicz
Julita Vassileva (Eds.)

User Modeling 2001

8th International Conference, UM 2001
Sonthofen, Germany, July 13-17, 2001
Proceedings

 Springer

Series Editors

Jaime G. Carbonell, Carnegie Mellon University, Pittsburgh, PA, USA
Jörg Siekmann, University of Saarland, Saarbrücken, Germany

Volume Editors

Mathias Bauer
German Research Center for Artificial Intelligence (DFKI GmbH)
Stuhlsatzenhausweg 3, 66123 Saarbrücken, Germany
E-mail: bauer@dfki.de

Piotr J. Gmytrasiewicz
University of Texas, CSE Department
Box 19015, Arlington, TX 76019-0015, USA
E-mail: piotr@cse.uta.edu

Julita Vassileva
University of Saskatchewan, Department of Computer Science ARIES
1C101 Engineering Bldg., 57 Campus Dr., Saskatoon, SK, Canada S7N 5A9
E-mail: jiv@cs.usask.ca

Cataloging-in-Publication Data applied for

Die Deutsche Bibliothek - CIP-Einheitsaufnahme

User modeling : 8th international conference ; proceedings / UM 2001,
Sonthofen, Germany, July 13 - 17, 2001. Mathias Bauer ... (ed.). - Berlin ;
Heidelberg ; New York ; Barcelona ; Hong Kong ; London ; Milan ; Paris ;
Singapore ; Tokyo : Springer, 2001
    (Lecture notes in computer science ; Vol. 2109 : Lecture notes in
    artificial intelligence)
    ISBN 3-540-42325-7

CR Subject Classification (1998): H.5.2, I.2, H.5, H.4, I.6, J.4, J.5, K.4, K.6

ISBN 3-540-42325-7 Springer-Verlag Berlin Heidelberg New York

Springer-Verlag Berlin Heidelberg New York
a member of BertelsmannSpringer Science+Business Media GmbH

http://www.springer.de

© Springer-Verlag Berlin Heidelberg 2001
Printed in Germany

Typesetting: Camera-ready by author, data conversion by Steingräber Satztechnik GmbH, Heidelberg
Printed on acid-free paper   SPIN: 10839786   06/3142   5 4 3 2 1 0

Preface

The study of the field of user modeling (UM) has resulted in significant amounts of theoretical work, as well as practical experience, in developing UM-based applications in traditional areas of human-computer interaction and tutoring systems. Further, it promises to have an enormous impact on recent developments in areas like information filtering, e-commerce, adaptive presentation techniques, and interface agents.

A user model is an explicit representation of properties of a particular user, which allows the system to adapt diverse aspects of its performance to individual users' needs. Techniques for UM have been developed and evaluated by theoreticians and practitioners in a variety of fields, including artificial intelligence, education, psychology, cognitive science, linguistics, and human-computer interaction.

The International Conferences on User Modeling constitute the major forum for presentation and discussion of both the latest developments in academic research on all aspects of user modeling and industrial experience in deploying adaptive systems in real-world applications. This volume contains the proceedings of the Eighth International Conference on User Modeling (UM 2001), held in Sonthofen, Germany. It follows UM99 (Banff, Canada), UM97 (Sardinia, Italy), UM96 (Hawaii, USA), UM94 (Hyannis, USA), UM92 (Dagstuhl, West Germany), UM90 (Hawaii, USA) and UM86 (Maria Laach, West Germany).

Until now, the proceedings of the conference have been published with university publishers. After discussions within UM Inc., it was decided from now on to publish the proceedings volume with one of the major publishing companies, to ensure wider availability of the volume in libraries and archives. After careful consideration Springer-Verlag was chosen.

The UM 2001 program includes tutorials, invited talks, technical paper and poster sessions, a doctoral consortium, workshops, and system demonstrations. There were a total of 79 technical submissions from 20 countries.

The submissions were reviewed by at least three, and in some cases by even five members of the program committee. The review process included discussions among the reviewers, and, ultimately, 19 submissions were accepted as full papers, resulting in a 24% acceptance rate. Another 20 submissions were accepted as posters.

Eight of the accepted full papers (highlighted in the table of contents by "(*)") were nominated by the program committee as candidates for the two outstanding paper awards:

- The Best Research Paper prize of $500, sponsored by Kluwer Publishers, publisher of the User Modeling and User-Adapted Interaction (UMUAI) journal.
- The Best Application Paper prize of $500, sponsored by HumanIT GmbH.

Three invited talks provided insight into important issues, applications and techniques for UM:

- Tailoring Privacy to the User's Needs by Alfred Kobsa,
- Heavyweight Applications of Lightweight User Models: A Look at Collaborative Filtering, Recommender Systems, and Real-Time Personalization by Joseph A. Konstan, and
- Eye Tracking: A Rich Source of Information for User Modeling by Sandra Marshall.

An integral part of the conference was the Doctoral Consortium. UM 2001 received 26 submissions for the Doctoral Consortium, 17 of which were accepted. Twelve of these have been published in the Doctoral Consortium section of this volume. The other five were submitted and accepted as papers or posters and appear in the corresponding sections of the volume.

This volume contains 19 full papers, summaries of the 20 poster presentations, contributions from the invited speakers, as well as summaries of 12 student presentations accepted at the doctoral symposium.

In addition to the contributions presented in this volume, the UM 2001 program featured three tutorials:

- User Modeling for Adaptive User Interfaces by Mark Maybury,
- Student Modeling for Adaptive Web-Based Educational Systems by Peter Brusilovsky, and
- Personalization for E-Commerce by Anthony Jameson.

Another major part of the UM 2001 program were the seven workshops, whose proceedings can be accessed via the web site of User Modeling Inc. (http://www.um.org). The workshops topics were:

- 3rd Workshop on Adaptive Hypertext and Hypermedia, organized by Paul De Bra, Peter Brusilovsky, and Alfred Kobsa.
- 2nd Workshop on Attitude, Personality, and Emotions in User-Adapted Interaction, organized by Fiorella de Rosis.
- Workshop on User Modeling for Context-Aware Applications, organized by Marcus Specht and Tom Gross.
- Workshop on Empirical Evaluations of Adaptive Systems, organized by Stephan Weibelzahl, David Chin, and Gerhard Weber.
- Workshop on Machine Learning, Information Retrieval, and User Modeling, organized by Ayse Göker, Fabio Abbattista, Ross Wilkinson, and Giovanni Semeraro.
- Workshop on Machine Learning for User Modeling, organized by Ralph Schäfer, Martin E. Müller, and Sofus Attila Macskassy.
- Workshop on Personalization in Future TV, organized by Liliana Ardissono and Yassine Faihe.

Acknowledgements

Putting together a program for UM 2001 was a difficult undertaking, and this year's conference owed its high quality to many people. The members of the Program Committee deserve great credit, for the considerable effort in reviewing the submissions, for their dedication in writing detailed and high-quality reviews, for their participation in the selection of invited speakers and the winners of the best paper awards.

Liliana Ardissono, Italy
Ben du Boulay, UK
Susan Bull, Canada
David Chin, USA
Abigail Gertner, USA
Russ Greiner, Canada
Anthony Jameson, Germany
Judy Kay, Australia
Neal Lesh, USA
Mark Maybury, USA
Antonija Mitrovic, New Zealand
Ann Nicholson, Australia
Cecile Paris, Australia
Fiorella de Rosis, Italy
Adelheit Stein, Germany
Loren Terveen, USA
Ingrid Zukerman, Australia

David Benyon, UK
Peter Brusilovsky, USA
Sandra Carberry, USA
Gerhard Fischer, USA
Brad Goodman, USA
Eric Horvitz, USA
Paul Kamsteeg, The Netherlands
Alfred Kobsa, USA
Diane Litman, USA
Michael McTear, UK
Riichiro Mizoguchi, Japan
Toshikazu Nishimura, Japan
Charles Rich, USA
John Self, UK
Carlo Tasso, Italy
Wolfgang Wahlster, Germany

We would also like to thank the additional reviewers:

Fabio Abbattista,Italy
Elisabeth Andre, Germany
Joseph Beck, USA
Rogerio DePaula, USA
Andy Gorman, USA
Martin Klesen, Germany
Gord McCalla, Canada
Yunwen Ye, USA

Taro Adachi, USA
Mathias Bauer, Germany
Leo Burd, USA
Hal Eden, USA
Jim Greer, Canada
Shin'ichi Konomi, USA
Eric Scharff, USA

The Doctoral Consortium chair was Gordon McCalla, from the University of Saskatchewan, Canada. He was assisted by the following members of his committee:

Leila Alem, Australia
David Chin, USA
Cristina Conati, Canada
Isabel Fernandez de Castro, Spain
Frank Linton, USA
Fiorella de Rosis, Italy

Paul Brna, UK
Robin Cohen, Canada
Helen Gigley, USA
Judy Kay, Australia
Riichiro Mizoguchi, Japan
Gerhard Weber, Germany

Special thanks for providing financial support for graduate students to attend the UM 2001 doctoral consortium and the conference go to

- Dr. Helen Gigley and the Office of Naval Research, and
- UM Inc.

We would like to thank the University of Twente for creating and allowing us to use CyberChair (http://www.cyberchair.org), a free web-based application facilitating the paper submission and reviewing process.

We are grateful to the University of Texas at Arlington for supporting the electronic paper and review submission process. In particular, we want to thank Bharaneedharan Rathnasabapathy who installed and adapted CyberChair and fine-tuned the scripts for generating author notifications.

Special thanks are due to the local organizers of the conference at DFKI in Saarbrücken, Germany:

Andrea Placzkova
Dietmar Dengler
Gabriele Paul

who contributed in many ways to the preparation of the conference and to Eric Schwarz-kopf for designing and maintaining the adaptive conference web-site.

Anthony Jameson has been the community spirit and memory of the UM conferences. He was a valuable source of expertise and encouragement and provided immediate responses to all of our questions and worries during the two years of preparation for this conference.

The UM 2001 conference was also made possible by generous contributions from our sponsors. These include: 7d AG (Germany), sponsor of the Conference Banquet; Atrada AG (Germany) and DFKI GmbH (Germany), sponsors of the conference organization and logistics; humanIT GmbH (Germany), sponsor of the Best Application Paper prize; Kluwer Academic Publishers, sponsor of the Best Research Paper prize; and the Trends in Cognitive Sciences Journal, which partially sponsored the invited talks.

May 2001   Mathias Bauer
                                                                                Piotr Gmytrasiewicz
                                                                                Julita Vassileva

Table of Contents

Doctoral Consortium

Invited Talks

Full Papers

Harnessing Models of Users' Goals to Mediate Clarification Dialog in Spoken Language Systems

Eric Horvitz and Tim Paek

One Microsoft Way
Microsoft Research
Redmond, WA 98052-6399
{horvitz,timpaek } @microsoft.com

Abstract. Speaker-independent speech recognition systems are being used with increasing frequency for command and control applications. To date, users of such systems must contend with their fragility to subtle changes in language usage and environmental acoustics. We describe work on coupling speech recognition systems with temporal probabilistic user models that provide inferences about the intentions associated with utterances. The methods can be employed to enhance the robustness of speech recognition by endowing systems with an ability to reason about the costs and benefits of action in a setting and to make decisions about the best action to take given uncertainty about the meaning behind acoustic signals. The methods have been implemented in the form of a dialog clarification module that can be integrated with legacy spoken language systems. We describe representation and inference procedures and present details on the operation of an implemented spoken command and control development environment called DeepListener.

Keywords : Dialog systems, clarification dialog, spoken command and control, speech recognition, conversational systems

1 Introduction

Science-fiction writers have long assumed that computer systems will one day have the ability to understand spoken input and to interact with people in a fluid, natural manner via conversational dialog. To date, most automatic speech recognition (ASR) research has centered on the refinement of acoustic and language models for identifying words from acoustic signals. Progress has been steady but incremental with this approach, with recognition error rates dropping on average by a small percentage each year.

We have pursued opportunities for making a qualitative leap forward in the robustness of ASR through the coupling of traditional low-level speech models with higher-level models of a user's intentions. The user models take into consideration the costs and benefits of taking dierent actions based on utterances, and the expected utility of seeking clarification about a user's intentions before taking action.

We focus in this paper on work to enhance the robustness of speech recognition for command-and-control systems. Spoken command-and-control systems

M. Bauer, P.J. Gmytrasiewicz, and J. Vassileva (Eds.): UM 2001, LNAI 2109, pp. 3–13, 2001.

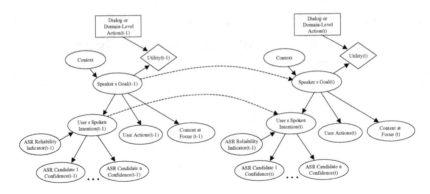

Fig. 1. A dynamic Bayesian network for reasoning about a user's goals given a sequence of utterances over time.

have been growing in popularity as a means for allowing people to control a variety of telephony and software services in a handsfree manner. A number of applications attempt to use speech recognition for guiding services in challenging acoustical contexts, such as interaction via a telephone or standard built-in laptop microphones. The perceived quality of such systems is limited by the error rate in interpreting spoken commands. We believe that advances in the robustness, flexibility, and naturalness of spoken command and control systems could make such applications of ASR more valuable and ubiquitous.

We have pursued endowing speech recognition systems with the ability to refine their understanding of acoustical signals through the process of engaging in human-oriented clarification dialog with the user. Clarification dialog centers on gathering evidence about the meaning of an utterance or to discriminate utterances from other sources of signal, such as ambient noise or overheard conversation. We harness, at the heart of the approach, a dynamic Bayesian network to perform inference about a user's intentions, and to integrate, in a cohesive manner, evidence from multiple acoustical signals over time gathered via clarification dialog. As we shall see, the Bayesian fusion of evidence over time, coupled with utility-directed dialog, allows an ASR system to refine the probability of a user's intention, by overlaying the information from adjacent responses.

We shall present a model for representing key probabilistic relationships among intentions and utterances, describe utility-directed procedures for making dialog and domain-level actions, and present details on the operation of an implemented spoken command and control development environment that has been packaged as a module that can be integrated with legacy spoken command and control systems.

2   Intentions, Context, and Uncertainty

We shall focus on representations and inferential machinery for enhancing the robustness of speech recognition for controlling automated services. As an example service, the Lookout system [4] developed at Microsoft Research provides an automated calendaring and scheduling service. Lookout learns a user model that is used to guide if, when, and how the service will be executed, and uses these models to drive a mixed-initiative interaction with users. In one of the chief modes of operation, users interact with Lookout in a handsfree manner, using voice commands to accept or reject oers of automated assistance, and to guide the calendaring activity.

We built our system on top of the command and control speech system provided with the Microsoft Agent (MS Agent) package. The MS Agent package is a freely available social agent development kit that provides a text-to-speech (TTS) generator and command and control ASR. MS Agent has been employed as the front end in a variety of software applications relying on speech recognition and TTS. Our approach centers on taking the action with highest expected utility for the typical case where there is uncertainty about the intentions of the user. We include in the set of decisions under consideration, several dialog actions that seek clarification from the user by sharing the state of the system's confusion with the user in a natural manner.

We employ dynamic Bayesian networks to model the uncertainty in a user's goals and utterances over time. Dynamic Bayesian networks are probabilistic dependency models that include temporal dependencies among random variables at dierent times [8,3,10,9]. Figure 1 displays two time slices of a larger iterative decision problem for inferring actions in response to output from a speech recognizer. Random variables are represented graphically as ovals with dependencies between variables as arcs. The dashed arcs indicate key temporal dependencies among variables in adjacent time slices.

Beyond reasoning about beliefs over time, we consider a decision problem at each time slice to identify dialog and domain-level actions in response to the user. As shown in the structure of the decision variable (square node) in Figure 1, the action associated with the largest expected utility is computed for each period, based on the inferred probability distribution over a user's goals.

To highlight the operation of the dynamic Bayesian network for increasing the robustness of speech recognition, let us consider the typical use of the ASR system for command and control. A listening session is initiated by a prompt from the TTS system inquiring if the user wants to activate a service in the current context. Following the initiation of a session, each recognition cycle, capturing the user's next turn in a dialog, is progressively represented by each time slice of a dynamic Bayesian network. At the end of each turn, the ASR system processes the acoustical signal and provides a set of recognized candidates.

At each step, a probability distribution over the goals of a user is inferred, based on observations about the user's activity,   e.g., events from the shell of a computer operating system or from a software application. Such computation of a user's goals based on activity and content has been a focus of work on probabilistic user modeling (e.g., [5,7,1,2,6]).

In addition to considering evidence about a user's activity, we analyze a set of variables representing the output from a speaker-independent ASR system for command and control. For the case of the Lookout system—the first application domain of our work on clarification dialog—speech commands are used for a variety of tasks including accepting or rejecting oers of service. We shall focus on the simple case of clarification dialog for interpreting such acceptances and rejections of a service. We defined a set of candidate utterances, including a large set of responses capturing a range of ways people respond with to an oer of assistance with an acknowledgment (e.g., "yes," "okay," "sure," "yeah," "go ahead," "right," "alright,""uh huh," etc.) or a rejection (e.g., "no," "go away," "not now," "later," "no way," "get out of here," "nah," "nope," etc.). We also included candidates that represent utterances associated with a user's potential deliberation about the desirability of initiating a service (e.g., "um," "hmmm," "let's see," "uh," etc.). Finally, we considered the cases where the ASR system detects an unrecognized sound, or where nothing is heard. The set of variables represented in the model were abstracted as classes of response, including armation , negation , reflection , no signal , and unrecognized signal .

Additional variables summarizing the status of a cycle of speech recognition can provide context-sensitive information about the overall proficiency of speech recognition. The variable labeled ASR reliability indicator in Figure 1 represents such a variable. We found it useful to consider the special case where the speech recognition analysis identifies a concatenation of two or more commands in a single turn (e.g., "yes..uh..no, no"). In such cases, we analyze the last term recognized by the system. As indicated in the Bayesian network model, we condition the user's spoken intention on the status of such a reliability indicator.

In response to a user's utterances, the speech recognition system provides a list of recognized candidates and a measure of confidence for each candidate. This measure of confidence is based on a common measure of uncertainty that is computed in many low-level speech models, referred to as perplexity . As represented in Figure 1, the user's spoken intention influences the classes of response and their confidences. We allow dialog designers to assess in the development environment prior conditional probabilities representing the likelihood of hearing dierent classes of response with specifi values of conflence, given the users actual utterance, referred to as the user's spoken intention .

3   Utility-Directed Decisions about Dialog and Action

At run-time, the low-level speech recognition system is called, the utterance is evaluated, the reliability variable is set, and a list of candidates and confidences for the current time slice are communicated to the dynamic Bayesian network. A probability distribution is inferred over the classes of response represented by the processed acoustic signal and the local decision with maximum expected utility is identified. In the current system, base-level actions include:

- Execute the service being oered
- Ask the user to repeat the spoken intention
- Note the hearing of a noise and inquire
- Try to acquire the user's attention
- Confm the users intention to bypass the oer of service

We constructed a utility model by assessing a space of outcomes defined as the cross product of the situations under consideration and these actions. In our prototype for Lookout, we assessed utilities, $u(A_i, S_j)$, for the twenty-five outcomes, constructed from the five actions A and five situations S.

4   Global Analysis of Conversational Progress

Beyond considering the best next action at each time slice, we worked to overlay a more global consideration of conversational progress. Such consideration involves monitoring the overall nature of the eciency of conversation by considering the number of turns and the convergence versus nonconvergence of the dialog system on a user's intentions over time. The function of this service is to notice when things are not going well, and to consider the utility of troubleshooting the overall conversation. Conversational troubleshooting makes use of representations of the growing frustration of users with increasing numbers of steps of clarification dialog. Just as a person who is hard of hearing might stop and mention that things are just not going well in the conversation and suggest an alternate strategy, the system considers stepping outside of the stepwise dialog to engage in troubleshooting, including such behaviors as describing the problem, reflecting about what was heard so far, and then trying again.

We explored several representations for integrating such capabilities into DeepListener, including the embedding of distinctions about progress into each time slice and the overlaying of a monitoring system at a higher conversational level of analysis. The current implemented version of DeepListener bases its decisions to troubleshoot on a model of frustration that grows with the number of explicit steps of interaction. Explicit turns include all interactions except for steps where the user is likely pausing to reflect about an intention or where the user is likely not attending to the dialog. The development environment allows users or system developers to encode preferences about the value of engaging in troubleshooting at each step as a function of the number of steps and the dynamics of beliefs.

5   DeepListener Implementation

We built and tested several implementations of DeepListener. At the heart of DeepListener is a dynamic Bayesian model constructed with the MSBNX Bayesian modeling tool developed at Microsoft Research. Run-time components for dynamic Bayesian inference and decision making and MS Agent components were meshed to create a run-time system and a set of development tools. The tools include controls that enable developers or users to assess utilities of outcomes. The development environment also provides a programmatic interface and methods for defining the relationship between an external user model used by the application being extended with a spoken dialog system. The interface includes a graphical representation of the dialog system's belief about the user's goals as a function of beliefs inferred in an external user model.

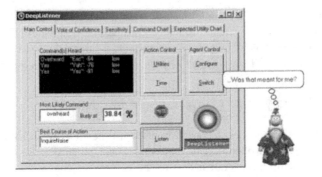

Fig. 2. Main screen of DeepListener system. The system provides tools for assessing utilities, displaying inferences over time, and interfaces for coupling DeepListener's beliefs to the beliefs of an external user modeling system.

To complement the dialog decision making machinery, a set of appropriate utterances and gestures for the animated agent were designed for each DeepListener action. To enhance the naturalness of interaction, gestures and utterances are drawn randomly at runtime from a pool of candidate gestures for each action.

Figure 2 shows the user interface provided by DeepListener to developers for coupling the system with legacy applications, viewing inferences, and testing interactive behaviors. The sequence of utterances and their confidences are displayed in an utterance-trace window at the upper left of the display. In this case, the system heard a "yeah," followed by a "yes," followed by the name of the user, all heard with low confidence. The best action here is for DeepListener to share it's belief that it is overhearing sounds that were not intended for the system. This action involves relaying the system's reflection via a thought cloud over the animated agent. At the lower right-hand corner of the interface, feedback on the system's listening and reasoning is provided in the form of a colored lens. A green glow indicates that the system is listening for a user response, yellow indicates that the system is confused, and red indicates that the system is peforming recognition or inference and, thus, is temporarily unavailable for listening. Such feedback on listening and reasoning status provides information analogous to the communication backchannel of expressions and gestures about understanding that listeners may relay to speakers in natural conversations.

Figure 3 shows DeepListener's preference assessment tools. The utility assessment tool on the right allows users to order their preferences about basic outcomes and to assess utilities using relative distance by moving sliders between the best and worst utilities. The figure displays outcomes for the case in which a user desires a service oered by the agent. The tool on the right demonstrates the facility for assessing a function that yields the utility of troubleshooting as a function of the number steps in a conversation without convergence on understanding.

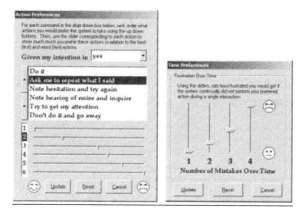

Fig. 3.   Views of DeepListener's preference assessment tools. Left: Interface for assessing stepwise outcomes, showing outcomes for the case where the user desires a service. Right: Tool for assessing a troubleshooting function representing the utility of troubleshooting with increasing numbers of steps in the dialog.

6   Real-Time Interaction with DeepListener

At run time, DeepListener executes dialog and real-world actions at each turn in a manner consistent with its current uncertainty about the observed sequence of utterances and the expected consequences of alternative actions.

In many situations, DeepListener hears well enough to simply perform the intended action within a single step. In such scenarios, the system performs just as a simple speech recognition would in response to an accurate recognition. However, the system's understanding of an intention may not be good enough to invoke an action in the world. The top portion of Figure 4 displays traces of the beliefs about a user's intentions, and the expected utility of alternate actions over time, for an interactive session where the user was in a relatively noisy environment (background noise was generated by HVAC and equipment fans) and sat approximately four feet from a standard built-in microphone embedded in a laptop computer. An automated service was oered per an inference about user goals, yielding prior probabilities on alternate intentions. The user uttered "ummm..." in the process of reflecting about the desire for the service, following by "okay." The system heard this response with a low confidence and requested a clarification, at which point the user said, "yes." Although this response was also heard with low confidence, the update to beliefs about the user's desire for the service led to an invocation of the service, given a consideration of the expected utilities of all actions. This example highlights how utility-directed clarification dialog can fuse evidence across time to converge on an intended action. The lower portion of Figure 4 shows the behavior of DeepListener at steps 2 and 3 of this case.

Overall, the experience of communicating with a DeepListener-enabled application diers qualitatively from interacting with traditional speech command

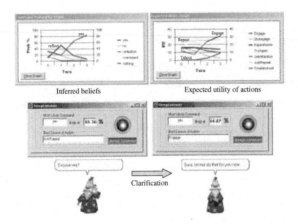

Fig. 4. Top Left: Beliefs about a user's intentions over a three-step interaction in a noisy environment. Top Right: Expected utilities inferred over the interaction, converging on an invocation of service. Bottom: Behavior of DeepListener at steps 2 and 3 of this session.

systems. In distinction to traditional ASR, DeepListener understands when it should gather additional information before taking (potentially erroneous) actions or simply expressing a failure to understand. For example, interacting with the system in noisy environments—or at a relatively long distance away from a microphone—invokes the impression of attempting to communicate with a person who is having diculty hearing but desires to work with the speaker to clarify the utterance. Also, users can assume, as they do with people they are interacting with, that there is a shared memory of the recent communication experience. Thus, during a cycle of clari&ation, a user can utter dierent words to describe an intention and expect the system to have considered the history of interaction, rather than assuming that each clarification is starting anew.

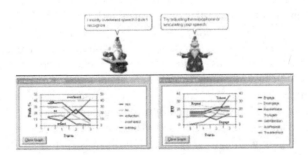

Fig. 5. Troubleshooting of the overall conversation following a sequence of poor recognitions and detection of background noise.

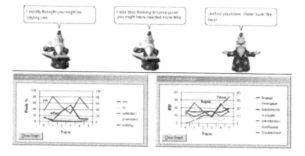

Fig. 6. Troubleshooting of conversation following clarification dialog demonstrating communication of a summary of DeepListener's time-varying beliefs about a user's intentions.

Figures 5 and 6 display inference over sample sessions that led to troubleshooting. For the case presented in Figure 5, the utility of troubleshooting eventually dominated other actions, following a sequence of poor recognitions and detection of background noise. The system shared a summary of its analysis and recommended that the user adjust the microphone and speak with greater articulation. For the session presented in Figure 6, the system heard low confidence utterances (e.g., a mued ÿeahÿ signaling an intention to go ahead with a service, interspersed with signs of reflection (e.g., "hmmm, let's see,"). After three steps of clarification dialog, the system initiated conversational troubleshooting, relaying to the user its sequence of beliefs about the user's intentions over time, and giving the user a tip about how to best communicate the most likely intention.

We are currently pursuing methodical tests of DeepListener in dierent kinds of environments to see how much better the system performs over a naive, spoken command and control system. We are also investigating the use of machine learning to learn key probabilistic dependencies from data and the extension of the system to consider additional sensory information about a user's context and attention. Some of this work is being pursued in the related Quartet project, focused on developing a multilevel conversational architecture [11].

7 Summary

We presented methods for extending traditional speech recognition systems with representations and inference machinery that consider the intentions associated with one or more utterances, and that continue to weigh the costs and benefits of alternate behaviors. The approach centers on the use of temporal probabilistic inference and expected utility to guide clarification dialog and domain-level actions. We described DeepListener, a clarification-dialog development environment that can be used to construct run-time spoken command and control systems. DeepListener employs utility-directed clarification dialog to acquire a growing sequence of utterances that is subjected to Bayesian analysis at each turn in a dialog. We reviewed the use of DeepListener to extend the robustness of spoken command and control for guiding the provision of automated services. We believe that the methods embodied in DeepListener show promise for enhancing the performance of spoken language systems in a variety of real-world situations and environments. We believe that the use of utility-directed clarification dialog transforms in a qualitative manner the overall experience of interacting with a spoken language system. Our ongoing work on DeepListener centers on quantitatively assessing the value of the approach in real-world settings, and on extensions to both the overall architecture and the methodology for constructing user models for clarification dialog.

Acknowledgments

We are indebted to Andy Jacobs for assistance with the software development. Carl Kadie provided support with the integration and automation of MSBNX components in DeepListener.

References

1. D.W. Albrecht, I. Zukerman, A.E. Nicholson, and A. Bud. Towards a bayesian model for keyhole plan recognition in large domains. In *Proceedings of the Sixth International Conference on User Modeling, Sardinia, Italy*, pages 365–376. User Modeling, Springer-Verlag, June 1997.
2. C. Conati, A.S. Gertner, K. VanLehn, and M.J. Druzdzel. Online student modeling for coached problem solving using bayesian networks. In *Proceedings of the Sixth International Conference on UserModeling, Sardinia, Italy*, pages 231–242. User Modeling, Springer-Verlag, June 1997.
3. P. Dagum, A. Galper, and E. Horvitz. Dynamic network models for forecasting. In Proceedings of the Eighth Workshop on Uncertainty in Artificial Intelligence, pages 41–48, Stanford, CA, July 1992. Association for Uncertainty in Artificial Intelligence.
4. E. Horvitz. Principles of mixed-initiative user interfaces. In *Proceedings of the ACM SIGCHI Conference on Human Factors in Computing Systems (CHI '99)*, pages 159–166. ACM Press, May 1999.
5. E. Horvitz and M. Barry. Display of information for time-critical decision making. In Proceedings of the Eleventh Conference on Uncertainty in Artificial Intelligence, pages 296–305, Montreal, Canada, August 1995. Morgan Kaufmann, San Francisco.
6. E. Horvitz, J. Breese, D. Heckerman, D. Hovel, and K. Rommelse. The Lumiere project: Bayesian user modeling for inferring the goals and needs of software users. In Proceedings of the Fourteenth Conference on Uncertainty in Artificial Intelligence, pages 256–265. Morgan Kaufmann, San Francisco, July 1998.
7. A. Jameson. Numerical uncertainty management in user and student modeling: An overview of systems and issues. *User Modeling and User-Adapted Interaction*, 5:193–251, 1996.
8. K. Kanazawa and T. Dean. A model for projection and action. In *Proceedings of the Eleventh IJCAI*. AAAI/International Joint Conferences on Artificial Intelligence, August 1989.

9. K. Kanazawa, D. Koller, and S. Russell. Stochastic simulation algorithm for dynamic probabilistic networks. In *Proceedings of the Eleventh Annual Conference on Uncertainty in Artificial Intelligence (UAI–95)*, pages 346–351, Montreal, Quebec, Canada, 1995.

10. A.E. Nicholson and J.M. Brady. Dynamic belief networks for discrete monitoring. *IEEE Transactions on Systems, Man, and Cybernetics*, 24(11):1593–1610, 1994.

11. T. Paek and E. Horvitz. Conversation as action under uncertainty. In *Proceedings of the Sixteenth Conference on Uncertainty in Artificial Intelligence*, pages 445–464. AUAI, Morgan Kaufmann, August 2000.

Modeling the Acquisition of English:
An Intelligent CALL Approach

Lisa N. Michaud, Kathleen F. McCoy, and Litza A. Stark

Department of Computer and Information Sciences
University of Delaware, Newark, DE 19716
{michaud,mccoy,stark }@cis.udel.edu
http://www.eecis.udel.edu/research/icicle

Abstract. In this paper, we present a methodology for the development of a user model for CALL which captures various levels of language acquisition using individualized overlays supported with stereotypes. Our current focus is the empirical analysis of the order of written English grammatical structure acquisition in our learner population used to develop stereotype layers in our model.

1 ICICLE: An Introduction

We are currently developing the system ICICLE (Interactive Computer Identification and Correction of Language Errors) to take a Computer-Assisted Language Learning (CALL) approach toward tutoring deaf students on their written English [12,13]. Our target learners are native or near-native users of American Sign Language (ASL), a language entirely distinct from English, so we approach the acquisition of skills in written English as a second language (L2) acquisition task. This allows us to develop a system for a population which can greatly benefit from access to individualized, adaptive tutoring [13] while contributing to the field of CALL a design and methodology which can be also generalized to other L2 learners.

Our system is a writing tutor intended to supplement classroom instruction by providing students with detailed feedback on the grammatical errors in their English compositions. Its primary concerns are the correct analysis of student-generated language errors and the production of tutorial feedback to student performance which is both correct and tailored to the student. Its interaction with a user begins when the user submits a composition to the system, which is analyzed for grammatical errors. The system then responds with tutorial feedback aimed at enabling the student to perform corrections. When the student has revised the piece, it can be re-submitted for analysis. As ICICLE is intended to be used by an individual over time and across many pieces of writing, the system should learn as much as it can about a user to perform the language analysis and constructive feedback as accurately as possible.

This work has been supported by NSF Grants #GER-9354869 and #IIS-9978021.

M. Bauer, P.J. Gmytrasiewicz, and J. Vassileva (Eds.): UM 2001, LNAI 2109, pp. 14–23, 2001.

1.1   User Modeling in SLALOM

ICICLE's current implementation is a windows-based application with a text parser that uses an English grammar augmented by a bug catalogue or "mal-rules" capturing typical errors made by our learner population [15]. The system recognizes and marks many grammatical errors, delivering "canned" one- or two-sentence explanations of each error on request. When the system finds more than one possible analysis of the grammar structure underlying a user's sentence, it currently chooses arbitrarily. Since the selection of parses may determine which error(s) it assumes the user has made, and the instructive text is canned, the system currently lacks adaptivity to its user. To change this, we intend to implement in ICICLE a model of the system user, based on our view of the student as an L2 learner.

Originally proposed in [11], SLALOM (Steps of Language Acquisition in a Layered Organization Model) captures the user's ability to use each of the grammatical "rules" of English in a hybrid of an overlay model and a stereotype-based model; each of the rules in the model is marked based on the system's observations of student performance, and this information will be supplemented by stereotype information about typical language learners in this population. The model will therefore reflect those rules which the student uses in his or her language production—correct English rules from those English structures the user has acquired, and mal-rules for those structures which the user has not yet learned. In addition, there may be some structures which exhibit variation between correct and incorrect form, introducing competing rules (both standard and mal-rule) into the model. We consider the realm of grammar covered by these competing rules to correspond to Vygotsky's   Zone of Proximal Development (ZPD), essentially that subset of language which the learner is about to master [17]. Krashen's observation that at each step of language learning there is some set of grammar rules which the learner is "due to acquire" [8], and the fact that elements which are on the verge of being acquired vacillate between correct and incorrect applications (cf. [7]), eectively reinforce the application of this concept to our domain.

The system's decision on how to interpret a user's text when there are multiple possibilities must depend upon the proficiency level of the learner and which rules are present in the user model. As this model represents those rules and mal-rules the user typically uses, parses can be selected whose hierarchical structure is composed of rules which most closely mirror those in the user model.

Once the text has been analyzed, ICICLE must generate a tutorial session, beginning by determining which of the errors will be the subjects of tutorial explanations. This decision is important if the instruction is to be eective. There should be a distinction in how the system addresses language "errors," which reflect grammatical competence, versus "mistakes," which are merely slip-ups [3]. We also want to avoid generating instruction which is beyond the user's understanding. The concept of "learnability" in second language instruction constrains knowledge that can be assimilated to those concepts the learner is ready to acquire [6]. We therefore focus instruction on that "narrow shifting zone dividing

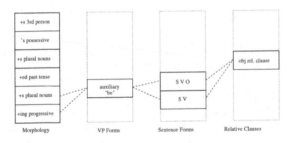

Fig. 1. SLALOM: Steps of Language Acquisition in a Layered Organization Model.

the already-learned skills from the not-yet-learned ones" [10], or the frontier of
the learning process. ICICLE will select those errors which involve items in the
ZPD and ignore both simple inadvertent mistakes by the user and errors that
are beyond the student's frontier of learning.

2   Compensating for Partial Evidence: Stereotypes in SLALOM

We have presented a model reliant on the recorded tendencies of the user with
respect to grammatical forms in English. This knowledge will sometimes be only
partial, particularly at the beginning of the system's interaction with a user.
We therefore must establish a method by which the system can infer a fuller
description of user proficiency than is directly displayed in his or her past use of
language forms. We propose to do this using a structure of relationships between
language concepts based on language learning stereotypes.

We first proposed a structure for SLALOM in [11]. Here we discuss how a
more mature version of this model can be used by ICICLE to fill in the gaps
in user observations. We partition grammatical knowledge into knowledge units
where each unit corresponds to a set of grammar rules (both standard English
and mal-rules) that realize a grammatical structure. A simplified representation
can be seen in Fig. 1.

Steps of Language Acquisition   refers to our intention to capture the order of
acquisition of these knowledge units. There is empirical support for stereotypical
sequences of English acquisition [5,9,8], and our model reflects this stereotype
by grouping units into related "hierarchies" (such as morphology markings, verb
phrase constructions, and relative clause formation), each of which has an order
represented in the figure by a vertical relationship; "easier" items which are
typically acquired earlier sit below those acquired later. The example hierarchy
in Fig. 1 demonstrates a possible SLALOM hierarchy based on the results of
empirical work by [5] on the acquisition order of morphology markers.

The Layered Organization Model   part of SLALOM's design is shown in the
figure by the dashed lines coordinating the acquisition steps across the hierarchies by indicating a "layer" of concurrent acquisition; elements connected at the

same layer are acquired at about the same time. Intuitively, one layer represents the structures currently being learned by the user. Because of the ordered nature of the hierarchies, those items below that layer have typically already been acquired, while those above have not been acquired. [1]

With the assistance of this stereotype information, ICICLE's syntactic analyzer will be enabled to make parse selections even when data on this individual does not cover all of the rules in the parsing grammar. A grammatical structure corresponding to a knowledge unit below those considered "acquired" or "ZPD" in the model can be considered previously acquired, and thus covered by a standard English rule in the grammar; conversely, those structures above the user's frontier of learning should be covered by mal-rules, and those in the same layer as the ZPD should be flexible, covered by either correct or incorrect rules.

Since this model is based on observations of an individual user, it will be initialized following the first analysis of a new user's writing. As actual data on the user's performance is delivered to the model over subsequent analyses, the inferences provided by the stereotype will be overwritten to reflect the individual, allowing the system to adapt to users who may learn outside of the stereotypical sequence due to dierent instructional programs. The model is also dynamic, maintaining statistics on user performance within a certain window of the present, including enough information from previous writing samples to give us a more complete view of user performance while excluding errors that are no longer being made. Because SLALOM's ordering of layers represents an expected order of acquisition, the most likely path of the ZPD layer is to move "up" in the model as the user learns.

3 Populating the User Model: An Empirical Study

A question not addressed in [11] has to do with "populating" the SLALOM model, determining where the knowledge units of the model go in our representation of stereotypic acquisition order. As mentioned in Section 2, support for the existence of such an order can be found in empirical studies on the acquisition of English. However, although there is support for a universal order of morpheme acquisition regardless of L1 (first language) [5], no existing work proposes an order for the entire body of grammatical structures covered in SLALOM and none addresses our learner group in particular.

The remainder of this paper describes how we have taken on the task of empirically deriving a stereotypic acquisition order for our own user population, whose L1 is American Sign Language. We seek to identify: (1) which aspects of English are mastered in what order, and (2) what groups of items are learned around the same time. This will allow us to group SLALOM contents into layers and impose upon those layers some stereotypic order.

---

[1] Note that what is considered a "layer" may be much larger than just one item per hierarchy. The important aspect of the definition is that each layer represents a grouping of language rules acquired at about the same time. The layer in the figure is for example purposes only and does not reflect any empirical findings.

id	Incorrect Determiner	mds	Missing Dummy Subject
md	Missing Determiner	ids	Incorrect Dummy Subject
sv	Subject/Verb agreement	mo	Missing Object
ht	Here/There as a Pronoun	bh	Be/Have Confusion
nf	Noun Formation	ii	Incorrect Intensifier

Fig. 2.   Examples of codes from our error coding manual.

Toward that end, we have been examining a corpus of 106 samples of writing by deaf college students at various levels of English proficiency. Since these samples represent dierent levels of grammatical ability, obtaining syntactic analyses of the samples would ideally provide us with information on which aspects of English are being executed with what levels of success across the dierent competence levels because the resulting parse trees would explicitly contain correct or mal-formed structures. However, we are still faced with the problem that the current analyzer (without a completed SLALOM) has no intelligent way to select between alternative parses. We therefore first need to provide the benefit of human intuition in distinguishing what interpretation of each sentence is the most accurate. From this, we can build a profile of performance across the levels represented by our corpus.

3.1   Grading User Performance

To provide the system with human judgments on interpretations of user text, we marked up our corpus by hand to indicate what errors had occurred in each sentence. For this task, we developed a taxonomy of "error codes," each of which addresses errors typical of our user population, based on the initial corpus analysis presented in [16,11]. Our codes have a close relationship to the mal-rules which the parser uses to recognize errors. The completed taxonomy had 68 error codes, primarily covering syntactic structures. Some example codes are shown in Fig. 2.[2]

We then divided the 106 samples between two coders, each receiving approximately half, with an overlap of 23 samples which both individuals coded in order to demonstrate consistency between the two perspectives.

To illustrate that our two coders were operating consistently with respect to each other, we needed to determine some measure of agreement between them. One diculty we faced in this task was that each sentence was tagged with a string of codes (see Fig. 3) which was organized linearly according to the order in which the errors occurred in the sentence but were not otherwise connected to the specific incidents they recorded. Furthermore, the strings tended to have gaps; when structures involved gray areas of grammaticality and were ungrammatical to one coder but acceptable to the other, a code in one string would not have a correspondent in the other. Therefore, we faced a task of comparing for each

---

[2] "Dummy Subject" refers to subjects which are not referents: There are books on the table / It is nice to see you.

Example:

Those who argue that it will have less hazing incidents here on campus if
the abolishment of fraternities and sororities are done.

Coder 1:   (mds ids bh ii sv) There are those who argue that   there will be fewer hazing
incidents here on campus if the abolishment of fraternities and sororities   is done.

Coder 2:   (mds ids sv) There are those who argue that   there will be less hazing
incidents here on campus if the abolishment of fraternities and sororities   is done.

Alignment:

mds	ids	bh	ii	sv
mds	ids	*	*	sv

Fig. 3.   Examples of coders' tags and alignment program output.

sentence in our corpus two lists of error codes without knowing which pairs of
codes referred to the same error.

For this problem we borrowed a page from bioinformatics research, which has
developed many algorithms to compare two strings of DNA in order to determine
the best alignment. In particular, we adapted the Smith-Waterman algorithm,
which computes a matrix of alignment scores where matches are rewarded and
mismatches or gaps introduced in one or the other string are penalized. After we
tuned the penalties and rewards to reflect the relative importance of matches,
mismatches, and gaps in our particular problem, we applied this algorithm to
the codes for the 23 overlap compositions. The alignment program produced a
very accurate alignment between the two coders' lists, consistent with human
judgment. An example output can be seen in Fig. 3.

Disagreement on the grammaticality of user text was the largest source of
conflict between our coders, and because both were equally qualified judges and
either interpretation could be correct, we discounted gaps as disagreements. In
some of the gap cases, one coder had a dierent semantic interpretation of the
changes required to bring the sentence into consistency with the surrounding
discourse, such as the tense context (should these verbs have been in present or
past tense?) or the discourse entities (should "friend" be "friends?"). In others,
including the example in Fig. 3, a code was absent from one string because of a
confusion on the definition of what needed to be explicitly coded. Fig. 4 shows
agreement between the coders when both coders agreed an error occurred (i.e.,
ignoring gaps). The number of "possible" codes for each sentence was determined
by the total length of the alignment sequence.

Measuring the frequency with which each of the coders used each of the 68
error codes, we determined the likelihood of chance agreement over this task and
calculated an adjusted "Kappa" value [2] of .78. Although this is just inside the
margin of what Carletta names the range of tentative conclusions ($.67 < K < .8$),
we are satisfied with the agreement level because it is strong enough to indicate
that our coders are providing our study with similar "human intuitions" in a
domain which has a lot of gray area, and if our parser sided with either coder's

794	Total Possible Errors
432	Both Coders Agreed Were Errors
352	Both Coders Assigned Same Code
81%	Bare Agreement
78%	Adjusted Agreement (Kappa)

Fig. 4.   Agreement statistics on overlapped coding.

interpretation, it would still be judging consistently with an experienced human; that is the best that we could require.

3.2   Clustering User Groups

The next step in our corpus analysis was to determine whether the coded samples were stratified in any way that corresponded to a judgment of general proficiency level. An important step in this was to have levels assigned by experienced judges. We distributed the samples to four instructors at the English Language Institute of the University of Delaware who are trained to grade compositions according to the standards of the national Test of Written English (TWE). Each sample was given a TWE score from 1 to 6 by two dierent judges, and a third judge arbitrated in the case of disagreement. We then prepared "error count" sets for each sample, indicating the number of occurrences of each of our error codes, normalized by the number of sentences in the sample in order to compensate for the fact that our samples varied greatly in length (from 2 to 58 sentences). We applied several clustering algorithms on the normalized data, seeking out clusters in which samples were minimally distant from each other, and so should represent samples which have the same errors in approximately the same magnitude.   [3]

We show the results of running the Ward clustering algorithm on our data in Fig. 5. Although we have a problem with sparse data (only 5% of the samples occurring at TWE levels 1, 5, and 6), there is a clear trend with lower and higher proﬁency levels showing a preference to dierent clusters, overlapping in Cluster 2. Together with MANOVA analyses we have run which further indicate trends of change between those errors committed by students at dierent levels, we have confirmed Corder's statement [3] that errors are a clue to the learner's current state of acquisition; however, we have also discovered that errors alone are not enough to precisely characterize the learner.

4   Future Work

Only by obtaining data on those structures a student can execute correctly will we be able to look at errors meaningfully by comparing the failed attempts to

---

[3] The ATULA-ATS system [14], uses statistical clustering to develop user groups into which to categorize a new user, based on non-knowledge attributes like attitude and background.

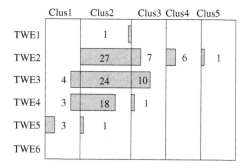

Fig. 5. Distribution of levels of proficiency across Ward clusters.

use a structure against the successes. We are currently in the process of adapting our syntactic analyzer so that we may explore the competing parse trees created for each input sentence in our corpus. Since we have specified the relationship between each of the mal-rules of our parsing grammar and our list of error codes, each parse tree can be converted to a string of error codes. These strings can then be compared against the human-generated codes to select which parse is the closest to a human's judgment using our alignment program.

With the "correct" parses indicated, we will know for each sentence which grammar constituents were formed correctly and which were made from mal-rules. From this we can derive a very detailed account of syntactic performance for each sample, supplementing our error information with the elements of English the user has executed   correctly as well. Stratified into the levels determined by our expert judges, this will flesh out our view of syntactic performance as proficiency develops, and give us our partial orders of acquisition on which to base the inferencing relationships in SLALOM; structures mastered by the lowest-proficiency writers will be grouped in the lowest layers of the model, structures mastered only by the higher-proficiency writers grouped toward the top, and indications of transitional performance will indicate which structures will be considered part of a single layer.

5   Related Work

The overlay/stereotype hybrid student model design is not unheard of in ITS student model design. Desmarais et. al's POKS (Partial Order Knowledge Structures) approach [4] builds an inferencing network incorporating order of acquisition information derived automatically from training data. Their approach, however, is strongly influenced by the fundamental assumption that while the user's mastery is measurable on any given knowledge unit, there is a poverty of such sampling because measurement must be done through explicitly querying the user. Our system, by contrast, will have access to large sets of user knowledge data via unobtrusive observation through the analysis process. SLALOM's partial ordering is both more robust (being based on a larger corpus with broadly-sampled data) and less relied upon, as the abundant individual data will always take precedence over inferences.

In the field of CALL, the student model Mr. Collins [1], has a design methodology similar to ours; the dynamic student model reflects more correct knowledge and fewer misconceptions as it moves toward the expert ideal. Also, a review of typical student errors in their learner group was applied toward the model's ability to expect future user performance and toward diagnosing the errors of the student. There are several distinctions between their approach and ours, particularly that Mr. Collins was developed in the restricted domain of the placement and use of Portuguese clitic pronouns, whereas the work we have described in this paper addresses student development over a broad range of grammatical structures. The system containing Mr. Collins is also designed to interact at a meta-level with the student, collaborating on the content of the model and explicitly providing tools for the student's learning strategies; since ICICLE does not have the liberty of interaction in the student's native language [4], our ability to communicate topics at the meta-level is perforce constrained.

6   Summary

We have embarked upon the implementation of a complex student model for a language instruction system and have presented a methodology for the empirical derivation of stereotypes for learners of written English as a second language. Since data on the specific user will be numerous, this stereotype information will only be used to supplement individual overlay data which will be more reliable as the system interacts with the individual. Since ICICLE is modular and only isolated aspects of the system (the mal-rules in the analyzer and the inferencing in SLALOM) are specific to the target user population, it is our intention that the methodology we have developed could be applied to adapt ICICLE to any L1 user group.

References

1. Susan Bull, Paul Brna, and Helen Pain. Extending the scope of the student model. User Modeling and User-Adapted Interaction, 5(1):45–65, 1995.
2. Jean Carletta. Assessing agreement on classification tasks: The Kappa statistic. Computational Linguistics, 22(2):249–254, June 1996.
3. S. P. Corder. The significance of learners' errors. International Review of Applied Linguistics, 5(4):161–170, November 1967.
4. Michel C. Desmarais, Ameen Maluf, and Jiming Jiu. User-expertise modeling with empirically derived probabilistic implication networks. User modeling and user-adapted interaction, 5(3/4):283–315, 1996.
5. Heidi C. Dulay and Marina K. Burt. Natural sequences in child second language acquisition. Language Learning, 24(1), 1975.

---

[4] We are currently investigating the integration of on-screen signed instruction.

6. Rod Ellis. The structural syllabus and second language acquisition.   TESOL Quarterly, 27(1):91–113, Spring 1993.

7. Rod Ellis. The Study of Second Language Acquisition . Oxford University Press, New York, 1994.

8. Stephen D. Krashen.   Principles and Practice in Second Language Acquisition . Pergamon Press, New York, 1982.

9. Diane E. Larsen-Freeman. An explanation for the morpheme acquisition order of second language learners.   Language Learning , 25(1):125–135, June 1976.

10. Frank Linton, Brigham Bell, and Charles Bloom. The student model of the LEAP intelligent tutoring system. In   Proceedings of the Fifth International Conference on User Modeling , pages 83–90, Kailua-Kona, Hawaii, January 2-5 1996. UM96, User Modeling, Inc.

11. Kathleen F. McCoy, Christopher A. Pennington, and Linda Z. Suri. English error correction: A syntactic user model based on principled mal-rule scoring. In Proceedings of the Fifth International Conference on User Modeling , pages 59–66, Kailua-Kona, Hawaii, January 2-5 1996. UM96, User Modeling, Inc.

12. Lisa N. Michaud and Kathleen F. McCoy. Supporting intelligent tutoring in CALL by modeling the user's grammar. In   Proceedings of the 13th Annual International Florida Artificial Intelligence Research Symposium , pages 50–54, Orlando, Florida, May 22-24 2000. FLAIRS.

13. Lisa N. Michaud, Kathleen F. McCoy, and Christopher A. Pennington. An intelligent tutoring system for deaf learners of written English. In   Proceedings of the Fourth International ACM SIGCAPH Conference on Assistive Technologies (AS-SETS 2000) , Washington, D.C., November 13-15 2000. SIGCAPH.

14. Sue Milne, Edward Shiu, and Jean Cook. Development of a model of user attributes and its implementation with an adaptive tutoring system.   User modeling and user-adapted interaction , 6(4):303–335, 1996.

15. David Schneider and Kathleen F. McCoy. Recognizing syntactic errors in the writing of second language learners. In   Proceedings of the Thirty-Sixth Annual Meeting of the Association for Computational Linguistics and the Seventeenth International Conference on Computational Linguistics , volume 2, pages 1198– 1204, Universite de Montreal, Montreal, Quebec, Canada, August 10-14 1998. COLING-ACL, Morgan Kaufmann Publishers.

16. Linda Z. Suri and Kathleen F. McCoy. A methodology for developing an error taxonomy for a computer assisted language learning tool for second language learners. Technical Report TR-93-16, Dept. of Computer and Information Sciences, University of Delaware, 1993.

17. Lev Semenovich Vygotsky.   Thought and Language . The MIT Press, Cambridge, Massachusetts, 1986. Translation revised and edited by Alex Kozulin; originally published in 1934.

Recognizing Time Pressure and Cognitive Load on the Basis of Speech: An Experimental Study

Christian Müller , Barbara Großmann-Hutter , Anthony Jameson ,
Ralf Rummer , and Frank Wittig

Department of Computational Linguistics, Saarland University
Department of Computer Science, Saarland University
Department of Psychology, Saarland University

Abstract. In an experimental environment, we simulated the situation of a user who gives speech input to a system while walking through an airport. The time pressure on the subjects and the requirement to navigate while speaking were manipulated orthogonally. Each of the 32 subjects generated 80 utterances, which were coded semi-automatically with respect to a wide range of features, such as filled pauses. The experiment yielded new results concerning the effects of time pressure and cognitive load on speech. To see whether a system can automatically identify these conditions on the basis of speech input, we had this task performed for each subject by a Bayesian network that had been learned on the basis of the experimental data for the other subjects. The results shed light on the conditions that determine the accuracy of such recognition.

1   Background and Issues

This paper is an experimental follow-up to the UM99 paper by Berthold and Jameson ([2]). Those authors argued the following points, among others:

- In a world of increasingly mobile and ubiquitous computing, it is becoming more important for a system ( ) to be able to recognize the situation-dependent resource limitations of its user ( )—for example, so as to be able to switch to a slower but less demanding style of communication where appropriate (cf. Jameson et al., [5]). While they focused on the variable of cognitive load, we will also consider the variable of time pressure.
- With systems that allow speech input, one source of information about   's resource limitations is the features of   's speech; many previous studies have revealed systematic influences of cognitive load (and to a lesser degree, time pressure) on specific features of speech.

On the basis of a synthesis of previous results, Berthold and Jameson ([2]) presented simulations that suggested that it might indeed be feasible to recognize a user's current cognitive load on the basis of a limited amount of speech input; but they noted that

The research described here was supported by the German Science Foundation (DFG) in its Collaborative Research Center on Resource-Adaptive Cognitive Processes, SFB 378, Projects B2 (READY) and A2 (VEVIAG). We thank Tore Knabe for contributions to the statistical data analyses and Sylvia Bach for help in conducting the experiment.

M. Bauer, P.J. Gmytrasiewicz, and J. Vassileva (Eds.): UM 2001, LNAI 2109, pp. 24–33, 2001.
c Springer-Verlag Berlin Heidelberg 2001

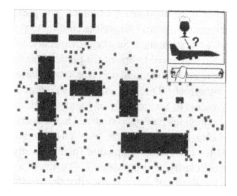

Fig. 1. *Environment used in the experiment, with a typical pictorial stimulus.*

specifically designed empirical studies would be required for a more definite answer to this question.

In the present paper, we first describe an experiment that was explicitly designed to fill this gap (Section 2). We then describe the learning of user models (in the form of Bayesian networks) on the basis of the data from this experiment (Section 3). Finally, we show how well the learned models succeed at recognizing subjects' resource limitations in the experimental data (Section 4).

2   Experiment

2.1   Method

Materials. The experimental environment simulated a situation in which a user is navigating through a crowded airport terminal while asking questions to a mobile assistance system via speech (see Figure 1). In each of 80 trials, a picture appeared in the upper right-hand corner of the screen. On the basis of each picture, the subject was to introduce and ask a question (e.g., "I'm getting thirsty. Is there ... will it be possible to get a beer on the plane?").

Design. Two independent variables were manipulated orthogonally:

- NAVIGATION? Whether or not the subject was required to move an icon on the screen through the depicted terminal to an assigned destination by pressing arrow keys, while avoiding obstacles and remembering a gate number that comprised five digits and one letter. When navigation was not required, the subject could ignore the depicted terminal and concentrate on the generation of appropriate utterances in response to the pictures.
- TIME PRESSURE? Whether the subject was induced by instructions and rewards (a) to finish each utterance as quickly as possible or (b) to create an especially clear and comprehensible utterance, without regard to time.

Procedure. After an extensive introduction to the scenario, the environment, and the 4 (   ) conditions, each subject dealt with 4 blocks, each of which comprised

20 stimuli distributed over 4 destinations. Each block was presented in one of the 4 conditions, the order being varied across subjects according to standard procedures.

Subjects. The 32 subjects, students at Saarland University, were paid for their participation. An extra reward was given to one of the participants who most successfully followed the instructions regarding the time pressure manipulation.

Coding and rating of speech. The first author transliterated the subjects' speech input and coded it with respect to a wide range of features, including almost all of those that had been included in previous published studies. On the basis of the transliterations (minus the coding symbols), four independent raters rated the relative "quality" of the 32 utterances produced for each stimulus picture (quality being defined in terms of grammaticality, relevance, clarity, and politeness). The raters also rated the pictorial stimuli in terms of the complexity of the responses that they tended to call for.

In this paper, we report results only for a representative subset of five speech-related variables, which we call symptomsbecause they reflect (albeit imperfectly) the psychological state of the subject induced by the experimental manipulations:

- DISFLUENCIES : The logical disjunction of several binary variables, each of which indexes one feature of speech that involves its formal quality: self-corrections involving either syntax or content; false starts; or interrupting speech in the middle of a sentence or a word.[1]
- ARTICULATION RATE: The number of syllables articulated per second of speaking time, after elimination of the time for measurable silent pauses.
- CONTENT QUALITY: The average quality rank—between 1 (worst) and 32 (best)—assigned to the utterance by the four raters.
- NUMBER OF SYLLABLES : The number of syllables in the utterance.
- SILENT PAUSES : The total duration of the silent pauses in the utterance, expressed relative to the length of the utterance in words (to take into account the fact that longer utterances offer more opportunities for pauses). A silent pause is any silence within the utterance that lasts at least 200 ms.
- FILLED PAUSES : The corresponding measure for filled pauses (e.g., "Uhh").

2.2   Results

Figure 2 shows, for each of the six dependent variables listed above, how it was influenced by the two independent variables TIME PRESSURE? and NAVIGATION?.

DISFLUENCIES . The disfluencies summarized by this variable increased to a significant extent when the speaker was distracted by a navigation task (   ).[2] Perhaps more surprisingly, they increased to almost the same extent when the speaker was not under time pressure (,   ). The reason may be that subjects in this condition tended to produce longer, more complex utterances (cf. the results for NUMBER OF SYLLABLES shown below), a tendency which is generally associated with a higher frequency of disfluencies (see, e.g., Oviatt, [7]).

---

[1] Filled and silent pauses are not counted here, because they are treated as separate variables.

[2] The statistical significance of the each of the effects to be discussed in this section was determined through a univariate analysis of variance (ANOVA), in each case after a multivariate ANOVA had shown that the univariate ANOVA was justified.

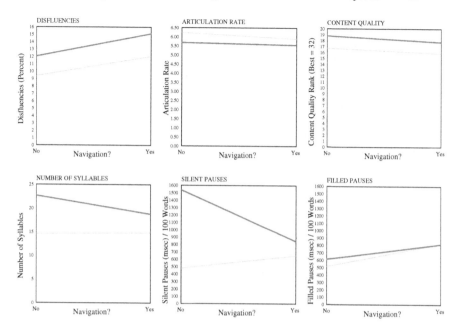

Fig. 2. *Mean values of the six speech symptoms for each of the four experimental conditions.*

(Thin lines: time pressure; thick lines: no time pressure.)

ARTICULATION RATE. On the average, subjects produced more syllables per second when they were under time pressure than when they were not ( ). Though this result is intuitively plausible, it is not logically necessary, given that there are many other ways of coping with time pressure. There is also a statistically highly reliable tendency to articulate less quickly when navigating (see the slope of the two lines;   ), as has been reported in a number of previous studies (cf. Berthold & Jameson, [2]). This effect is stronger under time pressure (interaction:).

CONTENT QUALITY. On the average, an utterance produced under time pressure ranks about 2 positions (out of 32) lower than one produced without time pressure (   ). The effect of having to navigate is even smaller, amounting to only about one rank position (   ).

NUMBER OF SYLLABLES. Although the subjects' attempts to produce higher-quality utterances in the absence of time pressure did not lead to much higher quality ratings, they did produce much longer utterances (   ). The most important impact of the navigation task was to reduce this tendency: The increase in length is about 50% without navigation and about 30% with navigation (interaction:). Evidently, when they had to navigate, subjects were less ambitious with regard to the goal of producing unambiguous, high-quality utterances.

SILENT PAUSES . The pattern just discussed is even more pronounced for the symptom of silent pauses: The sharp downward slope in the upper line of the graph shows that, when subjects had to navigate, they largely abandoned the goal of generating high-quality utterances that would require careful thought. This effect is especially striking when one considers that a secondary task would in itself tend to increase the number and/or length of silent pauses by demanding the subjects' attention at least intermittently—an effect which is in fact found in the condition with time pressure (lower line) and in previous studies (cf. Berthold, [1]). In sum, the presence or absence of time pressure makes a big difference with regard to silent pauses overall (   ), and the main impact of the navigation task is to reduce this difference (interaction:).

FILLED PAUSES . The last graph in Figure 2 shows that filled pauses behave very similarly to silent pauses in the two conditions with time pressure; in particular, they increase when there is a navigation task (as has been shown in previous studies; cf. Berthold, [1]). But in contrast to the case with silent pauses, they show a similar pattern when there is no time pressure. Overall, there is a significant effect of the navigation task (   ) but no significant effect of time pressure and no interaction. In sum, filled pauses might serve as a fairly straightforward index of the presence of a distracting secondary task.

We have seen that each of the dependent variables discussed here shows one or two statistically reliable effects of time pressure and/or the navigation task. These results suggest that observation of these variables in a person's speech might allow a system to infer their current resource limitations. But it is not obvious how successful such diagnosis will actually be in practice. This question is addressed in the next section.

3   Modeling

If we want to create a system that recognizes the resource limitations of its users on the basis of their speech, we need to take two basic steps:

1. Use machine learning methods to create some sort of model relating resource limitations to speech symptoms, using data such as those of this experiment (Sections 3.1 and 3.2 below).
2. Employ this model during an interaction with each user, using the features of their speech as evidence (Section 4).

3.1   Bayesian Network Structure

Regarding Step 1: Among the various techniques that could potentially be used, we employ Bayesian networks (BNs).[3] Within this framework, there are various ways of (a) learning a general user model on the basis of data from a sample of users and (b) adapting it to each individual user on the basis of data about that user (see Jameson & Wittig, [6]). The method employed in the present study is illustrated in Figure 3.

---

[3] Accessible introductions to BNs are now available from many sources; the classic exposition is that of Pearl ([8]).

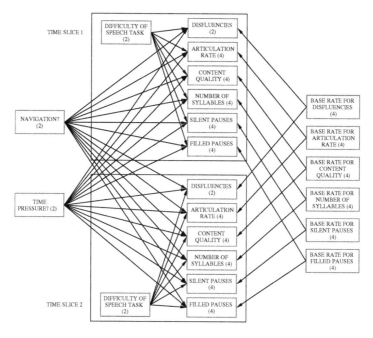

Fig. 3. *Structure of the dynamic Bayesian network used in the evaluation.*
(Nodes within the boxes correspond to temporary variables that index features of the current utterance. Each number in parentheses shows the number of discrete states for the variable in question.)

(The lower part labeled TIME SLICE 2 can be ignored for the moment.) The two nodes NAVIGATION? and TIME PRESSURE? on the left correspond to the two main independent variables of the experiment. The six nodes on the right in TIME SLICE 1 correspond to the dependent variables that we have discussed above.

The six nodes on the far right correspond to individual base rates for the six symptom variables. They are introduced to take into account individual differences in the overall level of the symptom variables. The value of each such variable is constant for each   : It is simply computed as the mean value of the variable in question for the entire experiment.[4]

---

[4] The BN structure in the figure implies that these base rate variables are statistically independent. This assumption was shown to be false by both structure learning algorithms and factor analyses. Nonetheless, this simplified model was found to perform better at the task of recognizing a speaker's time pressure and cognitive load than did more complex models that took into account the statistical dependencies. A possible reason is that in the more complex models the estimates of some probabilities in the learned BN are less accurate because they are based on relatively few observations. In any case, this result illustrates the general point (see, e.g., Greiner et al., [4]) that the goal in learning BNs is often to learn not the one "correct" model but rather the model which works best for a particular task in a particular setting.

The final node in the BN, DIFFICULTY OF SPEECH TASK , refers to the rated complexity of the speech task created by the stimulus picture (cf. Section 2.1).

Our question in the evaluation study will be: If a user   produces a sequence of utterances in a given experimental condition, how well can a system   recognize that condition? Therefore, the variables NAVIGATION? and TIME PRESSURE? can be viewed here as static variables whose value does not change over time. The six base rate variables are also static. By contrast, each of the variables inside the boxes labeled TIME SLICE 1 and TIME SLICE 2 refers to an aspect of just one utterance. Hence corresponding temporary nodes need to be created for each utterance. We are therefore dealing with a dynamic Bayesian network (DBN) that comprises a series of time slices.[5]

3.2   Learning of a BN

Since we want to test a learned BN model with the data of a given user   , we must not include   's data in the data that are used for the learning of the corresponding BN. Accordingly, we learned for each   the conditional probability tables (CPTs) for a separate BN using the data from the other 31 subjects. The learned BN has the structure shown in Figure 3 minus the nodes shown for TIME SLICE 2; the CPTs for the temporary variables within each time slice are the same as the ones learned for TIME SLICE 1.

The learning method we employed is the usual maximum-likelihood method for learning fully observable Bayesian networks (see, e.g., Buntine, [3]): The estimate of each (conditional) probability is computed simply in terms of the (relative) frequencies in the data.

4   Evaluation

The procedure for evaluating a learned BN is given in Table 1.

Figure 4 shows the results of the evaluation, aggregated over all 32 subjects.[6]

Looking first at the results for recognizing time pressure (left-hand graph), we see that the BNs are on the whole rather successful: The average probability assigned to the actual current condition rises sharply during the first few observations. Note that recognition of time pressure is easier when there is no navigation task.[7] This result is understandable given the overall effects shown in Figure 2: On the whole the effects of time pressure were greatest when there was no navigation task, since speakers could respond more sensitively to the time pressure (or lack of it).

---

[5] The general principles of dynamic Bayesian networks are explained, e.g., by Russell and Norvig ([9, chap. 17]). A discussion with regard to user modeling of the sort done here is given by Schäfer and Weyrath ([10]). A detailed understanding of DBNs is not required for the reading of this paper.

[6] The results for individual subjects are much less smooth than these aggregated results: The individual curves often show sharp jumps and extreme values.

[7]   for the difference between the average of the two upper curves and the average of the two lower curves. All statistical tests in this section are two-tailed sign tests based on the last 10 observations.

Relevant variables and their values

- A user U
- Values t and n of the Boolean variables T (time pressure?) and N (navigation?)

Task

Infer the values of T and N on the basis of symptoms in U's speech

Preparation of the test data

Select the 20 observations for U in which T = t and N = n, in the order in which they occurred in the experiment

Evaluating recognition accuracy

Initialize the model:

1. Create the first time slice of the BN for U
2. Instantiate each of the individual baseline variables with its true value for U (but leave the variables T and N uninstantiated)

For each observation O in the set of observations for U:

1. In the newest time slice of the BN, derive beliefs about T and N:
   - Instantiate all of the temporary variables for this time slice with their values in O
   - Evaluate the BN to arrive at beliefs regarding T and N
   - Note the probabilities assigned at this point to the true values of T and N, respectively
2. Add a new time slice to the dynamic BN to prepare for the next observation

Table 1. *Procedure used in evaluating the recognition accuracy of the learned Bayesian networks.*

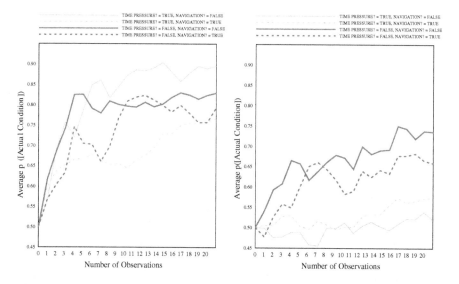

Fig. 4. *Accuracy of the learned BNs in inferring the correct value of* TIME PRESSURE? *(left) and* NAVIGATION? *(right).*

(Each curve shows the aggregated results for one combination of values of the variables TIME PRESSURE? *and* NAVIGATION?. *In each curve, the point for the ith observation shows the average probability which the BN assigned to the correct value of the variable in question after processing the first i observations.)*

Recognition of the navigation task is considerably less successful: The highest curve in the right-hand graph is significantly lower than the lowest curve in the left-hand graph during the last 10 observations (   ). This result is likewise understandable given the overall effects shown in Figure 2, where on the whole the effects of time pressure (reflected in the differences between the two lines in each graph) were more substantial than those of the navigation task (reflected in the slopes of the lines). In particular, the slopes of the lines in Figure 2 for the time pressure condition are especially flat, a tendency which corresponds with the very poor results for recognizing the navigation task when subjects are under time pressure. Essentially, since the speakers are trying to strip their utterances down to a bare minimum anyway, there is not much complex language processing that could be affected by a secondary task. Even the recognition accuracy when there is no time pressure is rather modest: After about 5 observations, the system assigns a probability of .60 to .65 to the correct hypothesis.

But note that it is not necessarily a problem if many users cope with a secondary task so well that it is difficult to recognize, on the basis of their speech, whether they are currently performing it or not. For these particular subjects, it may be less important to know whether they are performing a secondary task, since the secondary task may have little impact on their performance of other tasks (e.g., interacting with the mobile system). Further investigation of this issue will help to put the results just reported into perspective.

We could have made the navigation task easier to recognize simply by increasing its complexity in the experimental environment—perhaps to a point where it caused subjects' speech generation to break down completely. Instead, while developing the experiment we adjusted the level of complexity of the navigation task until it seemed typical of a situation in which a user is walking around a crowded airport while speaking into a device.

5   Summary of Contributions and Work in Progress

Our experiment differs from comparable previous experiments in (a) the number of independent variables examined simultaneously and (b) the relevance of the experimental tasks to mobile computing scenarios. A number of the specific effects identified had not been reported previously.

The evaluation of the learned user models is to our knowledge the first empirical evaluation of the feasibility of recognizing a person's time pressure and/or cognitive load on the basis of speech input.

We are currently pursuing the following extensions of this work:

- Use of more theoretically interpretable BN structures (cf. Wittig & Jameson, [11]) which will make it possible to analyze more clearly the reasons for particular aspects of the learned models' performance.
- Inclusion in the more articulate BN models of the remaining symptom variables that were recorded in the experiment but not included in the present study (cf. Section 3.1).

- Systematic studies of the reasons for the observed performance of the models (e.g., comparisons with tests in which some of the variables are omitted or not instantiated).

For practical use of these results, it will obviously be necessary to devise ways of coding the features of speech fully automatically, rather than largely manually as in the present study. Given that this goal is quite challenging for some of the features, our strategy has been to start by determining the diagnostic value of the features, so that the benefits of coding them automatically can be assessed. The results so far indicate that the features that would be most difficult to encode (e.g., content quality, self-corrections) have less diagnostic value than relatively easy features (e.g., duration of silent pauses, number of syllables).

References

1. André Berthold. Repräsentation und Verarbeitung sprachlicher Indikatoren für kognitive Ressourcenbeschränkungen [Representation and processing of linguistic indicators of cognitive resource limitations]. Master's thesis, Department of Computer Science, Saarland University, Germany, 1998.
2. André Berthold and Anthony Jameson. Interpreting symptoms of cognitive load in speech input. In Judy Kay, editor, UM99, User Modeling: Proceedings of the Seventh International Conference, pages 235–244. Springer Wien New York, Vienna, 1999.
3. Wray Buntine. A guide to the literature on learning probabilistic networks from data. IEEE Transactions on Knowledge and Data Engineering, 8:195–210, 1996.
4. Russell Greiner, Adam J. Grove, and Dale Schuurmans. Learning Bayesian nets that perform well. In Dan Geiger and Prakash P. Shenoy, editors, Uncertainty in Artificial Intelligence: Proceedings of the Thirteenth Conference, pages 198–207. Morgan Kaufmann, San Francisco, 1997.
5. Anthony Jameson, Barbara Großmann-Hutter, Leonie March, Ralf Rummer, Thorsten Bohnenberger, and Frank Wittig. When actions have consequences: Empirically based decision making for intelligent user interfaces. Knowledge-Based Systems 14:75–92, 2001.
6. Anthony Jameson and Frank Wittig. Leveraging data about users in general in the learning of individual user models. In Bernhard Nebel, editor, Proceedings of the Seventeenth International Joint Conference on Artificial Intelligence. Morgan Kaufmann, San Francisco, CA, 2001.
7. Sharon Oviatt. Multimodal interactive maps: Designing for human performance. Human-Computer Interaction, 12:93–129, 1997.
8. Judea Pearl. Probabilistic Reasoning in Intelligent Systems: Networks of Plausible Inference. Morgan Kaufmann, San Mateo, CA, 1988.
9. Stuart J. Russell and Peter Norvig. Artificial Intelligence: A Modern Approach. Prentice-Hall, Englewood Cliffs, NJ, 1995.
10. Ralph Schäfer and Thomas Weyrath. Assessing temporally variable user properties with dynamic Bayesian networks. In Anthony Jameson, Cécile Paris, and Carlo Tasso, editors, User Modeling: Proceedings of the Sixth International Conference, UM97, pages 377–388. Springer Wien New York, Vienna, 1997.
11. Frank Wittig and Anthony Jameson. Exploiting qualitative knowledge in the learning of conditional probabilities of Bayesian networks. In Craig Boutilier and Moisés Goldszmidt, editors, Uncertainty in Artificial Intelligence: Proceedings of the Sixteenth Conference, pages 644–652. Morgan Kaufmann, San Francisco, 2000.

The Learning Shell:
Automated Macro Construction

Nico Jacobs and Hendrik Blockeel

Katholieke Universiteit Leuven,
Department of Computer Science,
Celestijnenlaan 200A, B-3001 Leuven
tel +32 16327550
fax +32 16327996
{Nico.Jacobs, Hendrik.Blockeel   }@cs.kuleuven.ac.be

Abstract.   By analysing sequences of actions performed by a user, one can find frequent subsequences that can be suggested as macro (script) definitions. However, often these 'actions' have additional features. In this paper we combine an algorithm to detect frequent subsequences with an inductive logic programming system to automatically generate for each frequent subsequence the most specific 'template' for these additional features that is consistent with the observed frequent subsequences. The resulting system is implemented and used in an application where we automatically generate macros from logs of the use of a Unix command shell.

Keywords : machine learning, inductive logic programming, interface adaptation.

1   Introduction

When a user interacts with a computer, this can be seen as the user executing a sequence of actions. By analysing these sequences one can obtain useful information about the interaction between user and computer. An example of this is click-stream analysis   in which the sequence of visited webpages is analysed to get an idea of the way a website is visited in order to improve the site. In many situations the actions the user performs will also have additional features. Actions can take parameters (such as the filename on which the action needs to be performed), can return information (such as a return code) or can have other properties (such as a duration, cost, etc.). In the rest of this paper we call all these extra information the features of the action. These features can be very important. Consider the click-stream analysis example. When this analysis shows that a certain subsequence   A -> B -> A -> C occurs frequently one could conclude that B is an important page because it often happens that people on page A especially go to this page B even if they don't use any links on that page; they go back to A and then continue their web journey. However, if there would be a log of the duration of each visit and that feature would be used in the analysis,

M. Bauer, P.J. Gmytrasiewicz, and J. Vassileva (Eds.): UM 2001, LNAI 2109, pp. 34–43, 2001.

the result could be as follows: long visit to A -> very short visit to B
-> short visit to A -> long visit to C   . Given such an analysis, our first
conclusion is wrong. The user goes to page B, but since he returns to A very
quickly, probably he didn't want to see page B at all. So instead of concluding
that the link from A to B is important we can conclude that the user doesn't
like this link at all; maybe the link description is wrong?

In this paper we present a method to find frequent subsequences in a sequence of actions together with their features or other related information. We
explain why we use of inductive logic programming for this task. Then we apply
this method in a system that analyses sequences of commands typed at a Unix
command shell. The result of this analysis is a set of macro definitions that are
ready for use. We conclude with some directions for future work.

2   Finding Maximal Frequent Subsequences

We first introduce the concepts of sequence, subsequence and maximal frequent
subsequences as we will use them throughout the paper.

Definition 1.   Let s be a sequence of n elements: $e_{s,1}e_{s,2}e_{s,3}...e_{s,n-1}e_{s,n}$. A sequence s ($e_{s,1}e_{s,2}...e_{s,p-1}e_{s,p}$) of length p is a subsequence of the sequence s of
length n if 1   p   n   k, k   n − p : i $\in$ { 1...p} : $e_{s,i} = e_{s,k+i}$. The frequency
of a subsequence in a sequence is the number of dierent values for k such that
the previous condition holds.

For example the sequence 1 1 is a subsequence of the sequence 3 1 1 1 5 and the
frequency is 2.

When we consider sequences of user actions, we are interested in subsequences
with a high frequency: improving the ease to execute such frequent subsequences
of actions can improve the interaction between the user and the computer. Longer
subsequences are preferred over shorter ones, and since subsequences of a frequent subsequence are also frequent subsequences, we are looking for maximal
subsequences of a certain frequency.

Definition 2.   A sequence s is a maximal subsequence of frequency f of a sequence s if s is a subsequence of the sequence s with a frequency of at least f and
there is no sequence s , subsequence of s with frequency at least f, such that   s
is a subsequence of s .

The algorithm is an implementation of the minimal occurrences approach
described in [6]: to find these frequent maximal subsequences, we first find all
frequent subsequences of length 1, use these to calculate all frequent subsequences of length 2 etc. As soon as a frequent subsequence can't be extended to
a longer frequent subsequence, it has become maximal. It is important to notice
that each sequence s of length n > 1 $e_{s,1}e_{s,2}...e_{s,n-1}e_{s,n}$ has 2 frequent subsequences of length n − 1: $e_{s,1}e_{s,2}...e_{s,n-1}$ and $e_{s,2}...e_{s,n-1}e_{s,n}$. We call this first
subsequence leftparent (s) and the second rightparent (s). The left and right

parent of a sequence of length one is the empty sequence. For each sequence
we also store the positions in the input where this sequence starts. Given two
parents, it's easy to calculate the positions of the child-sequence: all positions of
the left-parent that are one less than a position of the right parent is a position
of the child sequence. Our algorithm is shown in figure 1.

```
length = 1
let S(1) be the set of all frequent subsequences of s of length 1
while S(length) =    do
        S(length+1) =
        foreach t    S(length)
                foreach u    S(length) such that    leftparent (u) = rightparent (t)
                        newsequence =   e_{t, 1}e_{t, 2}...e_{t,length}   e_{u,length}
                        if newsequence is frequent
                                add newsequence to S(length+1)
        length = length + 1
```

Fig. 1.   Calculating all frequent maximal subsets of s

We only have to read the input once to calculate S(1). Because we store the
positions of each frequent sequence, and we can calculate the positions of a new
sequence based on the positions of both parents, we can calculate all frequent
sequences with just one pass through the input. To reduce memory consumption
we do not store the subsequences   s but only their positions. This also reduces
computation time. The disadvantage is that after we computed all subsequences
we have to scan the input a second time to be able to output the actions of a
subsequence instead of their positions, but this usually requires less time than
the time saved by avoiding constructing and storing the real subsequences.

3   Finding Frequent Behaviour

We can apply the algorithm in figure 1 to analyse visits to a website. The sequence consists of the name of the files that a user retrieved, and the result of
the analysis are all sequences of pages that are often visited by that user.

When analysing the behaviour of users, especially in the above example of
webvisits, one wants to combine multiple sequences: analysing all the visits of
one person, or all the visits of certain groups of users. This can be done with a
very small modification to the above algorithm and by appending all sequences
one wants to analyse, in this way creating one combined sequence. This introduces 'artificial subsequences' at the border between two original sequences. To
overcome this problem we place special elements in the combined sequence at
the border between two original sequences: sequence s and t are combined in a
sequence $e_{s, 1}e_{s, 2}...e_{s,n}$ < special > $e_{t, 1}e_{t, 2}...e_{t,m}$. We modify the algorithm so
that it never considers subsequences that contain the special element.

Another problem when we use the above algorithm in analysing user behaviour is — as already mentioned in the introduction — that we often want to
take in account more information than just the action performed. For instance
we can try to analyse the webvisit data where we take into account the page
visited, the duration of the visit and two booleans: did the user save the page
and did the user print the page.

index.html 15 false false
research.html 124 false true
index.html 9 false false
research/publication.html 15 true false

Fig. 2.   Example of extended sequence

One way to analyse the data would be to consider all the information provided about one visit to a page as one element in the sequence (so in the above
example the first element in the sequence is   index.html 15 false false   which
is dierent from the third element   index.html 9 false false   ). This approach
however is not useful:

- in most applications an element consisting of an action and its features will
  not reoccurre often. We will find almost no frequent subsequences in such a
  sequence.
- we are interested in subsequences that use that extra information, but only
  when it is relevant. For instance, if in the above example a frequent subsequence of visited pages index.html -> research.html   is found, it may be
  that in all occurrences of the subsequence the research.html page is visited
  for less than 10 seconds, but that the other features are random. We then
  want a description of this subsequence that mentions only the duration of the
  visit to the research page and the . The algorithm presented in the previous
  section provides sequences that either mention all features or none.
- sometimes relations between features are more important than the value
  of the features themselfs. For instance when analysing commands typed at
  a shell, it is important to detect that two commands have the same (but
  unspecified) filename as parameter. An approach where sequences can only
  contain constants can not express such regularities.

We need to find an other way to incorporate the action features. We do
this by using Warmr [3], an inductive logic programming (ILP) system [7]. ILP
systems use (a subset of) first order logic for representing the input as well as
the learned rules, which makes such systems very flexible. We will first briefly
introduce the Warmr system and then illustrate how it is used in our system. In
this description we expect the user to be familiar with prolog (see [1] for more
information on prolog).

Warmr is a system which detects frequent patterns in relational data. It takes
as input a set of observations, background knowledge and a language bias and

searches for all legal patterns that are frequent in the set of observations. Each observation is written as a collection of prolog facts, the background knowledge is written as a prolog program and contains domain specific information that is valid for all observations. Background knowledge can be used to derive 'new' information based on the information available in the observation. The language bias defines the set of legal patterns and puts constraints on the variables that can be used in these patterns.

A pattern is either a literal that is legal by the definition in the language bias, or a legal conjunction of such literals. A pattern holds in an observation if the pattern succeeds as a query in a prolog program consisting of that observation and the complete background knowledge. The frequency (or support) for a pattern is the percentage of observations in which a pattern holds.

Fig. 3 shows how we use Warmr in our system. Each occurrence of a frequent maximal subsequence is transformed into an observation (which contains information about the features of the actions). Warmr will receive the set of all observations of a certain subsequence and search for all frequent patterns. Some of these patterns are redundant in the sense that they are part of an other frequent pattern; such patterns are filtered out. This process is repeated for each frequent maximal subsequence. All of these actions are automated except for writing the background knowledge (as mentioned earlier) and writing the language bias. This language bias defines the patterns we are interested in, and is application specific. In a later stage, grammar induction [8] could be useful to automatically generate this language bias.

```
find all frequent maximal subsequences in the sequence of all actions
foreach frequent maximal subsequence    t do
            foreach occurrence   oc of t in the input do
                        rewrite  oc as a Warmr observation
            run Warmr on the set of all observations of       t
            filter out redundant patterns
```

Fig. 3. Finding frequent behaviour

The next section shows an example of the use of this system.

4   Automated Macro Construction

Unix shells are still often used to interact with a Unix system. There have been previous eorts to analyse how users use this shell interface. [4] uses statistical techniques to analyse shell usage. Most user modeling approaches use machine learning techniques to learn a classifier that, given the history of previous typed commands, predicts what the next command will be. [2] compare dierent approaches, [5] presents an approach which can predict not only the next command, but some of its features as well.

Our approach to help the shell user is dierent. Instead of predicting the next command, we want to provide the user with automatically generated scripts (macros) that can replace sequences of actions. We log how a user interacts with the shell, then search for frequent sequences of actions, use Warmr to find a description for the features of these actions and rewrite these results so that we can present to the user a macro definition for the sequence of actions. It is up to the user to decide which of these macro descriptions to use. We chose this approach because previous work shows that

- the user often uses short commands [4]. For those commands, it is as little eort to type the command as to select or verify a prediction.
- long commands are dicult to predict correctly. Verifying and correcting the prediction can take as much time as typing the command (or even more).
- a special shell is necessary to integrate the results of the prediction, but users often want to keep using the shell they are used to. Because of the on-line learning, this special shell will also use more cpu time than 'normal' shells.

Our approach just oers the user a ħew' command (macro), which is a sequence of existing commands. The user has to verify these only once, and from then on use them: the overhead of using these macros is minimal. Since one macro replaces a   sequence of commands, there is an eort gain, even by replacing short commands. Almost all Unix shells have some mechanism to store a history of typed commands and allow the user to define new commands (often called functions, aliases or macros), so our approach can be integrated in nearly every existing Unix shell. Moreover, the user can easily share some macros with other users. Finally, this system can learn o-line, even on other machines than the user is using, so there is only a minimal extra cpu time necessary while the user is using the system: looking for new frequent sequences can be done when the machine is idle.

Let's illustrate this with an example. We have a history of shell use:

```
cd  tex
ls
vim  um2000.tex
latex  um2000.tex
xdvi  -hush  -keep  um2000.dvi
...
```

First we create a sequence   s of the command names:

```
cd  ls  vim  latex  xdvi     ...
```

We calculate all maximal frequent subsequences of   s. For each maximal frequent subsequence a learning task for Warmr is created. Suppose   s (vim latex xdvi) is one such subsequence. We extract from the input all occurrences of   s . These commands are parsed and written as prolog facts to be used as observations for the Warmr system:

command(1,1,vim).
attributestem(1,1,1,um2000).
attributeext(1,1,1,tex).

command(1,2,latex).
attributestem(1,2,1,um2000).
attributeext(1,2,1,tex).

command(1,3,xdvi).
switch(1,3,1,hush).
switch(1,3,2,keep).
attributestem(1,3,1,um2000).
attributeext(1,3,1,dvi).

command(2,1,vim).

...

We use a simple representation: the first argument of each fact is the index of the occurrence, the second argument is the position within the subsequence. A command can have more than one attribute and switch, therefor these facts have a third argument indicating their position within the command. Attributes are split up in a stem and an extension.

We can provide background knowledge to this learning task. For example, some users use the full name of some switches, while most use only the sort one. We can express in background knowledge for instance that the   -all   switch of the ls command is the same as the   -a switch:

switch(Ob,C,P,a) :- command(Ob,C,ls), switch(Ob,C,P,all).

Capital letters denote variables in prolog. The above rule can be read as follows: "if a switch all occurs at position P in the Cth command in the   Obth occurrence of the substring, and the associated command is   ls , then pretend like the switch a occurred at that position".

The language bias is constructed automatically by a small program written specially for this application. Given the language, the observations and background knowledge, Warmr can search for frequent patterns. We only accept patterns that occur at least in 50% of the observations. We show some of these frequent patterns.

attributestem(Ob,1,1,Stem), attributestem(Ob,2,1,Stem).
attributeext(Ob,1,1,Ext), attributeext(Ob,2,1,Ext).
attributeext(Ob,1,1,tex), attributeext(Ob,2,1,tex).

As mentioned in the previous section, we filter out all frequent patterns that are part of a longer frequent pattern. However, a rule can also be redundant because it reformulates with variables a rule that is already expressed with constants: e.g. if the rule   vim $1.tex -> latex $1.tex   is found, the rule   vim $1.$2 -> latex $1.$2   is redundant. Such rules are filtered out as well. If we apply this filtering to all frequent patterns, the result in our example is one pattern:

attributestem(Ob,1,1,Stem), attributestem(Ob,2,1,Stem),
attributestem(Ob,3,1,Stem), attributeext(Ob,1,1,tex),
attributeext(Ob,2,1,tex), attributeext(Ob,3,1,dvi), switch(Ob,3,1,hush).

The resulting patterns from all frequent maximal subsequences are sorted. As a sorting criterion we use the product of the length (in terms of actions) and the support of the pattern: longer macros and more frequent usable macros will probably the most interesting macros and will end in this way on top of the list.

The final step is transforming each pattern into a macro definition. We perform some extra operations in this translation. If the pattern doesn't provide any information about the attributes of a certain command, we compute the average number of attributes for that command in the observations, and use that many variables as attributes for that command. We show the resulting macro of our example:

```
function giveyourownname() {
    vim $1.tex
    latex $1.tex
    xdvi $1.dvi
}
```

The list of discovered macros is presented to the user to decide which macros to accept and to provide a name for the accepted macros.

We applied this to the Greenberg dataset [4]. Greenberg collected logs of 168 unix shell users: 52 computer scientists, 36 experienced programmers, 55 novice programmers and 25 non programmers. For each of these users we construct all maximal frequent subsequences, where a sequence was considered frequent if it occurs in at least 1% of the cases, with a minimum of 3 occurrences (because some logs are small). Within each group of users, we count the number of maximal frequent subsequences for each length, and divide these by the total number of logged commands within this group. The results are plotted in figure 4, with on the x-axis the length of a sequence, and on the y-axis the number of occurences of such sequences, expressed as a percentage of the number of commands. We see that sequences up till length 12 are found, although sequences longer than 8 commands are rare. Experienced programmers and computer scientists do not often perform identical sequences of commands. However, non programmers seems to be the group who can benefit most from this application, as they do have long sequences of commands that they repeat often.

5   Discussion

In this paper we presented a technique to find maximal frequent subsequences in a given sequence of actions and their features. Given such a frequent subsequence of actions, we use inductive logic programming to find a general description of the features of these actions. The result is a pattern of frequent user behaviour.

We used this technique to build a system that analyses the commands typed at a Unix shell to automatically generate macro definitions for frequently used sequences of commands. This approach can be applied in most existing shells and requires nearly no overhead of the user while it can save the user time and

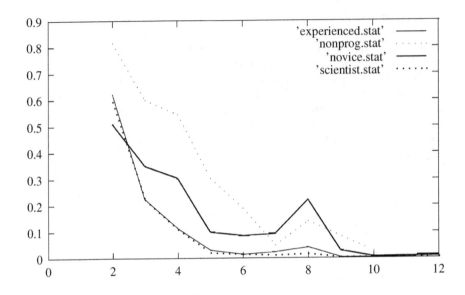

Fig. 4.   Macro length in Greenberg dataset

eort. Moreover, the user can edit and share these discovered patterns of frequent behaviour with others.

We tested the system on the Greenberg dataset. It shows that long sequences of repetitive behaviour are found in real user data and this for dierent types of users.

The current implementation is only a prototype. The parsing of commands is very basic: pipes, multiple commands on one line and I/O redirection are not yet supported. Also switches which have attributes on their own (such as   lpr -Pcolor) are not yet processed correctly. Background knowledge only contains a few rules like described in the previous section. A coupling with the   man pages (on-line manual of nearly all Unix commands) or a grammar induction system would make the system significantly smarter. The concept of edit distance [9] can be useful, because subsequences that match except for some commands (like ls) are much more similar than subsequences that match except for another command.

Besides this application there are other applications where this technique can be useful. As already suggested in this paper, analysing traces of visits to a website where each click is annotated with extra information can help the designer in understanding how users visit the site. The system can also be used in analysing other user interfaces: a prototype of the user interface is built and testers try this interface. All their annotated actions are logged and analysed. If important long subsequences of actions are found, the developer can consider redesigning the interface in such a way that these actions can be performed either shorter or more easily. All applications were sequential annotated data is involved and were frequent subsequences provide important knowledge are potential application domains for this technique.

Acknowledgements

The authors thank Luc Dehaspe for his help with the Warmr system, Luc De Raedt for the discussions on this subject and Saul Greenberg for providing the test data. Nico Jacobs is financed by a specialisation grant of the Flemish Institute for the promotion of scientific and technological research in the industry (IWT). Hendrik Blockeel is a post-doctoral fellow of the Fund for Scientific Research of Flanders (FWO-Vlaanderen).

References

1. I. Bratko. Prolog Programming for Artificial Intelligence . Addison-Wesley, Wokingham, England, 1990. 2nd Edition.
2. Brian D. Davison and Haym Hirsch. Experiments in UNIX command prediction. In Proceedings of the 14th National Conference on Artificial Intelligence and 9th Innovative Applications of Artificial Intelligence Conference (AAAI-97/IAAI-97) , pages 827–827, Menlo Park, July 27–31 1997. AAAI Press.
3. L. Dehaspe. Frequent Pattern Discovery in First-Order Logic . PhD thesis, Department of Computer Science, Katholieke Universiteit Leuven, 1998. http://www.cs.kuleuven.ac.be/~ldh/ .
4. Saul Greenberg. The Computer User as Toolsmith: The Use, Reuse, and Organization of Computer-Based Tools . Cambridge Series on Human-Computer Interaction. Cambridge University Press, 1993. QA76.9H85G73.
5. Benjamin Korvemaker and Russell Greiner. Predicting UNIX command lines: Adjusting to user patterns. In Adaptive User Interfaces: Papers from the 2000 AAAI Spring Symposium , pages 59–64, 2000.
6. H. Mannila, H. Toivonen, and A. I. Verkamo. Discovery of frequent episodes in event sequences. Data Mining and Knowledge Discovery , 1(3):259–289, 1997.
7. S. Muggleton. Inductive logic programming. New Generation Computing , 8(4):295–317, 1991.
8. Rajesh Parekh and Vasant Honovar. Grammar inference, automata induction and language acquisition, 1998.
9. Robert A. Wagner and Michael J. Fischer. The string-to-string correction problem. Journal of the ACM , 21(1):168–173, January 1974.

Learning Interaction Models in a Digital Library Service

Giovanni Semeraro, Stefano Ferilli, Nicola Fanizzi, and Fabio Abbattista

Dipartimento di Informatica, Universitàdi Bari,
Via Orabona 4, I-70125 Bari, Italy
{semeraro,ferilli,fanizzi,fabio}@di.uniba.it

Abstract. We present the exploitation of an improved version of the Learning Server for modeling the user interaction in a digital library service architecture. This module is the basic component for providing the service with an added value such as an essential extensible form of interface adaptivity. Indeed, the system is equipped with a web-based visual environment, primarily intended to improve the user interaction by automating the assignment of a suitable interface depending on data relative to the previous experience with the system, coded in log files. The experiments performed show that accurate interaction models can be inferred automatically by using up-to-date learning algorithms.

1 Introduction and Motivation

Functionalities that exploit machine learning techniques are the most characterizing feature of CDL (Corporate Digital Library), a prototypical intelligent digital library service under development at the University of Bari [4; 5; 11].

A key issue in digital libraries research is the support to the information access, retrieval and organization in order to make rapid decisions on what is relevant and which patterns exist among objects. Conventional interfaces, based on information retrieval viewed as an isolated task in which the user formulates a query against a homogeneous collection to obtain matching documents, are completely out of date. For example, users may realize what they are trying to ask and how to ask it by interacting with the system (iterative query refinement) [9].

One of the goals of our work is to investigate effective ways for endowing the interaction environment with appropriate representations of some meta-information, concerning the document content in particular, in order to provide users with proper cues for locating the desired data. The paradigms for content representation range from a textual description of what is stored in the information source to structured representations that adopt expressive knowledge representation languages. Our choice is to exploit visual techniques, whose main advantage is the capability of shifting load from user's cognitive system to the perceptual system.

When interacting with huge amounts of information, it is extremely useful to avail oneself of some meta-information on different aspects of the data, namely: what information is stored in the source (content), how this information is generated and maintained (a public source or a personal archive), how frequently it is maintained (provenance), the schemes for the items in the source, their attributes and their domains (form), the capability of the access services, such as the search paradigms

M. Bauer, P.J. Gmytrasiewicz, and J. Vassileva (Eds.): UM 2001, LNAI 2109, pp. 44–53, 2001.
©Springer-Verlag Berlin Heidelberg 2001

supported and their performance (functionality), measures about the usage, including previous use by the same user or others (usage statistics).

As regards the CDL visual environment, we will essentially focus on the module performing interaction modeling that is the basic component for providing a form of user interface adaptivity. This feature is achieved by automatically classifying the user by means of machine learning techniques based on new learning tools.

The remainder of the paper is organized as follows. An overview of the architecture of CDL and its interaction environment is given in Section 2, while Section 3 illustrates the Machine Learning toolset WEKA. Section 4 explains how interaction modeling is performed using the CDL Learning Server and the outcomes of a real experimentation are discussed. Conclusions are drawn in Section 5, where we also outline our planned future work on these topics.

2   The CDL Interaction Environment

A digital library is a distributed technology for the creation, dissemination, manipulation, storage, integration and reuse of digital information. We developed CDL as a prototypical digital library service, whose primary goal is to provide a common infrastructure that makes easy the process of managing corporate digital libraries, i.e. libraries that share mechanisms for searching information, updating content, controlling user access, charging users, etc., independently of the meaning and the internal representation of the items contained. This section gives an overview of the CDL architecture and visual interaction environment. A thorough and detailed description is reported in [4; 5].

The CDL project focuses on the development of effective middleware services for digital libraries and on their interoperability across heterogeneous hardware and software platforms [2]. Its main features are strictly related to the support of machine learning techniques for performing specific functions, namely: collection, organization and access. Therefore, supervised learning techniques are used to overcome the problem of cheaply and effectively setting information items free of the physical medium on which they are stored (information capture), as well as to perform document classification and interpretation [5], that are necessary steps to index information items according to their content (semantic indexing). Moreover, CDL provides users with an added value service, which helps novice users to understand the content and the organization of a digital library through a suitable visual environment and supports skilled users (those supposed to be familiar with the digital library) during retrieval by means of an appropriate interface modality. Interface adaptivity is pursued through an automated user classification based on machine learning techniques.

CDL is modeled along typical client/server architecture of a hypertextual service to be available on the Internet. Specifically, the current version adopts a three-tier thin-client stateful architecture [7]. In such a model, a Web browser is sufficient for running the client application. Besides, there is no need of storing data locally: documents are reconstructed and collected from the various library hosts by the middleware components, and then presented to the user through HTML pages, dynamically generated by means of Java applets, so to mirror the current content of the repositories in the library hosts. Furthermore, the architecture is characterized by the presence of a Learning Server [12] that, besides the other services related to document management, is able to infer interaction models concerning classes of users of the CDL, given the data collected in log files during usage sessions.

Three different kinds of roles have been identified [5] within the digital library service: 1) the Library Administrator, allowed to create/delete a digital library; 2) the Librarian, in charge of managing specific digital libraries; and 3) the Generic User (user for short), i.e. any person accessing the service to consult the available digital libraries. The user can query the libraries to retrieve the documents he is interested in and, then, he may display/view them in a digital format.

In the development of the CDL prototype, the first interface implemented was a standard form-based one [11], which turned out to be powerful and flexible, yet it soon appeared to be more appropriate for users who are already acquainted with the library organization and content. Casual users often perform queries yielding null results because they do not have an idea of the kind of documents stored in the libraries. Therefore, the CDL interaction environment has been enriched with other visual tools allowing users to easily grasp the nature of the information stored and the possible patterns among the objects, so that they can make rapid decisions about what they really need and how to get it.

One of the new features of the CDL environment is the possibility of interacting with the service through the topic map or interactive dynamic map, which gives a global view of the library content, by exploiting a geographic metaphor. A collection of topics is considered to be a territory containing resources (the topics themselves); maps of these territories can be drawn, where regions, cities, and roads are used to convey the structure of the set of topics: a region represents a set of topics, and the size of the region reflects the number of topics in that region. Similarly, the distance between two cities reflects the similarity relationship between them: if two cities are close to each other, then the topics are strongly related in a specific library. In order to generate the topic map in CDL, sets of topics or descriptors were identified defining the semantic content of the documents stored in a digital library; such topics constitute the library thesaurus, that was built along standard techniques.

Topics can be represented by vectors, which a standard practice for documents in information retrieval [10]. A number of correlations can be computed from these vectors and then visualized in the topic map. The thesaurus is partitioned in a set of p classes $\{A_1, A_2, ..., A_p\}$, where each A_i contains descriptors that are similar. For each class a centroid is computed and the other topics are assigned to the class with the highest similarity, this being computed with respect to the class centroid. Color-based coding techniques, representing the importance of a topic or a link, and other widgets are used to make more effective the overall visualization and provide mechanisms for flexible interaction in such a data intensive context.

The tree-based interface provides another visual tool to both browse libraries and perform queries. The user navigates into CDL along a tree structure, starting from the root and expanding the tree step by step, so that at each node the user can decide whether to further explore that path. By selecting any node, a pop-up menu appears with two items: the former explodes the selected node, the latter provides an explanation of the meaning of the node, in order to support the user in his choice. This helps a user that is familiar with a directory-tree structure to interact with the service.

3 Supervised Learning Schemes in WEKA

WEKA (Waikato Environment for Knowledge Analysis) has been developed at the University of Waikato in New Zealand [14] and it is written in Java. The system provides a uniform interface to many different learning algorithms, along with methods for pre/post-processing and for the evaluation of the results of learning schemes when applied on any given dataset.

Many exploitations of the WEKA learning schemes are possible. Indeed, the toolset provides implementations of state-of-the-art supervised learning algorithms, which can be applied to datasets expressed in a tabular format named ARFF. These algorithms are called classifiers. One way of using WEKA is to apply an algorithm and then test its output to evaluate the quality of the model inferred (e.g., decision trees or classification rules) from the training data. Another possible way is to apply different algorithms to the same learning problem and compare their performance in order to choose one for the best prediction or to adopt a voting procedure.

WEKA also includes implementations of algorithms for unsupervised learning, mining association rules and tools for the evaluation of the inferred models. For the purposes of this paper, we will focus on the supervised learning techniques. They are related to a specific learning task: starting from pre-classified examples of some target concepts (specifically, the familiarity with using a system), to produce a definition for them represented, for example, as a decision tree or a set of classification rules [14]. The aim is to induce the conditions to predict the correct classification of further unclassified examples.

Suppose that a dataset is available as a relational table. The problem of inducing decision trees can be defined recursively. First select an attribute to be placed at the root node and make one branch for each for each possible value. This splits up the example set into subsets, one for every value of the attribute. Now the process can be repeated recursively for each branch, considering only those instances that actually reach the branch. A node in a decision tree involves testing a particular attribute. Usually the test at a node compares an attribute value with a constant. Leaf nodes give a classification that applies to all instances that reach the leaf. To classify an unknown instance, this is routed down the tree according to the values of its attributes which are tested at each node traversed, and, when a leaf is reached, the instance is classified according to the class assigned to that leaf.

J4.8 is an algorithm that implements in WEKA an improved version of the C4.5 decision tree learner named C4.5 Revision 8 (Rel. 8). As an effect of the modification different thresholds were chosen and information gain rather information gain ratio is used, excluding attributes for which no threshold gives sufficient gain, and re-ranking potential tests, by penalizing those that involve continuous attributes [8]. The learner processes both training and test data in the ARFF format. The output produced can be divided in two parts: the first is a pruned decision tree while the second part gives estimates of the predictive accuracy achieved by such a tree.

Classification rules are an alternative to decision trees. The antecedent of a rule is a series of tests similar to the tests at decision tree nodes while the consequent defines the class that applies to instances covered by that rule. Generally, the preconditions are logically ANDed together and all the tests must succeed for the rule to fire. However, in some rule formulations, the preconditions are general logical expressions rather than simple conjunctions. Classification rules are generated directly off a decision tree. A rule can be produced for each leaf: the antecedent includes a condition for every node on the path from the root to that leaf, and the consequent of is the class assigned by the leaf. In general rules read off a decision tree are far more complex than necessary. For this reason they are usually pruned to remove redundant tests.

PART is a rule learner implemented in WEKA that can build rules from pruned partial decision trees built using C4.5's heuristics. Other interesting implementations of different classifiers based on the Naive Bayes probabilistic technique as well as an implementation of the k-nearest neighbors classifier (Ibk) are also available. Although these methods have been applied to User Modeling (see, e.g., [3]) we chose to embed the J4.8 and PART modules because of the similarity with C4.5 and C4.5RULES that had already been integrated in the CDL Learning Server described below, and for which experimental results were available [4].

4   Modeling Interaction through the Learning Server

An intelligent middleware component of the CDL architecture that is able to automatically classify users, is currently embedded in the CDL Learning Server.

The Learning Server can be defined as a suite of learning modules that can be exploited concurrently for performing several tasks related both to document management and to the inference of interaction models. We focus on this last task, intended as inferring user classification rules through supervised learning methods, according to historical data about his previous interaction with the service.

In fact, each user of a system has special capabilities, skills, knowledge, preferences and goals. This is particularly true in the case of a service that is publicly available on the Web. Since each user behaves differently from any other user, it seems virtually unfeasible to track and recognize a single user in order to adapt the system behavior. Nevertheless, it is desirable that an intelligent component be able to detect the kind of user that initiates an interaction so to ease the accomplishment of his goals. As a consequence, a problem concerns the identification of meaningful user classes for the system through features that properly describe users and characterize their interaction.

In this case, the main support of the Learning Server is the automatic assignment of one out of some predefined classes to each user, based on information drawn from previous sessions. This is known as interaction modeling [1]. In our view, such an approach can take advantage of Machine Learning methods, since it can be cast as a supervised learning problem by considering data on user interactions as training examples for a learning system, whose goal is to induce rules for classifying users [6].

In particular, the classification can be exploited to associate each class of users with an interface that is adequate to the degree of familiarity with the system, in order to speed up the process of understanding the organization and the content of a digital library and to assist the user in retrieving the desired information.

Furthermore, it is likely that, the user acquires familiarity with this service along the time, hence the system must be able to track out potential changes of the class the user belongs to. This problem requires the ability to identify the user and log his interaction. Thus, each new user receives an identity code - User ID – to be employed on any further access. Correspondingly, CDL creates and associates a log file to each User ID, in which historical data on the interactions are stored.

By examining the data stored in each log file, it is possible to extract some features that are useful to recognize the user model. Most of the features identified turned out to be application-dependent, while only few showed to be system-dependent. For instance, relevant features are those concerning the way users exploit the capabilities of the search engine, the search indexes chosen, the criteria for sorting the search results, the number of documents obtained as results of the search, the types of errors committed, etc. Data stored in the log files are then exploited to train a learning system in order to induce (a decision tree and/or) a set of rules used by the system to autonomously perform a classification of the users interacting with CDL (see [4; 5] for instances of such rules).

Fig. 1 illustrates how the Learning Server is employed in two phases: during the training phase, a number of log files relative to some users, together with their classification provided by an expert, is coded in ARFF format. The J4.8-PART module of the Learning Server then exploit this dataset in order to generate the Rule Set containing the models inferred per each class. When a user connects to CDL during the operational phase , the Application Server provides the Learning Server with the log relative to his UserId; this is converted into a new example that has to be classified consulting the available rules. Hence, a decision is made on the class to be assigned, which, in turn, determines the type of interface the user is to be prompted with. It is worthwhile to recall that the system works offline to infer the classification rules from the log files of the users whose interactions are selected to train the system. Furthermore, we are currently investigating the possibility of using online incremental learning systems [12] that avoid the drawback of starting over from scratch the learning process each time new log examples become available.

4.1   Setting Up the Experiment

The experimental setting for an automatic user classification consisted in collecting logs and generating from them a training set for J4.8 and PART. Each log file was used to draw the values taken by the attributes that describe user interactions in ARFF format. Like in previous experiments, we considered 128 attributes concerning the interaction (see [4; 5] for their description). Therefore, each training example was made up of a set of 128 values and was labeled with one of the three classes Novice, Expert and Teacher. One of the classes was also designated as a default, in order to classify those examples for which no rule left-hand side is satisfied. The choice of

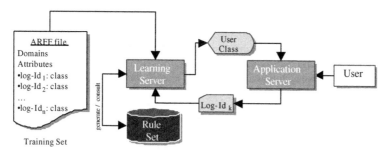

Fig. 1. Training phase and operational phase for the CDL Learning Server.

these three stereotypical classes is not restrictive. The learning mechanism presented above would apply also to a case where the domain expert decides to learn models for a more sophisticate taxonomy of users.

Table 1. Confusion matrix and average error rates relative to the first experiment.

	Novice		Teacher		Expert	
	error	#ex	error	#ex	error	#ex
Novice	0.038	13	0.029	2	0.0	2
Teacher	0.042	4	0.021	11	0.0	1
Expert	0.0	2	0.0	0.0	0.0	15

During the training phase, the decision trees were produced by J4.8 which were converted by PART into a set of classification rules. Rule generation aims at improving the comprehensibility of the resulting interaction models. Indeed, in our experiment, PART produced only 10 rules from the original 16-node decision tree, that seem to be more readable than the original tree-structured classification model. After the training phase, whenever any user accesses CDL through a client, the log file containing data generated along the previous sessions is exploited to provide a new example that the learning server will classify on the grounds of the rules inferred.

On the ground of the user classification, the Learning Server selects a distinct type of visual user interface, regarded as the proper one for that group of users. Specifically, the Learning Server prompts any user recognized as a member of the class Novice with the topic map interface, the tree-based interface is proposed to a user in the class Teacher and Expert users have the form-based interface as a default.

The main idea underlying the mapping between user classes and types of interfaces is that users unfamiliar with the system need an environment that allows them to preliminarily understand the content of a (probably unknown) digital library. More skilled users are supposed to already know both organization and content of the digital libraries, thus they may want a powerful tool that allows them to speed up the retrieval of the specific data they are looking for. However, the choice performed by the Learning Server is not mandatory for the user, hence he is allowed to choose another interface. The system should be able to follow up the user's evolution since user interaction is logged whenever he accesses the service. Thus, after a certain number of interactions, it is expected that CDL may propose a different interface to the same user.

4.2   Discussion of the Experim ental Results

This section describes the outcomes of some experiments that have been performed with the CDL Learning Server and gives a brief discussion. In order to validate the rule set obtained by using the Learning Server, a preliminary experiment was run with 50 real users that had been classified during previous interactions with the system, namely: 17 had been labeled as Novice, 16 as Teacher and 17 as Expert. Subsequently, these users interacted with the system and all information about these sessions has been used to enrich their personal log files, which generated a new set of test examples. The rules previously produced by PART have been applied to this set.

Table 1 shows the results of this experiment: the rows denote the starting class while the columns the class predicted by the Learning Server applying the set of rules previously obtained. The confusion matrix displays the number of users belonging to the ith class (in the rows) that have been included in the jth class (per column) after the application of the rules. Table 1 also presents the average error rates related to the new classification. These results show how the system classifies the users quite precisely: the average accuracy values are quite high (more than 0.95 in all cases) and the error is null when the system classifies users belonging to the Expert class.

Another experiment has been performed in order to compare the results obtained by the decision-tree learners J4.8 and C4.5. The effects of these changes were assessed in a series of a ten-fold cross validation runs. Specifically, the tree size, the error rate on the training set and the error rate on the test set have been compared. The data set consisted of 200 examples previously collected. 90% of them constituted the training set and the remaining was used as the test set, both with uniformly distributed class values. Hence, the groups of examples consisted of 181 training and 19 test instances. Two different sessions have been performed so to evaluate also the impact of pruning [14] which is a standard technique applied to decision trees to avoid the phenomenon of overfitting, i.e. to build trees that have a good performance on the training set but lack of predictive accuracy over other examples.

Tables 2 and 3 display the complete outcomes of this experiment per run before and after pruning, respectively. The last row shows the average values for each column. Note that both C4.5 and J4.8 perform the same pruning procedure, so the results obtained after pruning are comparable.

We can notice that the error rates on training set are quite similar, whereas they differ when the error rate on test instances is considered. The reason is that the test set is quite small (around 20 instances) hence a little misclassification leads to a high error value. The average results of these runs show the effects of the modification implemented in J4.8. This slightly improves C4.5's performance, leading to small trees both before and after pruning, and yields a decrease in error rates both on the training set (6.00 against 6.37 of C4.5) and on the test set (6.38 against 6.92 of C4.5). Specifically, choosing thresholds according information gain than on information

Table 2. Cross validation results before pruning.

run no.	C4.5			J4.8		
	tree size	error % training set	error rate on test set	tree size	error % training set	error rate on test set
0	41	6.7	52.4	49	5.9	33.3
1	41	7.8	4.8	53	6.1	33.1
2	41	5.6	33.3	37	6.7	33.3
3	41	7.3	26.6	41	6.7	19.4
4	49	4.5	33.3	45	5.6	28.4
5	41	8.4	38.1	47	6.7	52.4
6	43	6.1	33.3	47	5.6	33.3
7	37	7.3	28.6	51	5.6	19.2
8	43	4.4	52.6	47	6.0	63.1
9	39	5.6	33.3	49	5.0	23.8
	42	6.37	33.63	41	6.00	33.39

Table 3. Cross validation results after pruning.

run no.	C4.5			J4.8		
	tree size	error % training set	error rate on test set	tree size	error % training set	error % test set
0	35	6.7	52.4	41	6.7	42.9
1	39	8.4	4.8	29	11.8	14.2
2	35	6.7	33.3	25	10.0	28.5
3	33	7.8	23.8	35	7.2	19.4
4	45	5.0	33.3	41	6.1	28.6
5	27	10.1	38.1	33	9.5	47.7
6	39	6.1	33.3	35	7.8	33.3
7	31	7.3	23.8	41	6.7	19.4
8	33	5.5	57.9	25	7.5	63.1
9	33	5.6	23.8	29	8.5	23.9
	35	6.92	32.45	33	6.38	32.10

gain ratio leads to lower error rate while ruling out some tests on continuous attributes accounts for most of the reduction in tree size observed with J4.8.

Users' impressions on the CDL interface are discussed in [4]., while an empirical evaluation of the added value provided by a learning component in a similar domain will be available as a result of the COGITO Project [13].

5   Conclusions and Future Work

We presented a component of the Learning Server, which has been exploited in our prototypical digital library CDL for performing a form of interaction modeling. CDL is equipped with a web-based visual environment, offering different solutions for new users or already skilled ones. An effective user classification as that provided by a learning component may be fundamental for providing a form of interface adaptivity.

Being the new component based on Java technology, it seems particularly suitable for exploitation in online learning. We intend to apply to the same task incremental learning schemes that avoid the drawback of starting over the learning process from scratch each time new log examples become available for the classes to be recognized. Besides, unsupervised learning methods could be exploited too. Indeed, while for supervised methods the instances are labeled with a user class, in the unsupervised ones instances can be clustered together to form usage patterns, according to their degree of similarity. Hence, also the number of the classes is inferred directly from the available data.

Finally, we plan to apply learning tools to the inference of ontologies. This would make the search through the tree-based interface more knowledge-intensive. We also intend to complete the development of the learning server by integrating inductive reasoning capabilities in a first-order logic language.

Acknowledgments

This research was partially supported by the EC project IST-1999-13347 COGITO E-commerce with Guiding Agentsbased on Personalized Interaction Tools .

References

1. Banyon, D., and Murray, D.: Applying User Modeling to Human-Computer Interaction Design. Artificial Intelligence Review, 7 (1993) 199-225.
2. Bernstein, P. A.: Middleware: A Model for Distributed System Services, Communications of the ACM, 39(2) (1996) 86-98.
3. Billsus, D.and Pazzani, M.: Learning probabilistic user models. In: Proceedings of the 6th International Conference on User Modelling, Chia Laguna, Italy, 1996.
4. Costabile, M.F., Esposito, F. Semeraro, G. and Fanizzi, N.: An Adaptive Visual Environment for Digital Libraries. In International Journal of Digital Libraries, 2(2+3), Springer (1999) 124-143.
5. Esposito, F., Malerba, D., Semeraro, G., Fanizzi, N., and Ferilli, S.: Adding Machine Learning and Knowledge Intensive Techniques to a Digital Library Service. International Journal of Digital Libraries 2(1), Springer (1998) 3-19.
6. Moustakis, V. S., and Herrmann, J.: Where Do Machine Learning and Human-Computer Interaction Meet?. Applied Artificial Intelligence, 11 (1997) 595-609.
7. McChesney, M. C.: Banking in Cyberspace: An Investment in Itself. IEEE Spectrum, February (1997) 54-59.
8. Quinlan, J. R.: Improved Use of Continuous Attributes in C4.5, Journal of Artificial Intelligence Research, 4 (1996) 77-90.
9. Rao, R., Pedersen, J.O., Hearst, M.A., Mackinlay, J.D., Card, S.K., Masinster, L., Halvorsen, P.-K., and Robertson, G.G.: Rich interaction in the digital library. Communications of the ACM, 38 (4) (1995) 29-39
10. Salton, G., and McGill, M.J.: Introduction to Modern Information Retrieval, New York, NY, McGraw-Hill (1983).
11. Semeraro, G., Esposito, F., Malerba, D., Fanizzi, N., and Ferilli, S.: Machine Learning + On-line Libraries = IDL. In: C. Peters C. and Thanos C. (eds.), Proceedings of the first European Conference on Research and Advanced Technologies for Digital Libraries, ECDL'97, Pisa, Italy, Sept. 1997. LNCS 1324. Springer (1997) 195-214.
12. Semeraro, G., Costabile, M. F., Esposito, F., Fanizzi, N., and Ferilli, S.: A Learning Server for Inducing User Classification Rules in a Digital Library Service. In Z. W. Ras and A. Skowron (Eds.), Foundations of Intelligent Systems, LNAI 1609, Springer, (1999) 208-216.
13. COGITO Project IST-1999-13347 website: http://www.gmd.darmstadt.de/~cogito.
14. Witten Ian H. and Frank E: Data Mining: Practical Machine Learning Tools and Techniques with Java Implementations. Morgan Kaufmann, San Francisco CA (2000).

A User Modeling Approach to Determining System Initiative in Mixed-Initiative AI Systems

Michael Fleming and Robin Cohen

Department of Computer Science, University of Waterloo
Waterloo, Ontario, Canada N2L 3G1
Ph: 519-888-4567 x4457 ; Fax: 519-885-1208
{mwflemin,rcohen   }@uwaterloo.ca

Abstract. In this paper, we address the problem of providing guidelines to designers of mixed-initiative artificial intelligence systems, which specify when the system should take the initiative to solicit further input from the user, in order to carry out a problem solving task. We first present a utility-based quantitative framework which is dependent on modeling: whether the user has the knowledge the system is seeking, whether the user is willing to provide that knowledge and whether the user would be capable of understanding the request for information from the system. Examples from the application of sports scheduling are included. We also discuss a qualitative version of the model, for applications with sparse data. This paper demonstrates a novel use for user models, one in which the system does not simply alter its generation based on the user model, but in fact makes a user-specific decision about whether to interact at all.

Keywords: mixed-initiative systems, dialogue, exploiting user models to adapt interaction, interactive scheduling, clarification, tailoring generation

1 Introduction

A mixed-initiative artificial intelligence system is one in which both the system and the user have an active role to play in a dialogue or problem-solving process. In the past, most designers of mixed-initiative systems have simply come up with domain-specific solutions to their particular problem of interest. The aim of our research is to develop some guidelines to direct the design of mixed-initiative systems in a more principled manner. In particular, these guidelines should help to decide whether a mixed-initiative approach is suitable for a given problem and, if so, how to design and evaluate such a system. One crucial aspect of this research is the specification of when the system, in the process of reasoning, should take the initiative to request further assistance from a user. This is the central problem addressed in this paper.

We are interested in developing strategies that are user-specific and whereby the system can perform some reasoning to determine the "best" course of action. This requires a specific approach to user modeling and the use of user models in the determination of system initiative. We first present a quantitative approach and demonstrate it for the application areas of sports scheduling and translation. We then comment on the usefulness of a qualitative recasting of the formula, for applications with more sparse data. We

M. Bauer, P.J. Gmytrasiewicz, and J. Vassileva (Eds.): UM 2001, LNAI 2109, pp. 54–63, 2001.

compare this research to related work on user modeling to tailor interaction, on mixed-initiative design and on utility-based models of action and interaction. This work shows the importance of user modeling in designing mixed-initiative systems and has the new feature of employing user models to vary when to interact with a user (vs. simply altering the form or content of the interaction).

2   A Quantitative Model

The general situation addressed in this paper is the following. The system is working on a problem and is at a point where it might benefit from asking the user a question. Should it do so? In this section, we present a utility-based quantitative approach to designing systems that are capable of making this type of decision. In particular, we advocate that this type of decision-making should be dependent on the specific user who is involved.

Based on its user model, and on information about the difficulty of the task at hand, the system has the following information available. P_{UK} is the probability that the user has the knowledge required to answer the question. P_{UU} is the probability that the user would understand what the system is asking. P_{UMU} is the probability that the user could be made to understand, by means of a clarification dialogue, for example. EU_{ask} is the expected utility of the course of action that would be chosen after obtaining additional information from the user. EU_{no-ask} is the expected utility of the course of action that would be chosen by default if the user were not asked. $Cost_{ask}$ is the expected cost of the communication. This incorporates the time required for the interaction, the degree of bother for the user (modeling whether the user is willing to interact), and how crucial the decision is believed to be. $Cost_{clar}$ is the expected cost of engaging the user in clarification if the user does not understand the initial question.

Using these figures, we can calculate the benefits and costs associated with interacting with the user in a given situation. The general reasoning is as follows. The expected performance gain from the interaction is the difference between the expected utility of the best action that could be taken after further information is obtained, EU_{ask}, and the expected utility of the best default action, EU_{no-ask}. We would expect to achieve this improvement only when the user understands the question and has the needed knowledge to answer it (these conditions will hold with probability $P_{UU} P_{UK}$) or when the user has the knowledge, does not understand, but can be made to understand through a clarification dialogue (these conditions will hold with probability $(1 - P_{UU})P_{UMU} P_{UK}$).

Costs are a combination of $Cost_{ask}$, and the additional cost of $Cost_{clar}$, relevant only when the user does not understand (probability $= 1 - P_{UU}$).

$$
\begin{aligned}
Benefits &= P_{UU} P_{UK} (EU_{ask} - EU_{no-ask}) \\
&\quad + (1 - P_{UU})P_{UMU} P_{UK} (EU_{ask} - EU_{no-ask}) \\
&= P_{UK} [P_{UU} + (1 - P_{UU})P_{UMU}](EU_{ask} - EU_{no-ask}) \\
Costs &= Cost_{ask} + (1 - P_{UU})Cost_{clar} \\
Ask &= Benefits - Costs
\end{aligned}
$$

We would then ask the user if $Ask > 0$.

As a domain-independent example, suppose the system has a plan, and that its score is 0.7. If it can get further information from the user, it has a belief that it can construct a plan with a score of 0.95.[1] According to the user model, and its knowledge of the task, it computes the following values: $P_{UU} = 0.9$, $P_{UK} = 0.9$, $P_{UMU} = 0.8$, Cost $_{ask} = 0.15$, Cost $_{clar} = 0.3$.

Now, we can make the following calculations, which indicate that it makes sense to ask because the benefits exceed the costs.

$$\text{Benefits} = (0.9) [0.9 + (0.1)(0.8)] (0.95 - 0.7) = 0.2205 ; \quad \text{Costs} = 0.15 + (0.1)(0.3) = 0.18$$
$$\text{Ask} = 0.2205 - 0.18 = 0.0405$$

Several examples (including the one presented in detail above) are presented in the following table, with different values for the various factors:

P_{UK}	P_{UU}	P_{UMU}	Benefits	Costs	Ask?
1.0	1.0	x	0.25	0.15	Yes
1.0	0.8	0.5	0.225	0.21	Yes
1.0	0.5	0.8	0.225	0.30	No
0.7	1.0	x	0.175	0.15	Yes
0.5	1.0	x	0.125	0.15	No
0.8	0.8	0.8	0.192	0.21	No
0.9	0.9	0.8	0.2205	0.18	Yes

The system is most likely to interact with the user in cases where the user is considered quite likely to be knowledgeable and to understand the question.[2]

2.1 Sports Scheduling Examples

One application area which presents some interesting opportunities for a mixed-initiative approach is that of scheduling, especially scheduling sports leagues. Some work has been done on interactive scheduling (e.g. [1]). However, such systems cannot really be described as using mixed initiative because "the user is always in control, and the computer has no representation of the user's intentions or abilities" [1]. In scheduling scenarios, the constraints provided by the user may have to be changed or updated dynamically. In such cases, the user should be able to renegotiate the schedule by interacting with the system.

Suppose that a schedule is evaluated as follows. A perfect schedule is given a score of 1.0. If any hard constraints are violated, the score is 0.0. For each time that soft constraint i is violated, p_i points are subtracted from the perfect score, where p_i is the penalty associated with constraint i.

Example 1. Round-robin schedule; teams A-F; 15 available timeslots (7:30, 8:30, 9:30; Days 1-5).

Hard constraints:
H1. No team can play twice on the same day.   H3. B cannot play at 7:30.
H2. A cannot play at 9:30.   H4. C cannot play on Day 1.

---

[1] The system may not be able to select this better plan without additional input from the user, hence the difference in values.

[2] In this example, EU $_{ask}$ and EU $_{no - ask}$ are fairly close in value. If, for instance, EU $_{no - ask}$ were only 0.5, then all of the examples in the table would suggest that the user should be asked.

There is no way to satisfy all of these constraints, because of H1 and H4. Let us first assume that $EU_{no-ask} = 0$, since there is no way for the system to provide an acceptable schedule.

There are a few possible things we might learn from the user: (1) It may be possible to add a new time slot, which will fix the problem; (2) H1 can remain a hard constraint, but can be relaxed to say that no team should play two games in a row on the same day; (3) H1 can be turned into a soft constraint with some associated penalty.

The question is: how can we assign a value to EU_{ask}, the expected utility of the system's course of action if it does ask the user for help? One approach is to determine this value by reasoning about which of the three possibilities the user is likely to choose, and also about what penalty would likely be associated with the new soft constraint mentioned in the third option.

Suppose that we can estimate that there is a 50% chance that the user will add a new time slot that will solve everything, a 30% chance that he will modify H1 so that no team can play twice in a row, and a 20% chance that he will turn H1 into a soft constraint with a penalty of 0.1. In the first two cases, it is possible to come up with a perfect schedule (score = 1.0), while in the third case, the soft constraint would have to be violated for two teams, giving a score of 0.8. Now, EU_{ask} would be $(0.5)(1.0)+(0.3)(1.0)+(0.2)(0.8) = 0.96$.

Assume that we are certain that the user will understand the question and will have the required knowledge to help. Also, assume an interaction cost of 0.15. Then:

$$\text{Benefits} = (1.0)(1.0)(0.96 - 0) = 0.96 \quad ; \quad \text{Costs} = 0.15$$
$$\text{Ask} = 0.96 - 0.15 = 0.81, \text{ so the system will ask the user.}$$

Until now we have assumed that $EU_{no-ask} = 0$. Yet the system should be able to reason about some default course of action. Suppose the agent's default action is to design the best schedule it can, assuming that H1 has been turned into a soft constraint with some penalty p_1. It can come up with a schedule in which two teams play twice in one day, resulting in a score of $1 - 2p_1$. With an expected value of 0.1 for such a penalty, the utility of the expected outcome if we do not ask would be $1 - 2(0.1) = 0.8$.[3] Since EU_{ask} was computed earlier to be 0.96, the benefits would still outweigh the costs, and the user would still be consulted. Let us now consider a scenario where the system may decide not to interact.

Example 2. Round-robin schedule; teams A-F; 15 available time slots (7:30, 8:30, 9:30; Days 1-5).

Hard constraints:
H1. No team can play 2 games in a row.	H4. A cannot play at 9:30 on Day 4.
H2. A cannot play at 8:30.	H5. B cannot play at 9:30 on Days 1–3.
H3. B cannot play at 7:30.	

---

[3] Alternatively, the system might have a probability distribution on its belief about p_1 – e.g., 0.1 with 60% probability, 0.2 with 30% probability and 0.3 with 10% probability. This would mean that the expected value of p_1 would be 0.15, and the utility of the expected outcome would be $1 - 2(0.15) = 0.7$.

Soft constraints:

S1. A should play F on Day 5.   S2. No team should play twice on the same day.

No perfect schedule exists. By the hard constraints, A must play against B on Day 5. By S1, A should also play against F on Day 5, which would violate S2. The question is: should we violate S1 and move A–F to another day, or violate S2 and have A (and at least one other team) play twice in a day?

Suppose that the user has specified a penalty of 0.10 for violating S2, but we do not know what the penalty is for S1. However, from similar scheduling scenarios from the past, the system believes that S1 will have a penalty of 0.10 with probability 0.6 and a penalty of 0.50 with probability 0.4. The system has come up with two potential solutions, one which violates S1 and one which violates S2 twice (two teams have one day each on which they play twice).

Schedule 1						Schedule 2					
Time	1	2	3	4	5	Time	1	2	3	4	5
7:30	A-E	A-D	A-C	A-F	C-D	7:30	A-E	A-D	A-C	C-D	A-F
8:30	B-C	B-E	B-F	C-E	E-F	8:30	B-C	B-E	B-F	E-F	C-E
9:30	D-F	C-F	D-E	B-D	A-B	9:30	D-F	C-F	D-E	B-D	A-B

The utility of the second schedule is known to be 0.80. The expected utility of the first is $0.6(0.90) + 0.4(0.50) = 0.74$, so the system might make its best guess and choose the second one. The utility of this is $EU_{no-ask} = 0.80$.

The alternative is to ask the user to specify the correct penalty for violating constraint S1. Suppose the system does ask. With probability 0.6, it expects that the user will give the low penalty (0.1) for violating S1. In this case, it can come up with a schedule with utility 0.9. With probability 0.4, it expects the higher penalty for violating S1, in which case the other schedule (the one which violates S2 twice and has a score of 0.8) would be chosen in the end. Therefore, if we ask the user, we would expect a 60% chance of choosing a schedule with utility 0.9 and a 40% chance of a schedule with utility 0.8. The utility of the expected outcome is therefore $(0.6)(0.9) + (0.4)(0.8) = 0.86$.

Let $Cost_{ask} = 0.05$ and $Cost_{clar} = 0.20$. Again, assuming that we are sure that the user will understand and will have the needed knowledge, the utility of asking will be:

$$Benefits = (1.0)(1.0)(0.86 - 0.80) = 0.06 \; ; \; Costs = (1.0)(0.05) = 0.05$$
$$Ask = 0.06 - 0.05 = 0.01, \text{ so the system will ask the user.}$$

A few variations are shown below. This example is one where we need to be almost certain that the user has the knowledge and the ability to understand, in order to interact.

P_{UK}	P_{UU}	P_{UMU}	Benefits	Costs	Ask?
0.6	1.0	x	0.036	0.05	No
1.0	0.7	0.5	0.051	0.11	No
0.8	0.6	0.7	0.04224	0.13	No
0.9	0.9	0.9	0.05346	0.07	No
0.9	1.0	x	0.054	0.05	Yes

2.2   Translation Examples

To illustrate the calculation of cost factors, consider a different application for mixed-initiative interaction, interactive translation. A sample scenario is as follows. A system is translating a Spanish document into English. It has encountered a problematic word

– it believes (with a 60% probability) that translation A is better than translation B. It has access to a remote database of aligned documents which it could use to resolve the ambiguity. The expected utility of this approach is 0.9, but it would require a lengthy search, costing both time and money. The user needs the translation quickly, and the system is only 20% confident that the financial expenditure would be acceptable to the user. The user has been helpful with such problems in the past. There is an estimated 80% chance of success if the user is asked. The user is busy, but has indicated a willingness to help if necessary to achieve a high-quality translation, which is quite important in this case. The principal communication would last one minute, but there is an estimated 40% chance that the user will request additional contextual information, and such a clarification dialogue would require an additional two minutes of contact.

The cost of asking the user is $Cost_{ask} = max(0, w_t t + w_b b - w_c c)$, where t is the expected time required for communication, b is the estimated "bother level" of the user, c represents how crucial the decision is deemed to be, and w_t, w_b, and w_c are the weights associated with each of these components. These weights could be hard-coded into the system or could be learned from experience with the user. Time is measured in minutes, and we estimate the bother level to be 0.1 out of 1. The decision is given a score of 0.7 for criticality. The weights w_t, w_b and w_c are 0.3, 0.4 and 0.3, respectively. Note that the calculation for $Cost_{clar}$ uses t_{clar}, the time required for clarification, instead of t.

$$Cost_{ask} = (0.3)(1) + (0.4)(0.1) - (0.3)(0.7) = 0.13$$
$$Cost_{clar} = (0.3)(2) + (0.4)(0.1) - (0.3)(0.7) = 0.43$$

Now, we can compute the benefits and costs. The utility of the expected outcome without user interaction is calculated to be $(0.2)(0.9) + (0.8)(0.6) = 0.66$. (The system has a 20% chance of going to the remote database, which would yield an expected utility of 0.9, and an 80% chance of just going with its best guess, with an expected utility of 0.6). If the system does ask the user, there is an 80% probability of success ($P_{UK} = 0.8$). If the user does have this knowledge, then we assume that the correct choice will be made, and so the utility will be 1.0.

$P_{UK} = 0.8$ as shown above. P_{UU} can be interpreted as the probability that the user will not want the extra clarifying information (0.6). P_{UMU} will be assumed to be 0.8.

Benefits $= 0.8 [0.6 + (0.4)(0.8)] (1.0 - 0.66) = 0.294$; Costs $= 0.13 + (0.4)(0.43) = 0.302$
Ask $= 0.294 - 0.302 = -0.008$, so the system will not ask the user.

The effects of modifying some of the different values are shown in the following table. The original scenario is shown in the first row.

w_t	w_b	w_c	t	b	c	t_{clar}	$Cost_{ask}$	$Cost_{clar}$	$1 - P_{UU}$	Costs
0.3	0.4	0.3	1	0.1	0.7	2	0.13	0.43	0.4	0.302
0.3	0.4	0.3	2	0.1	0.7	2	0.43	0.43	0.4	0.602
0.3	0.4	0.3	1	0.7	0.7	2	0.37	0.67	0.4	0.638
0.3	0.4	0.3	1	0	0.7	2	0.09	0.39	0.4	0.246
0.3	0.4	0.3	1	0.1	0.9	2	0.07	0.37	0.4	0.218
0.3	0.4	0.3	1	0.1	0.1	2	0.31	0.61	0.4	0.554
0.3	0.4	0.3	1	0.1	0.7	2	0.13	0.43	0.8	0.474
0.3	0.4	0.3	1	0.1	0.7	2	0.13	0.43	0.2	0.216
0.3	0.4	0.3	1	0.1	0.7	5	0.13	1.33	0.4	0.662

In each of these examples, action would be taken if the benefits exceeded the costs. The results in the table show that the formula behaves intuitively: the costs increase as the time and bother factor grow, and the costs decrease as the problem becomes more critical. Although not shown in the table, similar effects can be observed by modifying the corresponding weights of these factors.

2.3   Extending the Calculation

In cases where it is determined that the benefits of interacting are less than the costs of interacting, it may be that the value of P_{UU} is the problem. This then necessitates deliberation about whether to engage in clarification to provide the user with the understanding needed to make the interaction succeed.

The formula in Sect.2 could then be extended as follows. If the benefits of asking the user outweigh the costs, then the system should interact. If this is not the case, but if the benefits of entering a clarification dialogue appear to outweigh the costs, then the clarification would be performed. Otherwise, no interaction would take place.

This then requires a calculation for the benefits and costs of clarification and a procedure for determining what to say to the user, in order to help him to understand. Our view of the process we have termed "clarification" is one of providing information to the user rather than adjusting the form of the generation. In fact, our view is that P_{UU} should be measured by the system projecting the generation and analyzing whether the user might have sufficient knowledge to comprehend the task.

3   Towards a Qualitative Model

For certain applications, there may be insufficient data on which to make reasonable estimates of the values required by the quantitative model. We have therefore developed a qualitative decision process, which is dependent on evaluating certain binary conditions about the user – a liberal strategy proposing that the system initiate interaction, unless it has reason to believe that interaction with this user would not be worthwhile.

Included in our decision process are some factors employed in the quantitative calculation: whether the user has the knowledge required and whether the user can understand the interaction. Since there is no independent calculation of expected utilities and costs, we incorporate two important conditions which are tied to these factors: whether the user is willing to interact and how important is the task to be performed by the system. We also allow for clarification, in cases where the system feels it is important to interact but the user would not be able to understand without further explanation. The overall algorithm is as follows:

```
If not (System Believes not (User-Knows-About(p)) then
    If not (System Believes not (User-is-Willing-to-Interact-about(p)) then
        If System Believes (User-Can-Understand-Interaction-about(p))then
            System Asks User (p)
    Else
            If System Believes (User-can-be-made-to-understand(p)) then
                System initiates learning phase for User
                System Asks User (p)
            Else
                System Acts without Asking User
    Else
        If System Believes (Very-Important(p)) then  /* interact even if User unwilling */
            System Asks User (p)
        Else
            System Acts without Asking User
Else
    System Acts Without Asking User
```

Although there are no numeric values to reason with during this deliberation process, information about the user still needs to be used. The system may determine that the user does not have the knowledge it is seeking during the interaction, by stereotyping the user and labelling certain classes of facts as unknown to this user class. Alternatively, the system can decide that it does believe the user has the knowledge it seeks, either from a stereotyping of the user or by examining the past history of interactions with this user, to conclude that this user knows facts of this type. Stereotypes and past history could also be used in the evaluation of the system's beliefs about the user's willingness and ability to understand. As for determining that the task at hand is "very important," this would be done on the basis of the system's view of the problem solving task.

The kind of reasoning required to determine the values for conditions in the qualitative model could also be employed in coming up with strategies for calculating the numeric values required in the quantitative formulation. For example, a user who has been unwilling to interact a certain number of times in the past could be assessed as having a certain bother cost in the cost calculation and a certain class of facts could suggest a default value for P_{UU} for users of a certain stereotype.

4   Discussion

In addressing the problem of specifying when a system should take the initiative, in a mixed-initiative artificial intelligence system, we are advocating a particular strategy for employing user models. Our algorithm clearly relies on having a user model which indicates information about a user's knowledge and attitudes. Other research in user modeling has studied how to employ user modeling information such as this for the purpose of tailoring output to users. Moreover, this related work has gone beyond simply suggesting a change in vocabulary, depending on the user's background. Paris [7], for instance, examines how an entire scenario of explanation may differ, depending on whether the user is novice or expert. Carberry et al. [3] highlight the difference between preferences and goals in the variation of output to a user. Ardissono and Sestero [2] study when to issue clarifying questions for a particular user, based on an evaluation of the user and the current task. Raskutti and Zukerman [8] examine what to say in light of a nuisance factor for the user. We are advocating a novel use for user models, namely to determine whether or not to interact with a user, depending on the perception of the user as indicated in the user model. This is distinctly different from altering the form or content of the generation based on information about the user.

In collaborative systems such as Collagen [5], there may indeed be different forms of dialogue, depending on the user, but this is determined by the user herself, through the responses she chooses to provide to the system. In other mixed-initiative systems, the user may also exercise some control over the extent to which she is engaged in dialogue, as in the work of Litman and Pan [6], where the user may globally choose to prefer mixed-initiative or system-initiative control or the work of Walker et al. [10], where a decision is made to prefer system-initiative or mixed-initiative, for all users, based on an evaluation of user satisfaction and efficiency. To some extent, we are similar but we are providing a strategy for interaction which is user specific, still with the aims of maximizing user satisfaction and efficiency, but more clearly specified to depend on the user herself and her capabilities.

Our work is also quite relevant to two research endeavours on utility-based decision-making. In the SPIRE project, Sullivan et al. [9] look at utility-based decisions in a multi-agent framework. There is a team of agents and a set of tasks that have been distributed among the various agents in the group. When an agent is presented with a potentially rewarding "outside offer," it must decide whether or not to default on its commitment to the team in order to accept the outside offer. The utility of defaulting is based in part on a measure of the total expected income, combining the immediate income from performing the new task, the cost of defaulting on the assigned task, and the expected future income, which may be affected negatively by its decision to default on its current commitment to the team. A similar computation is then done for the utility of not defaulting, and the decision is made according to which of the two values is higher. This work therefore has some similarity to our use of the utility of possible actions, as part of the determination of when to act. At the moment, our formula only takes into account the expected current benefits, but attempting to make projections about future benefits is certainly a possibility for future work.

In the Lumière project, Horvitz [4] presents a model for deciding whether to act on a user's behalf or to engage the user in dialogue, based on analysis of expected utility. The primary difference between our model and that of Horvitz is that his scenario is one in which the user would normally be performing the action in question, and the system's decision involves whether or not to offer to start the action on the user's behalf, while we are focusing on situations in which the system is working on something and might benefit from asking the user for help. Horvitz also considers the expected utility of dialogue with the user, compared to simply acting. This calculation is done by evaluating how likely it is that the user has the goal that the system is proposing and so is based on different factors than ours.

5   Conclusions and Future Work

In this paper, we have presented a quantitative framework for determining when the system should take the initiative to interact with a user, in a mixed-initiative system. This framework employs a user model, tracking specific information about the user, to allow the degree of interaction to vary according to the user. Since this quantitative model relies on having certain numeric values, we have developed an alternative qualitative framework. This decision process evaluates whether certain conditions about the user are true or false, and proposes that the system take the initiative, in the absence of evidence that interaction with this user would be prohibitive. One aim of our research is to determine which applications are well suited to mixed-initiative design. It would therefore be useful to examine for future work whether certain applications are better suited to a qualitative decision process than a quantitative one.

It would also be useful for future work to examine more closely the factors incorporated into our calculations and decision procedures, in order to fine tune the characterizations. For instance, whether the user is willing to interact and whether the task to be addressed is critical are incorporated into the cost calculation in the quantitative framework. Both of these factors appear as conditions in the qualitative algorithm. In fact, there is certainly a relationship between willingness of the user and cost, and between criticality of the task and utility of the interaction. Moreover, instead of interpreting the expected utility of asking in terms of an evaluation of possible plans, the system could consider the expected utility of actually asking for information, based on factors such as: how confident the system is in its preferred plan, how close the default plan of the system is to other possible choices, how critical it is to complete the task in a limited time frame and how critical it is to complete the task correctly. For future work, it is also important to elaborate on how the system would reason about whether the user could be made to understand, in order to enter into a repair phase before interaction. Finally, one crucial area for future work is to validate the proposed approach by selecting a small number of suitable applications, in order to provide empirical evidence for the value of the theories.

References

1. D. Anderson, E. Anderson, N. Lesh, J. Marks, B. Mirtich, D. Ratajczak, and K. Ryall. Human-guided simple search. In Proceedings of AAAI-2000 pages 209–216. AAAI Press, 2000.
2. L. Ardissono and D. Sestero. Using dynamic user models in the recognition of the plans of the user. User Modeling and User Adapated Interact ion, 5(2):157–190, 1996.
3. S. Carberry, J. Chu-Carroll, and S. Elzer. Constructing and utilizing a model of user preferences in collaborative consultation dialogues. Computational Intelligence, 15(3):185–217, 1999.
4. E. Horvitz. Principles of mixed-initiative user interfaces. In Proceedings of CHI '99, ACM SIGCHI Conference on Human Factors in Computing Systems, Pittsburgh, PA, pages 159–166. ACM Press, 1999.
5. N. Lesh, C. Rich, and C.L. Sidner. Using plan recognition in human-computer collaboration. In Proceedings of UM'99, Banff, Alberta, Canada, pages 23–32, 1999.
6. D. Litman and S. Pan. Empirically evaluating an adaptable spoken dialogue system. In Judy Kay, editor, Proceedings of UM'99, Banff, Alberta, Canada, pages 55–64, 1999.
7. C. Paris. The role of the user's domain knowledge in generation. Computational Intelligence, 7(2):71–93, 1991.
8. B. Raskutti and I. Zukerman. Query and response generation during information-seeking interactions. In Proceedings of UM'94, Hyannis, Mass, pages 25–30, 1994.
9. D. Sullivan, B. Grosz, and S. Kraus. Intention reconciliation by collaborative agents. In Proceedings of ICMAS-2000 pages 293–300. IEEE Computer Society Press, 2000.
10. M. Walker, D. Litman, C. Kamm, and A. Abella. PARADISE: A framework for evaluating spoken dialogue agents. In Proceedings of the 35th Annual Meeting of the Association of Computational Linguistics, pages 271–280, 1997.

M. Bauer, P.J. Gmytrasiewicz, and J. Vassileva (Eds.): UM 2001, LNAI 2109, pp. 64–73, 2001.

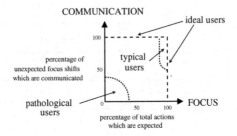

Improving User Modelling
with Content-Based Techniques

Bernardo Magnini and Carlo Strapparava

ITC-irst, Istituto per la Ricerca Scientifica e Tecnologica, I-38050 Trento, Italy
{magnini, strappa　}@irst.itc.it

Abstract.　SiteIF is a personal agent for a bilingual news web site that learns user's interests from the requested pages.

In this paper we propose to use a content-based document representation as a starting point to build a model of the user's interests. Documents passed over are processed and relevant senses (disambiguated over WordNet) are extracted and then combined to form a semantic network. A filtering procedure dynamically predicts new documents on the basis of the semantic network.

There are two main advantages of a content-based approach: first, the model predictions, being based on senses rather then words, are more accurate; second, the model is language independent, allowing navigation in multilingual sites. We report the results of a comparative experiment that has been carried out to give a quantitative estimation of these improvements.

Keywords:　Content-Based User Modelling, Natural Language Processing, WordNet　.

1　Introduction

SiteIF [9,10] is a personal agent for a multilingual news web site, that takes into account the user's browsing by "watching over the user's shoulder". It learns user's interests from the requested pages that are analyzed to generate or to update a model of the user. Exploiting this model, the system tries to anticipate which documents in the web site could be interesting for the user.

Many systems (e.g. [5,8]) that exploit a user model to propose relevant documents, build a representation of the user's interest which takes into account some properties of words in the document, such as their frequency and their co-occurrence. However, assuming that interest is strictly related to the semantic content of the already seen documents, a purely word based user model is often not accurate enough. The issue is even more important in the Web world, where documents have to do with many dierent topics and the chance to misinterpret word senses is a real problem.

In this paper we propose to use a content-based document representation as a starting point to build a model of the user's interests. As the user browses the documents, the system builds the user model as a semantic network whose nodes

M. Bauer, P.J. Gmytrasiewicz, and J. Vassileva (Eds.): UM 2001, LNAI 2109, pp. 74–83, 2001.
c Springer-Verlag Berlin Heidelberg 2001

represent senses (not just words) of the documents requested by the user. Then, the filtering phase takes advantage of the word senses to retrieve new documents with high semantic relevance with respect to the user model.

The use of senses rather than words implies that the resulting user model is not only more accurate but also independent from the language of the documents browsed. This is particularly important for multilingual web sites, that are becoming very common especially in news sites or in electronic commerce domains.

The sense-based approach adopted for the user model component of the SiteIF system makes use of MultiWordNet [1], a multilingual lexical database where English and Italian senses are aligned. A technique, recently proposed in [7], called Word Domain Disambiguation, has been adopted to disambiguate the word senses that define the user interest model.

As for the filtering phase, our approach is supported by experimental evidences (e.g. [3]) that have shown that a content based match can significantly improve the accuracy of the retrieval.

The paper also describes an empirical evaluation of a content-based versus a traditional word-based user modelling. This experiment shows a substantial improvement in performance with respect to the word based approach.

The paper is organized as follows. Section 2 gives a sketch of the kind of documents the system deals with and describes how MultiWordNet and the disambiguation algorithms can be exploited to represent the documents in terms of lexical concepts. Section 3 describes how the user model is built, maintained and used to propose new relevant documents to the user. Section 4 gives an account of the experiment that evaluates and compares a synset-based user model versus a word-based user model. Some final comments about future developments conclude the paper.

2   Content Based Document Representation

The SiteIF web site has been built using a news corpus kindly put at our disposal by AdnKronos, an important Italian news provider. The corpus consists of about 5000 parallel news (i.e. each news has both an Italian and an English version) partitioned by AdnKronos in a number of fixed categories: culture, food, holidays, medicine, fashion, motors and news. The average length of the news is about 265 words. Figure 1 shows an example of parallel (English-Italian) news.

The main working hypothesis underlying our approach to user modelling is that a content based analysis of the document can improve the accuracy of the model. There are two crucial questions to address: first, a repository for word senses has to be identified; second, the problem of word sense disambiguation, with respect to the sense repository, has to be solved.

As for sense repository we have adopted WordNet (version 1.6) [2], a large lexical database for English, freely available, which has received a lot of attention within the computational linguistics community. Nouns, verbs, adjectives

CULTURE: GIOTTO- PAID BY MONKS TO WRITE ANTI-FRANCISCAN POETRY	CULTURA: GIOTTO- PAGATO DA FRATI PER SCRIVERE POESIA ANTI-FRANCESCANA
Rome,10 Jan. -(Adnkronos)- Giotto was 'paid' to attack a faction of the Franciscans, the Spiritual ones, who opposed church decoration in honour of Poverello di Assisi. This has been revealed in the research of an Italian scholar who is a professor at Yale University, Stefano Ugo Baldassarri, who thinks he has solved the mystery of the only known poetry by the famous Tuscan painter: the Giotto verses have in fact always provoked wonder because they seem to be a criticism of the ideals of St. Francis and all the more so since their author was also the man who painted the famous frescoes of the Basilica at Assisi. ...	Roma, 10 gen. -(Adnkronos)- Giotto fu 'pagato' per attaccare una fazione dei Francescani, quella degli Spirituali, che si opponevano alla decorazione delle chiese in onore del Poverello di Assisi. Lo rivela una ricerca di uno studioso italiano docente alla Yale University, Stefano Ugo Baldassarri, che ritiene di aver svelato il mistero dell'unica poesia conosciuta del celebre pittore toscano: i versi giotteschi, infatti, avevano sempre destato meraviglia perch´ e apparivano come una critica agli ideali di San Francesco, tanto piu' mossa proprio dallàutore dei celebri areschi della Basilica di Assisi. ...

Fig. 1.   Sample of parallel news texts.

and adverbs are organized into synonym sets (i.e.   synsets), each representing one underlying lexical concept. Synsets are linked by dierent semantic relations (is-a, part-of   , etc...) and organized in hierarchies. The main advantage in using WordNet   is that versions in languages other than English are now available (even if none is still complete). In particular in SiteIF we use   MultiWordNet   , a multilingual extension of the English   WordNet   . The Italian part of   Multi-WordNet   currently covers about 35,000 lemmas, completely aligned with the English WordNet   (i.e. with correspondences to English senses).

The advantages of a synset-based document representation are that: (i) each ambiguous term in the document is disambiguated, therefore allowing its correct interpretation and consequently a better precision in the user model construction (e.g. if a user is interested in financial news, a document containing the word "bank" in the context of geography will not be relevant); (ii) synonym words belonging to the same synset can contribute to the user model definition. For example both "bank" and "bank building" bring evidences for financial documents, improving the coverage of the document retrieval.

As far as word disambiguation is concerned, we have addressed the problem starting with the hypothesis that many sense distinctions are not relevant for a document representation useful in user modelling. This line is also supported by several works (see for example [11], [4], and the SENSEVAL initiative) which remark that for many practical purposes (e.g. cross lingual information retrieval) the fine-grained sense distinctions provided by   WordNet   are not necessary. To reduce the WordNet   polysemy, and, as a consequence, the complexity of word sense disambiguation, we have used Word Domain Disambiguation (WDD), a technique proposed in [7] based on sense clustering through the annotation of the MultiWordNet   synsets with domain labels. Section 2.1 gives some details about WDD, while Section 2.2 shows how WDD is applied to represent documents in our context.

2.1   Word Domain Disambiguation

Word Domain Disambiguation is a variant of Word Sense Disambiguation where for each word in a text a   domain label (among those allowed by the word) has to be chosen instead of a   sense label. Domain labels, such as   Medicine   and Architecture   , provide a natural way to establish semantic relations among word senses, grouping them into homogeneous clusters. Figure 2 shows an example. The word book' has seven dierent senses in   WordNet   1.6: three of them can be grouped under the   Publishing   domain, causing the reduction of the polysemy from 7 to 5 senses.

In MultiWordNet   the synsets have been annotated with one or more domain labels ([6]). This resource currently covers all the noun synsets, and it is under development for the remaining lexical categories.

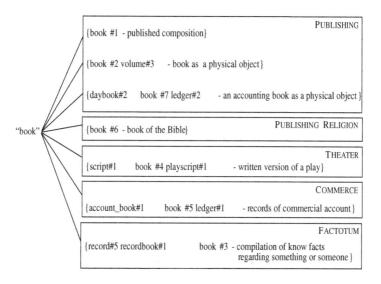

Fig. 2.   An example of polysemy reduction

The domain disambiguation algorithm follows two steps. First, each word in the text is considered and for each domain label allowed by that word a score is given. This score is determined by the frequency of the label among the senses of the word. At the second step each word is reconsidered, and the domain label with the highest score is selected as the result of the disambiguation. In [7] it is reported that this algorithm reaches .83 and .85 accuracy in word domain disambiguation, respectively for Italian and English, on a corpus of parallel news. This result makes WDD appealing for applications where fine-grained sense distinctions are not required, such as document user modelling.

2.2   Document Representations

Each document maintained in the SiteIf site is processed to extract its semantic content. Given that we relay on   MultiWordNet   , the final representation consists in a list of synsets relevant for a certain document. The text processing is carried out whenever a new document is inserted in the web site, and includes two basic phases: (i) lemmatization and part-of-speech tagging; (ii) synset identification with WDD.

As for lemmatization and part-of-speech tagging we use the LinguistX tools produced by InXight ™ , which allow to process texts in a number of languages including English and Italian. During this phase the text is first tokenized (i.e. lexical units are identified), then for each word the possible lemmas as well as their morpho-syntactic features are collected. Finally part of speech ambiguities are solved. This is the input for the synset identification phase, which is mainly based on the word domain disambiguation procedure described in Section 2.1. The WDD algorithm, for each word (currently just nouns are considered, due to the limited coverage of the domain annotation), proposes the domain label appropriate for the word context. Then, the word synsets associated to the proposed domain are selected and added to the document representation. As an example, Figure 3 shows a fragment of the Synset Document Representation (SDR) for the document presented in Figure 1. Words are presented with the preferred domain label as well as with the selected synsets. For readability reasons we show the synonyms belonging to each synsets in place of the synset unique identifier used in the actual implementation. In addition, only the English part of the synset is displayed.

3   Sense-Based User Modelling

In SiteIF the user model is implemented as a semantic net whose goal is to represent the contextual information derived from the documents. Previous versions of SiteIF were purely word-based, that is the nodes in the net represented the words and the arcs the word co-occurrences. However the resulting user models were fixed to the precise words of the browsed news. One key issue in automating the retrieval of potentially interesting news was to find document representations that are semantically rich and accurate, keeping to a minimal level the participation of the user.

A new version of SiteIF has been realized where the user model is still implemented as a network structure, with the dierence that nodes now represent synsets and arcs the co-occurrence of synsets. The working hypothesis is that the model can help to define semantic chains through which the filtering has a better

Word lemma	Domain label	Synsets
faction	Factotum	{ faction-2, sect-2 } { cabal-1, faction-1, junta-1, junto-1, camarilla-1 }
franciscan	Religion	{ Gray _Friar-1, Franciscan-1 }
church	Religion	{ church-1, Christian _church-1, Christianity-2 }
		{ church-2, church _building-1 } { church _service-1, church-3 }
decoration	Factotum	{ decoration-3 }
honour	Factotum	{ award-2, accolade-1, honor-1, honour-2, laurels-1 } { honor-3, honour-4 }
research	Factotum	{ research-1 } { inquiry-1, enquiry-2, research-2 }
scholar	Pedagogy	{ scholar-1, scholarly _person-1, student-2 }
		{ learner-1, scholar-2 } { scholar-3 }
professor	Pedagogy	{ professor-1 }
mystery	Literature	{ mystery-2, mystery _story-1, whodunit-1 }
poetry	Literature	{ poetry-1, poesy-1, verse-1 } { poetry-2 }
painter	Art	{ painter-1 }
verse	Literature	{ poetry-1, poesy-1, verse-1 } { verse-2, rhyme-2 } { verse-3, verse _line-1 }
wonder	Factotum	{ wonder-2, marvel-1 }
criticism	Factotum	{ criticism-1, unfavorable _judgment-1 }
ideal	Factotum	{ ideal-1 } { ideal-2 }
man	Factotum	{ man-1, adult _male-1 } { man-3 } { man-7 } { man-8 }
author	Literature	{ writer-1, author-1 }
fresco	Art	{ fresco-1 } { fresco-2 }
basilica	Religion	{ basilica-1 }

Fig. 3.   Synset Document Representation for a fragment of text

chance to catch documents semantically closer to the topics already touched by the user.

Possibly modelling with synsets or with words will bring to dierent choices and optimizations in the semantic network representation. However in this paper one purpose is to compare the results of word-based and of synset-based user model, and then we keep uniform the machinery of the user model data structures and algorithms.

3.1   Modelling Phase

In the modelling phase SiteIF considers the browsed documents during a user navigation session. The system uses the document representation of the browsed news. Every synset has a score that is inversely proportional to its frequency over all the news corpus. The score is higher for less frequent synsets, avoiding that very common meanings become too prevailing in the user model. Likewise, in the word-based case we considered a word list document representation, where every word has a score inversely proportional to the word frequency in the news corpus.

The system builds or augments the user model as a semantic net whose nodes are synsets and arcs between nodes are the co-occurrence relation (cooccuring presence in a document) of two synsets. Weights on nodes are incremented by the score of the synsets, while weights on arcs are the mean of the connected nodes weights. For each browsed news, the weights of the net are periodically reconsidered and possibly lowered, depending on the time passed from the last update. Also no longer useful nodes and arcs may be removed from the net. In this way it is possible to consider changes of the user's interests and to avoid that uninteresting concepts remain in the user model.

Figure 4 sketches the modelling process showing an example of user model augmentation.

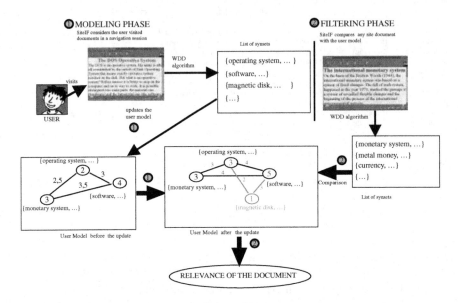

Fig. 4.   Modelling and Filtering Processes

3.2   Filtering Phase

During the filtering phase, the system compares any document (i.e. the representation of any documents in terms of synsets) in the site with the user model. A matching module receives as input the internal representation of a document and the current user model and it produces as output a classification of the document (i.e. whether it is worth or not the user's attention). The relevance of any single document is estimated using the Semantic Network Value Technique (see for details [9]). The idea behind the SiteIF algorithm consists of checking, for every concept in the representation of the document, whether the context in which it occurs has been already found in previously visited documents (i.e. already stored in the semantic net). This context is represented by a co-occurrence relationship, i.e. by the couples of terms included in the document which have already co-occurred before in other documents. This information is represented by arcs of the semantic net.

Here below we present the formula used to calculate the relevance of a document using the Semantic Network Value Technique:

$$\text{Relevance (doc)} = \sum_{i \in \{ \text{syns (doc)} \}} w(i) \; \text{freq}_{\text{doc}}(i) + \sum_{i,j \in \{ \text{syns (doc)} \}} w(i,j) \; w(j) \; \text{freq}_{\text{doc}}(j)$$

where $w(i)$ is the weight of synset-node i in the UM network, $w(i, j)$ is the weight of the arc between i and j.

See figure 4 for a summary sketch of the filtering process.

4   Evaluation

We wanted to estimate how much the new version of SiteIF (synset based) actually improves the performances with respect to the previous version of the system (word based). However, setting a comparative test among user models, going beyond a generic user satisfaction is not straightforward. To evaluate whether and how the exploitation of the synset representation improves the accuracy of the semantic network modelling and filtering, we arranged an experiment whose goal was to compare the output of the two systems against the judgements of a human advisor.

We proceeded in the following way. First, a test set of about one hundred English news from the AdnKronos corpus were selected homogeneously with respect to the overall distribution in categories (i.e. culture, motors, etc...). The test set has been made available as a Web site, and then 12 ITC-irst researchers were asked to browse the site, simulating a user visiting the news site. Users were instructed to select a news, according to their personal interests, to completely read it, and then to select another news, again according to their interests. This process was repeated until ten news were picked out.

After this phase, a human advisor, who was acquainted with the test corpus, was asked to analyze the documents chosen by the users, and to propose new potential interesting documents from the corpus. The advisor was requested to follow the same procedure for each document set: documents were first grouped according to their AdnKronos category, and a new document was searched in the test corpus within that category. If a relevant document was found, it was added to the advisor proposals, otherwise no document for that category is proposed. Eventually, an additional document, outside the categories browsed by the user could be added by the advisor. On average, the advisor proposed 3 documents for a user document set.

At this point we compared the advisor proposals with the results of the two systems. To simulate the advisor behavior (i.e. it is allowed that for a given category no proposal is selected), all the system documents whose relevance was less than a fixed dierence (20%) from the best document, were eliminated. After this selection, on average, the system proposed 10 documents for a user document set.

Standard figures for precision and recall have been calculated considering the matches among the advisor and the systems documents. Precision is the ratio of recommended documents that are relevant, while the recall is the ratio of relevant documents that are recommended. In terms of our experiment we have precision $= \frac{|H \cap S|}{|S|}$ and recall $= \frac{|H \cap S|}{|H|}$, where H is the set of the human advisor proposals and S is the set of the system proposals.

Table 1 shows the result of the evaluation. The first column takes into account the document news, the second only the   AdnKronos   categories. We can note that precision considerably increases (34%) with the synset-based user model. This confirms the working hypothesis that substituting words with senses both in the modelling and in the filtering phase produces a more accurate output. The main reason, as expected, is that a synset-based retrieval allows to prefer documents with high degree of semantic coherence, which is not guaranteed in case of a word-based retrieval.

Table 1.   Comparison between word-based UM and synset-based UM

	News		Categories	
	Precision	Recall	Precision	Recall
Word-Based UM	0.51	0.21	0.89	0.40
Synset-Based UM	0.85	0.36	0.97	0.43

As for recall, it also gains some points (15%), even if it remains quite low. However, this does not seem a serious drawback for a pure recommender system, where there is no the need to answer an explicit query (as it happens, for instance, in information retrieval systems), but rather the need is for an high quality (i.e. the precision) of the proposals.

5   Conclusions

We have presented a new version of SiteIF, a recommender system for a Web site of multilingual news. Exploiting a content-based document representation, we have described a model of the user's interests based on word senses rather that on simply words. The main advantages of this approach are that semantic accuracy increases and that the model is independent from the language of the news.

To give a quantitative estimation of the improvements induced by a content-based approach, a comparative experiment - sense-based vs. word-based user model - has been carried out, which has showed a significant higher precision in the system recommendations.

There are several areas for future developments. One point is to improve the disambiguation algorithms which are at the basis of the document representation. A promising direction (proposed in [7]) is to design specific algorithms which consider the synset intersection of parallel news.

A second working direction concerns the possibility to develop clustering algorithms over the senses of the semantic network. For example, once the user model network is built, it could be useful to have the capability to dynamically infer some homogeneous user interest areas. This would allow to arrange in uniform dynamic groups the recommended documents.

References

1. A. Artale, B. Magnini, and C. Strapparava.   WordNet   for italian and its use for lexical discrimination. In   AI*IA97: Advances in Artificial Intelligence   . Springer Verlag, 1997.

2. C. Fellbaum.   WordNet. An Electronic Lexical Database   . The MIT Press, 1998.

3. J. Gonzalo, F. Verdejio, Chugur, and J. Cigarran. Indexing with wordnet synsets can improve text retrieval. In S. Harabagiu, editor,   Proceeding of the Workshop "Usage of WordNet in Natural Language Processing Systems"   , Montreal, Quebec, Canada, August 1998.

4. J. Gonzalo, F. Verdejio, C. Peters, and N. Calzolari. Applying eurowordnet to cross-language text retrieval.   Computers and Humanities   , 32(2-3):185–207, 1998.

5. Henry Lieberman, Neil W. Van Dyke, and Adrian S. Vivacqua. Let's browse: A collaborative web browsing agent. In   Proceedings of the 1999 International Conference on Intelligent User Interfaces   , Collaborative Filtering and Collaborative Interfaces, pages 65–68, 1999.

6. B. Magnini and G. Cavagli` a. Integrating subject field codes into WordNet. In   Proceedings of LREC- 2000, Second International Conference on Language Resources and Evaluation   , Athens, Greece, June 2000.

7. B. Magnini and C. Strapparava. Experiments in word domain disambiguation for parallel texts. In   Proc. of SIGLEX Workshop on Word Senses and Multi-linguality   , Hong-Kong, October 2000. held in conjunction with ACL2000.

8. M. Minio and C. Tasso. User modeling for information filtering on internet services: Exploiting an extended version of the UMT shell. In   Proc. of Workshop on User Modeling for Information Filtering on the World Wide Web   , Kailia-Kuna Hawaii, January 1996. held in conjunction with UM'96.

9. A. Stefani and C. Strapparava. Personaliziong access to web sites: The siteif project. In   Proc. of second Workshop on Adaptive Hypertext and Hypermedia   , Pittsburgh, June 1998. held in conjunction with HYPERTEXT '98.

10. C. Strapparava, B. Magnini, and A. Stefani. Sense-based user modelling for web sites. In   Adaptive Hypermedia and Adaptive Web-Based Systems - Lecture Notes in Computer Science 1892   . Springer Verlag, 2000.

11. Y. Wilks and M. Stevenson. Word sense disambiguation using optimised combination of knowledge sources. In   Proc. of COLING-ACL'98   , 98.

An Integrated Approach for Generating Arguments and Rebuttals and Understanding Rejoinders

Ingrid Zukerman

School of Computer Science and Software Engineering, Monash University
Clayton, Victoria 3800, Australia
ingrid@csse.monash.edu.au

Abstract. This paper describes an integrated approach for interpreting a user's responses and generating replies in the framework of a WWW-based Bayesian argumentation system. Our system consults a user model which represents a user's beliefs, inferences and attentional focus, as well as the system's certainty regarding the user's beliefs. The interpretation mechanism takes into account these factors to infer the intended effect of the user's response on the system's argument. The reply-generation mechanism focuses on the identification of discrepancies between the beliefs in the user model and the beliefs held by the system that are relevant to the inferred interpretation.

Keywords: argumentation, Bayesian networks, plan recognition, discourse planning.

1 Introduction

An ideal interactive system would allow a user to request additional explanations, express doubt about the system's recommendations, and present his/her own views to the system. The interaction with such a system could continue indefinitely. In this paper, we present a first installment in the development of such a system. This is a WWW-based Bayesian Interactive Argumentation System (BIAS), which generates arguments, allows the user to question these arguments, and generates rebuttals to the user's rejoinders. In particular, we focus on the requirements placed by these capabilities on the system's user modeling component.

BIAS' active components are: (1) a WWW interface, (2) an inference mechanism, (3) an argument-generation mechanism, and (4) a rebuttal-generation mechanism. The interaction with BIAS starts with the presentation of background information regarding a particular scenario, which the user can explore further through the WWW interface. At any point the user can ask BIAS to present its argument regarding the goal proposition in this scenario; this argument is produced by the generation mechanism. The user can then accept this argument, explore the scenario further or pose a rejoinder. After receiving the user's rejoinder, BIAS activates the inference mechanism to recognize the user's intent, and then uses the rebuttal-generation mechanism to produce a rebuttal which takes into account the information in the rejoinder. The user can then continue exploring the scenario or generate another rejoinder, and so on.

In the next section, we present BIAS' WWW interface and the scenario used in our current implementation. In Section 3, we discuss our knowledge representation

M. Bauer, P.J. Gmytrasiewicz, and J. Vassileva (Eds.): UM 2001, LNAI 2109, pp. 84–94, 2001.

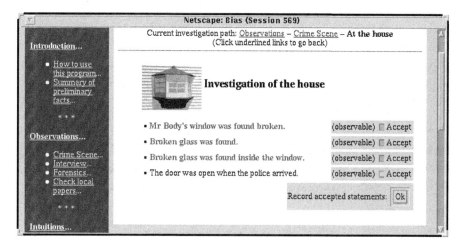

Fig. 1. Sample screen of the WWW interface

formalism and our user model. We then describe our procedure for inferring a user's line of reasoning, followed by our algorithm for rebuttal generation. In Section 6, we review related work, followed by concluding remarks.

2   WWW Interface and Sample Scenario

Our experimental set up is designed to model a situation where the user and the system are "true" partners (contrary to the usual mode of operation, where the system is omniscient). In our set up, both the user and the system start with the same amount of information, and both can obtain additional information from the "world".[1] Our experimental set up is realized by means of a "murder scenario", where BIAS and the user are partners in solving a crime. At the beginning of the interaction, the WWW interface presents a preamble that describes the preliminaries of the case. The following preamble is used for the interaction described in this paper:

> Mr Body was found dead in his bedroom, which is in the second story of his house. Bullets were found in Mr Body's body. A gun was found on the premises, and fingerprints were found on the gun. In addition, inspection of the grounds revealed footprints in the garden and circular indentations in the ground outside the bedroom window.

After receiving the preamble, the user can use a WWW interface to gather additional information about the world, e.g., from witnesses or the crime scene, or to post his/her intuitions about unobservable propositions, e.g., Mr Green had a motive to kill Mr Body. Figure 1 shows a screen where the user investigates the victim's house. The first three propositions (in red in the interface) have been accepted by the user, while the last

---

[1] At present, the relation between the system and the user is still asymmetrical, since the system is aware of all the information accessed by the user, while this is not the case for the user.

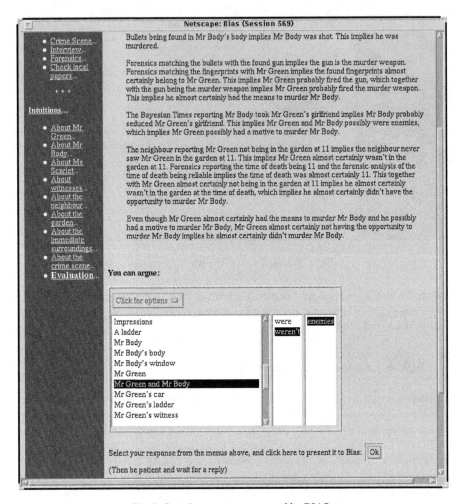

Fig. 2. Sample argument generated by BIAS

proposition (in black) was seen (but not accepted) by the user.[2] The information in the preamble, the seen and accepted facts and the intuitions entered by the user are stored in the user model. The investigated propositions and the preamble are also stored in BIAS' model of the world. In addition, during argument generation, BIAS investigates the world to obtain information necessary for argument formulation.

When the user asks for BIAS' opinion about the case, BIAS calls a Bayesian argument generator [9] to produce an argument for the goal proposition, which in our scenario is either Mr Green is guilty or Mr Green is innocent (whichever is most likely). The argument generator is given a desired level of belief for this goal. Initially, this level of belief is moderate so that the generator produces a preliminary argument which

---

[2] A user may forget to indicate explicit acceptance of a proposition, or may decide not to click the acceptance boxes in order to expedite the interaction.

Actually, it is quite likely that Mr Green and Mr Body were enemies. This is for the following reason.

A blue car being here last week and Mr Green having a blue car implies Mr Green's car was almost certainly here last week, which implies Mr Green almost certainly visited Mr Body last week. The neighbour reporting Mr Green arguing with Mr Body last week together with Mr Green almost certainly visiting Mr Body last week implies he almost certainly argued with Mr Body.

The Bayesian Times reporting Mr Body took Mr Green's girlfriend implies Mr Body probably seduced Mr Green's girlfriend. This together with Mr Green almost certainly arguing with Mr Body implies Mr Green and Mr Body probably were enemies.

Let's now go back to the main argument. Mr Green and Mr Body probably being enemies implies it is more likely that Mr Green had a motive to murder Mr Body, making it rather likely. This implies it is only slightly more likely that Mr Green murdered Mr Body.

Fig. 3. Rebuttal for the rejoinder But Mr Green and Mr Body weren't enemies

presents the system's "initial thoughts" about the case. If possible, our argument generator produces an argument that is compatible with both BIAS' beliefs about the world and the user's presumed beliefs. If this is not possible, BIAS' beliefs take precedence. Figure 2 shows the initial argument generated by BIAS in light of the above preamble and information gathered from the world.

The user can now continue investigating the world or s/he can pose a rejoinder. This is done by selecting the type of the rejoinder (but or consider) from a drop-down menu, and composing a sentence using three dynamic menus (Figure 2).[3] In this example, the rejoinder is but Mr Green and Mr Body weren't enemies. Rejoinders that begin with "but" correspond to an expression of doubt [2], which intends to undermine the system's argument. Rejoinders that begin with "consider" constitute requests for the consideration of the effect of a proposition on the argument.

After receiving a rejoinder, BIAS tries to determine the line of reasoning intended by the user. For the sample rejoinder in Figure 2, BIAS postulates that the user's rejoinder is aimed at increasing the belief in Mr Green's innocence through the following line of reasoning: Mr Green and Mr Body not being enemies implies that Mr Green less probably had a motive to murder Mr Body, which implies that Mr Green less probably murdered Mr Body. BIAS then generates the rebuttal in Figure 3, which presents a stronger sub-argument against the rejoinder proposition than that presented in the original argument.

3   Knowledge Representation and User Model

We have chosen Bayesian networks (BNs) as our main representational formalism owing to their ability to represent normatively correct reasoning under uncertainty. BIAS uses BNs to represent the information about the world, the system's beliefs about the world, and the user's presumed beliefs. The world-BN contains the nodes and links which represent the characters and props in a murder case and the relations between them. Different instances of a murder case may be created by instantiating particular observable

---

[3] Dynamic menus are used in order to avoid dealing with words and propositions not known by the system. The acceptance of free-form input is the subject of future research.

facts, e.g., The neighbour reports that Mr Green was in the garden. BIAS' BN and the user-model BN contain subsets of the world-BN, which represent BIAS' and the user's current beliefs about the murder case, respectively. These subsets are dynamically expanded using information obtained from the world-BN when the user investigates the murder case, when generating and presenting arguments and rebuttals, and when interpreting a user's rejoinders.

BIAS' BN and the user-model BN are used in different ways to perform these tasks. The interpretation process is performed in the context of the user model, since BIAS tries to "make sense" of what the user is saying relative to the system's view of the user's beliefs. In contrast, the processes for generating the initial argument and the rebuttals consult the user model and BIAS' model. When generating the initial argument, BIAS tries to rely on beliefs held by both BIAS and the user if possible [9], while during rebuttal generation, BIAS focuses on the discrepancies between the user-model BN and BIAS' BN [6].

Reasoning for generation and interpretation – extending BIAS' BN and the user-model BN. Different mechanisms are used to extend BIAS' BN and the user-model BN. BIAS' BN is extended by "looking over the user's shoulder" while the user is interacting with the WWW interface, and by accessing the world-BN directly during argument and rebuttal generation. This is done by considering propositions that are relevant to the goal, and if they are not directly observable, retrieving information about these propositions (i.e., their neighbouring nodes) from the world-BN. This process continues until the belief in the goal exceeds a particular threshold, which typically happens when BIAS retrieves observable propositions that have a large influence on the goal. For instance, in order to show that Mr Green had a motive to kill Mr Body, its neighbouring node in the world-BN, Mr Green and Mr Body were enemies, is retrieved. To determine the belief in this node, its two neighbours, Mr Body seduced Mr Green's girlfriend and Mr Green and Mr Body argued last week are retrieved, and so on [9]. Upon completion of this process, BIAS produces an argument in the form of a Bayesian sub-net, which is rendered in English and presented to the user (Figure 2).

The propositions in the user-model BN are obtained from a variety of sources: accepted propositions have been "clicked" by the user in the WWW-interface, while seen propositions have been shown to the user, but s/he has not indicated a belief in them. Propositions arguedByUser are mentioned in the user's rejoinder, while propositions impliedByUser are inferred from the rejoinder. Similarly, propositions in BIAS' arguments are arguedByBIAS or impliedByBIAS . These sources affect the system's certainty regarding the presence of the propositions in question in the user model. For instance, an accepted proposition is more likely to be believed by the user than a proposition impliedByBIAS . This certainty is represented by means of a numerical score, which is taken into account when interpreting the user's rejoinder (Section 4). The links in the user-model BN are obtained from the following sources: (1) BIAS' arguments and rebuttals, where they are presented by means of linguistic markers (e.g., therefore and this implies); (2) the interpretation of a user's rejoinders (links corresponding to the most likely interpretation or to the interpretation confirmed by the user); and (3) accepted propositions that are neighbours in the world-BN (e.g., Mr Body's window was broken, broken glass was found and broken glass was found inside the window in Figure 1).

Modeling Attention.   As indicated above, during argument and rebuttal generation, BIAS obtains information from the world-BN about the nodes in BIAS' BN that are likely to be relevant to the goal. We use attentional focus as a partial model of relevance to determine which propositions in BIAS' BN to inspect. In addition, we postulate that the line of reasoning intended by a user in a rejoinder is likely to include propositions in his/her focus of attention. In order to determine whether a proposition is in the user's or BIAS' focus of attention, we use a model of attention represented by means of a semantic network (SN) which contains associative links (rather than causal or evidential links). Activation is spread throughout this network from salient propositions [1]. One SN is incorporated into the user model (linked to propositions in the user-model BN), and one into BIAS' model (linked to propositions in BIAS' BN).

4   Interpreting a User's Rejoinder

The interpretation of a user's rejoinder consists of inferring the reasoning path intended by the user in the context of the user model (augmented by the BN corresponding to the presented argument). This process is implemented by algorithm IdentifyPath, which receives two inputs: a linguistic clue ("but" or "consider") and a rejoinder proposition (R) [8].

Algorithm IdentifyPath(linguisticClue,R)

1. Path construction   – Find paths that connect R to a proposition in the user model that is part of the argument-BN generated by BIAS.
2. Path evaluation   – Compute a score for each path based on its effect on the argument, its presence in the user's focus of attention, and BIAS' confidence in it.
3. Path selection   – Select the path with the highest score, or present promising paths to the user for confirmation if no single path is a clear winner.

4.1   Path Construction

Our path construction process copes with two types of inaccuracies in the user model: incompleteness (the user model does not represent all the user's beliefs), and high-granular ity (a one-step inference of the user corresponds to several links in the BN). This means that a path can be found between the rejoinder node and the argument-BN even if some nodes in this path do not appear in the user-model BN. Such gaps in the user model are filled during path construction by iteratively "growing" the user-model BN from two starting locations, R and the argument-BN, until R and the argument-BN become connected. Each iteration is similar to an argument-generation iteration in that the "horizon" nodes around R and around the argument-BN are passed to the world-BN in order to obtain information related to these nodes. However, in order to avoid the indiscriminate attribution of beliefs to the user, BIAS fills only small gaps (of at most two nodes). Since the path construction process often adds to the user model nodes that are not in the intended path, this process is performed in a temporary user model. The intended path is incorporated in the user model after path selection (Section 4.3).

To illustrate the path construction process, consider the user model in Figure 4(a), which contains an argument-BN (the tree whose root is the goal node G), the nodes

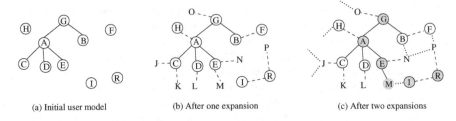

| (a) Initial user model | (b) After one expansion | (c) After two expansions |

Fig. 4. Path construction in a sample user-model BN

investigated by the user through the interface (F, H, I), and the user's rejoinder proposition R. After one expansion (drawn with dashed lines), propositions F, H and I become connected to R or to the argument-BN, and additional propositions from the world-BN, J, K, L, M, N, O and P (shown in italics in Figure 4(b)), are linked to R or to the argument-BN. After the second expansion (drawn with dotted lines), R becomes connected to the original argument-BN and the goal through several paths in the temporary user model, e.g., R-I-M-E-A-G (composed of grey nodes in Figure 4(c)).

The path construction process also takes into account the user's bounded reasoning capacity in that it finds interpretations which are direct and involve relatively short "inferential leaps" between the rejoinder and the goal. For instance, if the user says "But Mr Green was near the house at 11 : 15" after the argument in Figure 2, BIAS infers that the user is implying that Mr Green had the opportunity to kill Mr Body. However, if the user had said "But Mr Green owns a blue car", it is not reasonable for the system to postulate a convoluted inference between this rejoinder and the goal. BIAS achieves this behaviour by performing only three iterations when trying to connect R to the argument-BN, and by restricting the length of the paths being built.

4.2   Path Evaluation

The score of each path is a function of (1) the impact of R on BIAS' argument along this path according to the user model, (2) whether the nodes in this path are in the user's attentional focus, and (3) BIAS' confidence regarding the nodes in this path.

Impact of R along a path.   The impact of a rejoinder R on the nodes along a path is the change in the belief in these nodes due to R. This impact is moderated by the rejoinder's linguistic clue. A felicitous expression of doubt contradicts a proposition in the interlocutor's argument. Hence, its impact on a BN node is positive only when it moves the belief in this node in the "opposite" direction. In contrast, a request for consideration has no such negative connotations. Hence, it always has a positive impact.

When posing a rejoinder, a user may intend to affect the argument goal or another proposition in BIAS' argument. Therefore, when assessing the impact of a rejoinder along a path, we focus on two propositions: the goal and the highest-impact proposition. This is the proposition in the argument-BN on which the rejoinder had the highest impact along this path. For instance, given the rejoinder But Mr Green and Mr Body weren't enemies, the highest-impact proposition is Mr Green had a motive to kill Mr Body.

Attentional focus.   When posing a rejoinder, the user usually makes a small inferential leap along the path between the rejoinder and the proposition s/he intends to affect. For

Table 1. Conditions for the selection of a rebuttal strategy

	R is believed in BIAS' model and the user model	R is believed only in the user model
¬R is in the argument	N/A	Refute R
R has a strong effect on G in BIAS' model	Strengthen goal G	Refute R
R has a weak effect on G in BIAS' model	Dismiss Concede R	Dismiss Contradict R

Actually, it is very improbable that the found gun is available only to Mr Green. However, even if it was available only to Mr Green, this would have only a small effect on the likelihood that Mr Green murdered Mr Body. This is for the following reason.

The found gun being available only to Mr Green implies it is more likely that Mr Green fired the gun, making it almost certain. This implies it is more likely that he fired the murder weapon, making it almost certain, which implies it is even more likely that he had the means to murder Mr Body. This implies it is only slightly more likely that he murdered Mr Body.

Fig. 5. Contradictory dismissal for Consider that the found gun was available only to Mr Green

instance, when saying "But Mr Green and Mr Body weren't enemies", the user implies a short reasoning chain to Mr Green didn't have a motive to kill Mr Body and Mr Green didn't kill Mr Body. We postulate that such an inferential leap is more likely if it includes propositions in the user's focus of attention. The level of activation of the nodes along a path in the user model reflects their presence in the user's focus of attention.

BIAS' confidence in a path.   BIAS' confidence in a path depends on its certainty regarding the user's belief in each node along this path. This certainty is represented by the numerical score associated with the source from which a node was obtained (Section 3).

4.3 Path Selection

Path selection consists of choosing the paths with the highest scores returned by the path evaluation step, and presenting them to the user for confirmation if no single path is a clear winner. The recognition process fails if BIAS could not find a path between the rejoinder proposition and the argument-BN during path construction, or too many paths with similar high scores were found (so they could not be presented for confirmation), or the user does not select any of the presented paths. In the future, our interface will ask the user to further specify his/her rejoinder in these situations.

5 Rebuttal Generation

Given a user's rejoinder proposition R and a userPath – the user's line of reasoning inferred by BIAS or selected by the user, we consider three main types of rebuttals: (1) Refute R – which argues against the user's belief in R (Figure 3); (2) Strengthen G – which presents a stronger argument for the original goal proposition G; and (3) Dismiss userPath – which shows how the user's reasoning path fails to achieve its intended effect. The selection of a rebuttal strategy depends on (1) the belief in R according to

Refute R :
1. Deny the belief in R stated by the user.
2. Present a sub-argument for BIAS' belief in R.
3. If R was not mentioned in BIAS' argument, or the belief in R as a result of the sub-argument differs from that originally stated by BIAS, then follow the effect of R along userPath .

Strengthen G :
1. Acknowledge the user's belief in R.
2. While the belief in G is not as intended by BIAS, inspect each proposition P_i along userPath (starting from R towards G).
   (a) Generate a sub-argument for BIAS' belief in P_i.
   (b) If this sub-argument yields a significant change in P_i then store it for presentation, and propagate its effect on the beliefs in BIAS' model.
3. Present the line of reasoning along userPath with the planned sub-arguments.

Dismiss userPath :
1. Acknowledge/Contradict the user's belief in R.
2. Generate a sub-argument for each proposition that accounts for the discrepancy between the user's beliefs and BIAS' beliefs along userPath . These propositions (1) are directly connected to userPath , (2) have different beliefs according to the user model and BIAS' model, and (3) have a significant effect on the belief in a proposition on userPath . (It is possible that no such propositions are found, as shown in the example in Figure 5).
3. Follow the line of reasoning along userPath from R to G according to BIAS' model (this line is hypothetical for a contradictory dismissal).

Fig. 6. Rebuttal Strategies

the user model and BIAS' model, (2) whether R was mentioned in BIAS' argument, and (3) the impact of R on the goal according to BIAS' model (the selection policy is summarized in Table 1). For instance, a rejoinder that contradicts directly a statement in BIAS' argument is always refuted. This is the case for the rejoinder in Figure 2. In contrast, a rejoinder that has a small impact on BIAS' belief in the goal is dismissed. We distinguish between two types of dismissals depending on whether BIAS and the user agree on R: concessive if they agree, and contradictory if they disagree. Figure 5 illustrates a contradictory dismissal for the rejoinder Consider that the found gun was available only to Mr Green. The dismissal denies the user's rejoinder proposition, and shows that its hypothetical effect on Mr Green's guilt is marginal.

Figure 6 shows simplified schemas for our rebuttal strategies. These strategies call our argument-generation mechanism [9] to generate sub-arguments. The refutation strategy includes a sub-argument which contradicts the user's rejoinder proposition, the goal-stregthening strategy includes sub-arguments which affect the belief in the goal proposition, and the dismissal strategy may include such sub-arguments. The last two strategies differ in that the goal-strengthening strategy looks for new information in support of BIAS' belief in the goal (BIAS changes its belief in the goal if it fails to find this information), while the dismissal strategy usually takes advantage of information that is already present in BIAS' model.

6   Related Research

Our research builds on the system described in [9], which generated arguments from BNs, and the follow-on system described in [10], which enabled a user to explore the impact of different propositions on an argument by requesting the system to perform changes to this argument. Neither of these systems recognized a user's intentions from rejoinders or generated rebuttals that take into account these intentions, which BIAS does.

Quilici (1992) and Carberry and Lambert (1999) used a plan-based approach for argumentation. Quilici's system recognized the justification for a user's proposal and provided its own justifications in plan-related arguments. However, the rebuttals generated by this system were based on a single strategy: applying backwards chaining using a set of justification rules. This strategy is a special case of the more general rebuttal schemas presented here. Carberry and Lambert's system recognized a user's intentions during expert-consultation dialogues. Like BIAS, their system combined linguistic and contextual knowledge to recognize a user's intentions from rejoinders. However, it differed from BIAS in several respects: it covered a wider range of linguistic phenomena than those handled by BIAS, but it did not generate rebuttals, and it handled conversational turns in the context of interactions where each participant utters one or two propositions (compared to BIAS' complex arguments and rebuttals).

BNs have been used in several predictive tasks related to user modeling, e.g., [3,4,5]. BIAS resembles Gertner et al.'s system in that both systems use BNs for belief representation and plan recognition. However, the systems differ in the manner in which the BNs are obtained and in the usage of the BNs. Heckerman and Horvitz used a BN to infer a user's software assistance requirements from his/her input. Charniak and Goldman used BNs and marker passing (a form of spreading activation) for plan recognition during story understanding. However, neither of these two systems used BNs as a formalism for synthesis and analysis, as described in this paper.

7   Conclusion

We have offered a WWW-based interactive argumentation system which generates probabilistic arguments, recognizes a user's intentions from short-form rejoinders, and generates rebuttals to these rejoinders. The system consults a user model which represents a user's beliefs and inferences, the source from which these beliefs were obtained, and the user's attentional focus. The recognition mechanism, which is robust with respect to certain types of inaccuracies in the user model, connects the user's response with the system's argument. The rebuttal-generation process selects a rebuttal strategy on the basis of the beliefs in the user model and BIAS' model, and the impact of the user's rejoinder on the beliefs in BIAS' model. A preliminary evaluation of our interpretation mechanism indicates that people found BIAS' interpretations appropriate [8]. The rebuttal-generation mechanism will be evaluated in the near future.

Acknowledgments

The author thanks Sarah George, Nathalie Jitnah and Richard McConachy for writing the software for this project.

References

1. J. R. Anderson. The Architecture of Cognition. Harvard University Press, Cambridge, Massachusetts, 1983.
2. Sandra Carberry and Lynn Lambert. A process model for recognizing communicative acts and modeling negotiation subdialogues. Computational Linguistics, 25(1):1–53, 1999.
3. Eugene Charniak and Robert P. Goldman. A Bayesian model of plan recognition. Artificial Intelligence, 64(1):50–56, 1993.
4. Abigail Gertner, Cristina Conati, and Kurt VanLehn. Procedural help in Andes: Generating hints using a Bayesian network student model. In AAAI98 – Proceedngs of the Fifteenth National Conference on Artificial Intelligence, pages 106–111, Madison, Wisconsin, 1998.
5. David Heckerman and Eric Horvitz. Inferring informational goals from free-text queries: A Bayesian approach. In Proceedings of the Fourteenth Conference on Uncerta inty in Artificial Intelligence, pages 230–237, Madison, Wisconsin, 1998.
6. Nathalie Jitnah, Ingrid Zukerman, Richard McConachy, and Sarah George. Towards the generation of rebuttals in a Bayesian argumentation system. In Proceedings of the First International Natural Language Generat ion Conference, pages 39–46, Mitzpe Ramon, Israel, 2000.
7. Alex Quilici. Arguing about planning alternatives. In COLING-92 – Proceedings of the Fourteenth Internat ional Conference on Computational Linguistics, pages 906–910, Nantes, France, 1992.
8. Ingrid Zukerman, Nathalie Jitnah, Richard McConachy, and Sarah George. Recognizing intentions from rejoinders in a Bayesian interactive argumentation system. In PRICAI2000 – Proceedings of the Sixth Pacific Rim International Conference on Artificial Intelligence, pages 252–263, Melbourne, Australia, 2000.
9. Ingrid Zukerman, Richard McConachy, and Kevin B. Korb. Bayesian reasoning in an abductive mechanism for argument generation and analysis. In AAAI98 – Proceedngs of the Fifteenth National Conference on Artificial Intelligence, pages 833–838, Madison, Wisconsin, 1998.
10. Ingrid Zukerman, Richard McConachy, Kevin B. Korb, and Deborah A. Pickett. Exploratory interaction with a Bayesian argumentation system. In IJCAI99 – Proceedings of the Sixteenth International Jo int Conference on Artificial Intelligence, pages 1294–1299, Stockholm, Sweden, 1999.

Acquiring User Preferences for Product Customization

David N. Chin and Asanga Porage

Univ. of Hawaii, Dept. of ICS, 1680 East West Rd, Honolulu, HI 96822, USA
chin@hawaii.edu, tel: 808-956-8162, fax: 808-956-3548

Abstract.   Mass customization requires acquisition of customer preferences,
which can be modeled with multi-attribute utility theory (MAUT). Unfortunately
current methods of acquiring MAUT weights and utility functions require too
many queries. In Iona, the user is first queried for absolute/preferred constraints
and categorical preferences to cull the product pool. Next Iona selects queries to
maximally reduce the utility uncertainty of the remaining product choices.
Implemented queries include stereotype membership and contexts (the purchase
situation), which give probabilistic MAUT data modeled as ranges of weights.
The usefulness of a query is based on the reduction in uncertainty (smaller range)
weighted by the likelihood that the user belongs to a stereotype/context based on
similarity to the current user model. Querying proceeds until the usefulness of
the best query is below the threshold of user impatience.   Finally integer
programming is used to select the best product for the user.

Key words : Multi-attribute utility theory, stereotype, user preferences, mass
customization, travel planning, user model acquisition, constraints

1   The Problem: Acquiring User Preferences

Customers want products and services that satisfy their specific needs. Mass
customization produces individually tailored products that satisfy the specific needs
and preferences of each customer, but is costly because each customer requires
individualized attention. Multi-attribute utility theory [5], MAUT, can be used to
model user preferences for products that can be described by features (attributes).
Each attribute in MAUT has an importance weight (the utility of the attribute relative
to other attributes) and a value function (the relative utility of different values of the
attribute). The utility of a product is calculated as the weighted sum of the attribute
values over all product attributes.

Unfortunately, it is very time-consuming to determine weights and value functions
completely when a product has a large number of attributes. For example, a custom
home has hundreds of attributes such as choice of flooring for each room, doors,
windows, wall coverings/paint, roofing, etc. Each attribute in turn has many different
possible values (e.g., there are thousands of different carpets available, not to
mention linoleum, tile, wood, stone, etc.). Likewise, a customized travel package for
a trip to Hawaii (the domain for this paper) consists of dozens of attributes such as a
hotel's distance to the beach, price, and quality, an activity's type, distance from

M. Bauer, P.J. Gmytrasiewicz, and J. Vassileva (Eds.): UM 2001, LNAI 2109, pp. 95–104, 2001.
©Springer-Verlag Berlin Heidelberg 2001

hotel, time commitment, and price, and a restaurant's food style, price, atmosphere, and quality. To determine properly the weights and value functions for such complex products can take hours, even days of answering questions. Unfortunately, people are not willing to answer such long lists of questions even when they know the answers will be used to customize a product for them.

2   The Solution: Iona

Human architects design custom homes for clients and human travel agents design custom travel packages without determining exact MAUT weights and value functions for each client. They use a number of approximate methods instead. They determine which product specifications are most important to the client, identify the client type (stereotypes), and take into account the context (purchase situation). The Iona framework formalizes these techniques for mass customization. The Travel Planner implements most of the Iona framework in the domain of custom travel packages.

The Iona framework consists of the following functions: acquisition, assessment, elimination, selection and explanation/description. During acquisition, the following information is acquired: (1) absolute/preferred constraints (the most important product component specifications), (2) categorical preferences, (3) stereotype (customer type), and (4) context (purchase situation). Assessment consists of: (1) eliminating those choices that violate the absolute/preferred constraints, the categorical constraints, and the constraints inherent in the product (binary constraints between the different parts of the product and unary constraints such as availability), and (2) calculating the multi-attribute utility (usefulness to the customer based on the attribute levels) of the remaining choices. When asking for categorical preferences, descriptions of the discriminating attributes are given to users unfamiliar with the product. Questions regarding stereotypes/contexts are asked of the user to refine the utility estimates of the choices. The query to generate is based on the user's possible membership in the stereotype/context and the probable improvement in the utility estimates. A choice is selected for each part of the product when the usefulness of asking a query is less than the cost of querying. The selection is made using a binary integer-programming model to maintain global constraints such as price and time. The final solution is explained with emphasis on the attributes considered important by the user model.

This paper will concentrate on the acquisition function of Iona and its implementation in Travel Planner. More details can be found in [10].

2.1   Product Representation

The product to be customized is represented as a set of variables to be optimized. In Travel Planner, variables include possibly multiple instances of lodging, restaurants, activities, and transportation. Each variable can have many choices. For example, an activity could be going scuba diving at Hanauma bay, visiting the Arizona memorial, attending a hula competition, etc. Each choice is characterized by multiple attributes. Using MAUT, the best product maximizes the utility of the variable choices while still satisfying global constraints (price and time in Travel Planner). In MAUT, the attribute values are first mapped to a utility by a value function, which may vary from person to person. Next the utility of a choice is computed by summing the utilities of all its attributes weighted by the relative importance weights of the attributes, which also vary from person to person. The overall product utility (the travel package utility in Travel Planner) is the sum of the utilities of the choices made for each variable. If there are no global constraints (e.g., a very rich person on a long vacation), then the best product is simply the highest utility choices for each variable individually. With global constraints, tradeoffs must be made to stay within cost or time budgets. For example, a lower quality and hence lower utility, but cheaper hotel may be selected in order to have enough money left to go sailing. This tradeoff is made only if the differential utility between sailing and the next highest utility, but cheaper activity is greater than the differential utility between the lower quality hotel and the highest quality hotel that is still within budget. The choice of tradeoffs in MAUT is made to maximize the overall product utility to the user.

2.2   Constraints

Constraints include absolute/preferred constraints, categorical preferences, and inherent constraints. The user volunteers absolute/preferred constraints, such as restricting a lodging's location to Honolulu or an activity's description to kayaking. However, the user cannot provide constraints if unfamiliar with the product. For example, if the user has never been to Hawaii (or researched Hawaii), then the user would not know where to stay. Some users might just omit providing constraints. When the user does not provide absolute/preferred constraints that adequately reduce the set of alternatives, he/she is asked for categorical preferences (e.g., eating at a Japanese, Chinese, or Thai restaurant). This is necessary, because sometimes it is almost impossible to determine the utility of a choice purely based on stereotype/context information. When a traveler selects a water sports activity, it is hard to choose between surfing, parasailing, wind surfing, and snorkeling if the user does not provide additional constraints on the water sports activity. Although theoretically it is possible to determine from the stereotype/context information that a particular sports activity has higher value to the traveler, it would require building a very comprehensive user profile, which takes a lot of interaction. It is more time-efficient to ask direct questions of the user based on the classification of the available choices.

Attributes have classification hierarchies such as Waikiki and Ala Moana are in Honolulu, Honolulu, Aiea, Wahiawa and Pearl City are in central Oahu, and central Oahu, Leeward, North Shore, Windward, and Southeast Oahu are on the island of Oahu. These hierarchies are used to interpret absolute/preferred constraints at different levels of abstraction and to ask about categorical preferences at a suitable level of abstraction. A query with four or five answer options is easier to answer than a query with hundreds of options. The number of answer options for a query will depend on the attributes of the choices remaining in the solution. For example, if hotels are in 50 different cities, then the lodging location query will first have to be asked at a higher level of abstraction, such as district.

Inherent constraints include unary constraints for variable instances and binary constraints between variable instances. Examples of unary constraints include the seasonal availability of surfing on the North shore of Oahu and the temporary closure of fishing in a particular area. Examples of binary constraints are: activities are restricted to the same island as the lodging and restaurants must be less than 50 miles away from the hotel. These inherent constraints are maintained within the system and do not need to be given by the user. The product constraints are transparent to the customer and allow users to customize products without extensive knowledge of the product. The product constraints can be encoded at any level in the attribute classification hierarchy. For example, if lodging is on Oahu, then all activities should be on Oahu; if lodging is in Central Oahu, then the restaurants selected should also be in Central Oahu; if lodging is Hotel A, then the transport provider is Cab1. Currently implemented constraints include "equal to" and "not equal to" (negation).

2.3   Stereotypes

Stereotypes are helpful in determining people's general preferences regarding a product. For example, one study [16] investigated whether subjects from two culturally distinct regions in the United States would manifest different value orientations and if so, the extent to which these value differences may be related to attitudes toward automobiles and the relative importance of car attributes. One group preferred smaller, more fuel-efficient cars, which was consistent with their global and domain-specific economic values. They had a higher preference for automobile attributes that enhanced their desire for an exciting life, yet with non-polluting durable products. The other, more traditional group preferred larger more prestigious standard-size cars, which was consistent with their values. This study showed that stereotypes (area of residence) can be good indicators of people's attitudes and values towards the different attributes of products and services. It lends validity to using stereotypes to calculate the multi-attribute utility of alternative choices.

In Iona, stereotypes are used to represent the preferences of stereotypical users in a fashion similar to GRUNDY [14]. Iona replaces GRUNDY's facet values with MAUT attribute importance weights. In Iona, attribute weights are represented not as a single value with a confidence rating, but as a range of values representing the typical range of importance weights for members of that stereotype. The range allows very easy combination of stereotypes by taking the intersection of the ranges. As a comparison, [4] uses discrete reliability ratings (very-weak to very-strong) attached to discrete preference strengths (similar to importance weights), which does not allow for expression of uncertainty over a range weights such as complete uncertainty as to how strongly the user likes/dislikes something. PRACMA [6] uses a discretized probability distribution and combines evidence with Bayesian networks.

Unfortunately, the Bayesian network for the travel domain would be immense and it is unclear whether a more accurate discretized-probability-distribution representation would provide any benefits over a computationally-much-simpler range representation.

Individual users start out as members of the average person stereotype. Unlike other stereotype systems, there are no stereotype triggers in Iona.   Additional stereotypes membership is determined by asking the user.

Besides representing the range of importance weights for attributes, stereotypes in Iona also encode the value function for each attribute for which the stereotype has information. To reduce storage costs, value functions in Iona are represented as equations such as "$0.06x+0.4$" or "$\log_6 x$." A value function in MAUT maps attribute values to utilities.   These utilities are weighted by multiplying them by the importance weight range to give a range of utilities for each attribute of each choice.

The range also allows easy computation of the likelihood that the user belongs to a particular stereotype. The likelihood is based on the similarity of the current user model (a combination of the stereotypes in the user's model) to the suggested stereotype. It is easy to compare the similarity of weight ranges, but rather difficult to compare the similarity of value functions directly, so comparisons are made after value functions and weight ranges are used to compute ranges of utilities. Likelihood that a user belongs to a stereotype is directly proportional to the percent of overlap in utility ranges or inversely proportional to the percentage of non-overlap. More specifically, likelihood is the average percent overlap in utility ranges over all common attributes, which for one attribute is:

$$\text{Poss} = 1 - [(|\text{Exist}_l - \text{Sugg}_l| + |\text{Exist}_h - \text{Sugg}_h|) / ((\text{Exist}_h - \text{Exist}_l) + (\text{Sugg}_h - \text{Sugg}_l))] \qquad (1)$$

Sugg_h and Sugg_l are the high and low utilities given by the stereotype for this attribute. Exist_h and Exist_l are the high and low utilities of the current user model. The portion $((|\text{Exist}_l - \text{Sugg}_l| + |\text{Exist}_h - \text{Sugg}_h|)$ indicates the difference between the suggested and existing information. Poss may be negative if there is no overlap, allowing ranges with no overlap to contribute negatively (in proportion to the distance that the utility ranges are from each other) to the overall computation of likelihood.

2.4   The Best Query

As in [17], the best query is selected based on the utility of the query. To avoid confusion with the utility of the product, henceforth the utility of the query will be termed usefulness. Iona has a unique method of determining usefulness: usefulness is based on the ability of the query to help distinguish the utility of alternative products. This is similar in spirit to [15], which selected clarification questions to reduce the uncertainty among plan alternatives during interactive plan recognition. [2,12,13] also used information content gain to select the best query.

If the user model gave exact utilities, then there would be no question about the highest utility product. However, since the user model is uncertain, this leads to uncertainty about the best product. Queries are useful to the extent that they reduce this uncertainty. More specifically, usefulness is computed as:

$$\text{Usefulness} = (\text{Poss} * \text{UtilReduct}), \tag{2}$$

where UtilReduct is the potential reduction in the utility range. For a query about stereotype membership, usefulness is calculated using all the attributes of every remaining choice for which a utility estimate is indicated by the stereotype. The usefulness is weighted by Poss (see Equation 1), which is the likelihood that this user also belongs to this stereotype. Since most stereotype membership queries have multiple answers (e.g., income range, region of origin, age group), the total usefulness of such a query is simple the average of the usefulness of each stereotype answer (e.g., child, young-adult, middle-aged, and senior for age group). Note that the usefulness of each stereotype has already been weighted by the likelihood that the user belongs to the stereotype, so the average is really a weighted average.

2.5   The Interaction

Initially Travel Planner asks whether the user has been to Hawaii before (never, once, or many times) and for the duration of stay (as dates). Next Travel Planner asks the user to select the variables (components) of the travel package (any number of lodging, restaurant, activity, or transport) and provide absolute/preferred constraints for each variable as free-form text. The constraints are interpreted relative to Travel Planner's classification hierarchies with the help of a synonym list. For example, entering "Oahu" as a constraint for lodging would limit hotels to those listed under Oahu in the location hierarchy. A more specific constraint might be "Waikiki."

If the user does not provide sufficient constraints, he/she is asked for categorical preferences. An important problem is that the user might not be aware of the distinguishing factors between categories. Knowledge about the different categories of variable instance choices requires a familiarity with the product or service. Therefore, it is important for the system to provide a description when there is evidence to show that the user is unfamiliar with the product or service. Familiarity in Travel Planner is based on how many times the user has been to Hawaii and is similar to the expertise stereotypes in KNOME, the user modeling component of UC, the UNIX Consultant [3]. Descriptions should provide information about the discriminating attributes of these categories. It would also be useful if the attributes with higher importance to the traveler are emphasized in these descriptions, but this would require building the user model prior to asking about choice categories. The descriptions are computed from the database of choices. Parameters such as mean, standard deviation, and range of each attribute level are used for the description. For example, suppose there are significant differences (less than 60%) in average price and quietness for lodging at three areas of Oahu. The user would be told: Lodging in Honolulu is more expensive than in Ewa or Makaha. Lodging in Ewa is quieter than in Honolulu.

After the user has selected all of the desired variables, he/she is asked to provide a cost budget for these variables. The user is asked for a cost budget after selection of all variables, because now the user has a better idea of what the budget will cover. At this point, Iona performs constraint satisfaction to eliminate choices that violate the user's absolute/preferred constraints, the categorical constraints, other unary constraints such as seasonal closures, and binary constraints between variables such as restricting restaurants to the categorical location constraint of the lodging variable. If the user has over-constrained the problem, then the user must be informed of this and asked to relax the constraints (not yet implemented in Travel Planner).

In the next phase, the user is asked questions about stereotype membership and/or context (purchase situation). The best query is calculated based on its usefulness (Equation 2). The potential reduction in utility uncertainty is summed for all affected attributes of all remaining choices to give the usefulness of a query. Context queries are represented in a similar fashion to stereotypes (as ranges of attribute importance weights and value functions), so the usefulness of a context query is calculated in the same way as a stereotype membership question. The possibility of each answer (typically there are only two answers, yes or no, to a context query) is predetermined. Examples of context-related questions include: "are you going to Hawaii for the honeymoon?" and "are you visiting Hawaii for Spring Break?" Context-related questions are useful because people behave differently depending on the situation.

The query with the highest usefulness is asked until the usefulness of the best query is below the threshold of user impatience, which is similar to the nuisance factor used in RADAR [12,13]. At the end of querying, the problem is solved by integer programming using the mean value of the utility ranges. Finally the solution is presented to the user with emphasis on the attributes that the user model thinks are most important to the user. Currently, there are no opportunities for the user to provide feedback on the solution or ask for alternatives. For example, FindMe [1] allows the user to ask for choices that are further along a scale (e.g., cheaper, roomier). However user feedback would be essential in a real system.

2.6   A Comparison with Face-to- Face Travel Planning

The Travel Planner prototype was compared with actual face-to-face travel planning using the same database. The same user with the same problem interacted with Travel Planner and later a person acting as a travel agent (a student unassociated with this project who had extensive travel management experience). Both the user and the travel agent were asked to record their statements and their reasons for making the statements. The two participants were later asked to further explain the statements made during the interaction.

A qualitative analysis of the interaction shows some interesting differences. The human travel agent was motivated in part by earning commissions. For example, the human agent tried to persuade the client to extend his stay, took the initiative in suggesting variables (to sell more components), tried to sell activities aimed at the client's wife, and tried to sell a budget-breaking hotel, even adding a personal testimonial about the quality of the hotel. The human agent assumed the budget to be flexible and did not take responsibility for the overall budget, leaving that to the client. Indeed, the final travel package in the face-to-face interaction exceeded the initial budget by $100. The face-to-face interaction revealed the main objective of the client's trip (business), something that is not used by Iona, although it could provide important user model data. Finally, the human agent did not ask any stereotype questions, since these can be inferred from the client's appearance and the interaction.

Some of the similarities help validate the approach of Travel Planner. Both human and machine used discriminating attributes to describe differences in choices. Both asked for categorical constraints (e.g., restaurant type) to reduce the field of choices and both asked contextual questions (e.g., is the restaurant for a special occasion?).

Interestingly, the face-to-face interaction was considerably longer than the Travel Planner interaction. A lot of face-to-face time was spent providing the client with attribute values so that the client could make decisions. For example, the human agent showed the client pictures of the hotel and discussed price and quality of restaurants. In Iona, the program makes the decisions, so the client does not need to know attribute-level information such as which hotels have ocean views and the price of the different restaurants. Travel Planner only provides such information when describing the final travel package. Also, considerable time was spent in the face-to-face interaction determining the client's importance weights and value functions (such as the client's relative valuation of better food versus lower price, especially when the client's weights did not agree with the agent's weights). Iona can avoid this, since Iona gets attribute weights and value functions by asking about stereotype membership.

3   Conclusion

Iona is a unique framework and algorithm for the interactive customization of products and services. A customized product can be assembled based on the constraints provided by the user, the constraints inherent in the product, the stereotypes/contexts information, and the available choice alternatives for the product components. This algorithm can be used interactively as in Travel Planner or used on secondary databases containing customer information. Iona is the first to use stereotypes to estimate the multi-attribute utility of the alternatives. Suitable techniques are used to represent uncertainty and to combine information. The performance of the prototype was compared to a face-to-face situation of developing a customized travel package.

The algorithm uses a novel method to calculate the usefulness of each query based on the potential reduction in utility uncertainty of the remaining choices. It also takes into account the likelihood of different answers with similarity measures based on the possibility that the user might belong to a stereotype. The utility suggested by the stereotypes for each choice attribute level is compared with the utility estimates made up to that point. Similarity measures are calculated based on the utility estimates of the average user type for the first query. The first query is not the same for each user since the calculations are based on the attribute levels of choices remaining in the basic solution. Another unique feature is that attribute levels are converted to a utility value based on a continuous scale using value functions rather than on a categorical scale as in other related recommendation systems [7,8,9,11,14].

4   Future Directions

Travel Planner only considers queries about stereotype membership and context, however the Iona framework is not particular about the query type. For example, the Iona framework could easily accommodate more traditional MAUT parameter acquisition queries such as asking the user to: rate the importance of attributes on a sliding scale, rank two choices whose differences isolate one or two attributes, or draw a value function curve. For example, ATA [7] presents extreme alternatives to elicit importance weights. In cases where only a few attribute weights are uncertain, these types of queries may reduce uncertainty more than stereotype membership queries, which tend to give less specific information for any one attribute, but give information about several attributes.

An important factor overlooked by Iona is that attributes are not equally important to choice selection. For example, if all hotels are beachfront, then reducing the uncertainty in the user's utility or value function for distance to the beach would not help at all in deciding which hotel is best. The Iona framework would be improved by taking into account the distribution of the choice data. For example, Iona could compare the differences in average utility among the top choices both before and after the query. A query that reduces uncertainty in an attribute with little difference in the choices would not affect the average utility difference. Unfortunately, such computations become fairly intensive as the number of choices increase.

Instead of hand coding the Travel Planner stereotypes, the attribute weight ranges can be learned from sufficient demographic data and it may be possible to discover new stereotypes by correlating user characteristics to find clusters of users with similar attribute weights and attribute value functions. Finally, some attribute values such as cleanliness, luxury, and fun are highly subjective and so are difficult to determine for the choices. By polling large numbers of users, more accurate values for such subjective attributes can be determined. Even more accuracy is possible if user ratings are normalized. For example a fussy person may give consistently lower ratings to everything than someone who is easier to please. Finally, the Iona framework requires empirical evaluation to show that optimal or near-optimal solutions are obtained using Iona. However a lot of domain specific work is required before empirical evaluation would be possible.

Acknowledgements

This work was supported in part by the Office of Naval Research under contract N00014-97-1-0578.

References

1. R. D. Burke, K. J. Hammond and B. C. Young. Knowledge-Based Navigation of Complex Information Spaces. In Proceedings of the 13th National Conference on Artificial Intelligence, 462–468, 1996.
2. U. Chajewska, D. Koller and R. Parr. Making Rational Decisions using Adaptive Utility Elicitation. In Proceedings of the 17th National Conference on Artificial Intelligence, 363–369, 2000.
3. D. Chin. KNOME: Modeling what the user knows in UC, In A Kobsa and W. Wahlster, Editors, User Models in Dialog Systems, 74–107, Springer-Verlag, New York, 1989.
4. S. Elzer, J. Chu-Carroll and S. Carberry. Recognizing and Utilizing User Preferences in Collaborative Consultation Dialogues. In Proceedings of the Fourth International Conference on User Modeling, 19–24, 1994.
5. G. W. Fischer. Multi-dimensional Value Assessment for Decision Making, University of Michigan, Engineering Psychology Laboratory Technical Report 037230-2-T, June, 1972.
6. A. Jameson, R. Schfer, J. Simons and T. Weis. Adaptive Provision of Evaluation-Oriented Information: Tasks and Techniques. In Proceedings of the 14th International Joint Conference on Artificial Intelligence, 1886–1893, 1995.
7. G. Linden, S. Hanks and N. Lesh. Interactive Assessment of User Preference Models: The Automated Travel Assistant. In Proceedings of the Sixth International Conference on User Modeling, 67–78, 1997.
8. P. Maes. Agents that Reduce Work and Information Overload, Communications of the ACM, 37(7):31–40, 1994.
9. K. Morik and C. R. Rollinger. The Real Estate Agent: Modeling Users by Uncertain Reasoning. AI Magazine, 6(2):44–52, 1985.
10. A. Porage. A Framework for the Interactive Customization of Products and Services. Doctoral dissertation, University of Hawaii, Communications and Information Sciences Program, 1999.
11. B. Raskutti, A. Beitz, and B. Ward. A Feature Based Approach to Recommending Selections based on Past Preferences. User Modeling and User Adapted Interaction 7(4):179–218, 1997.
12. B. Raskutti and I. Zukerman. Query and Response Generation during Information-Seeking Interactions. Proceedings of the Fourth International Conference on User Modeling, 25–30, 1994.
13. B. Raskutti and I. Zukerman. Generating Queries and Replies during Information-seeking Interactions. International Journal of Human Computer Studies 47(6):689–734, 1997.
14. E. Rich, User Modeling via Stereotypes. Cognitive Science 3, 329–354, 1979.
15. P. van Beek and R. Cohen. Resolving Plan Ambiguity for Cooperative Response Generation. Proceedings of the 12th International Joint Conference on Artificial Intelligence, 938–944, 1991.
16. D. E. Vinson, J. E. Scott, and L. M. Lamont. The Role of Personal Values in Marketing and Consumer Behavior. Journal of Marketing 41(2):44–50, 1977.
17. D. Wu. Active Acquisition of User Models: Implications for Decision-Theoretic Dialog Planning and Plan Recognition. User Modeling and User-Adapted Interaction, 1(2):149–172, 1991.

Utility-Based Decision Tree Optimization:
A Framework for Adaptive Interviewing

Markus Stolze and Michael Ströbel

IBM Research, Zurich Research Laboratory, Säumerstr. 4,
CH-8803 Rüschlikon, Switzerland
{mrs,mis}@zurich.ibm.com

Abstract. An emerging practice in e-commerce systems is to conduct interviews with buyers in order to identify their needs. The goal of such an interview is to determine sets of items that match implicit requirements. Decision trees structure the interview process by defining which question follows a given answer. One problem related to decision trees is that changes in the selling strategy or product mix require complex tree restructuring efforts. In this paper we present a framework that represents the selling strategy as a set of parameters, reflecting the preferences of sellers and buyers. This representation of the strategy can be used to generate optimized decision trees in an iterative process, which exploits information about historical buyer behavior. Furthermore, the framework also supports advanced optimization strategies such as dynamic parameter adaptation and exit risk minimization.

1 Introduction

Many of today's e-commerce systems (online shops, business-to-business catalogs etc.) already use interviewing techniques. AOL, for example, features a system that helps users decide which digital camera they should buy by conducting them through a set of questions (http://www.personalogic.com/, 8 Nov, 2000). A slightly different system for digital camera selection is applied at mySimon (http://activebuyersguide.mysimon.com/, 8 Nov, 2000). This system asks a number of interview questions before coming up with a set of recommended items. A third example of an interview-based catalog can be accessed at eToys (http://www.etoys.com/giftfinder, 19 April, 2000). "Giftfinder" guides consumers through a mixture of item displays and questions to support the identification of the "right" toy for a child.

All three of these systems conduct an interview style of interaction to help users find the appropriate item. Decision trees offer a convenient way to represent such interviewing dialogues with buyers. For any given answer of a buyer, a decision tree specifies the next question to ask. The answers already given define criteria to select the relevant set of items.

Throughout this paper the decision tree scenario in Figure 1 is used as an example. In the sample tree, buyer X can answer question A with answer A1, A2 or A3. The tree definition defines that question B follows A1, question C follows A2, etc. This static decision tree is very efficient to interpret. However, the major drawback is the

M. Bauer, P.J. Gmytrasiewicz, and J. Vassileva (Eds.): UM 2001, LNAI 2109, pp. 105–116, 2001.
©Springer-Verlag Berlin Heidelberg 2001

effort needed to maintain the tree if the set of items changes or increased knowledge of the buyer behavior is to be incorporated in the interviewing process.

This paper introduces a framework for evaluating and optimizing decision trees for e-commerce system interviewing processes. In the next section the basic framework for decision tree optimization is presented in detail before more advanced optimization methods are outlined in Section 3. In Section 4 we review related work and finally, in Section 5, we discuss our results and point to areas of future research.

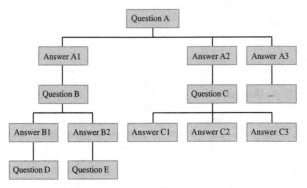

Fig. 1. Initial decision tree.

2   Approach

We approach the problem of finding an optimal decision tree in an iterative way that considers each branching point of the tree independently. To give an example, for the tree in Figure 1 it will be evaluated as follows: "if buyer X selects answer A1, is there a 'better' question than question B to ask buyer X in order to maximize the 'expected revenue' of the next question?" To answer this question, we define the revenue as the expected increase of the focus-set value (see Section 2.2) and, accordingly, the question with the highest increase of this focus-set value as the "best" question.
There are three underlying assumptions:

- The interview is conducted between one buyer and one seller offering a set of items.
- The items, which are subject to the interview process, are commodities. Item customization is not necessary.
- All sequence dependencies between questions are represented explicitly. This information is used to compute the set of possible questions. For example, if the answer F3 to question F requires that either question G or question H are asked as follow-up questions, then only these two questions will be evaluated and the question with the highest focus-set value gain will be selected.

Below we explain in more detail the steps needed for selecting the next best question.

2.1 Answer Probability Assessment

The starting point for the tree optimization is click-stream data that indicates how users traversed the currently active question tree. Using this data, answer probabilities can be calculated. The result of this assessment step is a tree structure with answer probabilities (AP) for all questions of the original decision tree (cf. Fig. 2).

These answer probabilities are dependent probabilities: AP(B2) depends on the precedent selection of answer A1. The total probability (TP) can be calculated on the basis of the totals for all answers of a single question independent of the precedent answers in the interview process. For the introduction of the framework in this section, the dependent answer probability AP is used. In Section 3.1, the application of total probabilities is discussed.

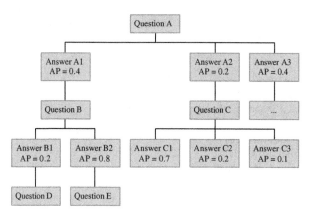

Fig. 2. Tree with answer probabilities.

2.2 Expected Focus-Set Calculation

The expected focus-set value (EV) is the goal criterion for the tree optimization. It expresses how well the currently considered set of items matches the preferences of the seller and the buyer. The focus set (FS) is the set of n items that, on the basis of the preceding answers in the tree, currently fulfill the requirements and preferences of the seller and the buyer. Initially, before the first answer, the focus set contains all items offered by the seller. The size of the focus set might also be restricted, as will be shown in Section 3.2.

Sellers' and buyers' preferences are formalized as utility functions. These functions are used to evaluate the items in the set of focused items. For the seller, this formalization is often a simple function of the item price margin, but might also incorporate other terms and conditions such as the delivery time or the return policy. The utility function of a buyer is constructed according to the answers given in the interview process. Let us assume that the buyer answers the question, "What is the minimum amount of RAM your desktop computer should have?" with "64 MB". This defines a filtering constraint that rules out all desktop computers with less than 64 MB of RAM. But this also defines the lower limit of the buyer RAM-utility function with a utility of 0 for computers with 64 MB of RAM and a utility of 1 for those computers with the highest available amount of RAM.

In general, the utility function for an attribute can either be deduced through direct questions regarding the attribute, as in the example above, or it can be established by rules that deduce attribute utility functions from buyer answers to needs-oriented questions. For example, a rule might state that buyers who indicate that they want to buy a PC for home use should look for a computer that has at least 64 MB of RAM.

The buyer utility of the focus set is determined by aggregating the utility of all the items in the focus set. To do this, the utility of each item in the set is computed by aggregating the individual attribute utility functions into a multi-attribute utility function [21].

The aggregated utility (AU) of a item is defined as the result of the combination function C_{AU} that takes buyer and seller utilities, and their respective weights, as the input. The combination function used in this paper is an additive combination function that computes the weighted sum.

Definition 1:
$A = \{a_1..a_n\} =$ the set of answers.
$I = \{i_1..i_k\} =$ the set of items
$PA_x = PA(a_x) = \{a_1..a_m\}$ is the set of precedent answers.
$FS_x = FS(PA_x \, 4 \, a_x) = \{i_1..i_k\}$ is the focus set of answer a_x.
$w_b =$ weight of buyer utility (U_b)
$w_b =$ weight of seller utility (U_s)
$AU(i_x) = C_{AU}(w_b, U_b(i_x), w_s, U_s(i_x))$
$\qquad = w_b * U_b(i_x) + w_s * U_s(i_x).$

The aggregated utility is not constant in the sense that a utility gain for the seller is not necessarily a utility loss for the buyer. Although a zero-sum situation is, in principle, possible, diverging preferences of the seller and the buyer towards the item choice and terms allow for win-win solutions [22], which result in an overall increase of the aggregated utility.

The setting of the weights formalizes the seller's selling strategy . High w_s will result in a strategy that mainly optimizes the seller benefit. On the other hand, high w_b results in a strategy that mainly optimizes buyer benefit. The focus-set value (FV) is defined as the average aggregated utility for all items in the focus set.

Definition 2:
$FV(FS_x) = (\,_{j=1..n}\, AU(i_j)) / |FS_x|, \, i_j \quad FS_x.$

Example continued: The weight structure was set by the seller to $w_s = 0.4$ and $w_b = 0.6$. The set of precedent answers for the answers B1 and B2 is $PA_{B1} = PA_{B2} = \{A1\}$. $FS_{B1} = \{i_1, i_2, i_3\}$. $FS_{B2} = \{i_1, i_4\}$. The resulting aggregated utilities and focus-set values are listed in Table 1 and Table 2:

Table 1. Focus-set value for answer B1.

Item	U_b	U_s	AU
		Answer B1	
I_1	0.8	0.4	0.64
I_2	0.6	0.5	0.56
I_3	0.7	0.5	0.62
			$FV_{B1} = 1.82/3 = 0.6$

Table 2. Focus-set value for answer B2.

Item	U_b	U_s	AU
		Answer B2	
I_1	0.4	0.7	0.52
I_4	0.9	0.8	0.86
			$FV_{B2} = 1.38/2 = 0.79$

Using the definition of the focus-set value and the answer probabilities, an expected focus-set value (EV) can be calculated for the questions in the decision tree.

Definition 3:
$Q = \{q_1..q_v\}$ = the set of questions.
$QA(q_x) = \{a_1..a_w\}$ = the set of answers to a question.
$EV(q_x) = {}_{i=1..w}\ (AP(a_i) * FV(FS_i)), a_i\ QA(q_x).$

That is, the expected focus-set value of a question is the expected value (i.e. probability weighted sum) of the focus-set values of the answers to that question.

Example continued:
The EV for question B after answer A1 is
$EV(B) = 0.2 * 0.6 + 0.8 * 0.79 = 0.752$.
The EVs of the other remaining questions after answer A1 shall be defined as follows:
$EV_C = 0.81$, $EV_D = 0.62$, and $EV_E = 0.68$.

2.3 Tree Optimization

The selection of the next question is based on a comparison of the expected focus-set value increase of all questions remaining after the application of sequence dependencies (see Section 0). The question q_{max} with the maximum focus-set value increase has to be determined:

Definition 4:
G $= \{a_1..a_y\}$ = set of given answers.
R $= \{q_1..q_z\}$ = set of remaining questions.
$FS(G)$ = focus-set value of the set of given answers.
IN_i $= IN(q_i) = EV(q_i) - FS(G)$
          = expected focus-set value increase of question q_i.
q_{max} $= q_{max}\ R |\ q_i\ R: IN(q_i) \bullet IN(q_{max})$
          = next best question to ask as it maximizes the expected focus-set value increase.

The final decision rule can be defined as follows:
If $IN_{max} > 0$, then q_{max} is the next question to ask.
If $IN_{max} [0$, then ask no further questions.

It can be seen that using the maximum expected focus-set value increase not only provides a means to determine the next "best" question to ask, but also a useful stop criterion.

Example continued:
The following values are used in the sample scenario:
$FS(G) = 0.5$.
$q_{max} = q_C$.
$IN_{qmax} = 0.81 - 0.5 = 0.31 > 0$.
The solution to the optimization problem is that question C should be asked after answer A1. This optimization process has to be executed for all branches in the initial decision tree, hence resulting in an optimized tree structure.

2.4 Iteration

After the tree adjustment, the optimized tree can be compiled and used to control the interviewing process in the seller's e-commerce system. The optimization process should be repeated if the item set changes, the FV/EV function specification changes, or if the results of the optimization can be verified on the basis of new answer statistics.

In addition to these events, which trigger the execution of the optimization cycle, there are other events that indicate the need to change the content of the underlying utility functions and deduction rules that are used for generating the decision tree. For example, an update of the user utility functions will be needed if situations occur repeatedly in which users with high item utility value refuse to buy an item. This indicates that there is a discrepancy between the calculated buyer utility in the e-commerce system and the utility implicitly perceived by the buyer. This should not be the case and, accordingly, the goal for the content update process is to modify the buyer utility function in such a way that the computed utility matches the collected sales statistics. Another more trivial event, which also triggers a content update, is the necessity to incorporate new questions or answers, if new features or new items are added to the buyer's portfolio.

3   Advanced Optimization Methods

The rule to pick the question with the maximum expected focus-set value increase introduced in the previous section is our basic method for optimizing the interviewing tree. This method might not be sufficient in some situations. In this section, four extensions of the selection rule are discussed. We do this to demonstrate the extensibility and flexibility of the framework, not its completeness.

3.1 Reasoning about Global   Focus-Set Properties

This extension of the optimization method deals with the fact that in some situations sellers might want to control the size of the focus set. A typical intention is to reduce this size step by step in order to finally suggest only one item to the buyer.

To incorporate this goal into the interviewing framework, an additional utility function can be added to the strategy formalization. This utility function assesses not only the characteristics of one item but, on a higher level, also the characteristics of the focus set: $U_{fs}(FS)$. To model the strategy of reducing the focus-set size, the utility value will increase with a decreasing number of items in the focus set, reaching 1 for a focus-set size of 1. The overall focus-set utility (FU(FS)) is then determined by applying the combination function C_{FU} to the aggregate utility and the focus-set utility, given their respective weights. In the simplest case, this is an additive combination function.

$$FU(FS) = C_{FU}(w_{au}, AU(P), wf_s, U_{fs}(FS))$$
$$= w_{au} * AU(P) + wf_s * U_{fs}(FS).$$

In general, "size" is just one easy-to-compute feature of the item set that can be evaluated in the U_{fs} function. Another useful measure is the "crispness" of the focus set, which can be measured as the entropy of the focus set, given the utilities of the contained items. This crispness is an estimate of how difficult it is for the user to choose between the items in the focus set.

In addition to buyer-related features, seller-related features can also be integrated. For example, sellers might favor a focus set containing items from a large number of different brands over a focus set of the same size that contains offers from only a small number of brands.

3.2 Adapting Strategy Parameters Dynamically

In some situations it can be useful to define the strategy parameters as dynamic functions that change during the course of the interview. For example, a seller might formalize a risk-friendly selling strategy in which initially w_b is high (e.g. to attract buyers) and only later in the dialog (after buyers were willing to invest some time and showed significant interest in the set of items) w_b is decreased to drive buyers towards items of superior value to the seller. Other sellers could choose (for other reasons) an inverse strategy that starts with a low w_b, which is then gradually increased on a step-by-step basis.

To enable sellers to experiment with such dynamic strategies, the definition of the aggregated utility (AU) of a item is extended to be dependent on the number of answers given. We can now define the aggregated utility as a dynamic function:

$$AU_{x,|G|} = AU(p_x, |G|) = w_{b,|G|} * U_b(p_x) + w_{s,|G|} * U_s(p_x).$$

3.3 Minimizing Exit Risk

A persistent problem with e-commerce systems is that users visiting these shops or catalogs exit before they have actually bought something. It is therefore a critical aim of any e-commerce system to reduce the number of user exits and to turn browsers into buyers. One way to achieve this for interviewing processes is to reduce the number of questions necessary to determine a meaningful focus set, which can be presented to the user. The stop criterion of the decision rule in the tree adjustment step is one element supporting this strategy, as it prevents useless questions, which do not increase the expected focus-set value. An advanced optimization of the number of questions can be achieved if the probabilities of consecutive answers are reflected in the selection of the next questions.

In addition to the number of questions, the nature of questions themselves might be irritating or too complicated, thus also causing the user to exit the interviewing process. To minimize the risk of losing users for this reason, the exit probability of a question can be integrated in the framework. This is possible in two ways:

One alternative is to multiply the EV of every question with $(1-p_{exit})$, where p_{exit} is the historical exit probability. The other option is to incorporate the risk of exit as an additional outcome of the question being given a negative value. The value lost in this case is the already achieved focus-set value FS(G).

When should questions with a high risk be asked? Using the first alternative, obviously not at the beginning of the interviewing process because of their decreased EV. Using the second alternative, they might be asked right at the beginning when the earned focus-set value is still low and the adjustment therefore relatively small.

4   Related Work

4.1 Decision Tree Induction

Methods for generating optimal decision trees to classify items according to their attribute values have been studied extensively in the areas of statistical pattern recognition [3], machine learning [19,20] and data mining.

In principle, the task of identifying the best item for a buyer can be seen as a classification problem in which the information elicited from the buyer determines (to a certain degree) the item he or she is going to buy. Standard decision tree induction algorithms can be used to build a decision tree if enough data about successful sales is available. However, this induced tree will often differ from the tree created by the method proposed in this paper. The reason for this is that traditional rule induction mechanisms use entropy gain [19], entropy gain ratio [20], or other entropy-related criteria (e.g. [15]) to decide on the next-best branching attribute. The resulting tree is optimized to lead buyers with as few questions as possible to the most "crisp" set of items.

Our contribution is the proposal of a domain-specific decision criterion for attribute selection that is useful for inducing decision trees for e-commerce interviewing processes. The traditional entropy-related tree-splitting criteria could be seen as special cases of the mechanism proposed here, in which seller utility is the same for all items, buyer utilities are determined directly by the sales records, and FU(FS) is defined to be dependent only on the entropy of the focus set.

4.2 Diagnostic Systems

The task of identifying the item that best matches an online buyer can be seen as a classification task similar to that of medical diagnosis [10] and technical troubleshooting [11]. Similar to the two cited diagnostic applications, we employ a probabilistic model to determine the likelihood of test results (i.e. answers to questions). However, our approach is different in that we use a utility model instead of a probabilistic model to predict the appropriateness of a item for a buyer. We do this because the set of items offered in an e-commerce site changes so rapidly that it is difficult to collect enough data to make valid predictions about the appropriateness of items on the basis of previous sales information.

Our approach is also similar to Heckerman's work [11] in that we use a single step look-ahead ("myopic") mechanism to determine the next best question to ask. However, our approach is different in that we try to optimize the joint benefit of buyer and seller (defined as the focus-set value) instead of trying to minimize the total cost of tests.

4.3 Adaptive Help and User Models

Our approach is also related to adaptive help systems like the Microsoft Office Assistants and follow-up research systems [12, 13]. These systems use Bayesian Networks to estimate the probability of users' goals. The resulting probabilities are then used as a basis to determine the expected utility of performing (and not performing) a communicative action. Here agents only engage in an action if the overall utility of that action is larger than zero and larger than the utility of all other possible actions. Our approach is similar to adaptive help systems in that it computes the utility of questions and uses it for selecting the next best question. However, the detailed methods for utility computation differ in both approaches.

Our approach also differs from adaptive help systems and similar user model-based approaches in that the product utility rules are not used directly for online user modeling. Instead, these rules are used during decision tree building for creating hypothetical user models for each node in the tree. These user models are used to determine the next best follow-up question and discarded afterwards. During an online interaction with a user, an explicit user model is not necessary because the model is compiled into the decision tree.

4.4 Recommender Systems

Our approach is also related to recommender systems [23], also called collaborative filtering systems [2] or social filtering systems [7]. According to Burke [6] "these systems aggregate data about customers and purchasing habits or preferences and make recommendations to other users based on similarity in overall patterns. For example, in the Ringo music recommender system [25], users who had expressed their musical preferences by rating various artists and albums could get suggestions of other groups and recordings that others with similar preferences also liked."

Recommender systems are related to the mechanisms presented here in that both mechanisms focus on helping buyers find appropriate items. The difference is that recommender systems rely on statistical correlation information generated from sales data to determine the potentially matching items. Instead, in our approach we use the sales data only to validate the buyer utility models. To determine the values of the potential next question we use the buyer utility models together with the seller utility and the overall focus-set utility. One advantage is that such an approach will also work if only little sales data is available and the product portfolio changes frequently. The second advantage is that the flexible weighting of the seller utility gives sellers a way to adapt item presentation to their preferences. This inclusion of seller concerns into the recommendation process is, to our knowledge, a unique feature of our approach to e-commerce buyer guidance. The only exception of which we are aware is [4] who use the expected sales margin together with statistics about frequent item sets in a data mining effort to optimize product placement in vending machines.

4.5 Evaluation-O riented Information Provisioning

A large group of related systems is performing evaluation-oriented information provisioning (EOIP) [14]. These systems are advisory systems or sales assistant systems that (a) predict the evaluation of candidate objects by a user and (b) elicit and interpret evidence about user preferences. The method proposed here fits this description of EOIP.

Similar to many EOIP systems [8, 9, 16, 17, 18, 24] we use a MAUT model for predicting the evaluation of candidates by the user. Compared to these systems our approach mainly differs in the way we elicit evidence from the user and interpret it. Most of the above-mentioned systems elicit evidence by showing users one or a few sample candidate objects, and having users express their preferences by selecting a preferred candidate object or by critiquing feature values of candidate objects. Our method also computes and evaluates the set of possible candidate objects, which could be presented to the user. However, computation of this set and its associated value to the buyer and seller is only a means to determine the next needs-oriented question that will optimize the expected focus-set value. It is quite likely that real world shopping interfaces will want to present both: a critiquable candidate list and needs-oriented questions. Furthermore, it is likely that such systems would also want to use methods studied in the area of adaptive hypermedia [5] to adapt the presentation of products to the preferences of individual users as for example discussed by Ardissono & Goy [1]. Creating systems that efficiently combine these different techniques will be an interesting challenge.

5   Discussion and Future Work

We believe that the proposed approach of supporting the generation and optimization of decision trees for e-commerce interviews with a utility-based formalization of the selling strategy is useful, as it provides a simple formula for the tree-splitting criterion, which can be extended to handle more complex optimization requirements. Changes in the selling strategy and product set as well as updated information about buyer behavior can be incorporated into an automatic regeneration of the interview decision tree. Hence, the framework enables adaptive interviewing in the sense that no manual tree editing is necessary to accommodate these changes.

If, for instance, a seller decides to change the selling strategy and to favor items with smaller guarantee timeframes to items with higher price, a new utility function for this seller can be compiled and injected into the interviewing process. The next tree optimization cycle then generates a decision tree, which will reflect this change. If, on the other hand, consumer feedback reveals decreasing satisfaction with the interview results (the set of proposed items) one potential countermeasure is to increase the weight of the buyer utility in the calculation of the aggregated item utility. In addition to this, we demonstrated the flexibility and extensibility of the framework by investigating advanced optimization strategies.

Given these benefits we are investigating possibilities for incorporating the described mechanism into commercial tools for e-commerce interview control.

An interesting area for further research is the investigation of mechanisms for online reasoning. In some e-commerce systems the initial set of items to be considered in the interview process will not be the same for all buyers due to the parallel use of other techniques such as pre-filtering (e.g. through shopping agents) or personalization. In the extreme case, every buyer will start with a different set of items, and in some systems this set of items might also change independently of the information collected in the interview. In such cases it will not be possible to pre-compile the decision trees in a "batch" procedure. As a result, reasoning about the next best question to ask has to be performed dynamically based on the available data about items in the focus set. Such online reasoning places stricter real-time requirements on the algorithms employed. Accordingly, mechanisms for partial compilation and other optimization techniques targeted at the algorithm's performance present an interesting future challenge.

Other areas for further research include advanced tree pruning mechanisms and support for multilateral relationships between buyers and sellers that can include more than one party at each end and also support the notion of intermediary brokers.

References

1. Ardissono, L., Goy, A.: Tailoring interaction with users in electronic shops. Proceedings of the 7th International Conference on User Modeling, Banff, Canada (1999) 35-44
2. Breese, J., Heckerman, D., Kadie, D.: Empirical analysis of predictive algorithms for collaborative filtering. Proceedings of the Fourteenth Conference on Uncertainty in Artificial Intelligence (1998) 43-52
3. Breiman, L., Friedman J., Olshen, R., Stone, C.: Classification and Regression Trees. Wadsworth International, Belmont (1984)
4. Brijs, T., Swinnen, G., Vanhoof, K., Wets G.: A Data Mining Framework for Optimal Product Selection in Convenience Stores. Proceedings of the Eighth European Conference on Information Systems (2000), Vienna
5. Brusilovsky, P.: Methods and techniques for adaptive hypermedia. User Modeling and User Adapted Interaction 3 (1996): 87-129

6. Burke, R.: Integrating Knowledge-based and Collaborative-filtering Recommender Systems. Proceedings AAAI-99 Workshop AI for Electronic Commerce (AIEC99), Orlando, Florida, July 18 (http://www.cs.umbc.edu/aiec/) (1999)
7. Dieberger, A., Hö, K.: Applying Social Navigation Principles to the Design of Shared Virtual Spaces. WebNet 1 (1999) 289-294
8. Dix, A., Patrick, A.: Query by browsing. Proceedings IDS'94: The 2nd International Workshop on User Interfaces to Databases. P. Sawyer. Lancaster, UK, Springer Verlag (1994) 236-248
9. Fischer, G., Nieper-Lemke H.: HELGON: Extending the Retrieval Reformulation Paradigm. Proceedings of ACM CHI'89 Conference on Human Factors in Computing Systems (1989) 357-362
10. Gorry, G.A., Barnett, G.O.: Experience with a model of sequential diagnosis. Computers and Biomedical Research 1 (1968) 490-507
11. Heckerman, D., Breese, J.S., Rommelse, K.: Decision-theoretic troubleshooting. Communications of the ACM 38(3) (1995) 49-57
12. Horvitz, E., Breese, J., Heckerman, D., Hovel, D., Rommelse, D.: The Lumiere project: Bayesian user modeling for interring the goals and needs of software users. Fourteenth Conference on Uncertainly in Artificial Intelligence, Madison, WI, July (1998)
13. Horvitz, E.: Principles of mixed-initiative user interfaces. Proceeding of the CHI 99 conference on Human factors in computing systems, May 15 - 20, 1999, Pittsburgh, PA USA (1999) 159-166
14. Jameson, A., Schäer, R., Simons, J., Weis, T.: Adaptive Pr ovision of Evaluation-Oriented Information: Tasks and Techniques. Proceedings of the 14th International Joint Conference on Artificial Intelligence (IJCAI), Montreal, August (1995) 1886-1893
15. Jun, B. H., Kim C.S., Kim, J.: A New Criterion in Selection and Discretization of Attributes for Generation of Decision Trees. IEEE Transactions on Pattern Analysis and Machine Intelligence 19(12) (1997) 1371-1375
16. Linden, G., Hanks, S., Lesh , N.: Interactive assessment of user preference models: The automated travel assistant. User modeling: Proceedings of the Sixth International Conference, UM97. A. Jameson, C. Paris and C. Tasso (eds). Vienna, New York:, Springer Wien New York (1997) 67-78
17. Nguyen, H., Haddawy, P.: The decision-theoretic video advisor. Proceedings of the AAAI Workshop on Recommender Systems, Madison, WI (1998) 77-80
18. Popp, H., Lüel, D.: Fuzzy Techniques and User Modeling in Sales Assistants. User Modeling and User-Adapted Interaction 5(3-4) (1996) 349-370
19. Quinlan, J.R.: Induction of Decision Trees. Machine Learning 1(1) (1986) 81-106
20. Quinlan, J.R.: C4.5: Programs for Machine Learning. Morgan Kaufmann, San Mateo (1993)
21. Raiffa, H., Keeney, R.: Decisions with Multiple Objectives. Wiley, New York (1976)
22. Raiffa, H.: The Art and Science of Negotiation, Harvard University Press (1982)
23. Resnick, P., Varian, H.R.: Recommender Systems. Communications of the ACM 40(3) (1997) 56-58
24. Rogers, S., Fiechter, C.-N., Langley, P.: An adaptive interactive agent for route advice. Proceedings of the Third International Conference on Autonomous Agents. Seattle, WA, June (1999) 198-205
25. Shardanand, U., Maes, P.: Social information filtering: automating the "word of mouth". Proceedings of the Conference on Human Factors in Computing System (CHI'95), Denver, CO, May 7-11, (1995) 210-219.

User Modelling in I- Help: What, Why, When and How

Susan Bull, Jim Greer, Gordon McCalla, Lori Kettel, and Jeff Bowes

ARIES Laboratory, Department of Computer Science, University of Saskatchewan,
Saskatoon, Saskatchewan, S7N 5A9, Canada.
bull@cs.usask.ca, greer@cs.usask.ca, mccalla@cs.usask.ca

Abstract. This paper describes user modelling in I-Help, a system to facilitate
communication amongst learners. There are two I-Help components: Private and
Public Discussions. In the Private Discussions learners take part in a one-on-one
interaction with a partner (possibly a peer). The Public Discussions are open -
everyone in the group has access to all discussion forums relevant to that group.
The Public Discussions are most suited to discussion of issues where there might
be a variety of valid viewpoints, or different solutions to a problem. It is also
useful for straightforward questions and answers that have wide-spread
applicability. The Private Discussions are better suited for more intensive
interactions involving peer tutoring or in-depth discussions. Because there is only
one helper in such situations, I-Help requires a method of selecting an appropriate
helper for an individual. We describe the user modelling that takes place in each
part of I-Help, in particular to effect this matchmaking for Private Discussions.
This modelling takes advantage of a distributed multi-agent architecture, allowing
currently relevant user model fragments in various locations to be integrated and
computed at the time they are required.

Keywords. peer help network, discussion forum, distributed student model

1 Introduction

Discussion forums and one-on-one peer help environments can be useful for
providing support outside normal class time. The two environments are best suited to
different types of interaction. Discussion forums allow learners to ask and answer
questions on a variety of topics, which is especially useful for discussion involving
multiple viewpoints or multiple problem solutions, or for straightforward questions
requiring a quick response. In contrast, one-on-one peer help networks can assist
open-ended intensive interactions between two individuals, such as tutoring. This
requires some kind of user modelling in order to locate appropriate helpers
(Mühlenbrock et al. [13]; Ogata et al. [14]; Yu et al. [17]). However, despite their
utility for different types of interaction, discussion forums and one-on-one peer help
networks are rarely integrated. I-Help combines a peer matching component to form
pairs for one-on-one help sessions (I-Help Private Discussions), and a discussion
forum for small group and large group participation (I-Help Public Discussions).

For peer matching, a method of selecting appropriate partners is a primary purpose
for user modelling. Other purposes include assessment and self-assessment, reflection, knowledge management, expertise location. This paper focuses on user model

M. Bauer, P.J. Gmytrasiewicz, and J. Vassileva (Eds.): UM 2001, LNAI 2109, pp. 117–126, 2001.
©Springer-Verlag Berlin Heidelberg 2001

data collected during use of I-Help, describing how this is applied to various purposes in I-Help under various circumstances and constraints. Attributes modelled include an individual's knowledge level in the various course topics; their eagerness to participate; their helpfulness; their cognitive style; their learning goals or interests; and their preferences in a learning partner. Sources of model representations are students themselves, peers, and information gathered by the two I-Help components.

I-Help is built on an agent architecture. Agents are also a fundamental part of the user modelling process. Each user has their own personal agent to take care of their interests. In addition to developing a model of their owner, an agent constructs partial models of users of all agents with which it comes into contact. The multi-agent approach results in distributed and fragmented user models which can be computed just-in-time, for the particular purpose at hand, using only the data required for that purpose. The data and user modelling representations and techniques are in place to do many things in I-Help. We demonstrate how our approach takes advantage of some of this user model power to successfully match partners, and suggest how the existing models may be used in the future, to develop the approach even further.

2   User Modelling in I-Help

User models in I-Help are fundamental and central to the system's function, but the models themselves are fragmented and distributed. There is no single monolithic user model describing an individual learner. Rather, learner models are represented, stored, computed, and applied in a distributed fashion and on an as-needed basis. Our overall notion of fragmentation and multi-agent communication in learner modelling has been termed "active learner modelling" (McCalla et al. [11]). In this paper we focus on the types of information used for modelling in I-Help and on techniques for integration of information into meaningful models for use in I-Help.

Various information types are modelled: knowledge; interests; cognitive style; eagerness; helpfulness; interaction preferences; opinions of peers; user actions. These are recorded, observed and inferred in various ways from a range of sources. One source is users themselves. Self-evaluation is employed in a number of user models to take into account a user's views of their competence (Beck et al. [1]; Bull & Pain [5]; Dimitrova et al. [7]; Kay [9]). In I-Help users provide profile information assessing their knowledge on topics of relevance in the I-Help groups to which they belong (topics are pre-assigned by the person in charge of an I-Help group).

Another source of information about users is peer assessment. Although a few examples exist (e.g. Bull et al. [3]), peer evaluations have been less frequently employed in student modelling. In I-Help Private Discussions, feedback on help sessions is sought from helpers and helpees. This updates the knowledge profile data for both helper and helpee. Judgements about content knowledge and interests from these various sources may be inconsistent, but attempts to reconcile this information are not made until some decision forces a summarisation. Indeed, there is no need for reconciliation prior to this point, as the various fragments of user model data will be successively updated as more data is gathered, but this will likely occur at different rates. For example, a person under consideration as a helper should be knowledgeable on the topic. If user-provided profile information on their knowledge level does not agree with observations made by other users, rationalisation of these conflicts is relevant only at that time: incoming data (such as additional peer evaluations) may at any moment increase the weighting of a particular point of view on such a conflict, affording greater credibility for that viewpoint.

As well as being sources of information for modelling, self and peer evaluation, even in this simple form, are useful activities in their own right – to raise awareness of domain issues and learning in general; and perhaps also to contribute to some form of learner assessment. Thus multiple modelling purposes are encompassed.

Browsing patterns and posting activity in the Public Discussions provide another source of information about users. Such activity is analysed to determine topics and concepts of interest through off-line data mining (Bowes [2]). Interest in particular forums, topics, users and individual postings can also be determined by monitoring notification preferences set by a user in the Public Discussions. Learners wishing to be notified by email about specific events in I-Help will likely have an interest in those events. In addition to enabling email notification of new postings of interest, user model representations derived from the Public Discussions are used in matching pairs in the Private Discussions – e.g. a user requesting notification of new postings by a specific author will usually do so because they find this user's postings helpful.

In addition to their knowledge of various topics, users also indicate interaction preferences in the Private Discussions: e.g. characteristics they seek in a helper and the maximum number of concurrent help sessions in which they can participate. They may also ban people with whom they do not wish to interact, and indicate people with whom they will preferentially interact. Topics may be banned if the user does not wish to give help in the area. Thus the learner sets the parameters within which their personal agent should operate when negotiating matches, affording them a degree of control (c.f. Kay [10]). This adds a social dimension to the user modelling.

Other information is also modelled. Data on eagerness to participate is inferred for a user, gathered from the user's I-Help usage patterns. Frequency of login to I-Help, the number of postings read and re-read in the Public Discussions, and time spent responding to help requests in both Public and Private Discussions contribute to the eagerness measure. Similarly, data on helpfulness of users is gathered from many sources. Users may register opinions about their helpfulness. Helpers in the Private Discussions are judged for helpfulness by the helpee. When a potential helper refuses to offer help, some evidence about helpfulness (or lack thereof) is gained. Helpfulness is also judged by the type of participation in Public Discussions – whether they often offer answers, and whether those answers are frequently read and endorsed. The Public Discussions have a voting mechanism where users can vote on the utility of postings. Endorsements of peers may be interpreted as a measure of helpfulness.

The Private Discussions contain a brief questionnaire from which inferences are made to help identify a user's cognitive style, to suggest suitable helpers with reference to different kinds of question. (Users indicate their question type by menu selection when submitting a help request.) The cognitive style categorisation is based on Riding and Cheema's [15] classification of the two dimensions of wholist-analytic and verbal-imagery style (see Bull & Greer [4]).

Table 1 summarises the attributes modelled, and the sources of information for these representations. As stated above, this information is integrated on an as-needed basis, using only the data that is relevant for the particular purpose (for example, knowledge level is relevant for assessment, but eagerness is probably not).

Table 1. User model attributes and information sources

Attributes	Sources of information			
	User	Peers	I-Help Private	I-Help Public
knowledge	•	•		
interests	•			•
eagerness	•		•	•
helpfulness	•	•	•	•
readiness (online)			•	•
cognitive style	•		•	
preferences in helper	•			
preferred people	•			
banned people	•			
banned topics	•			
help-load	•		•	

To enable I-Help to select the most appropriate helper for a particular request in the Private Discussions, it uses a matchmaker agent that communicates with the personal agents of users (Vassileva et al. [16]), which can, in turn, access various kinds of information about their 'owners' and about other users with which their owners have come into contact. The matchmaker performs a quick, coarse-grained survey of users who know about the topic in question. Other factors, such as cognitive style, eagerness and current help-load are also considered. A ranked list of potential helpers is then produced. To rationalise the possible diversity of opinions about a user, the current matchmaker constructs a composite estimate (weighted score). While this estimate is rather crude, preliminary studies have shown it to be sufficient for recruiting satisfactory helpers. A more subtle composite measure might further improve matchmaking. We have constructed a Bayesian modelling agent (service) to take a fragment of a Bayesian network and a set of observations and produce estimates of probabilities of nodes under various assumptions of new evidence (Zapata [18]). This service will be in integrated into an upcoming version of I-Help.

Modelling the helpee also plays a part in the selection of a helper. The preliminary helper list generated by the matchmaker is scanned to identify preferred helpers and banned people. If helpfulness is an important criterion for the helpee, helpers with higher levels of helpfulness are raised in the list. If urgency in finding a helper is an important criterion, then readiness (being on-line) is raised in priority, etc.

Once the helper list is prepared, the personal agent of the helpee is brought into negotiation with the agents near the top of the list. This, too, involves modelling. During negotiation local knowledge the user's agent has of the potential helper is consulted. Previous help interactions can be recalled; good or bad experiences with the helper that may have been shared by other users' agents may come into play. Negotiation over availability and willingness to accept the help request is then undertaken. A final list of five potential helpers is prepared, to which the request is sent. The first user to reply becomes the helper.

I-Help user modelling is important to protect helpers from unwanted interruptions and to spread the help-load. Any capable helper would become overwhelmed with requests in an open environment. In I-Help users and agents can set thresholds to regulate the number of requests received. A busy flag can be raised that can, for example, bar anyone but a friend with an urgent request. As agents in I-Help are further developed, inferences made by agents and the richness and independence of the models stored in the agents will grow. Agents will, in effect, each become expert systems able to compute user model information as needed for a particular purpose.

This section has illustrated that there is a substantial quantity of user model information that can be gathered and utilised in I-Help, and a range of uses. The multi-agent, distributed approach enables powerful modelling – much of which is already incorporated in I-Help. It must be emphasised that no effort is made to unify this data into a single user model for each user. The models that must be formulated depend on the purposes to which the models are put (e.g. helper location, information retrieval, promoting reflection, etc.) In fact the information used in the modelling processes may reside in different places – spread across the many agents in I-Help.

3   An Example

To illustrate the issues described in the previous section, we here look at an example drawn from a deployment of I-Help in a first year Computer Science course at the University of Saskatchewan (Spring 2000). We examine in more detail how the user modelling computations were used by the matchmaker agent to rank and select potential helpers in response to a particular help request in the Private Discussions. We then compare the matchmaker's rankings with other evidence of the potential helpers' capabilities drawn from their use of I-Help. The intention is to show how user modelling occurs in the context of a real example. We further explore the context of the help request by providing a snapshot of I-Help usage at the time of the request.

The computations described below are those used in the Spring 2000 version of I-Help, where the following attributes were used by the matchmaker agent in ranking potential helpers: knowledge level, helpfulness, eagerness, and readiness. These attributes are computed for each user and then combined (using a weighted linear equation) into an overall evaluation of each helper. Negotiations between the helpee's agent and the agents for the potential helpers then proceeds, to select the final helper. We consider this process in the context of the following (actual) help request, submitted to the Private Discussions:

> A simple question about looping: I want the program to enter the loop first time without trying the question. I know there is a way. There's the for loop, the while loop and…

```
    String currentline;
    while (currentline != null) {
        currentline = br.readLine();
```

As described previously, knowledge level information for user modelling is obtained in part from self assessment, and in part from peer evaluations. The self-evaluation of the knowledge level relates to the user's provision of information about their knowledge of the course topic on a scale of 1-10. Peer evaluations are based on previous evaluations of the potential helpers' knowledge of the topic of the current helpee's question. Peers rate knowledge level on a three point scale: low, medium or high. Peers are therefore not expected to rate a user's knowledge as precisely as the user him/herself, since peers only experience a user's understanding of a small area of a topic. However, since individuals may fail to update their own knowledge profile frequently, composite peer evaluations are weighted higher than self evaluations. (In the next version, relative recency of evaluations will also be taken into account.)

Helpfulness is calculated according to answers to questions on previous evaluation forms filled out by previous helpees: "Was the helper helpful?"; "Was the helper easy to understand?" This is used in conjunction with I-Help's observations of frequency and speed of response to questions in the Public and Private Discussions, thus again combining multiple sources of information for a single attribute.

Eagerness is more complex, taking into account a range of factors relating to individuals, in combination with the average and standard deviation of these factors across all users. These issues include logins to the Public and Private Discussions (which, at the time of the first large-scale deployment, were separate); postings made and read in the Public Discussions; information provided by the user to their agent (e.g. the act of updating their knowledge profile).

Readiness refers to whether the user is online. If they are, a weighting is added.

Using the above modelling information and sources, the following ranked list (showing the top eleven) was produced by the matchmaker in response to the above help request, for the purpose of locating a good helper for the question:

Prof1: 6.997   Peer1: 5.612   Prof2: 4.71   TA1: 4.612 banned   TA2: 3.91
Peer2: 2.836   Peer3: 2.232   Peer4: 2.18   Peer5: 2.178   Peer6: 2.14   Peer7: 2.126

Table 2. Potential Helper User Models

	Prof 1	Peer 1	Prof 2	TA 1	TA 2	Peer 2	Peer 3	Peer 4	Peer 5	Peer 6	Peer 7
eager	5.45	5.86	4.8	8.36	4.55	6.58	6.36	6.1	5.49	5.9	6.13
helpful	9.69	9	2.5	0	0	0	0	0	0	0	0
self eval	10	10	10	9	10	9	8	8	10	8	7
sys eval	10	4.75	10	10	10	2	2	2	2	2	2
ready	0	0	0	0	0	0.5	0	0	0	0	0

The ranked list includes two professors (Prof) and two teaching assistants (TA), whose score for system_evaluation was set to 10 (maximum) at the start. 5 of the top 6 were considered the most suitable potential helpers by the matchmaker – TA1 was not included as he banned the topic. This ranked list was computed at the time of the help request, integrating all currently available relevant information. Had the request been made three hours later, two lower ranked peers would have made it to the final selection, as peer evaluations of previous help sessions for these users occurred in the meantime, increasing their total score to above those of TA2 and Peer2.

Table 2 shows the breakdown of the scores according to self and system/peer evaluation, helpfulness, eagerness and readiness at the time of the request. All scores are out of 10. The help request in this example happened near the beginning of the course, therefore there are few helpee evaluations to take into account. This explains the low scores for most users for helpfulness and system evaluation.

At this stage negotiation between the helpee's agent and the agents of helpers at the top of the list commenced, with agents referring to many user model fragments at their disposal to act in the best interests of their user: i.e. the helpee's agent will be seeking the best possible helpers for their owner's particular question; agents of potential helpers will give preference to helpees with questions on topics in which they are interested, people they like, etc. Issues such as current help-load for helpers, and preferred helpers for helpees, come into play. In this case the matchmaker's suggestion was upheld, and the shaded individuals in Table 2 received the request. (Peer2 answered it, sending the response within 7 minutes of receipt of the question.)

It is difficult to validate matchmaker choices in I-Help, since so many factors are involved in helper selection. However, there are a number of things that may be considered as indicators. For example, we can look at how many helpees banned their helpers subsequent to the help session in the Private Discussions. In fact, no helpers were banned at any time. We can also look at helpee evaluations of helpers. At the time of data collection, 29 helpee evaluations (and 70 helper evaluations) had been completed. 27 of the 29 helpees found their helper to be helpful; 28 found the helper easy to understand; 14 evaluated the helper's knowledge as high, 14 as medium, and only one as low (this was one of the users who considered their helper unhelpful); 10 helpees added the helper to their preferred helper list (i.e. over one third of helpees requested the same helper to be given high priority in the future). Given the responses to the questions about helpfulness and ease of understanding, it seems that a 'medium' knowledge level is sufficient for help to be considered effective. Thus, from the viewpoint of helpees, the matchmaker appears to nearly always make successful selections even with the more restricted modelling in this earlier version of I-Help.

We can also look at Public Discussions usage statistics. Our purpose here is to show that matchmaker choices are reasonable – at least better than random matching or an open help environment (where the best helpers would be overwhelmed with requests). Focusing on peers (we assume professors and teaching assistants are eager, helpful, and knowledgeable), the two peers contacted as potential helpers for this help request in the Private Discussions were in the 5th and 15th position (of 318 users) in terms of responses to postings in the Public Discussions (24 and 7 replies made; average = 1.82). Prestige measures relating to the Public Discussions can also be used to consider the value of the matchmaker. Prestige of an author is calculated by measuring the average number of times that a user reads the same reply by the author (Bowes [2]). Individuals high on this list have generally been considered good, and they are therefore likely to be good helpers in the Private Discussions. The two peers chosen by the matchmaker were 15th and 16th on the "prestige" list.

Reviewing general activity in the Private Discussions, the two selected helpers were in 1st and 3rd position, suggesting they would probably see the request soon.

Looking briefly at the five peers who almost made the final helper list, two of these were consistently located between the scores of those selected as potential helpers, and one was consistently in first position, above those on the helper list. The remaining two peers that did not make the final list were well above average on the Private activity, Public replies and prestige lists. Other factors were involved in the final listing – for example, the lower ranked helper on the final list (Peer2) was the only one online at the time of the request. Lack of previous peer evaluations has already been explained as affecting the ranking of others. Further factors may have included banning of the topic by some peers, low level of knowledge on the particular topic of the question, the need to spread the help-load, etc.

These results illustrate that the I-Help matchmaker, drawing on information which is available at the time from distributed and fragmented user models, based on a range of data sources, generally makes good decisions about who is an appropriate helper for a particular help request. This applies even with the earlier, simpler modelling process. The current version of I-Help also models cognitive style and a range of choices of the user relating to characteristics important to them, in a helper. Once data from the current version is analysed, we hope to find evidence that the additional user model data further enhances the performance of matchmaking. This is important for planned larger deployments.

4   Conclusions and Future Directions

This paper has shown user modelling to be a crucial process in I-Help. There are many purposes: user modelling is needed in finding and ranking candidate helpers; in negotiation between personal agents over a help request; in protecting users from interruptions; in retrieving relevant information for a user; in providing open models of a user's content knowledge of a domain. There are many attributes: user modelling captures interests, goals, even cognitive styles of users, as well as domain skill levels, eagerness, and helpfulness factors. There are many perspectives on these attributes: user modelling happens from the user's own point of view, from the point of view of other users, from the point of view of application agents. Even though knowledge about users is drawn from a variety of sources with a variety of perspectives for a variety of purposes, thus meaning that user modelling in I-Help is pervasive, it is also essentially fragmented. There is no single, complex, unitary model for each user. Instead, user modelling is a "just-in-time" process, invoked as a by-product of achieving a particular purpose and using information relevant to that purpose. We feel that this perspective on user modelling is scalable and appropriate to the large, distributed, agent-based environments which are increasingly common.

We are extending I-Help, and deploying it ever more widely in University courses, both at the University of Saskatchewan and elsewhere (over 2000 students are currently using our more recent version of I-Help). As I-Help's sophistication and applicability increases in these course deployments, user modelling is becoming, if anything, even more important than in previous versions.

As well as a learning tool, I-Help can be viewed as a framework within which possible future directions are explored and evaluated, with successful projects later becoming integrated into the system. Current investigations include enabling agents to play a role in retrieving information for a use, rather than seeking a human helper, e.g. some FAQ or answer posted in the Public Discussions. To determine whether a resource document or a posting might be relevant to the user, simple keyword queries can be created, latent semantic analysis of the question and available answers can be performed, and/or semantic similarity indices may be used. Any of these methods are complemented through user modelling. For example, the help request itself may be augmented by knowledge of the kinds of browsing occurring prior to the formulation of the help request. If the user had viewed postings on a particular topic, or questions by a particular user, additional query terms could be added to the information retrieval process. Even the knowledge level or degree of eagerness that the user had previously exhibited might give clues as to the kind of information that would be most helpful.

A new project under development for the next version of I-Help is based on anticipating learner interests and offering useful information to users even before help is requested. This resembles a knowledge-based "tip-of-the-day" feature. Whenever information appears in the system, agents should be able to peruse that information and determine the possible relevance for their user. This is akin to information filtering, and once again, is based on the agent modelling its user's goals and interests.

User modelling in I-Help also has an important role in assessment and self-assessment of learners and in supporting reflection on learning. Opening learner models for inspection has been argued to promote reflection (Bull & Pain [5]; Dimitrova et al. [7]; Morales et al. [12]). Some of the current user model fragments of I-Help are open to viewing by the modellee – specifically those parts contributed by the modellee. We are working towards opening other areas: eagerness, helpfulness and a composite score of peer evaluations of knowledge which may be explicitly compared with self-assessments. Research into inspectable interfaces for Bayesian network learner models is also underway (Zapata & Greer [19]).

Another major goal of our investigations is to incorporate a more overt role for groups in I-Help. There are currently many kinds of groups in the system, both explicit and implicit (e.g. the students in a class or project team, friends, banned people, potentially good helpers, etc.). We want to make groups more fundamental, to capture aspects of group behaviour, to stimulate the formation of relevant groups, and to support group interaction. We feel that there is actually a graduated series of functionalities between the one-on-one Private Discussions and the many-on-many Public Discussions. User modelling and group modelling (as in Hoppe [8]) will be important in dealing with the issues raised by a more central role for groups in I-Help.

Even though I-Help has been presented as a learning tool in a University setting, it can be equally applied to a range of corporate and industry activities, e.g. for knowledge management and expertise location, illustrated by the fact that an early prototype of the Private Discussions was piloted in the Prairie Regional Psychiatric Centre of Corrections Canada (Collins et al. [6]); and the Public Discussion forums are now being adapted to serve as a knowledge management tool in a local company. Capturing interests and goals, as well as skill levels, eagerness and helpfulness factors are of great interest in corporate settings. Developing profiles of employees and modelling such nebulous attributes as being a 'team player' or a 'self-starter' become possible with the range of subtle data collected and analysed in I-Help.

References

1. J. Beck, M. Stern and B.P. Woolf. Cooperative Student Models. In B. du Boulay and R. Mizoguchi, editors, Artificial Intelligence in Education (Proceedings of AIED'97), pages 127-13, Amsterdam, 1997. IOS Press.
2. J. Bowes. Knowledge Management through Data Mining in Discussion Forums. MSc Thesis, Department of Computer Science, University of Saskatchewan, 2001.
3. S. Bull, P. Brna, S. Critchley, K. Davie and C. Holzherr. The Missing Peer, Artificial Peers and the Enhancement of Human-Human Collaborative Student Modelling. In S. Lajoie and M. Vivet, editors, Artificial Intelligence in Education (Proceedings of AIED'99), pages 269-276, Amsterdam, 1999. IOS Press.
4. S. Bull and J. Greer. Peer Help for Problem-Based Learning. In S. Young, J. Greer, H. Maurer and Y.S. Chee, editors, Proceedings of ICCE/ICAI'00 (Vol. 2), pages 1007-1015, 2000. National Tsing Hua University of Taiwan.
5. S. Bull and H. Pain. 'Did I say what I think I said, and do you agree with me?': Inspecting and Questioning the Student Model. In J. Greer, editor, Proceedings of World Conference on Artificial Intelligence in Education, pages 501-508, 1995. AACE.
6. J. Collins, J.E. Greer, V.S. Kumar, G.I. McCalla, P. Meagher and R. Tkatch. Inspectable User Models for Just-In-Time Workplace Training. In A. Jameson, C. Paris and C. Tasso,

editors, User Modeling: Proceedings of the Sixth International Conference, pages 327-337, Vienna, New York, 1997. Springer Wien New York.

7. V. Dimitrova, J. Self and P. Brna. Maintaining a Jointly Constructed Student Model. Technical Report, Computer Based Learning Unit, Leeds University, 2000.

8. H.U. Hoppe. The use of Multiple Student Modelling to Parameterise Group Learning. In J. Greer, editor, Proceedings of World Conference on Artificial Intelligence in Education, pages 234-241, 1995. AACE.

9. J. Kay. The UM Toolkit for Cooperative User Modelling. User Modelling and User-Adapted Interaction, 4:149-196, 1995.

10. J. Kay. Learner Know Thyself. In Z. Halim, T. Ottman and Z. Razak, editors, Proceedings of ICCE'97, pages 18-26, 1997. AACE.

11. G. McCalla, J. Vassileva, J. Greer and S. Bull. Active Learner Modelling. In G. Gauthier, C. Frasson and K. VanLehn, editors, Intelligent Tutoring Systems (Proceedings of ITS'00), pages 53-62, Berlin, Heidelberg, 2000. Springer-Verlag.

12. R. Morales, M. Ramscar, and H. Pain. Modelling the Learner's Awareness and Reflection in a Collaborative Learner Modelling Setting. Workshop on Current Trends and Applications of AIED, Fourth World Conference on Expert Systems Monterrey, 1998.

13. M. Mühlenbrock, F. Tewissen and H.U. Hoppe. A Framework System for Intelligent Support in Open Distributed Learning Environments. International Journal of Artificial Intelligence in Education, 9(3-4):256-274, 1998.

14. H. Ogata, T. Sueda, N. Furugori, and Y. Yano. Augmenting Collaboration Beyond Classrooms through Online Social Networks. In G. Cumming, T. Okamoto and L. Gomez, editors, Advanced Research in Computers and Communications in Education, pages 277-284, Amsterdam, 1999. IOS Press.

15. R. Riding, and I. Cheema. Cognitive Styles - An Overview and Integration. Educational Psychology, 11(3-4):193-215, 1991.

16. J. Vassileva, J. Greer, G. McCalla, R. Deters, D. Zapata, C. Mudgal and S. Grant. A Multi-Agent Design of a Peer-Help Environment. In S.P. Lajoie and M. Vivet, editors, Artificial Intelligence in Education (Proceedings of AIED'99), pages 38-45, Amsterdam, 1999. IOS Press.

17. Y-T. Yu, H-L. Shan, C-Y. Chou, and T-W. Chan. WWW-Based Mentoring System. In Z. Halim, T. Ottman and Z. Razak, editors, Proceedings of ICCE'97, pages 381-389, 1997. AACE.

18. J.D. Zapata. SMODEL Server: Student Modelling in Distributed Multi-Agent Tutoring Systems ARIES Lab Technical Report, University of Saskatchewan, 2000.

19. J.D. Zapata and J.E. Greer. Inspecting and Visualizing Distributed Bayesian Student Models. In G. Gauthier, C. Frasson and K. VanLehn, editors, Intelligent Tutoring Systems (Proceedings of ITS'00), pages 544-553, Berlin Heidelberg, 2000. Springer-Verlag.

An Adaptive User- Interface- Agent Modeling Communication Availability

Silke Höpner

Institut für Neue Medien e.V., Daimlerstr.32, D-60314 Frankfurt, Germany
Cork Institute of Technology, IRL-Cork, Ireland
silke@inm.de

Abstract. Communication availability is closely connected to workspace awareness and requires intelligent filtering, especially in Groupware-Systems. This paper introduces a personalized adaptive communication availability agent, which is currently in the process of implementation. The agent monitors user behavior, predicts from there the current degree of user availability and then displays it in a virtual world using an avatar.[1]

1 Introduction

In working spaces communication is an important means not only for information exchange, but also for social informal interaction. Functioning social group interactions result in a rise of working motivation because people enjoy themselves at work. Tele-workers often experience social restraints in an office group since they are not present as often as the rest of the regularly present local team members. This can lead to frustration and therefore a lack of working motivation. In order to support tele-workers and to give them a near-life and authentic office feeling as possible, we use a 3-d chat world [15] as a communication platform for formal and informal communication between tele-workers and regulars. Every user is presented by a finely featured human-like avatar and "lives" in his or her own virtual office rooms. Informal social interaction can take place in every office, in the corridors or in the lounge. If such a system is used on a permanent base running in the background on the computer, some situations can get very disturbing: If the user is under stress and the only reason why he is logged in is to be able to just ask information from his virtual desk neighbor A, he may not be inclined to engage in informal conversation with colleague B, who is not involved in the project. Nevertheless, the virtual world (VW) alerts the user in any case of a communication request. As a result a lot of situations occur where a working user is alerted in vain and interrupted in his concentration at work, leading to a lack of work efficiency. In order to avoid this and to enable a workspace awareness of the user's willingness to communicate to the outside virtual world, an intelligent personalized filtering system is needed: we call it a communication availability agent (CAA). The CAA is connected to PreMon [20], a

---

[1] This work was supported by the German BMWi (Bundesministerium für Wirtschaft und Technologie) and by the German DLR (Deutsche Luft- und Raumfahrtgesellschaft e.V.).

M. Bauer, P.J. Gmytrasiewicz, and J. Vassileva (Eds.): UM 2001, LNAI 2109, pp. 127–136, 2001.
©Springer-Verlag Berlin Heidelberg 2001

system for monitoring user activity, which serves simultaneously as an interface to the virtual world. The CAA obtains user data from PreMon, then either learns from the data or predicts the user's communication availability state and makes it transparent to potential visitors in the virtual world. This enables them to see if the user is available or not and not to disturb in the first place. The CAA is embedded into the general architecture shown in Figure 1:

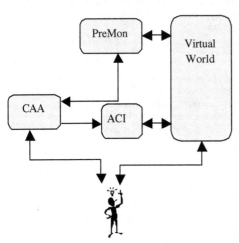

Fig. 1. The user interacts with the virtual world through a graphical user interface. As soon as the user is logged into the virtual world and does not use the VW as top application, the CAA monitors his/her actions. If another avatar tries to communicate with the user, while the user is busy, the CAA itself appears as avatar in the VW, acting as substitute on behalf of the user. Information on the user and on internal states of the VW is provided by PreMon [20], as well as the control of the user's avatar. The control of the CAA's avatar is realized by a COM-based avatar control interface (ACI) to the VW.

2 Related Work

While supporting communication and awareness in virtual [2,16] and real world [13] applications, recently first approaches in treating personal communication availability have been made. These are usually limited to manual configuration [10], to presentation of a rather general awareness state [2,16,13] or to approaching the subject by displaying video snapshots of the user to the group [6,8,11]. No autonomous agents considering the communication behavior of their users have been applied to this area yet.

As for user modeling, many user interface agents have been developed, learning user profiles by perceiving the user's actions [12, 19]. The CAA belongs to the class of modeling users' preferences (for classes see [9]). In this area statistical, connectionist and machine learning techniques are explored [21]. However, to the author's knowledge, time series classification with TDNNs [4] has not been used for this type of application yet.

3 Communication Availability

What is communication availability (CA)? Our approach to this complex topic is the following working definition [7]:

Communication availability:
-    Is an affective passive state of a person as reaction to a communication request from an other person,

- composed by an intersection of subjective (emotional) and objective aspects,
- depends on the situation, involved persons, time and addressed topics,
- appears short-termed,
- is characterized by expressive behavior (consciously or subconsciously), goal-oriented behavior (consciously) and emotional arousal states.

The objective aspects can be sensed and identified quite easily, but how can emotional aspects be recognized? Since communication availability depends (besides objective) on subjective and emotional aspects, a corresponding emotion theory was developed. From there a formal frame for embedding the concept of communication availability was established [7]. Derived from this theory the concept and the kernel architecture of the CAA were developed. This paper introduces the complete architecture of the agent.

We differentiate between three types of communication availability, which are to be predicted by the CAA. All types relate to a long list of measured parameters, which will be described later. However, they can be distinguished as follows:

1. General user communication availability: The state of the user may depend on a variety of reasons, i.e. stress because of a report deadline, early morning time before the first cup of coffee etc. However, it does not depend directly on a certain person or topic.
2. Person-related user communication availability: Besides the factors which occur in point 1, the readiness to communicate also depends to the one or more people involved in the communication request.
3. Person-Topic-related user communication availability: Here the readiness is additionally influenced by the topic, which is to be treated in the conversation.

In order to be able to evaluate the importance of certain persons to the user, the person whose CA profile is to be modeled must at first configure the CAA: To each known participant of the VW a private priority and a business priority value are assigned. For evaluating conversation topics, a list of keywords is also mapped on priority values.

4 Functionality

The following paragraphs introduce the functionality of the agent. For demonstration purposes, the agent's functionalities are described as they appear in the application scenario.

4.1 Human Computer Interaction

Avatars of colleagues meet in a virtual group office: They either stand or sit around and talk to each other or sit at their desks working. PreMon provides the CAA every three minutes with information about which avatars are present in the virtual office. Based on the configuration information on persons, the CAA determines the general communication availability of the user. This is performed by adding and averaging the priority values of all present virtual users and treating this value as a single person's priority. It is passed into a large n-dimensional vector of other values and the communication availability of the user is predicted.

The found degrees of CA are grouped in five classes (Table 1). The selected class is passed to PreMon, which reacts to it by presenting the avatar of the CAA's user in an action, which corresponds to the given level of communication availability. We consider it a communication request, if one or more avatars approach the user's avatar and pass through the minimum distance radius around it. If the user's avatar is called by name or nickname from one or more other avatars, this is also a communication request. In these cases a new person-related communication availability measurement is performed, only considering the avatars inside of the distance radius or the ones calling. Again all priorities are added, averaged and treated as a single person priority. Afterwards the new CA value is predicted:

If the agent finds the user available, he is alerted with a ping by a message box asking if the approaching/calling avatars are welcome. If the user agrees, the VW application is brought up as top application and the user can interact directly himself.

Table 1. This table presents the five classes of displayed communication availability. From left to right the columns contain: the CA value found by the CAA, the according CA class passed to PreMon, the semantics of this class, the translation of the semantics into messages which are supposed to be understood by the visitor, the resulting action presented by the avatar.

Degree of CA	Class	Meaning	Message Given To Visitor	Presented Avatar Action
[0; 0.2]	1	Not Available for Communication	Not present	User's avatar is turned gray
[0.2 ; 0.4]	2	Scarcely Available for Communication	User conducting a discussion	User's avatar is using the telephone
[0.4 ; 0.6]	3	Conditionally Available for Communication	User is thinking in deep concentration	User's avatar supports his head with his palm
[0.6 ; 0.8]	4	Rather well-disposed for Communication	User is busy working at the computer	User's avatar uses the laptop keyboard
[0.8 ; 1.0]	5	Fully Available for Communication	User would like to communicate	User's avatar looks around expectantly

If the user disagrees, this information is considered as feedback, the new CA class value is passed to PreMon and the avatar is accordingly presented. If already the first measurement finds the user unavailable, the found CA class value is passed to PreMon and presented accordingly while the avatars keep approaching/calling. Although this reaction should be pretty obvious, it is possible that the visiting avatars insist on communicating with the user's avatar and keeps calling or stays in the personal distance radius of the avatar. In this case the CAA is presented as avatar and starts a very simple conversation with the visitor. The text spoken by CAA is given in text balloons and contains the following: "Hello, I am the personal assistant of <username>. Unfortunately my user is currently unavailable. If it is important, I will see what I can do for you. Please select a keyword describing the topic you would like to address". Additionally a list of subjects, previously configured by the user, is displayed. After selecting a topic, the corresponding user-dependent priority value is found and also considered in a new CA value prediction. If the newly found CA value still points to unavailability, the avatar excuses the user, announces that the CAA will notify the user at the next possible opportunity and presents a text window, where the visitor can leave a message for the user.

Every time when the user was unavailable for a while and visits have occurred, the agent waits for a rise in the degree of the user's CA and presents the protocol of visits from participants of the virtual world (Figure 3).

Visitor	Topic	Person Priority	Topic Priority	Date	Time	Degree of CA	Application	Message	Feedback
Bill	Agents	4	10	11.11.2000	10:51	0,3	MS-Word	Message	Put Through
Gerhardt	Lunch	7	6	11.11.2000	10:58	0,1	MS-Excel		Put Through
Doris	Network	6	3	11.11.2000	11:03	0,2	Netscape		Put Through
Helmut	-	5		11.11.2000	11:19	0,1	MS-Word		Put Through
Hannelore	-	2		11.11.2000	11:22	0,1	MS-Word		

Change Communication   Close

Fig. 2. The graphical protocol interface of the CAA displays avatar visits during low communication availability states. From left to right are given: the visitor's name or nickname, the topic to be addressed, the configured priority of the person, the configured priority of the keyword, the date, the time, the predicted degree of communication availability, the topmost application used by the user at that time. If the visitor left a message, pressing the buttons can fetch it. If the user realizes while reading the protocol that the configured values are wrong or not up-to-date anymore, he can access them by pressing the left lower button. If the user feels that the agent failed in predicting his CA state, he can give an appropriate feedback at the right column.

4.2 Feedback

Since the agent not only prognoses the communication availability state of the user on a regular base, but also presents it in public, a tool is necessary which enables the user to control his agent. This holds several advantages:
1. Increase in control and user acceptance: the user always stays in control of the agent, although the agent works autonomously. It is easily possible to evaluate the agent behavior in all situations, therefore trust and user acceptance will increase over time.
2. Increase in online learning: The user can give explicit feedback to the agent. This results in an increase in learning and online adaptation.
3. Necessary configuration changes become obvious more quickly.

In order to keep the distraction of the user through such a tool as small as possible, feedback is presented in a very small graphical user interface, which appears at the low edge of the screen. Since the CA is expressed in percentages, a soft and intuitive presentation is sensible. Therefore we use a color scale with colors shifting from deep red (not available) to deep green (available).

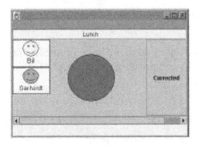

Fig. 3. Graphical User Interface for Feedback: If the CA is person-related, an icon of the visiting person is displayed additionally, if it is also subject-related, the topic is given in a text field. User feedback can be given through a slider, changing value and color.

5 Architecture

The CAA is currently being implemented in C++ and wrapped over JNI into Java. The agent is composed of four parts, which will be described below.

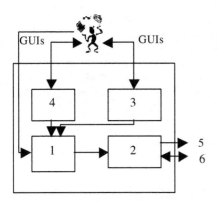

Fig. 4. Overview on the general architecture of the communication availability agent: The arrows show the data flow between the single internal and external components. The numbers denote as follows: Communication Availability State Prediction Component (1), Virtual World Perception and Avatar Control Component (2), Protocol and Configuration Component (3), Feedback Component (4), Virtual World Interface (5), Avatar Control Interface (6).

The Communication Availability State Prediction Component holds the intelligence of the CAA. It measures time series of n-dimensional data vectors and performs pattern recognition on these. Parameters, which are monitored for CA recognition, are either seized by sensors in combination with processing software or are determined by the user interface software in the computer. The parameter groups are specified as follows:

1. Reaction system parameters: These are parameters concerning the user's (re)actions[2] and can be divided into two groups:
   - Autonomous Reactions: All reactions of the user, which can be monitored by keyboard, mouse, camera, microphone, biometrics, etc. and which occur automatically without thoughtful goal-oriented planning (i.e. pulse differences, galvanic skin conductivity, ease of mouse movements, velocity differences in keyboard strokes etc.). A variety of methods have been

---

[2] Since communication availability is a state which appears as reaction to stimuli of the environment the actions of the user are referred to as reactions.

invented for the measurement of physiological data [i.e. 3, 5, 22], especially in the area of wearable computing [i.e. 18]. However, since an online measuring of physiological sources is required, only those parameters can be used whose values can be updated at every time step with minimal computational cost.

- Goal-directed actions: These refer to the consciously elaborated user reaction to a communication request (acceptance of request, duration of reaction[3], duration of talk in case of acceptance[4], etc.).

2. Environmental Parameters: Features, which represent the general environmental states of the user's situation and location, i.e.
   - Timely parameters (weekday, holiday, week-end, date, time, etc.),
   - Local parameters (temperature, luminance, locality, etc.),
   - Ambience parameters (noise level, existence of speech signals, etc.).

To the author's knowledge only limited work has been done on pattern recognition of affective or emotional states from physiological signals or other data. Many have argued that emotions might be recognizable from physiological signals given suitable pattern recognition techniques [comp. 3], but nobody has demonstrated which ones so far. First approaches have just recently been presented [i.e. 22], which suggest that emotions can be recognized from physiological signals at significantly higher rates than statistic probabilities.

The following graph gives an overview on the architecture of the Communication Availability State Prediction Component, whose implementation is currently in progress.

The measurement is triggered by a communication request in the virtual world at the point of time t_0 over a certain time interval t_0-t_2. The user reaction is considered to be over, when a goal-oriented user action occurs (like refusal to communicate etc.).

On the left hand side measurement takes place. The components are sorted by semantic groups of parameters. The reaction systems permanently measure (20 times per minute) the user behavior concerning the user's general body signals (mimic, gestures, voice), biometrics (pulse, expiration, galvanic skin conductivity) and computer based behavior (i.e. number of keyboard strokes per second, mobility and velocity of mouse movement, top application used etc.). The General Environment Situation Component measures surrounding aspects like the number of people in the office of the user, level of noise in the office, time etc. The problem situation in this context is a communication event: some user B uses the virtual world in order to contact user A. Parameters measured here are: contacting person, which topic is to be addressed, etc. The user reaction to this communication event, like responding directly or responding after hesitating or not responding at all is measured by the component goal-oriented behavior. Altogether we plan to extract about 150 parameters from the measurement components.

---

[3] How long does the user need to decide, if he wants to talk to the visitor? This can be interpreted as a measure for certainty

[4] Does the user try to get rid off the visitor? Very short (i.e. shorter than three minutes) communications are often used to delay or stop conversation attempts.

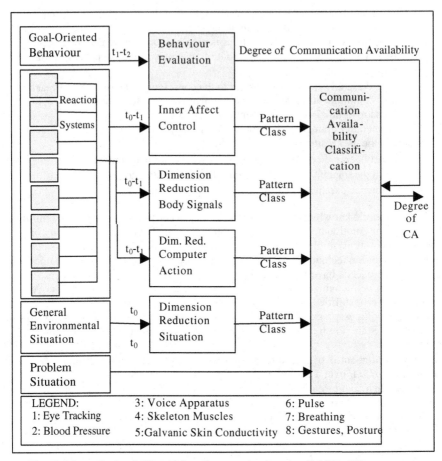

Fig. 5. Measuring and Classifying Communication Availability [7]

In the center level, dimension reduction takes place. Reaction system patterns consist of coordinated time series reactions of several reaction systems. Therefore a modeling structure is needed, which is able to model multi-dimensional time series. We use TDNNs (Temporal-Delay Neural Networks [4]) for all components of this level but the first and the last to evaluate time series in a length of about 5 seconds. The component Behavior Evaluation maps the measured user behavior on a closed interval [0;1], the component Dimension Reduction Situation uses an MLP (Multi-Layer Perceptrons [1]) for classifying the problem situation. Each component on the center level combines semantic groups of parameters in order to ease pattern recognition. The parameters of the communication request (i.e. person priority etc.) are passed through to the final network on the right hand side, because these parameters hold higher semantic values than the other groups, which require preprocessing.

The component on the right side is modeled by an RBF (Radial Based Function Network [17]) and maps the previously classified patterns on the measured user reaction. Measuring the goal-oriented communication availability user behavior, comparing it to the predicted user behavior and performing back propagation in the RBF on the right hand side realize learning. Since the neural networks in the center level only recognizes bodily patterns which usually represents the same type of states, we believe that backpropagation in this level is not necessary.

The other components only need to be described briefly: The Virtual World Perception and Avatar Control Component is structured fairly simple. The interface to the avatar's functions is based on Microsoft's Component Object Model [14]. The component basically activates the CAA's avatar in the virtual world, turns it to face the visitor and asks for the desired topic as described above. If the user is unavailable, the Protocols and Configuration Component is responsible for monitoring and logging communication requests. If the visitor has left messages, these are stored here and presented to the user as soon as the degree of CA rises. The component is also responsible for monitoring the Prediction of the CAA in the single situations and presenting them to the user. Feedback acquisition from the above described graphical user interface is the task of the Feedback Component. All situations, which were corrected by the user, are fed into the Communication Availability State Prediction Component for learning. For long-term training the corrected patterns are kept in logfiles and are repeatedly presented to the neural networks.

6 Summary

This paper presented a personalized adaptive user interface agent modeling communication availability, which is currently in the process of implementation. First communication availability was investigated; afterwards the functionality and the single components of the agent were presented, focusing on user modeling using artificial neural networks.

References

1.   Back, A.D.; Wan, E.; Lawrence, Steve; Tsoi, A.C.: A Unifying View of Some Training Algorithms for Multilayer Perceptrons with Filter Synapses. In: J. Vlontzos and J. Hwang and E. Wilson (Eds.): Neural Networks for Signal Processing 4. IEEE Press, 1995, pp. 146-154.
2.   Broll, W., Grther, W., Meier, E., Pankoke-Babatz, U., Prinz, W.: Place People in Context - the Awareness Forum. Proceedings of the HCI International '99 - 8th International Conference on Human-Computer Interaction (Munich, Germany, Aug. 22-27, 1999), 1999.
3.   Cacioppo, John T. / Tassinary, Louis G.: Inferring psychological significance from physiological signals, in: American Psychologist, 1990, 45(1), pp.16-28
4.   Clouse, S. Daniel; Giles, C.Lee; Horne, G. Bill; Cottrell, Garrison W.: Time-Delay Neural Networks: Representation and Induction of Finite State Machines. IEEE Transactions on Neural Networks, April 4th, 1997
5.   Essa, Irfan A / Alex Pentland: Coding, Analysis, Interpretation, and Recognition of Facial Expressions. IEEE Transactions on Pattern Analysis and Machine Intelligence, 19 (7), pp. 757-763, July 1997
6.   Greenberg, S. and Johnson, B. (1997) Studying Awareness in Contact Facilitation. Position paper for the ACM CHI'97 Workshop on Awareness in Collaborative Systems, organized by Susan E. McDaniel and Tom Brinck, Atlanta, Georgia, March 22-27.

7. Höppner, Silke: Modelling Emotions in Communication Availability Agents for Virtual Chat Environments. VWSIM' 01, 8-11th January 2001, Phoenix, Arizona.

8. Johnson, B. and Greenberg, S.: Judging People's Availability for Interaction from Video Snapshots. Proceedings of the Hawaii International Conference on System Sciences, Distributed Group Support Systems Minitrack, January, IEEE Press.1999.

9. Kobsa, A.: Recent Work, Prospects and Hazards. In: Schneider-Hufschmidt, M, Tuehme, T, und Malinowski, U, (Eds.): Adaptive User Interfaces: Principles and Practice. North-Holland, The Netherlands. 1993

10. Kuzuoka, H. and Greenberg, S.: Mediating Awareness and Communication through Digital but Physical Surrogates. ACM CHI'99 Video Proceedings (7 minute video) and Proceedings of the ACM SIGCHI'99 Conference Extended Abstracts (two page summary).1999

11. Lee, A. Awareness Research Based on NYNEX Portholes. Position paper for the CHI'97 Workshop on Awareness in Collaborative Systems, organized by Susan E. McDaniel and Tom Brinck, Atlanta, Georgia, March 22-27, 1997.

12. Maes, P., "Agents that Reduce Work and Information Overload." In: Software Agents, edited by Jeffrey M. Bradshaw, AAAI Press/MIT Press, 1997.

13. Masayuki Okamoto, et al.: Silhouettell: Awareness Support for Real-World Encounter, In Toru Ishida Ed., Community Computing and Support Systems, Lecture Notes in Computer Science 1519, Springer-Verlag, pp. 317-330, 1998.

14. Microsoft Corporation, Microsoft Component Services. Server Operating System: A Technology   Overview.   URL: http://www.microsoft.com/com/wpaper/compsvcs.asp

15. Moove gmbh: URL: www.moove.com from "Internet: Die virtuelle Welt der Chatrooms". In: Spiegel, Nr. 18, Mai 1999, pp.102.

16. Nakanishi, H. et al., FreeWalk: Supporting Casual Meetings in a Network, International Conference on Computer Supported Cooperative Work (CSCW-96), pp. 308-314, 1996.

17. Orr, J.L. Mark Recent Advances in Radial Based Function Networks. Update (1999) of "Introduction to Radial Based Function Networks", April, 1996, Centre for Cognitive Science, University of Edinburgh

18. Picard, Rosalind W.: Towards Agents that Recognize Emotion, in: Actes Proceedings IMAGINA, March 1998, Monaco, pp. 153-165

19. Robyn Kozierok and Pattie Maes, A Learning Interface Agent for Scheduling Meetings, Workshop on Intelligent User Interfaces, 1993.

20. Runde, Detlef et. al.: Providing Availability Information via a Chat System, a Virtual Environment, a WWW-Browser and Mobile Phones. Submitted to: ACM 2001 International Conference on Supporting Group Work (GROUP 2001), September 2001.

21. Terveen, Loren G. Overview of human-computer collaboration, KnowledgeBased Systems, 8 (2-3):67—81, 1995.

22. Vyzas, Elias: Recognition of Emotional and Cognitive States Using Physiological Data, M.Sc. Thesis, Dept. Of Mechanical Engineering, MIT, June 1999.

Cognitive Computer Tutors:
Solving the Two-Sigma Problem

Albert Corbett

Human-Computer Interaction Institute
Carnegie Mellon University
Pittsburgh, PA 15213, USA
corbett+@cmu.edu

Abstract. Individual human tutoring is the most effective and most expensive form of instruction. Students working with individual human tutors reach achievement levels as much as two standard deviations higher than students in conventional instruction (that is, 50% of tutored students score higher than 98% of the comparison group). Two early 20th-century innovations attempted to offer benefits of individualized instruction on a broader basis: (1) mechanized individualized feedback (via teaching machines and computers) and (2) mastery learning (individualized pacing of instruction). On average each of these innovations yields about a half standard deviation achievement effect. More recently, cognitive computer tutors have implemented these innovations in the context of a cognitive model of problem solving. This paper examines the achievement effect size of these two types of student-adapted instruction in a cognitive programming tutor. Results suggest that cognitive tutors have closed the gap with and arguably surpass human tutors.

1 Introduction

Individual human tutoring is perhaps the oldest form of instruction. Countless millennia since its introduction, it remains the most effective and most expensive form of instruction. Bloom [1] reports that students working with a "good" human tutor obtain average achievement levels that are two standard deviations higher than students in conventional instruction. That is, the average students in the individual tutoring condition obtain test scores as high as the top 2% of students in the comparison condition. Bloom labeled this result the "two-sigma" problem (sigma is the mathematical symbol for standard deviation): designing educational environments that are as effective as individual human tutors, but affordable enough to disseminate on a wide basis.

Two forms of student-adapted instruction were pioneered in the 20th century that tackle the two-sigma problem. One is machine-based individualized feedback on student performance via teaching machines and subsequently computers. The second is mastery learning in which the students move at their own pace through a curriculum, receiving the individualized instruction needed to "master" each unit before moving to the next. About 15 years ago the Carnegie Mellon PACT Center

M. Bauer, P.J. Gmytrasiewicz, and J. Vassileva (Eds.): UM 2001, LNAI 2109, pp. 137–147, 2001.
©Springer- Verlag Berlin Heidelberg 2001

began developing an intelligent tutoring technology called cognitive tutors that employs a cognitive model of student knowledge to implement both individualized feedback and mastery learning. This paper examines the separable impact of model-based (a) individualized feedback, (b) mastery learning and (c) a type of scaffolded mastery learning, all in the ACT Programming Tutor. The paper reviews meta-analyses of human tutors, computer-based instruction and mastery learning, describes the ACT Programming tutor, examines the impact of model-based feedback, cognitive mastery and scaffolded cognitive mastery and argues that the aggregate impact equals or exceeds the success of human tutors.

2   Meta-analyses and Effect Size

A meta-analysis is a quantitative review that computes the average impact of a treatment variable, for instance human tutoring, across multiple evaluation studies. The meta-analyses reviewed here examine the impact of educational interventions on student achievement. Because studies employ different achievement measures, the result of each study is converted to a standard measure of effect size with the formula

$$\frac{\text{(mean of the treatment group)} - \text{(mean of the comparison group)}}{\text{(standard deviation of the comparison group)}}$$

An effect size of +1 means the average score in a treatment group (students in an experimental instructional environment) falls one standard deviation above the average score in the comparison group (e.g., conventional instruction). As depicted in Fig. 1, 34% of a normal distribution falls between the mean and the first standard deviation. Since 50% of the distribution falls below the mean, an effect size of +1 SD means that the average student in the experimental treatment scored higher than 84% of the students in the comparison condition. As suggested in the opening section, about 98% of a distribution falls below +2SD, while about 69% falls below +0.5 SD and 63% falls below +0.33 SD.

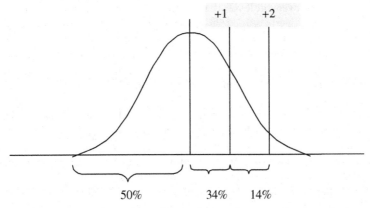

Fig. 1. The area of a normal distribution below the mean, between the mean and +1 standard deviations and between +1 and +2 standard deviations.

2.1. Meta-analysis of Human Tutors

Bloom [1] reports four dissertation studies comparing human tutoring to conventional classroom instruction. Learning time was held constant and the average achievement level in the human tutoring condition typically fell +2 standard deviations (SD) above the mean of the comparison group. Bloom characterizes the tutors in this study as "good" tutors, and this effect size should be thought of as an upper bound on what human tutors can achieve. Cohen, Kulik and Kulik [2] conducted a meta-analysis of achievement gains in 52 studies of human tutors in elementary and secondary schools and report a substantially smaller average effect size of +0.40 SD. One study yielded an effect size of 2.3, in Bloom's range, but only 16 of the 52 studies yielded an effect size of +0.50 or higher. These are primarily studies of peer (student-student) tutoring and paraprofessional tutoring, rather than professional tutors, so the tutors perhaps did not meet Bloom's standard of "good".

2.2 Meta-analyses of Computer-Based Instruction

Pressey's "teaching machine" [3] introduced machine-based individualized feedback in the early part of the 20th century. The teaching machine presented multiple-choice questions and could be set so that the student had to select a correct answer to each question before moving to the next. This early promise of prompt individualized feedback was more fully realized in the second half of the century with the advent of computer-based instruction. There have been several meta-analyses of first-generation computer tutors that present text and graphical displays, ask questions and provide feedback ([4], [5], [6], [7], [8]). The average achievement effect size across these meta-analyses ranges from +0.30 SD to +0.48 SD, in the same range as average human tutor effectiveness. Kulik and Kulik [6] also report that computer-based instruction reduces instructional time. The ratio of instructional time for the computer-based instruction group to that for the conventional group averaged 0.70.

2.3 Meta-analysis of Mastery Learning

The central idea of mastery learning is that virtually all students can achieve expertise in a domain if two conditions are met: (1) the domain is analyzed into a hierarchy of component skills and (2) students master prerequisite skills before moving on to higher level skills. Early interest in mastery learning arose in the 1920s, but it only achieved prominence in the 1960s. Two forms of mastery learning were developed. Bloom [9] proposed "learning for mastery" in which a group of students move through a curriculum together and individual students get extra assistance as needed. In Keller's [10] "personalized system of instruction", students move through the curriculum at their own pace. A meta-analysis of mastery learning [11] found an average achievement effect of +0.59 SD for group-based learning for mastery and +0.48 SD for personalized mastery studies. Mastery learning increases instructional time, but only slightly. Median instructional time was 4% longer in mastery learning than in the conventional conditions.

3 The ACT Programming Tutor

In the following sections we examine the impact of cognitive model-based feedback and mastery learning in the ACT Programming Tutor (APT). APT is a problem-solving environment in which students learn to write short programs in Lisp, Pascal or Prolog. Fig. 2 displays the APT Lisp Module midway through a problem. The student has previously read text presented in the window at the lower right and is completing a sequence of corresponding problems. The current problem description appears in the upper left window and the student's solution appears in the code window immediately below. The student selects operator templates and types constants and identifiers in the user action window in the middle right. In this figure the student has encoded the operator defun used to define a new operator, has entered the operator name, declared input variables and begun coding the body of the definition. The three angle-bracket symbols in the figure, <EXPR1>, <PROCESS1> and <EXPR0> are placeholders, which the student will either replace with additional Lisp code or delete. Communications from the tutor appear in the Hint window in the lower left. In this figure the student has asked for a hint on how to proceed.

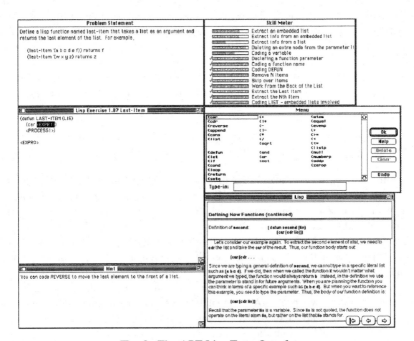

Fig. 2. The APT Lisp Tutor Interface.

3.1 Model Tracing, Knowledge Tracing and Cognitive Mastery

Like all cognitive tutors, APT is constructed around a cognitive model of the knowledge students are acquiring. APT uses this knowledge for two purposes. First, the cognitive model enables the tutor to trace the student's solution path, providing immediate step-by-step feedback on problem solving actions and advice on steps that achieve problem solving goals, in a process we call model tracing. Second, the tutor tracks the student's growing problem solving knowledge across problems in a process we call knowledge tracing, which in turn is used to implement cognitive mastery learning. In cognitive mastery learning, the student completes an individualized sequence of problems in each curriculum section until "mastering" each of the cognitive problem solving rules introduced in the section.

4 Cognitive Tutor Effect Sizes

This paper re-examines three studies of model-driven instructional interventions (a) model tracing, (b) cognitive mastery and (c) scaffolded cognitive mastery designed to support understanding and planning. It calculates the effect size of each intervention and examines the aggregate effect of these student-adapted interventions.

4.1 Model Tracing E ffect Size

In model tracing the tutor's cognitive model is employed to interpret students' problem solving actions, providing step-by-step feedback and advice as needed to ensure that the students successfully complete each problem. We have previously completed empirical evaluations that compare cognitive tutors for high school mathematics to conventional classroom problem solving activities. Students in the cognitive tutor group worked through a fixed set of problems with model tracing support (but without knowledge tracing and cognitive mastery), while the comparison group completed conventional classroom problem solving activities (boardwork and seatwork). Instructional time was held constant in these studies and the cognitive tutors yielded an achievement effect size of +1 SD [12]. This is 2 or 3 time the average effect of conventional computer based instruction and about half the effect of the best human tutors.

This paper examines the achievement effect size of model tracing in a recent study of the APT Lisp Tutor [13]. This study compared a group of students who completed a fixed set of problems with the APT Lisp Tutor to a conventional group who completed the same problem set on-line with an editor and Lisp interpreter, but no tutorial assistance. In contrast with the high school math tutor evaluations, this was a self-paced study in which both instructional time and achievement level can vary.

Procedure. Twenty college students worked at their own pace through the first two lessons of a Lisp programming text, completed a fixed set of 26 accompanying programming problems, then completed a paper-and-pencil programming test. Ten students completed the 26 problems with APT, which provided step-by-step feedback and advice as needed. Students in this condition always remained on a recognized solution path and always reached a successful conclusion to problem solving. Students in the non-tutor comparison condition completed the same programming problems on-line with a structure editor and Lisp interpreter and received no advice on how to write the programs. When the student signaled that he or she had finished a problem, the tutor tested the code and indicated whether the solution was correct. If not, the student was encouraged to continue working, but was not required to reach a correct solution, since it may not have been possible without assistance. If a student in the non-tutor condition gave up with an incorrect answer, the tutor presented a canonical solution to the problem. This approximates a common homework situation in which students can look up correct solutions in the back of the book.

Results. As displayed in Table 1, model tracing yielded an achievement effect size of +0.75 SD compared to the conventional problem solving condition. Students in the model tracing condition finished the fixed problem set in 1/3 the time required by students in the conventional group, as displayed in Table 2. The model tracing effect is smaller in this study than the +1 SD effect observed in the high school mathematics studies, but note that instructional time was held constant in those studies.

Table 1. Posttest accuracy (probability correct) in the Non-Tutor and Model Tracing conditions and effect size of Model Tracing

No Tutor		Model Tracing		
Mean	SD	Mean	SD	Effect Size
0.51	0.21	0.67	0.23	0.75

Table 2. Mean learning time (minutes) for the Non-Tutor and Model Tracing conditions and the ratio of learning times (Model Tracing/Non-Tutor)

No Tutor		Model Tracing		Ratio
Mean	SD	Mean	SD	MT/NT
32.1	9.7	102.0	64.7	0.31

4.2 Cognitive Mastery Effect Size

A second study [14] compared students working through the APT Lisp Tutor with just model tracing to students working with both model tracing and cognitive mastery (knowledge tracing). Students in the model tracing comparison group completed a fixed set of programming problems. Students in the cognitive mastery condition completed this fixed set plus additional problems as individually needed in each curriculum section to master the cognitive programming rules introduced in the section

Procedure. Twenty-two college students worked through the early sections in a Lisp text, completed corresponding programming problems, then completed an on-line programming test. Ten students were assigned to a "model tracing only" condition while twelve students were assigned to cognitive mastery condition. Students in both conditions completed a fixed set of 30 programming problems across the curriculum. In both conditions APT continuously updated its estimates that the student had learned the cognitive programming rules needed to solve the problems and displayed these estimates in a "skillmeter" (depicted in the upper right corner of Fig. 2). In the model tracing condition, these knowledge tracing estimates did not affect the curriculum and students completed just the fixed set of 30 problems. In the cognitive mastery condition, each student completed these 30 problems and completed an individually tailored sequence of problems until the probability that each of the rules had been learned reached a mastery criterion of 0.95.

Results. Students in the cognitive mastery condition completed an average of 42 exercises, compared to 30 in the fixed curriculum comparison condition. As displayed in Table 3, cognitive mastery yielded an achievement effect size of +0.89, compared to model tracing. Although students in the cognitive mastery condition completed 40% more problems than students in the fixed curriculum condition, they actually completed them in less time (50.3 minutes vs. 54.1 minutes). Students in the fixed curriculum condition took an unusually long time in the relatively easy first curriculum section – 3.5 times longer than the cognitive mastery condition. To obtain a more realistic estimate of the relative impact of cognitive mastery on learning time, we computed learning time for the remaining curriculum sections, excluding section 1. As displayed in Table 4, students in the cognitive mastery condition required about 15% more time than students in the fixed curriculum condition to complete these sections.

Table 3. Posttest accuracy (probability correct) in the Model Tracing and Cognitive Mastery conditions and effect size of Cognitive Mastery

Fixed Curriculum		Cognitive Mastery		
Mean	SD	Mean	SD	Effect Size
0.68	0.19	0.85	0.14	0.89

Table 4. Mean learning time (minutes) for the Model Tracing and Cognitive Mastery conditions and the ratio of learning times (Cognitive Mastery/Model Tracing) for curriculum sections 2 through 5.

Fixed Curriculum		Cognitive Mastery		Ratio
Mean	SD	Mean	SD	CM/MT
40.5	20.5	46.3	15.2	1.14

4.3 Augmented Support Effect Size

The knowledge tracing model used to estimate student knowledge can also be used to predict student problem solving performance. Studies show that the knowledge tracing model overestimates students' test performance by about 10% and does so because some students are learning suboptimal rules ([15], [16]). As a result, two model-driven forms of augmented support were developed for the early part of the APT Lisp Tutor curriculum. One enhancement employs animated feedback to make key data structure relationships salient. The second employs subgoal scaffolding to support students in developing simple programming plans. A recent study [17] compared a cognitive mastery condition in which students work to mastery with this augmented support to the standard cognitive mastery condition (like that in the previous study) in which students work to mastery without augmented support.

Procedure. Thirty-nine college students worked through the first five sections of the APT Lisp Tutor curriculum with both model tracing and knowledge tracing. Twenty-one students worked to reach cognitive mastery with augmented feedback and plan scaffolding. The other eighteen students worked to cognitive mastery without the additional model-based support.

Results. Students in the scaffolded cognitive mastery condition required an average of 35 problems to reach mastery, while students in the standard cognitive mastery condition required an average of 59 problems. As can be seen in Table 5 the achievement effect size of scaffolded support was +0.42 SD. Students in the scaffolded mastery condition reached mastery in about 25% less time, as shown in Table 6.

Table 5. Posttest accuracy (probability correct) in the Standard Cognitive Mastery and Augmented Cognitive Mastery conditions and effect size of Augmented Mastery

Standard Mastery		Augmented Mastery		
Mean	SD	Mean	SD	Effect Size
0.83	0.12	0.88	0.10	0.42

Table 6. Mean learning time (minutes) for the Standard Cognitive Mastery and AugmentedCognitive Mastery conditions and the ratio of learning times (Augmented Cognitive Mastery/Standard Cognitive Mastery)

Standard Mastery		Augmented Mastery		Ratio
Mean	SD	Mean	SD	AM/SM
83.2	74.7	63.1	36.2	0.76

4.4 Aggregate Effect Size

Model tracing yields a +0.75 achievement effect size compared to non-tutor conventional learning. Cognitive mastery yields a +0.89 effect size compared to basic model tracing. Scaffolded cognitive mastery learning yields a +0.42 effect size compared to standard cognitive mastery. Each innovation adds substantially to the impact on student achievement. What is the aggregate effect size the three instructional interventions? We cannot simply add the three effect sizes, because the unit (standard deviation of the comparison group) decreases across studies. But we can derive the aggregate effect size, since the comparison group in each successive study is the same as the experimental group in the previous study. Model tracing serves as the experimental treatment in experiment 1, then serves as the comparison group for standard cognitive mastery in experiment 2. Tables 1 and 2 reveal that test performance in the model tracing condition is almost identical across the studies, both mean (.67 vs. .68) and standard deviation (.23 vs. .19). Similarly, standard cognitive mastery serves as the experimental treatment in experiment 2 and as the comparison group for scaffolded mastery in experiment 3. Again, Tables 2 and 3 show that test performance in this condition is almost identical across the two studies, both mean (.85 vs. .83) and standard deviation (.14 vs. .12). As a result, we can reasonably estimate the aggregate effect size of model tracing, cognitive mastery and scaffolded cognitive mastery by computing the total difference between the scaffolded cognitive mastery mean in experiment 3 and the non-tutor mean in experiment 1 and dividing by the standard deviation of the non-tutor baseline in experiment 1:

$$(.88-.51)/.21 = +1.76 \text{ SD aggregate effect size}$$

5   Discussion

The aggregate effect of model tracing, cognitive mastery and scaffolding on achievement is virtually as large as that obtained by the best human tutors. Recall that instructional time was held constant in the human tutor studies. In experiment 1 above, students in the cognitive tutor condition completed problem solving in 1/3 the time required in the non-tutor condition. Even with the extra time cost of cognitive mastery students would be finishing in no more than 40% the time required by students working on their own. If we had held learning time constant, and allowed the cognitive tutor group to work as fast and far as they could through the curriculum, and tested both the cognitive tutor and non-tutor groups on all the material covered by the cognitive tutor group, we would expect the aggregate achievement effect size of cognitive tutoring to be substantially larger, arguably much larger than +2 SD. Not only have cognitive tutors reached and arguably surpassed Bloom's +2 SD goal, we also have empirical evidence that cognitive tutors have met Bloom's affordability criterion for widespread dissemination: In 2000-2001 our cognitive mathematics tutors are in use by more than 50,000 students in over 300 schools in 27 U.S. states.

Substantial work remains to be done. For example, the model-based scaffolding in the third study that accounts for approximately +0.25 SD of the aggregate cognitive tutor effect required interface modifications that were specific to the relatively small portion of the APT Lisp curriculum examined in these studies. In the NSF-funded CIRCLE Center, housed jointly at the University of Pittsburgh and Carnegie Mellon we are examining more general mechanisms to improve student-adapted instruction, including the use of eye-movements to trace student cognition at a finer grain size

[18] and natural-language processing to improve student-tutor dialogs [19]. We believe that these efforts will culminate in a cognitive mode-based tutoring technology that can reliably surpass the 2-sigma effect achieved by the best human tutors.

Acknowledgment

This research was supported by NSF grant number 9720359 to CIRCLE: Center for Interdisciplinary Research in Constructive Learning Environments.

References

1. Bloom, B.S.: The 2 Sigma Problem: The search for methods of group instruction as effective as one-to-one tutoring. Educational Researcher 13 (1984) 3-15
2. Cohen, P.A., Kulik, J.A., Kulik, C.C.: Educational outcomes of tutoring: A meta-analysis of findings. American Educational Research Journal 19 (1984) 237-248
3. Pressey, S.L.: A simple apparatus which gives tests and scores – and teaches. School and Society 23 (1926) 373-376
4. Kulik, J.A.: Meta-analytic studies of findings on computer-based instruction. In E. Baker & H. O'Neil (Eds.) Technology assessment in education and training. Lawrence Erlbaum, Mahwah, NJ (1994) 9-33
5. Kulik, J.A., Bangert, R.L., Williams, G.W.: Effects of computer-based teaching on secondary school students. Journal of Educational Psychology 75 (1983) 19-26
6. Kulik, C.C., Kulik, J.A.: Effectiveness of computer-based instruction: An updated analysis. Computers in Human Behavior 7 (1991) 75-94
7. Liao, Y.: Effects of computer-assisted instruction on cognitive outcomes: A meta-analysis. Journal of Research on Computing in Education 24 (1992) 367-380
8. Niemiec, R., Walberg, H.J.: Comparative effectiveness of computer-assisted instruction: A synthesis of reviews. Journal of Educational Computing Research 3 (1987) 19-37
9. Bloom, B.S.: Learning for mastery. In Evaluation Comment, 1. UCLA Center for the Study of Evaluation of Instructional Programs, Los Angeles, CA (1968)
10. Keller, F.S.: "Good-bye teacher...". Journal of Applied Behavioral Analysis 1 (1968) 79-89
11. Kulik, C.C, Kulik, J.A., Bangert-Drowns, R.L.: Effectiveness of mastery learning programs: A meta-analysis. Review of Educational Research 60 (1990) 265-299
12. Anderson, J.R., Corbett, A.T., Koedinger, K.R., Pelletier, R.: Cognitive tutors: Lessons learned. Journal of the Learning Sciences 4 (1995) 167-207
13. Corbett, A.T., Anderson, J.R.: Locus of feedback control in computer-based tutoring: Impact on learning rate, achievement and attitudes. Proceedings of ACTM CHI'2001 Conference on Human Factors in Computing Systems (in press)
14. Corbett, A.T., Anderson, J.R.: Knowledge decomposition and subgoal reification in the ACT Programming Tutor. Artificial Intelligence and Education, 1995: The Proceedings of AI-ED 95. AACE., Charlottesville, VA (1995) 469-476
15. Corbett, A.T., Knapp, S.: Plan scaffolding: Impact on the process and product of learning. In C. Frasson, G. Gauthier, & A. Lesgold (Eds.) Intelligent tutoring systems: Third international conference, ITS '96. Springer, New York (1996) 120-129
16. Corbett, A.T., Bhatnagar, A.: Student modeling in the ACT Programming Tutor: Adjusting a procedural learning model with declarative knowledge. User Modeling:

Proceedings of the Sixth International Conference, UM97. Springer, New York, (1997) 243-254

17. Corbett, A.T., Trask, H.: Instructional interventions in computer-based tutoring: Differential impact on learning time and accuracy. Proceedings of ACTM CHI'2000 Conference on Human Factors in Computing Systems. Springer, New York (2000) 97-104

18. Anderson, J.R., Gluck, K.: What role do cognitive architectures play in intelligent tutoring systems. In D. Klahr & S. Carver (Eds.) Cognition and instruction: 25 years of progress. Lawrence Erlbaum, Mahwah, NJ (in press)

19. Aleven, V., Koedinger, K. R.: Toward a tutorial dialog system that helps students to explain solution steps. Building Dialogue Systems for Tutorial Applications: AAAI Fall Symposium 2000, (2000)

Applying Interactive Open Learner Models to Learning Technical Terminology

Vania Dimitrova, John Self, Paul Brna

Computer Based Learning Unit, Leeds University, Leeds LS2 9JT, UK
{V.Dimitrova,J.A.Self,P.Brna}@cbl.leeds.ac.uk
Phone: (+44) (0)113 233 4626, Fax: (+44) (0)113 233 4635

Abstract. Our work explores an interactive open learner modelling (IOLM) approach where learner diagnosis is considered as an interactive process involving both a computer system and a learner that play symmetrical (to a certain extent) roles and construct together the learner model. The paper presents an application of IOLM for diagnosing and fostering a learner's conceptual understanding in a terminological domain. Based on an experimental study, we discuss computational and educational benefits of IOLM in terms of improving the quality of the obtained learner model and fostering reflective thinking.

Keywords . Intelligent tutoring systems, student modelling, meta-cognitive skills.

1   Introduction

A recent trend in student modelling has focused on overt approaches that envisage the diagnostic process open for inspection, discussion and direct influence from the learner [12]. Involving the learner in diagnosis originated from ideas of decreasing the complexity of learner model (LM) maintenance and tackling dynamics of student's behaviour [14]. Furthermore, overt diagnostic methods are expected to yield pedagogic gains in providing the means for reflective learning [4].

Our work explores an interactive open learner modelling (IOLM) approach and conceives diagnosis as an interactive process involving both a computer system and a learner that play symmetrical (to a certain extent) roles and construct together the LM. IOLM goes beyond open learner modelling [10,11,13] and elaborates the notion of interaction, which allows challenging the robustness of the learners' knowledge and provoking the users' active engagement in diagnosis (while learners may happen to browse passively through open learner models). We have expanded the idea of LM negotiation [4] where the interaction is triggered chiefly by conflicts between the computer and the student's views. Instead, IOLM manifests a constructive dialogue guided by the computer that flexibly switches between different diagnostic tactics.

A framework for IOLM has been presented elsewhere [8,9]. It includes distinctive components: a discourse model manages diagnostic interactions providing both a diagnoser and diagnosee a common communication method and symmetrical power in dialogue maintenance [8] while a formally defined mechanism maintains a jointly constructed LM [9]. To validate the framework we have developed STyLE-OLM - an IOLM system in a terminology domain. This paper presents an experiment with

M. Bauer, P.J. Gmytrasiewicz, and J. Vassileva (Eds.): UM 2001, LNAI 2109, pp. 148–157, 2001.

STyLE-OLM and discusses computational and educational benefits of IOLM in terms of improving the quality of the LM and engaging the learners in reflective activities.

In the next two sections, we present the task (conceptual understanding in learning technical terminology) and outline the system. An application of STyLE-OLM for diagnosing and fostering conceptual understanding is demonstrated in section 4. Section 5 and 6 discuss some advantages of the approach, based on which we draw conclusions about a possible utilisation of IOLM in intelligent learning environments.

2   The Task: Conceptual Understanding in Terminology Learning

We have explored the task of learning technical terminology in a foreign language, particularly non-English speakers studying Finance terminology in English. Learning environments concerned with terminology, see e.g. [5, 16], suffer from the lack of adaptability. It may well be the case that the provided information contains terms a user is not familiar with. A major obstacle is the scarce attention paid to modelling a learner's cognition in this domain, which requires a sophisticated LM embracing diverse aspects of terminology competence.

Understanding term meanings is important for comprehension and production of terminological texts. This follows a more general argument about the importance of word meanings in language learning [15]. Most linguists believe that the meaning of the words is decomposed in concepts whose understanding entails acquiring a large system of knowledge where concepts are related to each other. Generally, concept learning research refers to acquiring a domain conceptualisation by applying correctly corresponding methods, such as generalisation (inferring from examples), explanation (justifying certain properties), deduction (inferring specific knowledge about category exemplars), and analogy (reasoning using similarities) [17]. This is often not the case with learners who may misapply or fail to apply the correct classification rule. In educational contexts, both finding possible explanations for learners' conceptual errors and fostering learners' conceptual understanding play an essential role. STyLE-OLM addresses these tasks as outlined in the following sections.

3   The STyLE-OLM [1] System

STyLE-OLM is an environment for interactive diagnosis where a learner can inspect and discuss aspects of his domain knowledge and influence the content of the LM. The architecture of the system is presented in Fig. 1.

STyLE-OLM imports a domain knowledge base (KB) built with conceptual graphs (CGs). The instantiation presented here is in a Finance domain[2]. The experiment described below was carried out with a preliminary KB, which at that time included a type hierarchy with 96 concept types, and 19 CGs. The KB is being developed by a

---

[1] STyLE-OLM is the Open Learner Modelling component in STyLE (Scientific Terminology Learning Environment) being developed in the framework of the EU funded Larflast project.

[2] The STyLE-OLM architecture does not depend on the subject area. Another instantiation of the system, which is in a Computer Science domain, has been utilised in [8] and [9].

Bulgarian team [1] and used in the Larflast project. STyLE-OLM elicits the domain knowledge needed for IOLM utilising type hierarchy operations, basic CG operations (copy, join, restrict, and simplify), and some advanced operations (e.g. generalisation, specialisation, common generalisation).

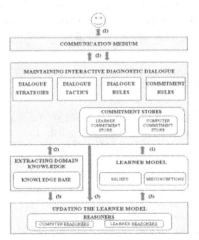

Fig. 1. The STyLE-OLM architecture. There are three main interaction stages: (1) - Initialisation, (2) - Discussion, and (3) - Learner model update.

The LM incorporates beliefs and misconceptions (Fig. 2). The beliefs, which can be correct, erroneous and incomplete, are encoded with CGs. The beliefs in the LM are open for inspection and discussion. Misconceptions are defined in our work as explanations for the learner's errors at conceptual level. At present, we consider several misclassifications and misattributions.

The communication medium in STyLE-OLM combines text and graphics. There are two modes - DISCUSS and BROWSE. In DISCUSS mode (Fig. 3), a learner discusses his domain knowledge with the system. Both the learner and the system construct dialogue utterances by creating a CG that represents the proposition of their communicative act and adding some illocutionary force to this proposition. In BROWSE mode (Fig. 4), a learner inspects the LM beliefs, elicited from the interaction and assigned a level of correctness by the system. At any time, the learner can switch between the two modes.

```
know(student1,money_market,[203]).
know(student1,money_market,[502]).
know_wrongly(student1,financial_market,[200]).
not_know(student1,capital_market,[501]).

misconception(misattribution(financial_market,200),
             misattribution_1,[203,502]).
%  Error: The learner believes wrongly that
%      "On financial markets securities are converted into cash" (graph 200)
%  Explanation: Because the learner believes          that
%      "Money markets are financial markets" (graph 502) and
%      "On money markets securities are converted into cash" (graph 203).
```

Fig. 2. Beliefs and a misconception from a LM in STyLE-OLM, the numbers indicate graph IDs.

The LM discussion is maintained in a dialogue game manner [8]. Dialogue moves are used to indicate the illocutionary force of the agents' communicative acts (see Fig. 3). Dialogue rules define when the moves are permitted. Beliefs the agents have committed to in the dialogue are accumulated in commitment stores. The learner's commitment store contains his beliefs about the domain, while the computer's store includes its beliefs about the beliefs of the learner (see Fig. 5). Commitment rules define changes to the commitment stores as results of the dialogue moves.

We consider interactive diagnostic dialogue to consist of dialogue games that represent the interaction episodes and correspond to certain diagnostic goals. The goals define game tactics, e.g. explore aspects of the learner's knowledge, explain a learner's error by discovering a possible misconception, or negotiate a different view. Tactics define sequences of communicative acts to be address in the dialogue. CG schemata are used to obtain domain content for the tactics. To select a game to 'play' at each time of the dialogue, STyLE-OLM consults dialogue strategies - rules that suggest which dialogue game should be active in the current situation. The strategies may require that the current game is interrupted and a new or an interrupted one is activated.

Graphical tools for constructing CGs

Graphical area for creating CGs with the propositions of the dialogue utterances

Textual representation of the last dialogue utterance

Buttons for going through the discussed CGs

Button for switching to BROWSE mode

Selected dialogue move

Dialogue history

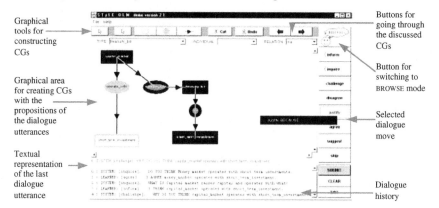

Fig. 3. STyLE-OLM in DISCUSS mode - a learner's justification after a system's challenge.

Graphical area to present CGs with beliefs from the LM

Degree of correctness the system assigns to the belief, represented with the CG

Buttons for browsing through the beliefs in the learner model

Button for switching to DISCUSS mode

Dialogue history

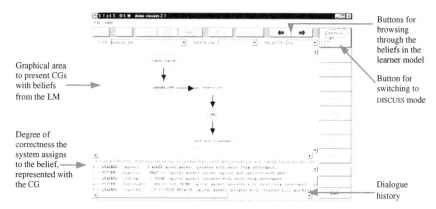

Fig. 4. STyLE-OLM in BROWSE mode where the learner can inspect the learner model.

```
      from the system commitment store
believe(system,believe(learner,502).
believe(system,believe(learner,203)->believe(learner,502)).
believe(system,notbelieve(learner,501).
not_believe(system,believe(learner,201).

      from the learner commitment store
believe(learner,200).
believe(learner,200->203).
not_believe(learner,501).
```

Fig. 5. Example beliefs from the commitment stores. The numbers present IDs of CGs.

A modal logic operator maintains the changes in the commitment stores and extracts what the agents have agreed about the student's beliefs [9]. When a belief contradicts with a commitment store, STyLE-OLM removes the beliefs inconsistent with the one stated last and initiates a confirmation dialogue. Having the agents' explicit commitments represented in the commitment stores, STyLE-OLM applies reasoners to infer potential consequences of these commitments. It elicits agreements and conflicts in the system and learner's views about the learner, e.g. an agreement that believe(learner,203)   can be inferred from the commitment stores presented in Fig. 5 assuming that the learner might apply a modus ponens reasoner and the computer applies a default reasoner over its beliefs about the learner. The agreements are used as a source for updating the LM. The conflicts are to be addressed in following negotiative dialogues.

As shown in Fig. 1, the interaction with STyLE-OLM comprises three main stages:

(1)   Initialisation - an initial LM (built by traditional diagnostic methods) is imported and converted into commitment stores. It is assumed that both agents support the initial LM and corresponding beliefs are added to both commitment stores.

(2)   Discussion - a loop that involves the agents' turns taken in a sequential order - each learner's turn is analysed by the system and a system's response is generated.

(3)   Learner model update - after the interaction is terminated (the learner quits the session) or suspended (the learner switches to BROWSE mode for inspecting the LM), the agreements and conflicts between the commitment stores are extracted and the beliefs in the LM are updated. Possible learner's misconceptions may be assigned.

4   Diagnosing and Fostering Conceptual Understanding

4.1   The Experiment

An experiment with seven subjects, postgraduate students at the authors' department, was conducted primarily to examine the behaviour of STyLE-OLM, specifically the use of the communication medium, the dialogue management, and the LM maintenance. The experiment also allowed us to examine some advantages of IOLM.

Each learner attended an individual session. Prior to the session, a learner was given an introductory text with target Finance terms to study for a while and then asked to answer several drill questions about these terms without using the text. The learners' drill performance was assessed and initial LMs obtained (by hand). The learners were given some training to get acquainted with the communication medium.

In a session with STyLE-OLM, the learners were asked to help the computer system to obtain a better model of their domain conceptualisations, which would facilitate adaptability in pedagogical situations like generating explanations, providing feedback, selecting instructional materials. The learners were encouraged to inspect the LM, discuss their domain knowledge, and influence the content of the learner model. Generally, the interactions lasted about half an hour and were terminated by the learners. The sessions with STyLE-OLM were observed and monitored by the experimenter. Log files were recorded to study aspects of the system's behaviour.

4.2   An Example: Articulating Aspects of a Learner's Conceptual Knowledge

The excerpt here is from a session with a learner whose initial LM showed a reasonably strong knowledge in FINANCIAL MARKETS, the topic in the evaluative study. We use textual form to represent to represent the dialogue, although all communication is actually done graphically (see Figs. 3 and 4). At particular places we give learner's comments, experimenter's observations and details about the behaviour of the system.

The initial LM contains information that the learner knows the domain facts:

"MONEY MARKET operates with   SHORT TERM INVESTMENTS",
"CAPITAL MARKET operates with   LONG TERM INVESTMENTS",
"CAPITAL MARKET supports   BUILDING NEW HOMES, FACTORIES, SCHOOLS, HIGHWAYS AND SHOPS".

The learner does not know   that

"On the   MONEY MARKET SECURITIES are converted into   CASH".

The initial situation is that the learner confuses the terms CAPITAL MARKET and MONEY MARKET. STyLE-OLM initiates a dialogue game to explore the similarity and the difference between both terms. The system starts with the definitions of these terms and tries to confirm the beliefs in the learner model (so it uses inform   moves).

0. STyLE-OLM$_{[inform]}$ YOU THINK that CAPITAL MARKET operates with LONG TERM INVESTMENTS.

1. Learner$_{[agree]}$I AGREE that CAPITAL MARKET operates with LONG TERM INVESTMENTS.

2. STyLE-OLM$_{[inform]}$ YOU THINK that MONEY MARKET operates with SHORT TERM INVESTMENTS.

3. Learner$_{[disagree]}$ I DISAGREE that MONEY MARKET operates with SHORT TERM INVESTMENTS.

STyLE-OLM continues with the comparison of the terms and addresses a situation about CAPITAL MARKET that was included in the initial LM.

4. STyLE-OLM$_{[inform]}$ YOU THINK that CAPITAL MARKET supports BUILDING NEW HOMES, FACTORIES, SCHOOLS, HIGHWAYS and SHOPS.

5. Learner$_{[inform]}$ I THINK that CAPITAL MARKET supports BUILDING NEW HOMES, FACTORIES, SCHOOLS, HIGHWAYS and SHOPS.

The system continues by exploring the type hierarchy.

6. STyLE-OLM$_{[inquire]}$ DO YOU THINK CAPITAL MARKET is a FINANCIAL MARKET?

7. Learner$_{[agree]}$ I AGREE that CAPITAL MARKET is a FINANCIAL MARKET.

To further explore the domain about CAPITAL MARKET, STyLE-OLM generates CGs that specialise the definition of the term by using exemplars of LONG TERM INVESTMENTS. As these beliefs are not in the commitment stores, the system uses inquire   moves.

8. STyLE-OLM$_{[inquire]}$ DO YOU THINK CAPITAL MARKET operates with CORPORATE STOCKS?

9. Learner$_{[disagree]}$I DISAGREE that CAPITAL MARKET operates with CORPORATE STOCKS.

10. STyLE-OLM$_{[inquire]}$ DO YOU THINK CAPITAL MARKET operates with TAX EXEMPT BONDS.

Learner's comments: "I see, it's asking me about tax exempt bond now… It might be true if tax exempt bond is a kind of long term investment. I can ask the system this."

At this point, the robustness of the learner's domain expertise is challenged. In searching for clarifications of domain aspects, he inquires the system.

11. Learner$_{[inquire]}$IS IT TRUE that TAX EXEMPT BOND is a LONG TERM INVESTMENT.

STyLE-OLM now changes the current plan to include an answer to the question.

12. STyLE-OLM$_{[inform]}$ I KNOW that TAX EXEMPT BOND is a LONG TERM INVESTMENT.

Learner's comments: "I see. Then I can answer the question it asked me earlier... "

13. Learner[inform] I THINK that CAPITAL MARKET operates with TAX EXEMPT BONDS.

STyLE-OLM continues the game exploring exemplars of LONG TERM INVESTMENTS.

14. STyLE-OLM[inquire] DO YOU THINK CAPITAL MARKET operates with MORTGAGE LOANS.

Learner's comments: "Perhaps, I shall change the topic... I shall think of which market operates with mortgage loans..."

The learner reads through the Finance terms. He does not seem to find the term he is looking for. He decides to see his model and goes to BROWSE mode. The learner browses through the graphs presenting beliefs from the LM. He seems happy with the information in the LM, goes back to DISCUSS mode, and continues the dialogue.

15. Learner[inform] I THINK that NEGOTIATED MARKET operates with MORTGAGE LOANS.

The strategies accept the focus change suggested by the learner. The current game is suspended, a game that explores domain aspects with the new focus is initiated. The dialogue continues with MORTGAGE LOAN as it is more relevant to the preceding discourse.

16. STyLE-OLM[inquire] DO YOU THINK MORTGAGE LOAN is a LONG TERM INVESTMENT?

In the dialogue follow up, MORTGAGE LOAN is to be further elaborated.

After the session, the LM is updated. The interaction revealed facts that the learner does not know:

"MONEY MARKET operates with   SHORT TERM INVESTMENTS" (which was presented as known before the interaction)

"CAPITAL MARKET operates with   CORPORATE STOCKS,   CONSUMER LOANS, and NEGOTIABLE CERTIFICATES OF DEPOSIT".

In addition to the explicitly stated beliefs, the system makes a plausible inference that the learner does not know   that

"CORPORATE STOCKS and   TAX EXEMPT BONDS are   LONG TERM INVESTMENTS".

The following belief is erroneous, i.e. marked as known wrongly   , because the domain knowledge base does not support it.

"NEGOTIATED MARKET operates with   MORTGAGE LOANS".

The experiment is presented in more detail in [7]. Next, we discuss the results in respect to some computational and educational advantages of IOLM.

5   On the Quality of the Updated Learner Model

In order to analyse the quality of the LM we need criteria for comparing the initial and the updated LMs. We will define that a LM L_{new} is of a better quality than a LM L if: (1) L_{new} removes the inconsistencies in L if such exist; (2) L_{new} presents a larger scope of learner's beliefs; (3) L_{new} provides more explanations of the learner's errors; (4) L_{new} includes a higher proportion of valid assertions about the learner's knowledge; (5) L_{new} minimises the number of not valid assertions about the learner's knowledge.

The first criterion refers to problems with LM consistency often experienced by observational diagnosis, e.g. a belief contradicting the previous beliefs needs to be added. The inconsistencies were addressed in confirmation episodes. Few conflicting beliefs were left due to limitations in the CG inference, e.g. it did not recognise that two CGs represented propositions which were rephrasing one another.

The second criterion concerns articulating learner's beliefs and expanding the LM. The mean number of added beliefs to the LMs was 7 (S.D.=4). Some beliefs were deleted from the LMs as a result of the interactions with STyLE-OLM.

The third criterion refers to finding possible learner's misconceptions, addressed in some dialogue tactics. Although several misconception searches were initiated, few misconceptions were added to the LMs. Users often discovered their errors and made claims that changed LMs. Thus, potential misconceptions were not confirmed.

The last two criteria refer to validating the changes in the LM. We consider that a LM obtained from a computer diagnoser is valid if it satisfies the diagnosee, the student who has been diagnosed, and a human diagnoser, a teacher who can perform the diagnosis instead of the computer. We gave each learner questions concerning the resulting LM. Five learners considered that the LM corresponded to their domain knowledge, one was neutral, and one disagreed with the LM because it had facts presented as 'known' which he did not actually know. These facts were not discussed with STyLE-OLM but were present in the initial LM of the user. While such cases fortify the benefits of IOLM, they also show potential pitfalls for missing necessary discussion topics (and leaving invalid pieces in the LM) because either dialogue tactics may not capture them or a learner could terminate the session before their discovering.

The dialogue transcripts, the initial and the obtained LMs from some sessions were given for validation to a human diagnoser - a foreign language teacher in a Finance domain. Differently from the diagnosees, the teacher was rather neutral validating (on the basis of the observed interactions) the LMs she inspected. She questioned principally the approach of assigning correctness to someone's knowledge when a deficient system's expertise was employed. The teacher pointed at inadequacies in strategies that may have hindered the articulation of students' knowledge, e.g. when a learner made a wrong claim the system did not initiate a game to explore the error (see 3 in the excerpt above) and thus relevant beliefs might have been missed.

6   Fostering Reflective Conceptual Understanding

Involving learners in situations where they can inspect and discuss their models is a reflective activity which leads learners to think about their knowledge, to articulate, validate, and challenge the robustness of their own domain competence.

Predominantly, we observed that the learners were fostered to render statements about their domain beliefs, which caused recalling and reconsidering domain aspects [2]. The more knowledgeable students tended to make more claims about their beliefs. The mean percentage of this reflective activity calculated in respect to all reflective activities each learner experienced is 79% (S.D.=12) for the more knowledgeable group and 53% (S.D.=7) for the less knowledgeable group. The difference in the means was found to be significant (Mann-Whitney for very small samples, n_1=3, n_2=4, U=0, p=0.028). The discussions with the more knowledgeable learners contained relatively varied types of exchanges where participants made claims about their beliefs, while typically the less knowledgeable learners made claims about their domain beliefs challenging aspects of the LM after inspecting it in BROWSE mode.

Students went back to claims about their beliefs and (at times) changed these claims, i.e. they were recalling and reconsidering domain aspects [2] and validating their domain beliefs [6]. These reflective activities were usually observed in situations where learners were challenged by STyLE-OLM and looked back at their claims both in the dialogue history and the obtained LM. Less knowledgeable learners experienced such situations more often (mean 27%, S.D.=9) since their claims were more frequently challenged by the system. These participants tend to browse their LMs in order to check the correctness of the claims they had made. Two more knowledgeable learners did not go back to claims they had made (mean 9%, S.D.=13).

The students investigated arguments to support their beliefs, i.e. they were searching for grounds of their beliefs [6]. The users grounded their domain beliefs by asking questions to clarify aspects of the domain relying on the system's domain expertise (mean for the more knowledgeable 12%, S.D.=5; mean for the less knowledgeable 21%, S.D.=6). While more knowledgeable learners constructed questions exploring aspects not discussed yet but following the preceding discourse (as in 11 in the dialogue above), the less knowledgeable students often asked questions after browsing the LM. Sometimes, these users 'answered' a question by posing it back to the system (the reflectiveness of such inquiries is dubious).

The occurrence of the above situations in interactions with STyLE-OLM has allowed us to argue about the presence of reflection. As a whole, the more knowledgeable users were relatively well-engaged in discussions about the LMs. They experienced on average a total of 12.5 (S.D.=4) reflective activities in a session. While the interactions with the less knowledgeable students were shorter and had frequent focus changes, these users browsed their models more often when provoked by system's inquiries or challenges. The mean total number of reflective activities that the less knowledgeable users were involved in was slightly lower: 11.3 (S.D.=1). We argue that STyLE-OLM is capable of engaging both groups of learner in reflective activities.

The study showed that the scope of articulated domain beliefs was extending in a coherent manner so that learners had not only recalled aspects of the domain but been able to build a consistent picture connecting related domain facts. We also found that in each session different alternatives related to one piece of knowledge were explored, e.g. the excerpt above shows term definitions, situations with domain terms; hierarchical relations, and exemplars of generic terms. These factors address the effectiveness of the reflection. They are by no means comprehensive and further investigations of this issue, e.g. considering the learning effect, are required.

7   Conclusions

This paper has elaborated on the potential of interactive open learner modelling, illustrated in a terminological domain. We have presented a system that exemplifies the approach. Based on an experiment with the system, we have shown that IOLM can both improve the quality of the LM and provide means for engaging the learners in reflective activities. STyLE-OLM is based on a fairly general framework for IOLM. Generalisation of the approach shown here to other declarative domains is likely [7].

The benefits of the approach allow us to argue about the twofold role of IOLM in intelligent learning environments. On the one hand, IOLM can be part of the diagnostic component to target problems with traditional, observational, diagnosis. On the other hand, IOLM may well be included in the learning activities of an educational system and approached as a pedagogical activity by an instructional planner. These issues have been addressed in the integration of STyLE-OLM in STyLE [3] - a learning environment that supports non-native speakers to learn English Finance terminology.

Acknowledgements

The first author is supported by the British ORS programme. The research is part of the Larflast project. We thank the anonymous reviewers for their helpful comments.

References

1. Angelova, G., Nenkova, A., Boycheva, Sv., & Nikolov T. (2000). CGs as a knowledge representation core in a complex language learning environment. In B. Ganter & G. W. Mineau (eds.), Proc. of int. conference on conceptual structures . Shaker Verlag, 45-58.
2. Boud, D., Keogh, R., & Walker, D. (1996). What is reflection in learning. In D. Boud, R. Keogh, & D. Walker (eds.), Reflection: turning experience into learning . Kogan Page,7-17.
3. Boytcheva, S. Kalaydgjiev, O. Nenkova. A. & Angelova G. (2000). Integration of resources and components in a knowledge-based web environment for terminology learning. In S. Cerri & D. Dochev (eds.), AI: methodology, systems and applications. Springer, 210-220.
4. Bull, S. (1997). Collaborative student modelling in foreign language learning. PhD Thesis. University of Edinburgh.
5. Chanier, T. (1996). Learning a second language for specific purposes within a hypermedia framework. Computer Assisted Language Learning, 9 (1), 3-43.
6. Dewey, J. (1960). How we think - a restatement of the relation of reflective thinking to the educational process. D.C. Heath and Company.
7. Dimitrova, V. (in preparation). Interactive open learner modelling. PhD Thesis. Computer Based Learning Unit, Leeds University, expected submission in April 2001.
8. Dimitrova, V., Self, J.A. & Brna, P. (1999). The interactive maintenance of open learner models.In S.Lajoie & M.Vivet (eds.),Artificial intelligence in education. IOS Press, 405-412.
9. Dimitrova, V., Self, J.A. & Brna, P. (2000). Maintaining a jointly constructed student model. In S.Cerri & D.Dochev (eds.), AI: Methodology, Systems and Applications Springer, 221-231.
10. Kay J. (1999). A scrutable user modelling shell for user-adapted interaction. Ph.D. Thesis, Basser Department of Computer Science, University of Sydney, Sydney, Australia.
11. Morales, R., Pain, H., & Conlon, T. (2000). Understandable learner models for a sensorimotor control task. In G.Gauthier & C.Frasson, ITS'2000, Berlin: Springer, 222-231.
12. Morales, R., Pain, H., Bull, S., & Kay, J. (1999). Workshop on open, interactive, and other overt approaches to learner modelling . AIED'99, Le Mans, France.
13. Paiva, A. & Self, J.A. (1995). TAGUS - a user and learner modelling workbench, User Modeling and User-Adapted Interaction, 4, 197-226.
14. Self, J.A. (1990). Bypassing the intractable problem of student modelling. In C. Frasson & G. Gauthier (eds.),ITS: At the crossroad of artificial intelligence and education, NJ:Ablex.
15. Singer, M. (1990). Psychology of language: An introduction of sentence and discourse processes, Lawrence Erlbaum Assoc.
16. Smith, J. (1998). Everyone's ABC of accounting language www.soc.staffs.ac.uk/~cmrjs/agloss.htm.
17. Thagard, P. (1992). Conceptual revolutions. Princeton University Press.

Student and Instructor Models: Two Kinds of User Model and Their Interaction in an ITS Authoring Tool

Maria Virvou and Maria Moundridou

Department of Informatics, University of Piraeus,
80, Karaoli and Dimitriou St., Piraeus 185 34, Greece
{mvirvou, mariam}@unipi.gr

Abstract. WEAR is a Web-based authoring tool for Intelligent Tutoring Systems in Algebra related domains. Apart from modelling the student which is a common practice in almost all ITSs and ITS authoring tools, WEAR deals also with modelling the other class of its users: the instructors. Student and instructor models in WEAR interact with each other by exchanging information. This is in favour of both classes of WEAR's users, since they are affected by each other in a way similar to the one in a real educational setting. This paper describes the two kinds of user model and the type of information that they exchange. The issues raised in this research may be applied to other authoring tools by the addition of an instructor modelling component.

1   Introduction

One-to-one tutoring is believed (e.g. [1]) to be one of the most effective methods of instruction. Unfortunately, the large number of expert instructors that would be needed in such an educational setting make this ideal form of instruction unfeasible. Intelligent Tutoring Systems (ITSs) are computer-based instructional systems aiming at providing each student with a learning experience similar to the ideal one-to-one tutoring. In particular, ITSs have the ability to present the teaching material in a flexible way and to provide learners with tailored instruction and feedback. A number of successful evaluations of ITSs (e.g. [5; 9]) have managed to show that such systems can be effective in improving learning by increasing the students' motivation and performance in comparison with traditional instructional methods. However, ITSs are still seen with scepticism due to the fact that they have not been extensively used in real educational settings such as workplaces and classrooms. The main reason for this limited use is probably the fact that the task of constructing an ITS is complex, time-consuming and involves a large number of people including programmers, instructors and experts of a specific domain. Moreover, once constructed, an ITS for a specific domain can not be re-used for different domains without spending much time and effort. An approach to simplifying the ITS construction is to develop ITS authoring tools/shells. The main aim of such systems is to provide an environment that can be used by a wider range of people to easily develop cost-effective ITSs.

In the last decade a lot of research energy has been put in building ITS authoring tools; for a thorough and in-depth analysis of the state of the art for ITS authoring tools/shells the reader is referred to [6]. The users of ITS authoring tools are

M. Bauer, P.J. Gmytrasiewicz, and J. Vassileva (Eds.): UM 2001, LNAI 2109, pp. 158–167, 2001.
©Springer-Verlag Berlin Heidelberg 2001

instructors who are responsible for the authoring procedure and learners who work with the produced ITSs. While learner modelling is a common task that is performed in almost every ITS and in many ITS authoring tools, instructor modelling has not gained any attention yet. This is an observation made also by Kinshuk and Patel [4]: "Whereas the work on student modelling has benefited by the user modelling research in the field of HCI, the research on the role of a teacher as a collaborator in the computer integrated learning environments is almost non existent." However, the role of instructors as users/authors of ITS authoring tools is very important for the effectiveness of the produced ITSs. In order for authoring tools to benefit the most from the involvement of instructors, they should provide individualised feedback to them throughout the ITS's life cycle. This can be achieved by an instructor modelling component incorporated in the architecture of the authoring tool.

Indeed, this paper is about an ITS authoring tool for the Web that models not only its students-users but also the instructors who author the ITSs to be generated. The authoring tool is called WEAR, which stands for WEb-based authoring tool for Algebra Related domains [10; 11]. WEAR provides a learning environment in which students can learn how to solve problems in various algebra-related domains (e.g. economics, physics, chemistry, etc.). In particular, WEAR deals with the generation of instruction, since it offers the ability of problem construction. In addition, it performs student error diagnosis by providing a mechanism that can be applied to many algebra-related domains. Finally, WEAR is also concerned with managing the sequence of the curriculum.

In particular, this paper focuses on the student and instructor modelling components of WEAR and their interaction. WEAR's user models (instructor and student model) interact with each other by exchanging information. This communication mimics in some sense the interaction that takes place in a real setting of a one-to-one tutoring: both the instructor and the student build models of each other and these models affect their attitude towards the learning process.

WEAR's design and development is based on the results of an empirical study that we conducted and which involved students and instructors of various algebra-related domains. What is of interest from the results of the empirical study in respect to the focus of this paper are the following: Instructors usually wish to know how students have performed so that they may evaluate their courseware with respect to their teaching goals. On the other hand, students always seek information about their instructor's teaching style, so that they may have a better understanding of what to expect from the course they are taught.

In the main body of this paper we will present WEAR's architecture and operation, describe how instructor and student modelling are incorporated in it, and also how and on what grounds these two models interact with each other.

2   Student and Instructor Models in WEAR's Architecture

WEAR is implemented in JAVA and PROLOG and resides on a Web server. Students and instructors can access WEAR and work with it using a conventional Web browser. The system's underlying architecture is shown in Figure 1. The "Tutoring components" consist of components that interact with students while they are solving problems, diagnose the cause of the errors a student may make, adaptively present the teaching material and form individualised advice for students. These components update the "Student model" at every interaction of a student with the system and use the information kept in that model to perform the tasks mentioned above. The "Tutoring components" use information that they obtain from the "Authoring components" which interact with the instructor. In particular they use the domain knowledge provided by the instructor in order to compare the students' solutions to the correct one.

The domain knowledge which is provided by the instructor to the "Authoring components" consists of the domain description in terms of variables, equations and units of measure, and all the information needed to construct a problem (known and unknown variables, level of difficulty, etc.). In addition, the instructor provides information concerning the structure of the course and the teaching material. The "Authoring components" are taking the input from the instructors and in return they assist them in constructing new problems, retrieving previously created ones, and delivering teaching material and problems to students. The "Authoring components" also provide information to the "Instructor model" which is updated at the end of each interaction of the instructor with the system. This model holds information acquired from the instructors in an explicit and implicit way. For example, instructors may be explicitly asked questions such as what their preferences are concerning the course, what their teaching expertise is, etc.; implicit information inferred by the system may concern the instructors' interests in some categories of problem etc. Using the information stored in the "Instructor model", the "Authoring components" render the system more flexible and adaptable to particular instructors' interests and needs.

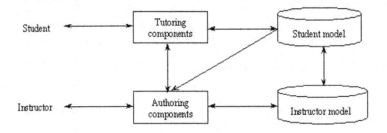

Fig. 1. WEAR's architecture

Most systems exploit the user models they build for the sake of the users to whom these models belong; for example a student model is used for the sake of students. However, WEAR uses its instructor and student model for instructors and students respectively and vice versa. This means that the model of each class of user is also used as a source of information to be passed to the other class of user. This is done in two ways: either explicitly by informing the other class of user or implicitly by affecting the model of the other class of user. As it can be seen from the system's architecture (the arrow connecting the "Student model" with the "Authoring components"), the information that is explicitly provided, concerns the case of the student models, which pass information to instructors. For example, instructors may be given some information about students' performance from the student model in order for instructors to evaluate their own teaching strategy.

Furthermore and most importantly the models of the two classes of user interact with each other and affect the modelling process itself. For example, the students' performance recorded in the student models is used to calculate the degree of an instructor's tendency to overestimate or underestimate the level of difficulty that s/he assigns to problems. If a high degree of such a tendency seems to exist, it is recorded in the instructor's model and used to provide individualised help to him/her (e.g. to remind him/her of this when constructing new problems). Similarly an instructor model may affect student models. For example, the students' level of knowledge, which is recorded in student models, is assessed taking into account the students' errors. These may either be mathematical or domain errors. By default WEAR considers the two kinds of error equally important; however, if an instructor model indicates a specific instructor's preference to weigh more one kind of error than the other, then the students' level of knowledge is calculated taking into account the instructor's preference.

WEAR functions in two different modes: the instructor's and the student's mode. The student's mode is in fact the ITS that WEAR produces, while the instructor's mode is the authoring tool itself. In the student's mode, students are presented with a number of problems to work with and are provided with individualised feedback while they are solving them. In the instructor's mode the instructor is able to construct new problems and/or retrieve previously created ones. In both cases, WEAR provides automatic assistance, as it will be discussed in the subsequent sections.

3   WEAR's Operation for the Instructor

The tool takes input from a human instructor about a specific equation-related domain (e.g. physics). This input consists of knowledge about variables, units of measure, formulae and their relation and can be provided to the tool at the same rate as lessons progress in a course. An example of input to the system that an instructor could provide to describe a portion of the domain of physics could be the following:

Variables: period - T, frequency - f, speed - u, wavelength - ë, time - t, distance - d
Equations: $T=1/f$, $u=f*ë$, $U=d/t$

Furthermore, instructors can upload HTML files and create a list of topics for the students to study. In that case, instructors are requested to provide some more information (e.g. they are asked to specify the prerequisite relationships among topics, associate the topics with the domain concepts, etc.). At this mode, instructors are also asked to answer some questions of the system concerning their preferences in teaching strategies and their level of expertise.

When an instructor wishes to create problems s/he is guided by the system through a step by step procedure. At each step of this procedure the instructor should specify values for some parameters needed to construct a problem. In particular, the problem construction procedure is the following: the system displays every variable that the human instructor has entered when describing the domain and requests the unknown. The system considers automatically all the variables as possible given data. Such variables depend on the "unknown" according to the domain equations. These variables are shown to the instructor who should now select the ones that will be "known" in the problem to be constructed and enter their values. The system follows the instructor's actions and reports any inconsistencies. For example, if the instructor enters values for fewer variables than those needed for the problem to be solvable then the system points out the error. Finally, the system produces a simple problem text describing the given and asked data. After the construction of a problem, the tool asks the instructor to assign to the problem the appropriate "level of difficulty". While in student's mode the system uses this measure in order to suggest to each student what problem to try next.

Beyond constructing a problem by himself/herself, the instructor has the ability to explore the problems constructed by other instructors and choose the ones that s/he desires to be accessible by his/her class. Instructors are allowed either to browse the collection of problems by selecting the categories of problem that match their needs and interests, or to search the entire collection using some keywords. Problems are categorised according to the domain they belong. At a second level the problems of each domain are categorised according to the variables that they involve and their level of difficulty.

4   Instructor Modelling

The instructor modelling component monitors each instructor's interactions with WEAR and constructs and/or updates his/her user model. As we have already mentioned, an instructor either searches for an already constructed problem or constructs a problem by himself/herself. WEAR infers from these two actions the user's interest or contribution to something, respectively. This is similar to a system called InfoVine [3], which infers that users are interested in something if they are repeatedly asking the system about it whereas they are expert in something if they are repeatedly telling the system about it. In WEAR, when a user frequently searches for specific categories of problem then it is inferred that this particular user is "interested" in these categories of problem; when a user frequently constructs problems that belong to the same category and these problems have been solved by a number of students, the inference made is that this user is a "major contributor" in that sort of problem. In particular, the instructor aspects that are being modelled in WEAR, are the following:

Instructor's preferences: In WEAR the instructor may explicitly give some long-term preferences as to whether s/he wishes the course to be difficult, average or easy or whether s/he wishes it to be very popular or fairly popular or whether s/he is not interested in this feature. The preference about the difficulty level of the course is associated with a percentage of failure in performances of class students. The preference about the level of popularity of the course is associated with the students' interest in the course (e.g. how many times students access the course, and/or the proportion of problems solved to the total number of available problems). In addition, the instructor may state if s/he considers equally important the two categories of students' error (mathematical and domain errors). In other words, the instructor is asked to specify how the students' level of knowledge will be calculated: if an instructor has stated that s/he considers more important the domain errors, then the weight of these errors will be higher in the formula calculating the students' level of knowledge.

Instructor's usual activities and special interests: Instructor's activities that are frequent are recorded in his/her long-term model. For example, if an instructor constructs exercises frequently then s/he is recorded as a major contributor. The instructor's interests are inferred and also recorded in the long-term instructor model. For example, what kind of exercises the instructor is interested in or whether s/he is interested in the diagnostic statistics about students depending on the number of times s/he visits the relevant page.

Instructor's level of expertise in teaching: In WEAR the instructor model records the teaching expertise of the instructor. This is explicitly stated by the instructor himself/herself. Each instructor may situate himself/herself in one of three categories: novice, having little experience, experienced. In the case of novice tutors and those having little experience, the authoring tool offers more detailed help concerning the teaching strategies that tutors may select and shows them the results of the consistency checks. In addition, WEAR after consulting the student models infers and records in instructor models the instructors' tendency to overestimate or underestimate the level of difficulty they assign to problems.

This user model is utilised by the system in the following ways:

Provide individualised help to the instructor. WEAR uses the instructor model in order to offer individualised help to the instructor with respect to his/her teaching strategies. For example, if an instructor has stated a long-term goal that s/he wishes to render the course popular within the class students then the authoring tool will examine whether the instructor's short term goals are consistent with his/her long-term goals and let him/her know accordingly. Student models provide information about how many students have attempted certain exercises and how many times they have seen certain lectures. This information is used to let the instructor know how well s/he does with his/her predefined teaching strategy. Similarly, if an instructor has been recorded in his/her long-term model as having the tendency to overestimate or underestimate the level of difficulty of problems, s/he will be reminded of that by the authoring tool when inserting new problems.

Adapt the interaction with its users. When a user wishes to find a problem and decides to browse the available categories, s/he will see that in the categories' list the ones that s/he frequently explores are pre-selected for him/her by the system. Of course, the instructor is free to select some other categories as well, or even ignore the already selected ones. In addition, if new problems belonging to the categories that a particular user is interested in are added, the system informs him/her when s/he logs in.

Promote co-operative or collaborative work among instructors. Users are offered the choice of seeing what other users have done along two dimensions: the course structure and the constructed problems. Concerning the former, the information that is presented to the instructor is the structure of a similar course created by another instructor. The similarity of courses is calculated in terms of the domain to which they belong and in terms of the difficulty level assigned to them by their authors. In particular, the instructor may see an enriched Table of Contents presenting not only the topic hierarchy but also the relationships between topics. In that way, instructors who may be novice as course designers could be assisted by more experienced peers who have previously used WEAR. When selecting to see problems constructed by others, the instructor is presented with a list of problems constructed by users who are considered by the system as "major contributors" in the categories that this specific user is considered "interested". In addition, while an instructor is constructing a new problem by himself/herself the system is checking whether there is any similar problem already constructed by another instructor who is considered "major contributor". If this is the case, the instructor is offered the choice to see the similar problems and use them instead of completing the construction of his/her own. In that way, the system avoids the repetition of problems, facilitates the instructors' work and advances the co-operation and collaboration among them.

5   WEAR's Operation for the Student

Each student is assigned a level of knowledge by the system according to his/her past performance in solving problems with the tool. WEAR adaptively annotates the links to the problems that a student sees based on the student's "level of knowledge" and the "level of difficulty" that is assigned to each problem by the instructor. This is done in order to facilitate the student's choice about which problem to solve next resulting in adaptive navigation support [2]. In a similar manner WEAR provides adaptive navigation support to students concerning the topics that they should study.

When a student attempts to solve a problem the system provides an environment where the student gives the solution step by step. At first the student is presented with a problem statement such as: "The annoying sound from a mosquito is produced when it beats its wings at the average rate of 600 wingbeats per second. What is the frequency in Hertz of the sound wave? Assuming the sound wave moves with a velocity of 340 m/s, what is the wavelength of the wave?"[1]. The student is requested to write down the equations that are needed to solve the problem and then s/he is requested to mathematically solve the problem. To detect the erroneous answers the system compares the student's solution to its own at every step. The system's solution is generated by the domain knowledge about algebraic equations and about the specific domain where the problem belongs to (e.g. physics). During the process of solving a problem the student's actions are monitored by the system. In case of an erroneous action, the diagnostic component of WEAR attempts to diagnose the cause of it.

6   Student Modelling

A "history mechanism" embodied in WEAR records certain student features that have been inferred during past interactions, such as persistence of a certain type of error (e.g. mathematical error). These features form the long-term student model [7; 8] which represents the student's knowledge both in the domain being taught and in solving linear equations. This student model is a combination of a stereotype and an overlay student model. The stereotype student model (formed either directly by the instructor or after a preliminary test posed to the student) classifies initially the student according to his/her knowledge of the domain and his/her mathematical skills. As a result of this, the student is assigned to a stereotype (novice, beginner, intermediate, or expert). For example, a student may be assigned to the stereotype "expert" for his/her mathematical skills and to "beginner" for his/her knowledge of the

---

[1] This example problem statement is taken from:
   http://www.glenbrook.k12.il.us/gbssci/phys/Class/waves/u10l2e.html

domain taught. The stereotype model also defines initial values for the overlay student model. The latter is represented by a set of pairs "concept-value" which are explained below.

The concepts are domain concepts and concepts concerning the process of solving equations (e.g. separating known from the unknown). Domain concepts include domain variables. For example, in the domain of Physics the variables "Velocity", "Force", etc. are seen as concepts. It is assumed by the system that a student knows a concept if in a given problem that this variable-concept is needed, s/he enters the correct equation that defines this variable. The value for each concept is an estimation of the student's knowledge level of this concept.

The student model is used by the system in various ways. There are cases when an error that a student makes can be attributed to more than one cause. In such cases the student model that holds information concerning the student's tendency to particular types of error is used to resolve the ambiguity as to what the cause of the error has been. In addition, the student model is used to form individualised progress reports of the student, which could be requested by the student and/or the instructor, as well as to provide adaptive navigation support to students concerning which problem to solve next and which topic to study. Furthermore, student models are used by the system to inform the instructor about problematic situations (e.g. when the majority of students fail to comprehend something, as may be indicated by their low scores in the corresponding tests). Finally, student models provide evidence as to whether the instructor's long-term goals (popularity and/or difficulty of the course) are far from being achieved or not.

7   Interaction between Student and Instructor Models

As already discussed in the above sections, instructor and student models acquire information about instructors and students respectively, in an explicit and implicit manner. An important source for the implicit acquisition of information for the model of each class is the model of the other class of user. This is done so that each class of user may receive help and feedback taking into account the relevant issues that are determined by the other class.

In the case of instructor modelling, student models provide information about how many problems the students have attempted to solve and how many times they have visited certain topics of the teaching material. This information is used to let the instructor know how well s/he does with his/her predefined goal of popularity of the course.

Another issue that concerns the instructor model comes up while students are tackling the given problems. In this case, the system collects evidence about the level of difficulty of these problems so that it can provide feedback to the instructor. For example, if the majority of the students of a certain level have failed in solving a particular problem, which has been assigned by the instructor to this level, then the instructor is informed. In a case like this, perhaps the instructor may wish to reconsider the level of difficulty since there is evidence that the problem may be of a higher level of difficulty. On the other hand, if many students have managed to solve a problem of a higher level of difficulty than the one proposed by the instructor, the level of difficulty may have been overestimated by the instructor. In this case too, the system informs the instructor. In both cases, the tool does not take the initiative to alter the level of difficulty by itself: it suggests the instructor to increase or decrease this measure according to the observed students' performance in a specific problem. In this way an instructor is being assisted by the system in the classification of problems.

Finally, instructor models hold information about the instructors' contribution to particular categories of problem. For an instructor to be considered a "major contributor" in a specific area, s/he should have created many problems in that area and these problems must have been solved by a number of students. This information is again provided by the student models.

In the case of student modelling, the students' level of knowledge is affected both by the domain and mathematical errors that they may make. The students' level of knowledge is calculated taking into account the instructor's preference to assign more weight to one or the other category of error. In this way the instructor model affects the student modelling procedure.

Another piece of information that is implicitly passed from the instructor model to the student model concerns the level of difficulty of the course. In particular, students have the choice of seeing what their level of knowledge is, not only in absolute terms but also in relation to the level of difficulty of the course, as stated by the instructor when defining his/her long-term goals. For example, a student's performance in a course may be average instead of very good due to the fact that the instructor's goal was to create a quite difficult course. Having the ability to see his/her real knowledge level and also a knowledge level affected in some way by the course's level of difficulty, the student can better realise where s/he stands in the domain being taught.

8   Conclusions

In this paper we presented WEAR, a Web-based authoring tool for Intelligent Tutoring Systems in Algebra related domains, and focussed on its user modelling capabilities. In WEAR we model two classes of user: the students and the instructors - unlike most ITS authoring tools that only model the students. We argued that an instructor modelling component may render the system more flexible and adaptable to particular instructors' interests and needs. Moreover, we discussed an issue that we consider important: the interaction between the instructor and student models. Information stored in student models is passed either to the instructor himself/herself or to his/her user model. The same happens with instructor models that pass information to students and student models. What motivated us to implement this information exchange between user models, was the observation that in a real one-to-one tutoring setting, both students and instructors build models of each other and based on that models they adjust the way they respond during the learning process.

From an empirical study we conducted involving both students and instructors, there is strong evidence that the user modelling mechanisms that WEAR embodies may be really in favour of both classes of user. However, in the near future we plan to evaluate WEAR in whole and especially the user modelling aspects discussed in this paper.

References

1. Bloom, B.: The 2 sigma problem: The search for methods of instruction as effective as one-to-one tutoring. Educational Researcher. 13(6) (1984) 4-16
2. Brusilovsky, P.: Methods and techniques of adaptive hypermedia. User Modeling and User-Adapted Interaction. 6 (2-3) (1996) 87-129
3. Harvey, C.F., Smith, P. & Lund, P.: Providing a networked future for interpersonal information retrieval: InfoVine and user modelling. Interacting with Computers. 10 (1998) 195-212
4. Kinshuk & Patel, A.: Intelligent Tutoring Tools: Redesigning ITSs for Adequate Knowledge Transfer Emphasis. In Lucas, C. (ed.): Proceedings of 1996 International Conference on Intelligent and Cognitive Systems IPM, Tehran (1996) 221-226
5. Koedinger, K.R. & Anderson, J.R.: Intelligent Tutoring Goes to School in the Big City. International Journal of Artificial Intelligence in Education . 8 (1997) 30-43
6. Murray, T.: Authoring Intelligent Tutoring Systems: An analysis of the state of the art. International Journal of Artificial Intelligence in Education . 10 (1999) 98-129
7. Rich, E.: User Modelling via Stereotypes. Cognitive Science. 3 (4) (1979) 329-354
8. Rich, E.: Users as Individuals: Individualizing User Models. International Journal of Man-Machine Studies. 18 (1983) 199-214
9. Shute, V., Glaser, R. & Raghaven, K.: Inference and Discovery in an Exploratory Laboratory. In Ackerman, P.L., Sternberg, R.J. & Glaser, R. (eds.): Learning and Individual Differences. Freeman, San Francisco (1989) 279-326
10. Virvou, M. & Moundridou, M.: A Web-Based Authoring Tool for Algebra-Related Intelligent Tutoring Systems. Educational Technology & Society. 3(2) (2000) 61-70
11. Virvou, M. & Moundridou, M.: Modelling the instructor in a Web-based authoring tool for Algebra-related ITSs. In Gauthier, G., Frasson, C. & VanLehn, K. (eds.): Intelligent Tutoring Systems, Proceedings of the 5th International Conference on Intelligent Tutoring Systems, ITS 2000 Lecture Notes in Computer Science, Vol. 1839. Springer, Berlin (2000) 635-644

METIORE:
A Personalized Information Retrieval System

David Bueno[1] and Amos A. David[2]

[1] Department of Languages and Computer Science, University of Má laga,
29071, Má laga, Spain
bueno@lcc.uma.es
[2] LORIA, BP 239, 54506 Vandoeuvre, France
adavid@loria.fr

Abstract. The idea of personalizing the interactions of a system is not new. With stereotypes the users are grouped into classes where all the users in a class have similar characteristics. Personalization was therefore not on individual basis but on a group of users. Personalized systems are also used in Intelligent Tutoring Systems (ITS) and in information filtering. In ITS, the pedagogical activities of a learner is personalized and in information filtering, the long-term stable information need of the user is used to filter incoming new information. We propose an explicit individual user model for representing the user's activities during information retrieval. One of the new ideas here is that personalization is really individualized and linked with the user's objective, that is his information need. Our proposals are implemented in the prototype METIORE for providing access to the publications in our laboratory. This prototype was experimented and we present in this paper the first results of our observation.

1 Introduction

The idea of personalizing the interactions of a system is not new. One of the approaches is the concept of stereotype [16; 17]. With stereotypes the users are grouped into classes where all the users in a class have similar characteristics. Systems interaction and response are based on the knowledge of the characteristics of the users in a class. Personalization was therefore not on an individual basis but on a group of users. This approach was however refined to take into consideration information that is specific to a particular user. This concept has been implemented in many systems in many application areas. In the area of Intelligent Help System, the concept was used in the Unix Consultant, KNOME [8] for the use of Unix. KNOME provides answers according to the stereotype where the system had placed that user after a few interactions. Other personalized systems in the area of ITS are ELM-ART [6; 21] and InterBook [5; 7]. A lot of work has also been done in the area of Information Filtering, from personalized newspaper [3; 9], news filters [4] or e-mail filtering.

The techniques used in Information Filtering can be easily adopted in Information Retrieval because these two fields are very close as [13] said, "The information

M. Bauer, P.J. Gmytrasiewicz, and J. Vassileva (Eds.): UM 2001, LNAI 2109, pp. 168–177, 2001.
ⒸSpringer-Verlag Berlin Heidelberg 2001

filtering problem can be seen as a information retrieval process, where the user has a number of long-term queries". Most of our ideas have therefore been used either in tutoring or in information filtering systems.

Our proposals have been implemented in a prototype called METIORE. The system allows users to access the bibliographic references of research publications available at the library of the computer laboratory center LORIA, France. In the following sections, we first present the functional characteristics of METIORE followed by a description of our user model. We have also carried out an experimentation of the prototype. Our observation during this experimentation is presented in section 4 before presenting a brief conclusion and our prospective. Most of the examples we give in this paper are from METIORE.

2   The Functional Characteristics of METIORE

For a better understanding of how personalization is done in METIORE, we first present in this section the main functional characteristics of the system.

2.1 The User's Objective

When the user launches the system we ask him to specify his objective for the session. The use of the system for a given objective is considered a session. Also in WebWatcher [1] the concept of objective (also called goal) is used. In their approach, the keywords of the goal are used to look for the links that the system will propose to the user as interesting. For us the objective is the expression of the user's information need formulated in natural language. Presently, we do not process the text in natural language to extract the keywords even though it constitutes our research objective in order to calculate similarities between objectives. The objective is presently used to group the set of queries, concepts and decisions that the user makes on the system having the objective in mind. Our hypothesis is that grouping the user's interactions into objectives will help the user to find information in his history and help the system to build a specific model of the user from one or more sessions. Our approach of personalization is based on this concept of objective. Every aspect of the system is organized around the system's proposals and the user's interactions.

This concept is very important to us since we believe that every user has a minimum knowledge of his information needs before attempting to use an IRS. This knowledge can of course be improved with the use of the system and with a consequence on the user's ability to express his information need through the system's interaction. For us, the queries do not necessarily express all the information needs of the user but rather his approach towards solving the problem of his information needs.

2.2 The Search Functions

For the user to obtain solutions to his information needs, we provide several search functions in the system. The search interface allows the user to make simple or complex queries. Search queries are defined using the attributes of a publication such as title, authors, year, keywords, etc. One of the problems in IRS is that information retrieval is content based. This means that a user must have minimum information on what he is looking for. In order to ease this form of query, we provide search characteristics that allow the user to discover the contents of any attribute of the publications. For example, the user can specify only one attribute and the system will provide the values used for the attribute as well as the associated references.

The equation of a query is (attribute1 [attribute2 [,attribute3]]; {constraints})   where attribute1, attribute2, attribute3   are any of the attributes of a publication and constraints are conditions to be satisfied by the publications. For example attribute1=author, attribute2=author, Author=John   provides the list of co-authors and their number of publications in which one of the authors is John. The attributes and the selector of constraints are the same (author, keyword, year, editor...).

2.3 The Results of a Query

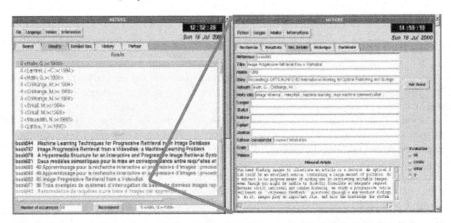

Fig. 1. The two result windows: a) General result with menus in English (left) b) Detailed result with menus in French (right)

The result of a query is displayed in a general result window (Fig. 1.a). It is composed of a list of clusters with their frequencies. For our example (attribute1=author, attribute2=year; keywords=retrieval)   the result, as commented before, has the frequency and the instance of the two attributes (see Fig. 1.a). For example "9 <Halin G><1989>" means that Halin G had 9 publications in 1989. When the user selects one of the clusters, its components are shown in the down side of the window. The list is sorted using the personalization algorithm that will be explained with the user model. After going through the titles of the solutions, the user can select one of them to see it in detail as shown in the window of Fig. 1.b It is in this window where the user can give his feedback that will be used to update the user model. In the next subsections we will explain the meaning of the feedback and the importance of the color codes used for the list of solutions.

Feedback. The user's feedback is based on the various reasons for accepting or refusing a solution. This is different from the classical types of feedback restricted to interesting/not interesting as in [18] or like the proposal in [2] where the possible evaluations are interesting/not interesting or indifferent. In these classical types of feedback the reasons for the user's decisions are not known. The following four types of feedback are implemented presently in our applications:

- The solution is relevant (ok). This means that the solution is valid for the user.
- The solution is not relevant because the user knows it already (known). This means that the solution is interesting for this objective but already known.
- No opinion on the relevance of the solution (?). This evaluation applies to the case where the user is unable to give another judgment on the solution.
- The solution is not relevant because it doesn't correspond to the user's objective (wrong). The user judges the solution as irrelevant to his objective.

Also we have:

- Unvisited solution (normal). This is the default evaluation for all proposed solution to signify unvisited.

Color Codes. Brusilovsky [5] justified the utilization of link annotation (equivalent to our color codes) through experiments done with their system InterBook. This system is also used in the lisp tutorial ELM-ART [6; 21]. The use of this kind of annotation makes the user feel that there is some extra help in his interactions with the system, even if a "cognitive overhead may distract users from the content" [5]. In our case we also use this kind of annotation for all the documents proposed as solution to a query. We try to give additional and visual help to the user so that he can know the documents that he had already evaluated and how he had evaluated them in relation to the present objective. Document that have never been evaluated by the user are also presented in color code with the degree of relevance calculated by the system.

2.4 The History of the User's Activities

The user can exploit his past history. The concept of history is also presented in [11] but in our model we sort the history by the user's past objectives and evaluations. The exploitation of the user's history constitutes for us another category of activity. Through this category, the user can review his past objectives, the associated solutions and his evaluations associated with each solution. This category of activity may be used for several reasons: a) Recollect past solutions b) Modify the evaluations of past solutions, c) Look for already presented objects in order to find related ones c) Analyze past solutions for some past objectives and the current one.

3   The User Model

If we want a system to give personalized responses, it's necessary to have a model that can represent explicitly and individually each user. One of the most difficult tasks is therefore to identify the most important parameters for representing a user and to what extent personalization is envisaged. We present in the next two sections the components of our model and the algorithm that we use to exploit it for personalization.

3.1 The Parameters of the User Model

In the user model of METIORE we have some general information about the user, such as his personal data (name, login, language of the interface, default mode, etc...). To obtain the real user preference for documents in the model we keep for each objective all the documents evaluated with their evaluation. Each document has some features that represent it (keywords, author, year, etc...). They inherit the evaluation of the document that contains them. This information will be very important for the personalization algorithm.

3.2 Algorithm for Personalization

The problem that we want to solve is a problem of classification. When the user makes a query, we want to sort the solution in the order of his preferences, giving the most relevant solution at the beginning. To do that for each document, that is the result of the query, the system will look for the class of evaluation that is more suited to this document. To make this classification, each document must be parameterized. The selection of parameters for the documents is also an important task. Many systems use only keywords but other parameters can be as important to take into account, like the year, the author or even the journal of publication. Lantz [13] has also analyzed this problem in information filtering. In our system, the number of parameters to use can be configured.

In our user model, we keep the documents evaluated (separately for each objective). Also after each evaluation of the user, for each parameter that belongs to the document evaluated, we increment the value of this evaluation by one. In Fig. 2 is shown the way the parameters are represented. For example, an objective could have the attribute keyword with the value UM and the evaluations 5 3 0 5 that will mean the number of times that some document that contains this keyword has been evaluated as ok, known, ?, wrong respectively. Using those values, we calculate the relevance degree of the document using the algorithm that we explain below.

```
{objective1 {attribute1 {value ev1 ev2 ev3 ev4} {value ...}} ...
        {attributen {...}}} ...
{objectivem {attribute1 {value ev1 ev2 ev3 ev4} {value ...}}...
        {attribute        n {...}}}
```

Fig. 2. User evaluation history

Many studies have been done to compare the different methods of classification: Neural Network, ID3 and Bayesian. Most of them have a high complexity. However, naive Bayes, even with its simplicity, due to the assumption of independence between parameters, is able to give similar results and sometimes better than the others with a much simpler calculation. Those comparisons are done in [10; 12; 15; 19], and others versus Winnow and Rocchio algorithms can be found in [20].

Our algorithm is based on the Naive Bayes theory using the precedent evaluations of the user. As stated earlier, the result of the algorithm will be the degree of relevance of an object to the present objective for a user   . In other words, we try to calculate the probability of the user giving a particular type of evaluation for a given object in the context of the present objective. With this objective in mind we use an adaptation of Naive Bayesian Algorithm [13] to our specific objective. The original formula is shown in (1)

$$P(C/V_{i,J_1},...,V_{n,J_n})=P(C)\prod_{i=1}^{n}Q_i(C,J_i) \tag{1}$$

Where

$$Q_i(C,J_i)=\frac{P(V_{i,J_i}|C)}{P(V_{i,J_i})} \tag{2}$$

In (1) and (2), C is one of the possible classes (ok, known, ?, wrong). V_{iJi} is a Boolean variable with value 1 if the current instance has value J_i and P(C) is the probability of the class C. For example, if the keyword retrieval (J_i) appears in the document the algorithm calculates Q(ok, retrieval). Equation (1) is only valid if the possible attributes are independent, as we assume in our case.

The modification of equation (1) that we propose gives similar results but is less restrictive because we use the average of the weights of each attribute as shown in (3). This reduces the impact of probability 0 for new attributes. The results that we obtain will be already normalized (0-1) with the characteristic that equation (4) is true and we will use this value as the percentage of relevance of the results.

$$P(C/V_1,J_1,...,V_n,J_n)=P(C)\frac{\sum_{i=1}^{n}Q_i(C,J_i)}{n} \tag{3}$$

$$\sum_i P(C/V_{i,J_1},...,V_{n,J_n})=1 \tag{4}$$

Having those values, we can now show to the user, the list of articles sorted in the next steps.

1   We show the classes in the order of ok, known, ?, wrong
2   Inside each class, we put the documents already evaluated on top of the list
3   Then we put the documents that the algorithm has attached to this class, sorted by the values that they have obtained in (3).

4 Experimentation of METIORE

In this section we will explain our methods of evaluation and the first results that we obtained.

4.1 The Methods

One way of evaluating a system for personalized response is using the data that the system compiles after each of the user's interaction. This means that if the system proposes a solution, we can use as a measure, the percentage of success of this proposal. This kind of evaluation was employed in the personal assistant of Tom Mitchell [14]. We use this method to calculate the accuracy of the results from the point of view of the system. We present some of our hypothesis below. We use a questionnaire and also the information of the system to validate the answers of the users. The hypotheses are:

- The integration of the user's activities and its association with the objective for the calculation of solutions should give the solutions that the user will evaluate as more relevant.
- The exploration of the active history by the user should facilitate information retrieval and provide more relevant solutions
- When the user hasn't a history, the system can give help by the integration of the history of other users.
- The exploitation of the history of other users should also accelerate the access to relevant solutions
- The possibility of the user to give a feedback on the solutions should give a better understanding of his information need.
- The classification of the solutions by kind of evaluation and the association of color codes should facilitate the retrieval of solutions
- The possibility of a cooperative retrieval should help to accelerate the finding of relevant solutions.

4.2 The First Results

Low percentage of success with the system's recommendation does not necessarily signify a failure as indicated by Armstrong [1]: "Even a modest reduction in the number of hyperlinks considered at each page leads to an exponential improvement in the overall search". This sentence can be applied to our system in the sense that even if only a few of the recommendations are really interesting, that is much better than no recommendation at all. But with our experiments we realized that the results were much better than what we expected, as we will see now.

Our experiments have been done at the computer research laboratory LORIA in France. The database that we used was the database of the publications of this laboratory. The people that were involved in the experiment were 20 Ph. D. students and research members of the laboratory. The experimentation was carried out over three months, divided into sessions of about one hour. The experimentation was also carried out in three phases: the phase of explanation of the functional characteristics of the prototype; the phase of independent use where users selected their own objectives and the phase of feedback with questionnaire.

To be able to generate statistics of the predictions of the system after each evaluation of the user, some information is kept by the system. We save the prediction that the system made for each document and the evaluation that the user made. It should be noted that at the beginning, the system hasn't enough information to recommend a document to the user and the system is not able to know if a given document would interest the user. This is when the prediction is considered as normal . Even in those cases the documents are relevant in a good number of cases.

	ok	known	bof	wrong
pok	30	8	9	13
pknown	21	7		
normal	14	14	0	8
pbof	8	8	8	
pwrong	10	0	7	13

% of evaluations	
ok	47%
known	21%
?	13%
wrong	19%

Fig. 3. Summary for all users interactions: a) Predictions vs. Real evaluations b) frequency of evaluations

The most interesting result of the evaluation is the final solution for all users. Fig. 3 presents a tabular representation for all the predictions made by the system and what the users really evaluated. From that we can conclude the following:

- The percentage of (ok/pok) is very interesting. 50% of the times that the system proposed a solution as correct, it was really correct for this user. 13,33% of the times that the system predicted that it will interest him and it is true but the user already knew that. That means that the 63,33% of the prediction of the system is correct. We consider this a good result.
- The prediction of known has a high evaluation as ok 75%. This can be considered reasonable because when a user evaluates a document as known it means that the document interests, and similar documents can also be interesting but perhaps are unknown.
- We have also observed during the experimentation that the number of successes increased over time. As we had suspected, the more the user uses the system, thus training the system on his preferences, the better the proposals he receives from the system.
- Another observation that could also explain the high percentage of good evaluated solutions is that most of the users accepted the recommendation of the system, and rarely they evaluate the suggested ones as wrong. This action can be a little dangerous at the beginning when the system doesn't have a lot of information about the user and the recommendations may not be accurate. That's why we have thought to put a threshold, such as a minimum number of evaluated solutions before which the system won't give any advice. This could be also configured.

The development of the questionnaire has also passed by a process of refinement through some initial tests. From the observation of the results of the questionnaires and the observation of the experiments we have also observed the following:

- Nearly all the users were satisfied with the solutions that the system gave them and they felt that the system had learnt their objective. In particular, some users at the end of the evaluation asked for automatic recommendation without making any query

- We thought at the beginning that giving the feedback on all proposed documents would be a task that the users wouldn't like. Many of them had commented that giving feedback to the system is the only way to get the most correct assistance. So they didn't hesitate to do it.
- Mostly the regular users have used the active history and they found it an interesting tool. But the first time users (or users of only a few sessions) couldn't appreciate its utility.

5   Conclusions

We have presented in this paper how personalization is carried out through the use of a user model. We also presented the algorithm used for this personalization. The prototype METIORE, in which our proposals have been implemented, was briefly presented and our observations during the experimentation to evaluate the performance of the system were summarized.

We noticed that the first phase of the experimentation in which we explained the functional characteristics of the prototype was decisive. We thought that we would need thirty minutes to explain them but an average of ten to fifteen minutes was sufficient. Unfortunately, this observation cannot be generalized because we had users that are already familiar with the user of graphic user interface. We therefore intend to continue our experimentation in a university library where many users are not familiar with the use of graphic user interface.

We have observed that the algorithm for personalization was efficient and simple to implement. We have tested it on a database with about 5000 bibliographic references. We intend to test the system on a more important database and to compare it with other algorithms as the pure Naïve Bayes or random recommendations.

The objective provided by the user has not been fully exploited. We intend to apply natural language processing techniques on them in order to calculate the degree of similarity between two objectives. This approach can be used by the system for first time or casual users. We also intend to provide an interface to navigate through the objectives for long-term users that may have a long list of past objectives. The objectives are presently listed simply in the order in which they are given. Finally, we are making the system available on the network of our laboratory for the researchers to use for information access.

References

1. Armstrong, R., Freitag, D., Joachims, T., & Mitchell, T. (1995). "Webwatcher: A learning apprentice for the world wide web". AAAI Spring Symposium on Information Gathering from Heterogeneous Distributed Environments
2. Benaki, E., Karkaletsis, V. A., & Spyropoulos, C. D. (1997). "Integrating User Modeling Into Information Extraction: The UMIE Prototype". UM'97 . URL= http://um.org.
3. Billsus, D., & Pazzani, M. (1999). "A Hybrid User Model for News Story Classification". Proceedings of the Seventh International Conference on User Modeling (UM '99) Banff, Canada

4. Billsus, D., & Pazzani, M. (1999). "A Personal News Agent that Talks, Learns and Explains". Proceedings of the Third International Conference on Autonomous Agents (Agents '99) . URL= http://www.ics.uci.edu/~pazzani/Publications/agents99-news.pdf.
5. Brusilovsky, P., & Eklund, J. (1998). "A Study of User Model Based Link Annotation in Educational Hypermedia". Journal of Universal Computer Science, 4(4), 429-448
6. Brusilovsky, P., Schwarz, E., & Weber, G. (1996). "ELM-ART: An intelligent tutoring system on World Wide Web". Intelligent Tutoring Systems (pp. 261-269). BerlinIn Frasson, C., Gauthier, G., & Lesgold, A. (Eds.) Springer Verlag
7. Brusilovsky, P. (1996). "Methos and thecniques of adaptative hypermedia". UMUAI, 6(2-3), 87-129
8. Chin, D. N. (1989). "KNOME: Modeling What the User Knows in UC". User Models in Dialog Systems,
9. Kamba T. , & Bharat K. (1996). "An Interactive, Personalized Newspaper on WWW.". Multimedia Computing and Networking California
10. Keogh, E., & Pazzani, M. (1999). "Learning augmented Bayesian classifiers: A comparison of distribution-based and classification-based approaches.". Uncertainty 99, 7th. Int'l Workshop on AI and Statistics, (pp. 225-230). Ft. Lauderdale, Florida
11. Kobsa, A., Nill, A., & Dietmar MIler. (1996). "KN-AHN: An Adaptative Hypertext Client of the User Modeling System BGP-MS". Review of Information Science 1(1). URL= http://www.inf-wiss.uni-konstanz/RIS.
12. Kononenko, I. (1990). "Comparison of Inductive and Naive Bayesian Learning Approaches to Automatic Knowledge Acquisition". Current Trends in Knowledge Adquisition, 190-197
13. Lantz, A., & Kilander F. (1995). "Intelligent Filtering; Based on Keywords Only? ". Computer Human Interaction (CHI'95)
14. Mitchell, T., Caruana, R., McDermott, J., & Zabowski D. (1994). " Experience With a Learning Personal Assistant". Communications of the ACM, 37(7)
15. Mitchell, T. M. (1997). "Machine Learning". The McGraw-Hill Companies, Inc.
16. Rich E. (1979). "User Modeling via Stereotypes". International Journal of Cognitive Science, 3, 329-354
17. Rich, E. (1983). "Users are individuals: individualizing user models". Int. J. Man-Machine Studies, 18, 199-214
18. Schwab I. , & Pohl W. (1999). "Learning Information Interest from Positive Examples". User Modeling (UM'99)
19. Singh, M., & Provan, G. M. (1996). "Efficient learning of selective Bayesian network classifiers". . Proceedings of the 13th International Conference on Machine Learning
20. Versteegen, L. (2000). "The Simple Bayesian Classifier as a Classification Algorithm". URL= http://www.cs.kun.nl/nsccs/artikelen/leonv.ps.Z.
21. Weber, G., & Specht, M. (1997). "User modeling and adaptive navigation support in WWW-based tutoring systems". (pp. 289-300). Wien Springer-Verlag

Personalizing Delivered Information in a Software Reuse Environment

Gerhard Fischer[1] and Yunwen Ye[1,2]

[1] Center for LifeLong Learning and Design, Department of Computer Science
University of Colorado, Boulder, Colorado 80309-0430, USA
Tel: +1-303-492-1502 Fax: +1-303-492-2844
{gerhard, yunwen   }@cs.colorado.edu
[2] Software Research Associates, Inc., 3-12 Yotsuya, Tokyo 160-0004, Japan

Abstract. Browsing- and querying-oriented schemes have long served as the principal techniques for software developers to locate software components from a component repository for reuse. Unfortunately, the problem remains that software developers simply will not actively search for components when they are unaware that they need components or that relevant components even exist. Thus, to assist software developers in making full use of large component repositories, information access need to be complemented by information delivery. Effective delivery of components calls for the personalization of the components to the task being performed and the knowledge of the user performing it. We have designed, implemented, and evaluated the CodeBroker system to support personalized component delivery to increase the usefulness of a Java software reuse environment.

Keywords: Task modeling, discourse modeling, user modeling, software reuse, information delivery.

1 Introduction

Browsing- and querying-oriented schemes have long served as the principal techniques for people to retrieve information in many applications, including systems for locating software components and for exploring the World Wide Web. However, these conventional retrieval techniques do not scale up to large information stores. More innovative schemes, such as query by reformulation [18] and latent semantic analysis [10], have introduced new possibilities. Unfortunately, the problem remains that users simply will not actively search for information when they are unaware that they need the information or that relevant information even exists. Thus, to assist users in making full use of large information repositories, information access methods need to be complemented by information delivery methods.

Evidence exists that the lack of support for information delivery has long been a significant obstacle to the success of software reuse [5,19]. Before software developers can reuse components, they have to either know the components already or locate them quickly and easily. Component location is often supported by component repository systems, most of which, like other information systems, support browsing and querying only. They fall short in helping software developers who make no attempt to locate components [5]. Even if software developers are aware of the components, they may

M. Bauer, P.J. Gmytrasiewicz, and J. Vassileva (Eds.): UM 2001, LNAI 2109, pp. 178–187, 2001.

not be able to retrieve them because of the mismatch between the situation model and the system model [9]. The situation model refers to the understanding of the task by developers or users, and the system model refers to the names and descriptions of components in repository systems, which are predetermined by system designers. Instead of passively waiting to be discovered, component repository systems need to be more active in supporting reuse by delivering potentially reusable components to software developers when they are engaged in development activities.

2 Information Delivery Systems

High-Functionality Applications.   Component repository systems are high-functionality applications (HFAs) [3]; they often include thousands of components and evolve quickly. The design of HFAs must address two problems: (1) the unused functionality must not get in the way, and (2) unknown existing functionality must be accessible or delivered when it is needed.

Most current component repository systems are passive, meaning users (software developers) have to initiate the search process through information access methods— either browsing or querying—to locate components. These passive systems are designed under the assumption that users are aware of their information needs and that they know how to ask for it. Our empirical studies have shown, however, that a user's knowledge on an HFA does not match the system itself. Typically, a user has four levels of knowledge in an HFA:

- level 1 knowledge (L1): elements are well known and regularly used;
- level 2 knowledge (L2): elements are known vaguely and used occasionally;
- level 3 knowledge (L3): elements are believed to exist in the system;
- level 4 knowledge (L4): all elements of the system.

Elements falling in the area L4 – L3 become information islands, and passive systems cannot help users to find them because their existence is not even known [19]. Information delivery, a method by which the system initiates the information search process and volunteers information to users, can build a bridge to the information islands. Moreover, compared with passive systems, information delivery systems make it easier for users to locate information in L3.

The Limitations of Task- and User-Independent Information Delivery Systems.
Systems that just throw a piece of decontextualized information at users are of little use because they ignore the working context. The working context consists of the task being performed and the user performing it. The challenge for information delivery is to deliver context-sensitive, or personalized, information, related to both the task at hand and the background knowledge of the user. Task- and user-independent information delivery systems (or "push" systems) such as Microsoft's "Tip of the Day" suffer from the problem that concepts get thrown at users in a decontextualized way. Despite the possibility for interesting serendipitous encounters of information, most users find this feature more annoying than helpful.

CodeBroker—An Active Component Repository System.   We have designed, implemented, and evaluated an active component repository system, named CodeBroker, that supports information delivery [20]. CodeBroker delivers task-relevant and user-specific components to Java developers by (1) constructing a task model to capture the programming task through continuously monitoring the programming activities in a software development environment, (2) identifying the domain of users' current interest by creating a discourse model based on the interaction history between the system and the user, and (3) creating a user model to represent each user's knowledge about the repository to assure that only unknown components are delivered.

3   Task-Relevant Component Delivery

General Approaches to Task Modeling.   Tasks can be modeled through either plan recognition or similarity analysis [4,6]. The plan recognition approach uses plans to specify the link from a series of primitive user actions to the goal of a task. When actions of a user match the action part of a plan, the system deems the user to be performing the corresponding task, and information about the task is delivered. The similarity analysis approach examines the self-revealing information in the context surrounding the current focus of users and uses that information to predict their needs for new information. The system then delivers information from the repository that has high similarity to the contextual circumstance. Plan recognition-based task modeling systems are difficult to scale up because it is difficult to create plans. Unlike plan recognition, by which the system tries to infer the task goal, the similarity analysis approach matches a task to the information sharing the same contextual circumstances.

Task Modeling in CodeBroker.   CodeBroker adopts similarity analysis to find relevant components. It utilizes the descriptive elements of programs and finds components that have similar descriptions. A program has three aspects: concept, code, and constraint. The concept of a program is its functional purpose, or goal; the code is the embodiment of the concept; and the constraint regulates the environment in which the program runs.

Important concepts of a program are often contained in its informal information, such as comments and identifier names that are important beacons for program comprehension [19]. Modern programming languages such as Java further enforce the inclusion of self-explaining informal information by introducing the concept of doc comments. A doc comment begins with "/** " and continues until the next "*/ ". Contents inside doc comments describe the functionality of the following module, either a class or a method.

Constraints of a program are captured by its signature. A signature defines the syntactic interface of a program by specifying the types of input and output data. For a component to be easily integrated, its signature should be compatible with the environment in which it will be incorporated.

CodeBroker models tasks by extracting doc comments and signatures of the program under development. It tries to find relevant components with similar concepts and constraints. Relevance of components to the task at hand is determined by the combination of concept similarity and constraint compatibility. Concept similarity is the similarity existing from the concept of the current task, revealed through comments and identifiers, to the concept revealed in the documents of components in the repository. Constraint compatibility is the type compatibility existing from the signature of the program under development to the signatures of repository components.

Concept similarity is computed by Latent Semantic Analysis (LSA) [10]. After being trained with a large volume of domain-specific documents, the semantic space created by LSA for that domain can capture the latent semantic association among words, and thus it bridges the gap between the situation model and the system model [9]. Constraint compatibility is computed by signature matching. Two signatures match if their input types and output types are both in structural conformance [19]. Figure 1 shows

Fig. 1. Task-relevant delivery of components. Components delivered when a doc comment is entered (a) or a signature is defined (b). The third component in (a) has a similar concept but incompatible signature (shown in the mini-buffer). The delivery in (b) is based on the task model including both doc comments and signatures, and its first component matches the task.

an example of task-relevant delivery of components. A programmer wants to create a random number between two integers, and expresses his task in the doc comment: Create a random number between two limits   . The comment serves as a task model, based on which the system delivers several components (Fig. 1a). However, the task model is not complete because it does not say the method must take two integers as input. When the signature (int x int -> int   ) is defined (Fig. 1b), the system acquires a more precise task model combining both the concept (doc comment) and the constraint (signature), and gives a better delivery. In Fig. 1b, the first delivered component matches the task and can be immediately used.

Developing a Discourse Model through Retrieval by Reformulation.   The components delivered solely based on the task model may not be precise enough. First, because the task model is not directly represented—a direct representation is the program code—it is partial and biased. Second, doc comments do not always reflect what software developers want to do. Similarly, descriptions of components in the repository are not complete and precise enough, either.

CodeBroker supports retrieval by reformulation [18] to complement the impreciseness of task models. Retrieval by reformulation is a dynamic, interactive information location approach that allows users to develop their queries incrementally [18]. After evaluating the delivered components, software developers can either refine the query or directly manipulate the delivered components.

Through direct manipulation of each delivered component, software developers can tell the system explicitly what does not interest them currently. In CodeBroker, each delivered component is associated with the Skip Components Menu   (Fig. 2), which has three items: the component itself, its class, and its package. If the developer does not want to have the method, or all the components in the class or the package, delivered again in this development session because they are irrelevant to the current project, the developer can choose the appropriate item and then the This Session Only command. Then the system will remove the method or all methods from the class or the package from automatic delivery. Direct manipulation can incrementally create, between

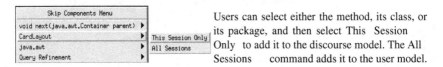

Users can select either the method, its class, or its package, and then select This Session Only to add it to the discourse model. The All Sessions   command adds it to the user model.

Fig. 2. The Skip Components Menu

the developer and the system, a shared understanding of the larger context of the current task. Components in a repository are organized in hierarchy according to their application domains (packages) and inheritance relationship. Most projects need only a part of the repository. If the system knows in which part the developer is currently interested, it can deliver more relevant information.

This shared understanding of a developer's current interest is captured in discourse models. A discourse model represents the previous interactions between the user and the system in one development session and serves as a filter to remove irrelevant components in later deliveries in the same development session. It also reduces the delivery of irrelevant components caused by polysemy—a difficult problem for any information retrieval system—by limiting searching domains because polysemous words often have different meanings in totally different domains. For example, if the programming task is to shuffle a deck of cards, the developer may use the word "card" in doc comments. That would make the system deliver components from the class java.awt.CardLayout   , a GUI class in which "card" means a graphical element. If the project does not involve interface building, this whole class is irrelevant. Developers can add the class or even the whole package (java.awt   ) to the discourse model to prevent components of it from being delivered in the development session.

```
;; Discourse model for the session started at Thu Nov 2 08:53:12 2000.
(("java.util.zip") ;; Package added at Thu Nov 2 08:55:53.
 ("java.awt" ("CardLayout"))) ;; Class added at Thu Nov 2 09:20:30.
```

Fig. 3. A discourse model, which is a Lisp list of items with the format: (package-name (class-name (method-name)))   . An empty class-name   or method-name   area indicates the whole package or class should not be delivered in this development session.

A discourse model in CodeBroker is in the format of a Lisp association list (Fig. 3). Every development session starts with an empty discourse model, and its contents are gradually added by developers, during the use of the system, through the Skip Components Menu   (Fig. 2).

4   User-Specific Component Delivery

Information delivery [3] is meant to inform software developers of those components that they do not know. Therefore, the system needs to know what they know already. We use user models to represent software developers' knowledge about the component repository. User models in CodeBroker are both adaptable and adaptive [2,17].

User Models in CodeBroker.   A user model in CodeBroker contains a list of components known to the software developer (Fig. 4). Each item in the list is a package, a class, or a method. Each component retrieved from the component repository is looked up in the user model before it is delivered. If a method component matches a method in the user model, and the user model indicates that the developer has used it more than three times (adjustable by developers), the system assumes the developer knows it already and removes it from the delivery. If the method has no use-time   , it means the method was added by the developer, who had claimed he or she had known it very well and did not want it delivered. If the class of the method (which has no method list in the user model), or the package of the method (which has no class list) is included in the user model, the method is also removed.

Adaptable User Models.   Software developers can explicitly update their user models through interactions with CodeBroker. If they find one known component is delivered, they can click the component to bring up the Skip Components Menu   (Fig. 2), where they can choose one abstraction level (method, class, or package) and then select the All Sessions   command. The method (or its class or package) will be added to the user model. User-added components have no use-time   field (Fig. 4).

Adaptive User Models.   Due to the large volume of components and the constantly evolving nature of repository systems, for software developers to maintain their user models is a time-consuming task. Therefore, user models in CodeBroker are adaptive. CodeBroker continuously monitors developers' actions in the development environment. Whenever a method component from the repository is used by the developer, the system adds the component with the current time as use-time   to the user model. The system adds only methods to the user model; it does not add classes or packages because the use of a class or a package does not mean that the developer knows the whole class or package.

```
;; user model for Jeff
(
("java.applet"
    ("Applet"
        ("getParameterInfo")) ;; Added by Jeff at Thu 2 08:20:10 2000
)
("java.io"
    ("File"
        ("exists" "Thu Nov 2 08:35:49 2000" "Nov 2 08:15:10 2000" "Nov 2 08:10:22 2000")
        ("isAbsolute" "Thu Nov 2 08:36:31 2000" "Nov 2 08:19:15 2000" "Nov 2 08:20:21 2000"))
    ("CharArrayWriter"
        ("toCharArray")) ;; Added by Jeff at Thu 2 09:00:11 2000
)
("java.net") ;; Added by Jeff at Thu 2 09:15:11 2000
)
```

Fig. 4. A user model, which is a list of items with the format: (package-name (class-name (method-name use-time use-time ...)))   . When the use of a component is detected by the system, it is added to the list with the current time as use-time   . If the component is added by the user, there is no use-time   . As with discourse models, an empty class-name   or method-name   area means the whole package or class is included.

Initialization of User Models. Initial user models are created by analyzing the programs that software developers have written so far. CodeBroker analyzes those programs to extract each component used, and if the component is contained in the indexed component repository, it is added to the initial user model with the program modification time as the use-time   .

5   Related Work

CodeBroker builds upon our previous experience with critiquing systems [4] that model tasks by plan recognition to give feedback to users who have developed a suboptimal solution. CodeBroker tries to predict information needs and provide feedforward [16] for users so that they can avoid suboptimal solutions. Some information agents also aim to provide feedforward. For example, Remembrance Agent [15] augments human memory by autonomously displaying old emails and notes relevant to the email being written by the user. Letizia [11] assists users in browsing the WWW by suggesting and displaying relevant web pages. By observing the programmer's Java programming, Expert Finder [11] can refer the programmer to expert helpers who display significant experience in the area in which the programmer is troubled.

Research on component repository systems has mostly focused on the retrieval mechanism only, aiming to improve the relevance of retrieved components to the query submitted by users. The retrieval mechanism of CodeBroker is similar to that of those systems using free-text indexing [12]. Many sophisticated retrieval mechanisms have been proposed, such as multifaceted classification, frames and semantic networks, and associative networks [13]. Despite their sophistication and the simplicity of free-text indexing, no significant difference is found in retrieval effectiveness [14]. CodeBroker is unique because it is active and it strives to improve the relevance to the task and user, not to the query per se.

6   System Evaluation

To investigate the effectiveness of the system in supporting programmers to reuse by actively delivering personalized components, and to understand the distinctive role that task models, discourse models, and user models play in achieving this personalization, we have conducted 12 experiments with 5 subjects whose expertise in Java programming ranged from medium to expert level. In each experiment, the subject was asked to implement one predetermined programming task with the CodeBroker system. Days before the experiments, CodeBroker created an initial user model for each subject by analyzing the Java programs that the subject had written recently.

Task models based on similarity analysis in CodeBroker were quite effective in delivering task-relevant components. In 10 of the 12 experiments, the subjects reused components delivered by the system. The 12 programs created reused 57 distinct components (if a component was used more than once in a program, it was counted as one), and 20 of them were delivered by the system. Of the 20 reused components delivered by the system, the subjects had not known the existence of nine components. In other words, those nine components were from information islands (see Sect. 2), and they could not have been reused without the support of CodeBroker. Although subjects somehow anticipated the existence of the other 11 components (belonging to L3, as discussed in Sect. 2), they had known neither the names nor the functionality, and they had never used them before. They might have reused those 11 components if they could manage to locate those components by themselves. In follow-up interviews, all subjects acknowledged that CodeBroker made locating those anticipated components much easier and faster.

Discourse models (Fig. 3) improved the task-relevance when they were created by subjects. In five experiments, subjects used the Skip Components Menu   (Fig. 2) to create discourse models, which removed a total of 10% of retrieved components from the deliveries. All the components removed by discourse models were not relevant to the programming tasks. The programming tasks of these experiments were rather small, and each development session was short. We expect discourse models to improve the task-relevance of delivered components even further in real programming tasks, which require more interactions between programmers and the system.

User models (Fig. 4), however, removed only 2% of the retrieved components. The following two reasons might have belittled the role of user models in the experiments: (1) initial user models of subjects were not complete because many of the programs that the subjects had written for companies were not available for the creation of initial user models; (2) to observe the effectiveness of task models, subjects were assigned tasks that involved the part of the repository that they did not know well, and as a result, most retrieved components were not known to them and were not included in their user models. Nonetheless, in follow-up interviews, subjects said that they did not notice the delivery of too many components they already knew. A careful examination of those components removed by user models showed that those removed components could not be reused in the tasks. User models helped and are needed to reduce the number of irrelevant components to be delivered, although more experimental data based on long-term use [8] of the system are needed to investigate the contributions of user models.

Overall, the subjects rated the system an average of 6.9 on a scale from 1 (totally useless) to 10 (extremely useful).

7   Summary and Future Research

This paper presents a new approach—component delivery—to assist software developers in reusing components from large repositories. The approach combines task models, discourse models, and user models to improve the context relevance of delivered components. Task-relevant components are first retrieved based on task models, and the retrieval results are the same for all developers and development sessions. The task relevance is further improved by discourse models to reflect the difference of the larger context. Moreover, user models make the delivery specific to users so that different users may be given different information, depending on their particular experiences. Evaluations of the CodeBroker system, developed based on this approach, have illustrated each model's contribution to the context relevance.

The challenge in an information-rich world (where human attention is the most valuable and scarcest commodity) is not only to make information available to people at any time, at any place, and in any form, but to reduce information overload by making information relevant to the task-at-hand and to the background knowledge of the users [3]. Information delivery methods will be successful and adopted by users only if they are able to achieve the right balance between the costs of intrusive interruptions and the loss of context-sensitivity of deferred alerts [7].

Currently, the repository is located in the same machine as the development environment of developers and is created statically before its use because most current repositories are closed and proprietary. As the movement of Open Source Systems attracts more and more developers, we can expect more software components to become open-source, for example, the Jun system (a 3D Smalltalk/Java library) [1]. It will then become increasingly difficult for software developers to know newly available open-source components. We envision a distributed CodeBroker system running on several computers where software developers contribute open-source components. The system will dynamically index components from those constantly evolving repositories and then will deliver components through networks to other developers. Through the mediation of CodeBroker, software developers can thus benefit from each other's work and improve the productivity of software development through avoiding unnecessary repetition of work.

Acknowledgments

The authors thank the members of the Center for LifeLong Learning & Design at the University of Colorado, who have made major contributions to the conceptual frameworks described in this paper. Kumiyo Nakakoji provided many helpful comments. The research was supported by (1) the National Science Foundation, Grants REC-9631396 and IRI-9711951; (2) Software Research Associates, Tokyo, Japan; (3) PFU, Tokyo, Japan; and (4) the Coleman Family Foundation, San Jose, CA.

References

1. A. Aoki, K. Hayashi, K. Kishida, K. Nakakoji, Y. Nishinaka, B. Reeves, A. Takashima, and Y. Yamamoto. A case study of the evolution of Jun: An object-oriented open-source 3D multimedia library. In Proc. of 23rd International Conference on Software Engineering (to appear), Toronto, Canada, 2001.

2. G. Fischer. Shared knowledge in cooperative problem-solving systems—integrating adaptive and adaptable components. In M. Schneider-Hufschmidt, T. Kuehme, and U. Malinowski, (eds.), Adaptive User Interfaces: Principles and Practice, pp. 49–68. Elsevier Science, Amsterdam, 1993.

3. G. Fischer. User modeling in human-computer interaction. User Modeling and User-Adapted Interaction (to appear), 2001.

4. G. Fischer, K. Nakakoji, J. Ostwald, G. Stahl, and T. Sumner. Embedding critics in design environments. In M. Maybury and W. Wahlster, (eds.), Readings in Intelligent User Interfaces, pp. 537–559. Morgan Kaufmann, 1998.

5. W. Frakes and C. Fox. Quality improvement using a software reuse failure modes model. IEEE Transactions on Software Engineering, 22(4):274–279, 1996.

6. B. Gutkauf. Improving Design & Communication of Business Graphs through User Adaptive Critiquing. Ph.D. Dissertation, Universitat-GH Paderborn, Paderborn, Germany, 1998.

7. E. Horvitz, A. Jacobs, and D. Hovel. Attention-sensitive alerting. In Proc. of Conference on Uncertainty and Artificial Intelligence 1999, pp. 305–313, San Francisco, CA, 1999.

8. J. Kay and R. Thomas. Studying long-term system use. CACM, 38(7):61–68, 1995.

9. W. Kintsch. Comprehension: A Paradigm for Cognition. Cambridge University Press, 1998.

10. T. Landauer and S. Dumais. A solution to Plato's problem: The latent semantic analysis theory of acquisition, induction and representation of knowledge. Psychological Review, 104(2):211–240, 1997.

11. H. Lieberman. Personal assistants for the web: An MIT perspective. In M. Klusch, (ed.), Intelligent Information Agents: Agent-Based Information Discovery and Management on the Internet, pp. 279–292. Springer-Verlag, 1999.

12. Y. Maarek, D. Berry, and G. Kaiser. An information retrieval approach for automatically constructing software libraries. IEEE Transactions on Software Engineering, 17(8):800–813, 1991.

13. A. Mili, R. Mili, and R. T. Mittermeir. A survey of software reuse libraries. In W. Frakes, (ed.), Systematic Software Reuse, Annals of Software Engineering 5, pp. 317–347. Baltzer Science, Bussum, The Netherlands, 1998.

14. H. Mili, E. Ah-Ki, R. Grodin, and H. Mcheick. Another nail to the coffin of faceted controlled-vocabulary component classification and retrieval. In Proc. of Symposium on Software Reuse, pp. 89–98, Boston, MA, 1997.

15. B. Rhodes and T. Starner. Remembrance agent: A continuously running automated information retrieval system. In Proc. of 1st International Conference on the Practical Application of Intelligent Agents and Multi Agent Technology, pp. 487–495, London, 1996.

16. H. Simon. The Sciences of the Artificial. The MIT Press, 3rd edition, 1996.

17. C. Thomas. To Assist the User: On the Embedding of Adaptive and Agent-Based Mechanisms. Oldenbourg Verlag, Munich, 1996.

18. M. Williams. What makes RABBIT run? International Journal of Man-Machine Studies, 21:333–352, 1984.

19. Y. Ye and G. Fischer. Promoting reuse with active reuse repository systems. In Proc. of 6th International Conference on Software Reuse, pp. 302–317, Vienna, Austria, 2000.

20. Y. Ye. Supporting Component-Based Software Development with Active Component Repository Systems. Ph.D. Dissertation, University of Colorado, Boulder, CO, 2001.

Automating Personal Categorization
Using Artificial Neural Networks

Dina Goren-Bar, Tsvi Kuflik, Dror Lev, and Peretz Shoval

Department of Information Systems Engineering
Ben Gurion University of the Negev
Beer-Sheva
Israel
(dinag,tsvikak,dlavie,shoval)@bgumail.bgu.ac.il

Abstract. Organizations as well as personal users invest a great deal of time in assigning documents they read or write to categories. Automatic document classification that matches user subjective classification is widely used, but much challenging research still remain to be done. The self-organizing map (SOM) is an artificial neural network (ANN) that is mathematically characterized by transforming high-dimensional data into two-dimensional representation. This enables automatic clustering of the input, while preserving higher order topology. A closely related method is the Learning Vector Quantization (LVQ) algorithm, which uses supervised learning to maximize correct data classification. This study evaluates and compares the application of SOM and LVQ to automatic document classification, based on a subjectively predefined set of clusters in a specific domain. A set of documents from an organization, manually clustered by a domain expert, was used in the experiment. Results show that in spite of the subjective nature of human categorization, automatic document clustering methods match with considerable success subjective, personal clustering, the LVQ method being more advantageous.

1 Introduction

1.1 Motivation

Information users define subjective topic trees or categories, based on personal preferences, and assign documents they read or write to categories according to this subjective definition. Now that the amount of publicly available information on the web is increasing rapidly by roughly a million pages every day [3], automation of categorization and filtering of documents has become an essential procedure. For years, manual categorization methods were defined and employed in libraries and other document repositories based on human judgment.

Organizations and users searched for information and saved it in categories in a way that was meaningful to them. Obviously, the categories used by information users may be idiosyncratic to the specific organization or user, but not to an automatic classification system. A major problem in generating an automatic, adaptable system is how close can the automatic system reflect the subjective point of view of the user, regarding his/her domain(s) of interest. Users are usually inconsistent, having a

M. Bauer, P.J. Gmytrasiewicz, and J. Vassileva (Eds.): UM 2001, LNAI 2109, pp. 188–198, 2001.
©Springer-Verlag Berlin Heidelberg 2001

tendency to change the document classification they use over time. Moreover, users may find a document relevant to more than one category, choosing usually just one, arbitrarily, to host the document. So, how can an automatic clustering system "guess" the users subjective classification? Moreover, we may see in organizations that there is no objective, defined topic tree, which is supplied or adopted by the employees but, instead each worker, creates its unique categorization-tree according to subjective criteria. To test this issue, taking a well-defined set of categorized documents agreed upon several experts does not reflect the real problem.

The motivation for the current study was to evaluate the actual use of automatic categorization techniques, to support the manual categorization in a company that performs this task on daily basis by human experts. In our experiment, the system performed a task similar to one of the human categorizers, based on his data.

In this study we implemented and evaluated two artificial neural net methods that address the specific user's preferences and deal with his/her varying subjective judgment We used a set of manually categorized documents from a specific domain of interest (documents about companies and financial news), and trained a SOM and LVQ ANN to automatically categorize them. Then, we measured the distance between the automatically generated set of clusters (or categories) and the pre-defined manual clustering. Our assumption is that if the distances are marginal, we can use the following method for automatic clustering using that ANN: A user provides a training set of pre-clustered documents, this set is used for training the system, after training is completed, the system provides an automatic clustering based on the user preferences.

The present study specifically addresses the following questions:

1. How close can automatic categorization come to personal, subjective user categorization?
2. What is the effect of the training set size on automatic categorization performance?
3. What is the difference between supervised (LVQ) and unsupervised (SOM) training on the above questions?

1.2 Background

Clustering is defined as the unsupervised classification of patterns into groups [5]. A wide variety of clustering methods have been presented and applied in a variety of domains, such as image segmentation, object and character recognition, data mining, and information retrieval [5].

Artificial neural networks (ANN) have been used in recent years for modeling complex systems where no explicit equations are known, or the equations are too ideal to represent the real world. The ANN can form predictive models from data available from past history. ANN training is done, by learning from known examples. A network of simple mathematical "neurons" is connected by weights. Adjusting the weights between the "neurons" does the training of the ANN. Advanced algorithms can train ANN models, as much as thousands of inputs and outputs. By analysis of the trained ANN useful knowledge can be extracted. Information retrieval and information filtering are among the various applications where ANN has been successfully tested [2].

Two main branches of ANN are presently in use today, which are distinguished by their training methods namely, supervised and unsupervised:

1. The supervised ANN branch uses a "teacher" to train the model, where an error is defined between the model outputs and the known outputs. Error back-propagation algorithm adjusts the model connection weights to decrease the error by repeated presentation of inputs.
2. The unsupervised ANN branch tries to find clusters of similar inputs when no previous knowledge exists about the number of the desired clusters.

In both cases, once the ANN is trained, it is verified by presenting inputs not used in the training.

The self-organizing maps (SOM), a specific kind of ANN, is a tool that may be used for the purpose of automatic document categorization [4,6,7]. The SOM is an unsupervised competitive ANN that transforms highly dimensional data to a two dimensional grid, while preserving the data topology by mapping similar data items to the same cell on the grid (or to neighboring cells). A typical SOM is made of a vector of nodes for input, an array of nodes as an output map, and a matrix of connections between each output unit and all the input units. Thus, each vector of the input dimension can be mapped to a specific unit on a two-dimensional map. In our case each vector represents a document, while the output unit represents the category that the document is assigned to.

Closely related to the SOM algorithm is the Learning Vector Quantization (LVQ) algorithm. LVQ is a supervised competitive ANN which also transforms high dimensional data to a two dimensional grid, without taking into account data topology. To facilitate the two dimensional transformation, LVQ uses pre-assigned cluster labels to data items, minimizing the average expected misclassification probability. Unlike SOM, where clusters are generated automatically based on item similarities, here the clusters are predefined. In our case the cluster labels represent the subjective categorization of the various documents supplied by the user.

LVQ training is somewhat similar to SOM training. An additional requirement of the LVQ is that each output unit has a cluster label, a priori to training [6].

In order to use a clustering mechanism, such as an ANN based approach, an appropriate document representation is required. The vector space model, in which a document is represented by a weighted, vector of terms, is a very popular model in the information retrieval community [1]. This model suggests that a document may be represented by all meaningful terms included in it. A weight assigned to a term represents the relative importance of that term. One common approach for term weighting is TF ("term frequency") where each term is assigned a weight according to its frequency in the related document [8]. Sometimes documents relations are also considered, combining TF weighing with IDF ("inverse document frequency") into TF*IDF weights. Using the SOM algorithm relives the necessity since it already takes this combination into account document relations during the training phase. The TF method was adopted in this study in order to define meaningful terms for document representations for both, SOM and LVQ processing.

1.3 Related Work

A need for personalized categorization has existed for some time now, and a great deal of work has been done in various application areas. For example, various mail filing assistants have been developed such as the MailCat system [9], which propose folders for email that are similar to the categories or labeling process performed by the ANN. MailCat employs the TF*IDF algorithm, where every folder has a centroid representative vector. The MailCat system provides the user with categories (folders) from which the user chooses the appropriate one. The authors mention that MailCat "does not even require that the classifier be based upon TF-IDF", suggesting it should be based on another representation. They rather highlight the importance of other factors other than the representation methods, such as reasonable accuracy, incremental learning, and producing a ranking of several possible categories, for personalized categorization systems. As can be understood from SOM definition and from the following results, SOM can be used to provide more automation for systems like MailCat.

Clustering methods can define similar groups of documents among huge collections. When this approach is employed on the result of a search engine, it may enhance and ease browsing and selecting the relevant information. Zamir & Etzioni [11], evaluated various clustering algorithms and showed precision improvement of the initial search engine results, from 0.1- 0.4 to 0.4 – 0.7. Rauber & Merkl [7], showed that clustering, applied on general collections of documents, can result in an ordered collection of documents, grouped into similar groups, that is easily browsable by users.

Other studies resembling the "one button" (one category) implementation of MailCat, reported roughly similar precision results on automatic categorization [9].

The main difference between MailCat and similar systems and the method we propose is that their systems are built to support and adapt towards specific user interests, based on the development of specific algorithms to achieve "reasonable accuracy", while in our case we use a well-known categorization method to represent subjective, personal behavior. Therefore, the major difference between us, in the classifier used, specifically in our proving of the feasibility of an unsupervised algorithm. The different approach may have interesting implications about the generalization of results to different domains, considering that in our study we reach the same improved levels of precision reported by Zamir and Etzioni (from 0.45 – 0.75) [11]. It is also conceivable, that our system can be extended to more than two categories.

The rest of this paper is structured as follows: The next section describes the experiment performed for the evaluation of the training methods, followed by the presentation of the experimental results. We conclude with a discussion and planned future work.

2 Experiment

2.1 Data

The experiment was performed in a company, which deals with information extraction and categorization, in order to evaluate the possible automation of data items categorization within the company's domain, using actual, available data. We chose this environment in order to deal with real-life data in a real-life organization. The data collection method resembled a field study. We did not asked the information expert to do an experimental task, which could have based our experiment in the sense that he would think over on each data categorization. Instead, we took the already clustered items done in natural daily conditions. A data set containing 1115 economics and financial data items was used. The data was extracted from an online Internet based source (Yahoo.com). An information specialist read each item and manually clustered the items into one of 15 possible clusters. The size of the cluster varied from 1 to 125 documents per cluster. This approach represents a daily, normal operation of information seeking and categorization in organizations today.

Table 1. Original data clusters

\set cat\	1	2	3	4	5	6	7	8	9	10
1				1	0\1					
2		1\0	1\0							
3	0\1	0\1				0\1		1		1\0
4	0\1	0\1	0\1	1	1	1	1	1	0\1	1
5	2\1	2	1\3	2	2\3	2	2\1	2\1	2\3	1
6	5	4\5	5\4	5	5\4	5\4	4\5	5	5\4	5
7	6	6	6	6	7\6	6	6	6	6	6
8	11	11	11	11	10\11	11	11	11	11	11
9	19\18	19\17	18\17	18	19\18	20\19	18\17	18	18	17\18
10	21\20	20	22\21	18\20	19\20	18\19	20\21	19\20	21\20	21
11	21	21	21	22\21	22\21	22\21	21	22	22\21	21
12	26\27	27\26	25	26	27\26	27	27\26	27	26	26
13	29	29	30	31\29	29\30	29\30	29	29	29	30\29
14	39	39\40	39\40	39	38\39	38\39	40\41	38	39\40	40
15	44	44	44	43\44	44\43	44	44	44	44	43\44

2.2 Method

All 1115 documents were analyzed, using a classical text analysis methodology. "Stop words" were removed. The resulting terms underwent further stemming processing, using the Porter stemming algorithm [Frakes and Beiza-Yates 1992]). Finally, normalized weighted term vectors were generated to represent the documents. In order to reduce the vector length, a low frequency threshold was implemented as a means of dimensionality reduction. Non-informative terms, which appeared in less than 100 documents (less than 10%), were excluded from the matrix. Then, the SOM and LVQ simulations were implemented using the SOM Toolbox for Matlab 5 [10].

Since experimental results may be influenced by the selection of the test and training sets, ten test sets were randomly selected. The size of each was 20% of the overall set (223 items). The size of 223 documents for test set and initial training set was selected in order to allow (when available) sufficient number of examples for each original cluster to be used (an average of 15 documents from each cluster). For each test set, several training sets of different sizes were generated from the remaining 892 items, by random selection, so that the test set items were never part of the training set. Training sets sizes comprised 20%, 40%, 60% and 80% of the original data set (223, 446, 669, and 892 items).

The experiment was repeated ten times for each algorithm, with a randomly pooled test set to overcome the possibility of biasing effects resulting from data sets selection.

The labeling process of the auto-generated clusters consisted of the following steps: First we observed the original manual classification of the documents clustered at each output unit (automatic cluster). The manual cluster with the highest frequency, indicating where most of the documents belong to, rendered its name to the automatic output unit.

In order to evaluate the ANN performance two popular measures were used: precision and recall. Recall, in a specific category, is the number of documents that were automatically clustered correctly by the system, divided by the overall number of documents that belong to that cluster originally (given by the expert). Precision is the number of documents automatically clustered correctly, divided by the overall documents clustered by the system to the same category (correct + incorrect).

2.3 Set Up

Maps of different sizes were generated to match the different training sets. The initial weights of each map were generated randomly just before the learning phase. Two runs were performed, one for SOM and one for LVQ. Hence, slight differences were found in the randomly selected test and training sets. Table 1 represents document distribution among the ten sets, the columns representing the test sets and the rows representing the categories. Whenever a difference appeared in a test set between the SOM and the LVQ runs, the number in the left-hand side belongs to LVQ test set while the number of the right-hand side, is from the SOM test set.

3   Experimental Results

In order to evaluate the performance of the automatic classifications with each method, we computed the average precision and recall on the ten different test-training sets.

3.1 LVQ Results

The results of LVQ-based recall and precision, are summarized in Table 2. The rows represent each of the initial 15 manually defined "original" categories, while the columns represent the four different sizes of training sets. Precision and recall results are denoted "P" and "R" respectively. The results for each training-set are the average result of the ten runs. The nature of the data used (variation of categories sizes) resulted in several "empty" categories in the training/test sets (see table 1 for a summary of the actual number of documents for each category for every test set).

The results show that recall improves significantly as the size of the training set increases to 60% (669 documents). For the 80% training set size the results are mixed, which may indicate that at 60% enough data is accumulated to learn and adapt the ANN to the user's subjective references and no more data is needed.

There is a noticeable difference between categories 1-7 and the other categories, which may result from the small number of documents in these categories. This difference implies that learning is not possible in categories where a training set is not available (or has a marginal size).

Table 2. LVQ

\Training \ Category\	Set	Size						
	80%	(892)	60%	(669)	40%	(446)	20%	(223)
	R	P	R	P	R	P	R	P
1*	0	0	0	0	0	0	0	0
2**	0	0	0	0	0	0	0	0
3*	0	0	0	0	0	0	0	0
4	0	0	0	0	0	0	0	0
5	0	0	0	0	0	0	0	0
6	0.46	0.97	0.26	1	0.20	1	0.04	1
7	0.77	0.59	0.80	0.58	0.63	0.57	0.30	0.44
8	0.95	0.81	0.94	0.74	0.93	0.71	0.81	0.69
9	0.77	0.88	0.72	0.84	0.71	0.88	0.69	0.77
10	0.52	0.59	0.60	0.59	0.60	0.57	0.59	0.53
11	0.70	0.51	0.62	0.53	0.60	0.46	0.51	0.44
12	0.78	0.68	0.74	0.65	0.73	0.64	0.68	0.59
13	0.69	0.81	0.69	0.83	0.65	0.82	0.65	0.76
14	0.81	0.84	0.81	0.82	0.80	0.83	0.80	0.82
15	0.79	0.84	0.82	0.83	0.79	0.78	0.75	0.74

* All marked categories contained minimal number of documents and appeared as specific categories only in part of the 10 randomly generated sets – see Table 1 for details.

Table 3. SOM

\Training \ Category\	Set	Size						
	80%	(892)	60%	(669)	40%	(446)	20%	(223)
	R	P	R	P	R	P	R	P
1*	0		0		0		0	
2**								
3*	0		0.33		0		0	
4	0.50	0.53	0.50	0.61	0.20	0.42	0.10	0.25
5	0		0.15	0.5	0	0	0	
6	0.39	0.71	0.22	0.77	0.23	0.56	0.17	0.25
7	0.47	0.45	0.35	0.51	0.35	0.49	0.40	0.45
8	0.92	0.74	0.88	0.69	0.79	0.67	0.73	0.68
9	0.68	0.87	0.67	0.86	0.68	0.86	0.52	0.83
10	0.78	0.56	0.79	0.53	0.75	0.52	0.72	0.45
11	0.53	0.61	0.50	0.58	0.47	0.61	0.41	0.50
12	0.70	0.66	0.69	0.57	0.64	0.53	0.60	0.50
13	0.66	0.80	0.66	0.78	0.62	0.77	0.57	0.66
14	0.79	0.85	0.76	0.90	0.76	0.91	0.76	0.85
15	0.79	0.72	0.74	0.71	0.70	0.71	0.67	0.69

* Marked categories appeared as categories only in part of the 10 randomly generated sets
** No such category at all (was not defined by SOM during learning sessions)

It is also noticeable that precision improves as the size of the training set grows, but in this instance 80% training yielded the best results, with the exception of group 6 which contained a minimal number of documents, group 11 which is a collection of un-categorized documents and group 13.

These results imply that when there are enough examples, the LVQ method support personal categorization to a reasonable degree.

3.2 SOM Results

The results of SOM-based recall are summarized in Table 3, where, each "original" category is represented by a row, while columns represent the four different sizes of training sets. The results for each training-set are the average result of the ten runs. The nature of the data used (variation of category size) resulted, like the LVQ results, in several "empty" categories in the training/test sets. Table 1 summarizes the actual number of categories for each test set.

Results show that recall improves significantly as the size of the training set grows, with the exception of groups 1-5 that had nearly no documents. For the 80% training set size some of the results approximate the results obtained at 60%, which may mean that at 60% enough data has been accumulated and the ANN has succeeded to learn the user's specific preference and no more data is needed.

Category 2 was not represented at all by the SOM, for some unknown reason.

Category 11 included all documents that could not be assigned (by the human expert) to any category, hence generated a special category of items that were not well defined.

Results show, that precision also improves as the size of the training set grows, but this time the 80% training yielded the best results, with the exception of groups 1-5 that had nearly no documents and 6 and 7, that contained a minimal number of documents, and group 14.

These results show that, given there are enough examples, the SOM method, (which is an unsupervised automatic system) can match personal categorization to a reasonable degree.

3.3 Overall Results and a Comparison of SOM and LVQ Methods

Performing automatic clustering by SOM and LVQ save the following results (an overall average, summarized in Table 4): Recall of LVQ ranged from 49% to 60%, while recall of SOM ranged from 45% to 57%. Precision of LVQ ranges from 65% to 75% while precision of SOM ranges from 55% to 69%.

Given enough training documents (a learning set of 892 documents), both methods yielded similar results of about 70% precision and about 60% recall. As expected, in the case of the 223 document training sets supervised learning yielded better initial results: 49% recall using LVQ vs. 45% recall using SOM, and 65% precision using LVQ, but only 55% precision using SOM.

Table 4. Overall results

Learning set	Percentage	80%	60%	40%	20%
	Actual size	892	669	446	223
Measure	Method				
Recall	LVQ	0.60	0.58	0.55	0.49
	SOM	0.57	0.54	0.50	0.45
Precision	LVQ	0.75	0.73	0.71	0.65
	SOM	0.69	0.63	0.60	0.55

The experimental results becomes problematic when examining the original categories that contained a minimal number of documents, or no documents at all at some of the test-sets, as showed in Table 1. Table 5 summarizes those categories with more than 10 documents per category (categories 8-15). It can be seen that recall improves significantly while precision of SOM improves and LVQ stays the same. This result supports the assumption that categories with only a few documents actually lower the overall level of precision and recall since the system could not be trained to cluster them.

Table 5. Overall results – "full" categories

Learning set	Percentage	80%	60%	40%	20%
	Actual size	892	669	446	223
Measure	Method				
Recall	LVQ	0.75	0.74	0.73	0.69
	SOM	0.73	0.71	0.68	0.62
Precision	LVQ	0.75	0.73	0.71	0.67
	SOM	0.73	0.70	0.70	0.65

4   Conclusions and Future Work

The purpose of this work was to test the possibility of automating the classification of subjectively categorized data sets. For that purpose we chose to work with real data from a company, which deals with information search and categorization on a daily basis. Our results show that from the initial 10 test sets (Table 1) of data, categories 1-3 get eliminated in the process because of their sparseness. Category 4 performed slightly better. Categories 5-7 are somewhat more problematic, probably because the small amount of documents is insufficient for training and therefore result in incorrect clustering on. In spite of these problematic data sets (that represent real life), the overall results confirm the hypothesis that it is possible to cluster (with reasonable error), a subjective classification. Performing automatic clustering using either SOM or LVQ provided an overall match of 73% to 75% recall and 73% to 75% precision for the two methods, this degree of match was achieved with a learning set of 892 documents. This level of precision and recall outperform the results reported by Segal & Kephardt [9]. Another not unexpected finding is that the supervised learning yields better results initially (69% vs. 62% recall and 67% vs 65% in precision for the 223 documents training set), the surprising issue though was that the overall performance is quite similar given enough documents.

A major question for the adoption of automatic subjective classification systems is the size of training set required. If the training set needed is large, it is most likely that users will not use such a system. In our case, the size of the training set varied from ~200 to ~900 data items, an average of 15 to 60 data items per category. While 15 data items may be a reasonable size for a data set, bigger sizes may be problematic. However even initial small training set yields results that are quite close to the overall performance achieved by the larger set. This implies that an initial, small set (with some ongoing adaptation) may be sufficient for a start.

In conclusion, despite the subjective nature of human categorization, an automatic process can perform that task, with considerable success. Given an automatic classifier just the number of clusters, as were determined by the user, and a training set, enables the system to "learn" the human classification. The idea that the system classifies items in a similar way humans do, is even more interesting in the unsupervised learning case. Usually, there exist several possible ways to classify the same set of data items but, the results show, that even in this case the machine and the user were quite close. This result supports the rationality of the human classifier, meaning that human and machine referred to similar dimensions for the performance of the task. These first results require further study. For one thing, we will try to define the various types of errors occurring during the classification process, especially automatic classification errors by the human expert, in order to validate the initial subjective classification. In the present study we compared the automatic classification to the manual one, assuming that the manual classification is 100% correct. But people are inconsistent and change their minds frequently. It would be interesting to give user the classification, with the mismatches, and let him/her decide who was right.

We also intend to compare the classifiers already implemented with new ones. This will enable us to assess our overall level of performance, comparing our results with other automated methods.

Finally, it might be worthwhile to investigate the correlation between the size of the initial cluster and the learning and classification process (the influence of the "sparse" clusters on the overall results).

References

1. Baeza-Yates and Ribiero-Neto (1999) Modern Information Retrieval, Addison-Wesley, 1999.
2. Boger, Z. Kuflik, T., Shapira, B. and Shoval, P. (2000) Information Filtering and Automatic Keywords Identification by Artificial Neural Networks Proccedings of the 8th Europian Conference on Information Systems.pp. 46-52, Vienna, July 2000.
3. Chakrabarti, S., Dom, B. et al. (1999). Hypersearching the Web. Scientific American, June, 54-60.
4. Honkela, T., Kaski, S., Lagus, K., and Kohonen, T. (1997). WEBSOM - Self-Organizing Maps of Document Collections. In Proceedings of WSOM'97, Workshop on SelfOrganizing Maps, Espoo, Finland, June 4-6, pages 310-315. Helsinki University of Technology, Neural Networks Research Centre, Espoo, Finland.
5. Jain, A. K., Murty, M. N., Flynn, P. J. (1999) Data Clustering: A Review, ACM Computing Surveys, Vol 31, No. 3 pp. 264-323, September 1999

6. Kohonen, T. (1997). Self-Organizing Maps. 2nd ed., Springer-Verlag, Berlin.
7. Rauber A. and Merkl. D. (1999). Using self-organizing maps to organize document archives and to characterize subject matters: How to make a map tell the news of the world Proceedings of the 10th Intl. Conf. on Database and Expert Systems Applications (DEXA'99), Florence, Italy.
8. Salton, G., McGill, M. Introduction to Modern Information Retrieval. McGraw-Hill New-York (1983).
9. Segal, B. R., and Kephart, J. O., (1999) MailCat: An Intelligent Assistant for Organizing E-Mail, Proceedings of the Third International Conference on Autonomous Agents. Pp. 276-282
10. Vesanto, J., Alhoniemi, E., Himberg, J., Kiviluoto, K., & Parviainen, J. (1999). Self-Organizing Map for Data Mining in Matlab: The SOM Toolbox. Simulation News Europe, (25):54.
11. Zamir, O., and Etzioni O. (1998), Web Document Clustering: A Feasibility Demonstartion, Proceedings of SIGIR 98, Melbourne, Australia.

Posters

User Modelling as an Aid
for Human Web Assistants

Johan Aberg and Nahid Shahmehri

Department of Computer and Information Science
Link"oping University, S-581 83 Link" oping, Sweden
{johab,nahsh } @ida.liu.se
Phone, Fax: +46-13-281465, +46-13-282666

Abstract.   This paper explores how user modelling can work as an aid
for human assistants in a user support system for web sites. Information
about the user can facilitate for the assistant the tailoring of the consultation to the individual needs of the user. Such information can be
represented and structured in a user model made available for the assistant. A user modelling approach has been implemented and deployed in
a real web environment as part of a user support system. Following the
deployment we have analysed consultation dialogue logs and answers to
a questionnaire for participating assistants. The initial results show that
assistants consider user modelling to be helpful and that consultation
dialogues can be an important source for user model data collection.

1   Introduction

Previous research and recent commercial developments have highlighted the importance of so-called web assistant systems [1]. A web assistant system is a user
support component that can be added to any kind of web information system
(e.g. for electronic commerce, digital libraries, or home banking). The system is
a collaboration between computer-based and human-based support, for example
forcing the computer-based support to handle routine user support problems,
and thus allowing the human assistants to deal with more complex issues.

Information about a user can allow a human assistant to provide high quality
support by tailoring the consultation to the individual user. Having such information readily available can also make consultation dialogues more ecient and
thus save time and other resources. A step towards a more ecient and personalised support could be to provide the human assistants with a user modelling
tool. This kind of tool should present the assistant with relevant information
about the user when it is needed in the consultation dialogue.

The aim of this paper is to explore the value and feasibility of user modelling
for web assistant systems. We have chosen to implement and deploy a simple user
modelling tool for human assistants and study it in a real web environment. The
system was deployed at a non-profit site called Elfwood, with a focus on science-
fiction and fantasy related art and literature. Voluntary assistants from around
the world participated and made use of the user modelling tool when assisting

M. Bauer, P.J. Gmytrasiewicz, and J. Vassileva (Eds.): UM 2001, LNAI 2109, pp. 201–203, 2001.

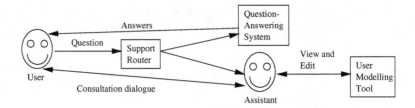

Fig. 1.   Overview of the web assistant model

users during a period of three weeks. Apart from testing technical feasibility our study focuses on two questions: 1) What are the subjective opinions of assistants towards the concept of such a user modelling tool? 2) What kind and amount of user model data can be collected from consultation dialogues?

2   Web Assistant System

An overview illustration of our web assistant model is presented in Fig. 1. The user's support process is initiated when the user asks a question in natural language. The user's question is fed to the automatic question-answering system (analysed further in [3]). FAQ items which closely match are returned as potential answers to the user's question. If the user does not find the returned answers satisfactory, the support router will connect the user to a human assistant with expertise matching the topic of the question. If all the appropriate assistants are currently busy, the user can choose to wait in a queue. Once an assistant is available the user is connected to that assistant and can proceed with a consultation dialogue via textual chat.

In the user modelling component, information about a user is stored in a predefined attribute hierarchy, in an overlay style. The attribute structure was defined in cooperation with several expert artists and writers that were members of Elfwood. A user's model is displayed for an assistant as soon as a consultation dialogue starts. The assistant can then make use of the information in the model to tailor the consultation to that individual user. No automatic inference is performed on the data in the user model, although the assistant is of course free to make inferences as a part of his or her interpretation of the user data. The assistant can also update the model by filling in attribute values based on what is learned from the consultation dialogue with the user.

3   Field Study and Results

The overall objective of our work on web assistant systems has been to explore this kind of system in a real-world application. Thus a field study is a natural research method. During the period of deployment at Elfwood, 636 users registered with the support system, and 129 of these users worked through the system to have consultation dialogues with assistants. The collected data that we have analysed in this paper is: 1) the results from a questionnaire for the participating assistants, and 2) the logs from the text chat consultation dialogs that took place. For more information about the field study, please refer to [2] where we present complementary results from other questionnaires for users and assistants considering the usability of the web assistant system as a whole.

The questionnaire for assistants regarding the user modelling tool was sent out via e-mail directly after the deployment period. The questionnaire contained questions about the tool and about the process of working with the tool. Respondents had to express their agreement or disagreement with statements on a scale from 1 to 10. We also asked for textual explanations for the quantitative answers. A total of 14 assistants responded with completely filled out questionnaires (response rate of roughly 47%). The main result here is that the assistants did indeed find the user modelling tool helpful. If we disregard the scores of three assistants who never got to assist users with any information in their model, we got a mean of 8.27 with a standard deviation of 1.35, where a 10 indicates that the tool was helpful and a 1 indicates that the tool was of no help.

In our initial analysis of the consultation dialogue logs we have considered in what conversational circumstances user model information becomes available. Following the circumstances identified in [4] we have counted each occurrence of user information that could possibly be useful for the user tasks that we supported, and associated each such occurrence with a corresponding conversational circumstance. The main result from this analysis is that the assistants have an important role to play in gathering personal information about the user. Approximately half of all the user information came up from a direct question by the assistant. In the remaining cases users volunteered personal information, or volunteered information as background information for a problem description. On average, around 1.5 pieces of new user information came up in each consultation dialogue.

References

1. Johan Aberg and Nahid Shahmehri. The role of human Web assistants in e-commerce: an analysis and a usability study. Internet Research: Electronic Networking Applications and Policy, 10(2):114–125, 2000.
2. Johan Aberg and Nahid Shahmehri. Collection and Exploitation of Expert Knowledge in Web Assistant Systems. In Proceedings of the 34th Hawaii International Conference on System Sciences, Maui, Hawaii, USA, January 3-6 2001.
3. Johan Aberg and Nahid Shahmehri. An Empirical Study of Human Web Assistants: Implications for User Support in Web Information Systems. In Proceedings of the CHI Conference on Human Factors in Computing Systems, pages 404–411, Seattle, Washington, USA, 2001.
4. Stephanie Elzer, Jennifer Chu-Carrol, and Sandra Carberry. Recognizing and Utilizing User Preferences in Collaborative Consultation Dialogues. In Proceedings of the Fourth International Conference on User Modeling, pages 19–24, 1994.

Modelling the Interests of a News Service User

Fredrik Åman and Annika Waern

Swedish Institute of Computer Science
Box 16 33 Se-164 29 Kista Sweden
fred@hig.se annika@sics.se

We have developed a filtering service for an on-line news channel. In this domain, both content-based and collaborative filtering proved difficult to apply. Our solution was make extensive use of user involvement. In particular, we use the information gathered when users send tips about news articles to their friends. The paper describes the types of user involvement that our system allows, the techniques used for user modelling, and how these are used to generate relevant user-adaptive behaviour.

1 A Social and Personal News Media

Filtering for news media must take into account the fact that the media represents a continuous flow of information. Traditionally, this has been taken very literally: news has been seen as a stream of messages flowing from one or several news publishers, broadcasted to a set of consumers. This stream of information is then to be filtered at the consumer end to fit the individual user's interests (see e.g. [5]).

This view of news consumption is however very distant from research in news media consumption (see e.g. [3]). News media consumption is an activity that is firmly rooted in our local social interactions – news is to some extent gossip. In the project 'news in the year of 2003' we have designed and developed a novel model for news media, where consumer activities, as well as the production of news, are seen as relevant for the filtering activity. We consider all types of activities around the media as part of the flow: an article is news to someone, somewhere, when it is written, read, or sent to someone. There are several different types of activities that can influence what information is deemed most relevant at a particular point in time,

– Someone has recently added it to the pool,
– Some people have recently read it,
– Someone recently sent a tip about it to a friend,
– Someone recently commented upon an article, or added a link to it from a newer article,
– Lot of people that have read it think it is a highly relevant article.

From this list of criteria, we see that with our view of news media, they become inherently social.

M. Bauer, P.J. Gmytrasiewicz, and J. Vassileva (Eds.): UM 2001, LNAI 2109, pp. 204–206, 2001.
c Springer-Verlag Berlin Heidelberg 2001

1.1 The Conceptual Design

The news media we have designed is split into two distinct levels: one conceptual level and the surface design. A major issue for the full project is to develop a set of surface designs that inspire different types of behaviour. This article is however concerned with the lower layer, the conceptual design of the system and the implementation of its filtering function.

The news media we have designed consists of two essential functions. The first is a web site where different news forum can be visited. The surface design of a news forum vary with the desired level of user participation. The second are tips about interesting articles, that are sent out by email or SMS (the mobile phone short messaging service). Tips can be manually sent from one user to another, as well as generated automatically as part of the personalised news filter functionality. Automatic tips are triggered by recent changes to forum that match users' profiles.

2 Background

Our conceptual design is inspired by recent work on social navigation [4], which aims to make the trails of other users a visible part of the navigational structure for information. The design also draws its motivations from research in news media consumption (see e.g. [3]), which shows that news media consumption is an activity that is firmly rooted in our local social interactions – news is to some extent gossip.

The algorithmic implementation is inspired by work from two different fields: work on information filtering, and work on neural network modelling. Information filtering can be either content-based or collaborative [1]. In content-based filtering, the information items to be filtered are given an explicit description. When a new information item arrives, its description can be directly compared to the user's interest profile. Collaborative filtering approaches rely on information about how the information items previously have been used, rather than on their semantic content.

In the case of news filtering, both approaches present us with problems. Pure content-based approaches will not make use of the kind of social clues present in our news domain. On the other hand, pure collaborative filtering will require that users read and rate a singular document, before it will become available to other users. Neither do standard techniques for collaborative filtering make use of the kind of complex information available in explicit recommendations. This forced us to adopt a different approach to filtering.

3 A Neural Network Model for Social News Filtering

Most algorithms for filtering are specialised to the task, and consequently, content-based and collaborative filtering have been implemented using very different algorithms. Neural network [6] on the other hand is a more general approach to machine learning, and could be used for either task. We selected to use a neural network approach as a way of combining content-based and collaborative filtering, as well as make use of the more complex information provided by social clues (such as explicit recommendations). The design has been implemented and is currently being evaluated through simulations.

As a framework we use a neural network approach to generalisation [2]. Users activities are classified into a set of features with different possible values. In particular, we classify every read action as consisting of three features.

- The person or news source that supplied the read article ,
- the forum in which the reading action occurs, and
- the news value of the article.

Tipping activity is classified in a very similar manner, adding the person that the tip is intended for as a fourth feature. The news value is calculated on the basis of how often the article has been read over a certain time interval. This way, the evaluation becomes time dependent: more recent activities influence the network more than old activities.

Our implementation is based on a single-layer neural network [6]. The single-layer network can be passively trained from observations of user's reading actions. Each reading action by a particular user can be used to modify corresponding perceptron-weights to reflect the user's most typical reading behaviour. To enable active feedback, we must add a third layer, an output layer, to the perceptron model. This layer reflects the different possible filter messages that the service provides. Perceptrons within the layer can be trained on feedback, the user can explicitly or implicitly tell the system if a tip was useful.

References

1. Balabanovi`c, Marko and Yoav Shoham. Fab: content-based, collaborative recommendation. Communications of the ACM Vol 40 No 3, 1993, pages 66-72.
2. Bloedorn, E., I. Mani, and T.R. MacMillan. Representational issues in machine learning of user profiles. AAAI Spring Symposium on Machine Learning in Information Access, 25-27 March, 1996, Stanford University, CA.
3. Giddens, Anthony Modernity and Self-Identity. Self and Society in the Late Modern Age Cambridge: Polity Press 1991.
4. Munro, A., Höök, K., and Benyon, D. (eds.) (1999)   Social Navigation in Information Space, Springer, August 1999.
5. Pazzani, Michael J. Representation of Electronic Mail Filtering Profiles: A User Study. In proceedings of the Intelligent User Interfaces conference, New Orleans, Louisiana, January 2000.
6. Rosenblatt, F., "Principles of neurodynamics," Spartan books, 1962.

Category Based Customization Approach for Information Retrieval

Kenro Aihara and Atsuhiro Takasu

National Institute of Informatics
2-1-2 Hitotsubashi, Chiyoda-ku, Tokyo 101-8430, Japan
{kenro.aihara,takasu   }@nii.ac.jp
Phone:+81-3-4212-2577 Fax:+81-3-3556-1916

Abstract.   This paper proposes an customization technique to supporting interactive document retrieval in unorganized open information space
like WWW. We assume that taxonomical thought is one of the most
important and skilled operations for us when we organize or store information. The proposed methodology, therefore, handles hierarchical
categories of documents. The system can be customized through users'
modification of categories. The features of the proposed approach are (1)
visualization of document categories for interaction, (2) initialization of
categories by hierarchical clustering method, (3) customization of categories by support vector machine techniques, (4) additional attributes
for individual implicit cognitive aspects.

Keywords.   User Feedback, Customization, Visualization, Text Categorization, Human-Computer Interaction, Support Vector Machine, Information Retrieval

1   Introduction

Human-computer interaction (HCI) has become one of the key issues for information retrieval (IR) systems. Many of existing IR systems require its user's
declaration of keywords related to his/her information needs or the range of attribute values to support the user to access the required information. However, it
is dicult to externalize users'requirement with necessary and sucient words.
In addition, it is not easy to recognize or evaluate the answered results.

This paper proposes an HCI methodology to supporting interactive document
retrieval in unorganized open information space.

2   Methodology

We guess that taxonomical thought is one of the most important and skilled operations for us when we organize or store information. And usually classification
may change dynamically according to one's mental and physical situation. On
that assumption, dynamic clustering or classification techniques can be applied
to interactive interface.

M. Bauer, P.J. Gmytrasiewicz, and J. Vassileva (Eds.): UM 2001, LNAI 2109, pp. 207–209, 2001.

The proposed system, therefore, provides two-dimensional space to visualize information space and categorized information objects, such as documents. Objects are placed in the space as icon. The system also manages the hierarchy of categories. Hiearchical categories can keep the number of items or concepts which users must handle at once small.

2.1   Interactive Scenario

At first, the system stores "the document-term matrix" which has entries a weight $f(i, j)$ of term j for document i from a collection. Currently we use tf-idf which is the very standard method in IR community [1].

Then the system produces initial categories of documents by a clustering method with the complete linkage algorithm.

Next, the system shows document icons in two-dimensional space. Arrangement of icons are computed using similarities of documents.

From previous research, we know that the user typically does not agree the shown categories produced by the system initially. When he/she unagrees, he/she often tries to modify such visualized information as he/she likes. We suppose that that action must include the user's implicit cognition, such as an intent which cannot be verbalized by him/herself. The system, therefore, can exploit such actions as the feedback information.

When its user wants to retrieve information or browse the information space, he/she can use his/her own customized IR interface. When a user inputs an query by keywords, the system determines the most relevant object and returns the category including the object. Although existing IR systems return ranked list of answers, our system visualizes relations of objects and that can help users to recognize their contents.

Finally, new documents will be classified into an appropriate category. This approach, therefore, can be used for information filtering system.

2.2   User Feedback

The feedback will be given by users' modification of categories which shown in the system.

If document d (or cluster of documents) in cluster A is moved into cluster B by a user, the system appends a new attribute for the user. In our research[2] or many relevance feedback studies, systems usually process feedback in given dimensions. We, however, suppose that such original dimensions couldn't represent the user's feedback well enough. For extrapolation of insucient dimension related to users' cognitive factor, the system appends user attributes.

2.3   Initial Categories

The proposed IR interface shows document categories to users. We expect that visualized document categories can help users to recognize the shown information space regardless of its user's familiarity with the domain of the information.

Initial categories can be obtained by clustering. We use a hierarchical clustering and the complete link algorithm which can produce small and tight clusters.

2.4   Customization of Categories

After a user modifies categories, the system learns the new boundary of cluster B with support vector machine (SVM).

SVM[3] is a classifier for multi-dimensional data to determine a boundary curve between two classes. The boundary can be determined only with vectors in boundary region (so-called "margin") of two classes (so-called "support vectors") in training examples. From the training examples SVM finds the parameters of the decision function $D(\bar{x})$ which can classify two classes A and B and maximize margin during a learning phase. SVM need to re-learn only when support vectors changes. This feature is very important for a large-scale and open document collection which changes constantly.

As mentioned above, the system appends user attribute after modification. For learning of SVM, the system sets 1 to the value of the attribute of moved document d (or documents which belong to the moved category). This attribute can be used for distinguishing between the moved documents and ones in the previous category. It might be dicult to classify them without this appended attribute. And SVM learns the ordinality from the original attributes within the new category.

The user-dependent weight for categorization $f_{cat}(u, i, j)$ of attribute j of document i for the user u is given by Eq. (1) and Eq. (2).

$$f_{cat}(u, i, j) = \begin{array}{ll} f(i, j) & (j = 1, 2, ..., m) \\ U_{cat}(u, i, k) & (j = m + k, \quad k = 1, 2, ..., N_a(u)) \end{array} \tag{1}$$

$$U_{cat}(u, i, k) = \begin{array}{l} 1 \text{ (if } i \text{ was modified in } k\text{-th action)} \\ 0 \text{ (otherwise)} \end{array} \tag{2}$$

where m stands for the number of terms and $N_a(u)$ stands for the number of feedback actions of the user u. Thus categories can be customized with user attributes and SVM.

The system needs to re-learn not all SVMs of categories but only one of the target category when a new attribute is appended.

References

1. Salton, G., Buckley, C.: Term weighting approaches in automatic text retrieval. Information Processing and Management.   24(5)   (1988) 513–523
2. Aihara, K., Hori, K., Ohsuga, S.: Aiding the process of building knowledge out of chunks of information. Journal of Japanese Society for Artificial Intelligence.   11(3) (1996) 432–439 (in Japanese)
3. Boser, B., Guyon, I., Vapnik, V.: A training algorithm for optimal margin classifiers. Proceedings of the Fifth Annual ACM Workshop on Computational Learning Theory. (1992) 144–152

Using Rollouts to Induce a Policy from a User Model

Joseph E. Beck and Beverly Park Woolf

Computer Science Department
University of Massachusetts
Amherst, MA 01003. U.S.A.
Phone: (413) 545-0582, Fax: (413) 545-1249
beck,bev   @cs.umass.edu

Abstract. This research describes the application of an executable user model to generate policies to adapt software to best t the user. Our approach rst gathers data describing how users behave, and uses these data to induce a computational model that predicts how users will perform in a particular situation. Since system designers have differing goals, our architecture takes an arbitrary goal that the designer would like to see users achieve. Our architecture than using rollout techniques to determine how software should act in a particular situation with the user in order to achieve the desired goal.

1 Introduction to ADVISOR

Most student models describe behavior or knowledge, usually represented in a declarative form, such as "With some probability   the student understands skill   ." However, this is not sufcient to control the decisions of an intelligent system. In order to act, a system must have some policy of mapping the state of the software and the contents of the user model to some action that it will perform. This process of encoding knowledge of how to act is expensive [3].

To address this issue, we have constructed ADVISOR. Our objective is to design an architecture that can determine how to act on the basis of a user model and a desired goal, without it having to be told how to achieve the goal. Figure 1 provides an overview of how ADVISOR reasons with its knowledge about the users. First, data about how users behave when working with the system are gathered. Then, these data are used to derive a predictive model of student behavior. Finally, this predictive model is used to nd a method of acting that achieves a desired goal. We have previously done work in this area [1] using reinforcement learning.

This work reports on the use of rollouts [2] to construct a policy for how a system should act. Briey, rollouts (or Monte Carlo estimation) are a technique for estimating the value of a state by performing a very narrow search until the "end" of the simulation run. Normally, a search cannot lookahead indenitely because of the combinatorial explosion produced by having multiple branches to examine after each decision. By only considering one branch, rollouts overcome this difculty. An obvious drawback is that, due to the narrowness of the search, rollouts potentially overlook very useful decisions, and ones that would affect how the agent should perform. This can either be overcome

M. Bauer, P.J. Gmytrasiewicz, and J. Vassileva (Eds.): UM 2001, LNAI 2109, pp. 210–212, 2001.
c Springer-Verlag Berlin Heidelberg 2001

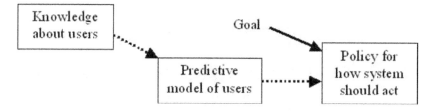

Fig. 1. Flow of knowledge in ADVISOR

by using a good heuristic that selects which branch the rollout should select, or by performing many rollouts in the hopes that at least some of them will result in information useful to making a good decision.

Our approach is to use many rollouts and randomly select which branch to select when searching ahead. The advantage of this is that almost no knowledge is required to build the reasoning agent. With no information other than observing traces of users, it is possible to construct a policy for how to act. Learning techniques require fussing with learning parameters and state representations, which is a considerable drawback.

ADVISOR was integrated into AnimalWatch, a tutor for teaching fraction arithmetic, to act as its pedagogical module and make teaching decisions.

2   Results

To determine if ADVISOR is capable of reasoning using rollouts we constructed a target time task. For this task, ADVISOR was required to have (simulated) students solve a problem in a certain amount of time. This could be useful to ensure that students do not spend too little time on a problem (i.e. received too much help) or too much time (i.e. the exercise was too challenging). For a target time of 35 seconds, ADVISOR was given a score of 1.0 for having a student take exactly 35 seconds to solve the problem. For taking 30 seconds, the score would be   . In this case,
was set to 0.025, so the score would be 0.875.

We tested ADVISOR across a wide range of time goals per problem: all values up to 120 seconds. That is, we ran 120 simulations, one with a goal of taking 1 second per problem, one with a goal of taking 2 seconds per problem, etc. For each target time, we ran ADVISOR 1000 times and reported the average score. Figure 2 shows how varying numbers of rollouts perform on the target time task. For all target times, there is a moderate but constant gain for performing more rollouts. This performance is near optimal for this task. For low target-times, AnimalWatch is not well congured to provide problems. Only for high target times do rollouts perform relatively poorly.

Ideally, ADVISOR would achieve performance of 1.0, the maximum, for each time goal. This is not possible for three reasons: the AnimalWatch tutor is not capable of hitting all times goals precisely; the predictive model is not perfectly accurate; and rollouts will not reason perfectly with the available data. The rst two questions are beyond the scope of this paper, and the third can be addressed by using a stronger reasoning mechanism (e.g. more rollouts).

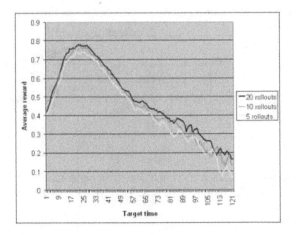

Fig. 2. Performance across different numbers of rollouts

3   Conclusions and Open Issues

We have previously attacked the problem of deriving a policy from a user model using reinforcement learning, and tested the result with human students [1]. An advantage of rollouts is that it is unnecessary to retrain ADVISOR when the teaching goal changes. The teacher could even use goals the tutor's designers did not consider; this would be much harder in a system that used machine learning.

ADVISOR's approach should generalize to other adaptive systems. Given an executable model of user performance and a desired goal, it is possible to use automatic reasoning techniques to cause the system to behave in the desired manner.

A limitation of ADVISOR is that it cannot model long term teaching goals. For example, one might like to say "Find a way to teach so that students master the curriculum in a minimum amount of time and still maintain 90% performance on all items." Unfortunately, this is currently beyond the scope of the simulation and architecture.

However, within its limitations, ADVISOR is capable of taking a user model, a goal, and determining a policy of acting with the user to achieve the goal without prior knowledge of "good" methods of acting.

References

1. Joseph E. Beck and Beverly P. Woolf. Learning to teach: A machine learning architecture for making teaching decisions. In Proceedings of the Seventeenth National Conference on Artificial Intelligence, 2000.
2. Dimitri P. Bertsekas and John N. Tsitsiklis. Neuro-Dynamic Programming. Athena Scientic, Belmont, Massachusetts; U.S.A., 1996.
3. H. Nwana and P. Coxhead. Towards an intelligent tutoring system for fractions. In Proceedings of First International Conference on Intelligent Tutoring Systems, pages 403–408, 1988.

Tailoring the Content
of Dynamically Generated Explanations

Kalina Bontcheva

University of Sheeld, Regent Court, 211 Portobello St., Sheeld S1 4DP, UK
kalina@dcs.shef.ac.uk

Abstract. This paper describes briefly an approach for tailoring the content of automatically generated hypertext explanations. The implemented pilot system hylite + has a dynamically updated user model, which is used by the language generation modules to adapt the explanations to the user beliefs and preferences. The goal is to provide suciently detailed information which, on one hand helps the user by explaining the unknown terms, and on the other, avoids repeating already known facts.

hylite + generates encyclopaedia-style explanations of terms in two specialised domains: chemistry and computers. The user interacts with the system in an ordinary Web browser (e.g., Netscape, Internet Explorer) by specifying a term she wants to look up. The system generates a hypertext explanation of the term; further information can be obtained by following hypertext links or specifying another query (see Figure 1).

The analysis of a corpus of encyclopaedic texts and terminological glossaries [1] showed that such texts often provide additional definitions of key vocabulary, background information and examples, in order to help inexperienced readers with the specialised terminology. Our empirical studies also showed that users prefer dierent content tailoring techniques, depending on the hypertext formatting and desired explanation length. This variation of user preferences motivated us to provide users with the ability to customise the system content tailoring behaviour. The adaptivity techniques preferred by the majority of users were enabled by default and the interface allows this behaviour to be changed easily, including disabling all personalisation (see Table 1).

When the user requests information about a topic (e.g., emulsion), hylite + needs to select a set of relevant propositions, from which the generation algorithms [1] produces the hypertext page in the following manner:

1. Obtain relevant propositions from the system's viewpoint given the user request, i.e., a domain concept C or an instance of such a concept.
2. Determine which propositions are already known by the user and mark them as such. In case of contradictory beliefs between system and user, both system and user beliefs are added to the propositions to be conveyed (e.g. believe(system, believe(user1,isa(photo _emulsion, emulsion))) and believe(system,isa(photo _emulsion, gel))).
3. Inspect each proposition for unknown related concepts and mark them as such.

M. Bauer, P.J. Gmytrasiewicz, and J. Vassileva (Eds.): UM 2001, LNAI 2109, pp. 213–215, 2001.

Table 1.   Some of the implemented content tailoring (adaptivity) features

Type of adaptivity	Default behaviour	User choices
Links to related pages	after the explanation	disable
Return to a visited page - using Back - using a link	show same page modify page opening	disable modification customise the phrase
Already seen material	include with a cue phrase	disable
Clarify unknown terms - short, to-the-point text - more informative text	known superconcept in parenthesis short definitions	choose links only switch to definitions switch to superconcepts

Unknown concepts in definitions, as well as unknown properties, parts, and super-/sub-concepts, trigger the inclusion of additional information (usually their definition) (see Figure 1).

The user model is also used to detect partially known facts which are then verbalised by the generator using contextual phrases such as   besides and as well as. For example, if the user has already seen an explanation of   TAPE DRIVE and follows the link to STORAGE DEVICE then the description of the types of storage devices is generated using such a phrase:

As well as tape drives, other types of data-storage devices are ...

Incorrect beliefs, detected in the user model, are explained by providing them in parallel with the correct fact. In the   photographic emulsion   example shown above, the system generates the following sentence as part of the   EMULSION explanation [1]:

A common error is to believe that photographic emulsion is emulsion, whereas, in fact, it is a gel.

The system was evaluated in a task-based experiment where subjects were asked to complete tasks with two versions of the system – the adaptive and a baseline, non-adaptive one [1]. The results showed that the users found both systems easy to use and intuitive to navigate. The majority of the users preferred the adaptive system, where they also had a higher task success rate.

The novel aspects of this work, in comparison to other related NLG work (e.g., PEBA [4], ILEX [3], TAILOR [5]), are two: (i) adaptable NLG – the user has control over the generator's decisions, including disabling all tailoring;   (ii) architecture which combines the   eciency   of sequential module execution and the flexibility oered by interleaved and revision-based approaches (see [2]).

---

[1] The a common error is... expression is used to express the uncertainty of this assumption which has been made on the basis of a stereotype. The generator can also deal with incorrect beliefs of individual users.

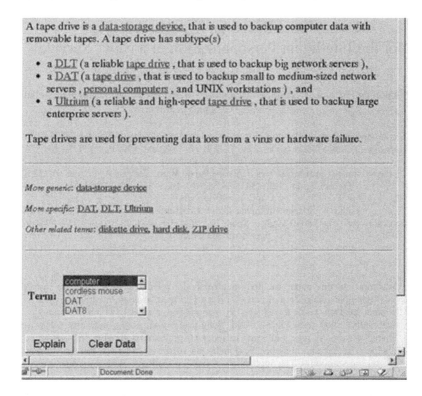

Fig. 1.   An example of a generated page with additional definitions and links to related material

References

1. Kalina Bontcheva.   Generating Adaptive Hypertext Explanations with a Nested Agent Model. PhD thesis, University of Sheeld, 2001. Forthcoming.
2. Kalina Bontcheva and Yorick Wilks. Dealing with dependencies between content planning and surface realisation in a pipeline generation architecture. In   Proceedings of the International Joint Conference in Artificial Intelligence (IJCAI'2001)   , Seattle, USA, August 2001.
3. Alistair Knott, Chris Mellish, Jon Oberlander, and Mick O' Donnell. Sources of flexibility in dynamic hypertext generation. In   Proceedings of the 8th International Workshop on Natural Language Generation (INLG'96)   , 1996.
4. Maria Milosavljevic, Adrian Tulloch, and Robert Dale. Text generation in a dynamic hypertext environment. In   Proceedings of the 19th Australian Computer Science Conference , Melbourne, 1996.
5. Cécile L. Paris.   User modelling in text generation   . Francis Pinter Publishers, London, 1993.

A User Model Based on Content Analysis
for the Intelligent Personalization of a News Service *

Manuel de Buenaga Rodríguez [1], Manuel J. Maña López [2], Alberto Díaz Esteban [1],
and Pablo Gervás Gómez-Navarro[3]

[1] Departamento de Inteligencia Artificial, Universidad Europea de Madrid – CEES, 28670
Villaviciosa de Odón, Madrid, Spain. Tel.: (34) 91 6647800 ext. 670. Fax: (34) 91 6168265
{buenaga, alberto}@dinar.esi.uem.es
[2] Departamento de Informá tica, Universidad de Vigo, Campus As Lagoas s/n, 32004
Orense, Spain. Tel.: (34) 988 387014. Fax: (34) 988 387001
mjlopez@uvigo.es
[3] Departamento de Sistemas Informá ticos y Programació, Universidad Complutense,
Ciudad Universitaria, 28040 Madrid, Spain. Tel.: (34) 91 3944739. Fax: (34) 91 3944662
pgervas@sip.ucm.es

Abstract. In this paper we present a methodology designed to improve the
intelligent personalization of news services. Our methodology integrates textual
content analysis tasks to achieve an elaborate user model, which represents
separately short-term needs and long-term multi-topic interests. The
characterization of user's interests includes his preferences about content, using
a wide coverage and non-specific-domain classification of topics, and structure
(newspaper sections). The application of implicit feedback allows a proper and
dynamic personalization.

Keywords. Information dissemination, short/long-term models, multi-topic
user profile, adaptive user model, personalized information service.

1   Introduction

Most of the newspaper publishers and news agencies supply information search and
delivery engines, as well as different personalization options. Thus, web sites of
leading newspapers, as e.g. The New York Times, offer personalization methods
specially focused in adaptation based on structure, i.e. newspaper sections. Others
also provide personalization based on content, but much remains to be said on this
issue.

The aim of this paper is to present a methodology designed to improve the
intelligent personalization of news services. The purpose is to offer a personalized and
especially synthetic version of a newspaper, improving the functionality currently
provided by commercial services. Most of the ideas presented in this paper have been
applied in a personalization service for a relevant Spanish newspaper: ABC [4].

---

* This work has been partially supported by Spanish Ministry of Industry (TS203/1999)

M. Bauer, P.J. Gmytrasiewicz, and J. Vassileva (Eds.): UM 2001, LNAI 2109, pp. 216–218, 2001.
c Springer-Verlag Berlin Heidelberg 2001

2   Modeling User's Interests

Users of any information access system have needs of different kinds. A user may have an occasional curiosity in knowing about some matter, but perhaps he is not interested in having new stories related to this topic in his personalized newspaper of the following days. The very different characteristics of both kinds of needs suggest the inclusion of general and sporadic interests in two separate representations: long and short-term models.

The user model proposed represents separately short-term needs and long-term multiple interests. Users can express their preferences both in terms of newspaper sections and news stories content. A wide coverage classification of topics non-specific to the newspaper domain, together with an initial representation of each category, is used to characterize user's interest. This representation works like a stereotypical definition that avoids starting with an empty user model that is trained by user feedback [1, 3, 2]. Application of implicit feedback allows these initial definitions to be enhanced and evolve together with user's interest.

The kind of necessity determines the news access method. Short-term needs are handled by the ad hoc retrieval subsystem, whereas long-term needs are managed by the dissemination information subsystem, which selects relevant news according to user's models and sends an e-mail message to the readers containing them. In following sections we will deal the long-term model because it integrates more advanced characteristics.

3   Preferences about News

User's preferences about news may be expressed in terms of contents, i.e. subjects of interest, or in terms of the structural element they belong to, i.e. sections of interest. To allow representation of multiple interests in the user model, users can show their preferences about sections and subjects giving their degrees of interest on each one.

We believe sections are not the best candidates to represent user's interests about news contents. An alternative is that the system provides a wide coverage classification about general subjects, non-specific to the newspaper domain, but known and understandable by the users. We have selected Yahoo! categories because it is the largest directory and it offers a specialized version in Spanish. The category system of Yahoo! Spain provides a first level with 14 categories and a second level with more than 200.

It is possible to obtain a representation for each category applying text categorization techniques [5] and using a set of training documents[1]. In our case, the set of training documents is the collection of web pages indexed by Yahoo! within these categories.

As well as the predefined hierarchy of categories, the system has to allow that users define alternative categories that are less generic and closer to their own interests. In this definition, users set for each new category a name and a list of

---

[1] A set of documents labeled manually with the suitable categories.

keywords. However, this option, due to its difficulty, is probably more appropriate for experienced users than for beginners.

Both features (sections and categories) have an associated weight that represents their importance for the user's interests. It is a fine-grain tuning mechanism that allows users to obtain a flexible characterization of their needs.

4   Adapting the Model to User's Preferences Changes

To achieve a long-term dynamic model that evolves together with user's interest, it is necessary to apply feedback techniques that provide information about this evolution. However, in practice, many users are unwilling to provide relevance judgments on retrieved documents. An alternative is to use implicit feedback, i.e. to inference document relevance from user's behavior, which has successfully applied in the learning of user models [1]. Then, we use the documents read by the user as feedback. The system provides numerous context elements, including a user-adapted summary [6] that can assist users to decide about document relevance without inspecting the full text. If a user accesses the full text of a piece of news, the system can infer that it is relevant and use its term weight vector to improve the long-term user model.

Before a new dissemination process starts, the user models, i.e. the term weight vectors that represent categories, are updated. For each piece of news read by the user, the vector category with the greatest value of similarity (according to cosine measure) is modified.

References

1. Balabanovic, M.: An Interface for Learning Multi-topic User Profiles from Implicit Feedback. In: AAAI Workshop on Recommender Systems, Madison, Wisconsin (1998)
2. Billsus, D., Pazzani, M.J.: A Hybrid User Model for News Story Classification. In: Proceedings of the Seventh International Conference on User Modeling, Banff, Canada (1999)
3. Chen, L., Sycara, K.P.: WebMate: A Personal Agent for Browsing and Searching. In: Proceedings of the Second International Conference on Autonomous Agents, Minneapolis, (1998)
4. Díz Esteban, A., Gervá s Gńez-Navarro, P., Garcá Jimé nez, A.: Evaluating a User-Model Based Personalisation Architecture for Digital News Services. In: Proceedings of the Fourth European Conference on Research and Advanced Technology for Digital Libraries, Lisbon, Portugal (2000)
5. Lewis, D.D.: Representation and Learning in Information Retrieval. PhD Thesis, Technical Report UM-CS-1991-093, Department of Computer and Information Science, University of Massachussetts (1992)
6. Mañ a Lṕez, M.J., Buenaga Rodŕguez, M., Gńez Hidalgo, J.M.: Using and Evaluating User Directed Summaries to Improve Information Access. In: Proceedings of the Third European Conference on Research and Advanced Technology for Digital Libraries, Paris, France (1999)

Modeling Exploratory Behaviour

Andrea Bunt and Cristina Conati

Department of Computer Science, University of British Columbia
201-2366 Main Mall, Vancouver, B.C. V6T 1Z4
phone: (604)822-4912 fax: (604)822-5485
bunt@cs.ubc.ca , conati@cs.ubc.ca

Abstract.   In this paper we propose a user model that aims to assess
the user's exploratory behaviour in an open environment. The model is
based on a Bayesian Network and consists of several components that allow diagnosis of the causes of poor exploratory behaviour. Among these
components are the user's knowledge of exploration strategies, the user's
motivation level, personality traits and emotional states.

Keywords.   Bayesian Networks, exploration, exploratory environments

1   Introduction

Many researchers have examined the potential of exploratory learning environments as tools to stimulate active, constructive student learning (e.g [2]). However, empirical studies show that these environments are not always eective
(e.g.[3]). One of the key problems is that not all users are always capable exploring properly.

Eective exploratory behaviour is inflenced by a number of user-dependent
factors including exploration knowledge, domain knowledge, motivation, personality traits and emotional states [4][3]. Ideally, exploratory environments should
provide support for users who are not exploring properly without disrupting or
restricting users who are. Therefore, these systems would greatly benefit from a
detailed user model that gauges the eectiveness of the users exploration. While
a few systems exist that provide feedback on the results of a user's exploration
process (e.g [5]), none of these systems include a student model that can assess
and guide the exploration process itself.

The following sections describe preliminary work on building a user model
to assess and support a user's exploratory behaviour. Section 2 describes the
current state of the model. Section 3 describes the plans for extension.

2   Components of the User Model

Currently, a preliminary user model that assesses exploratory behaviour has
been implemented in the context of the Adaptive Coach for Exploration (ACE),
an intelligent exploratory learning environment that allows students to freely

M. Bauer, P.J. Gmytrasiewicz, and J. Vassileva (Eds.): UM 2001, LNAI 2109, pp. 219–221, 2001.
c Springer-Verlag Berlin Heidelberg 2001

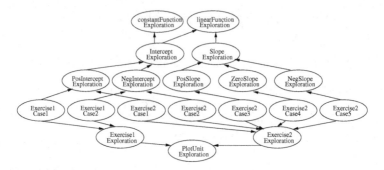

Fig. 1.   An example portion of the exploration model

explore concepts associated with mathematical functions. For example, the user
can explore how a function behaves given a variety of inputs and how manipulating the graph of a function alters its corresponding equation. With the aid
of the student model, the system attempts to detect when the student is not
exploring eectively and is able to provide hints to improve the exploration [1].

The student model within ACE is a Bayesian Network that contains nodes
representing the eectiveness of the students exploratory behaviour. Fig.   ??
shows an example portion of the network for ACE's graph manipulation unit
(labeled PlotUnit Exploration). Exploratory behaviour is assessed at dierent levels of granularity including the exploration of individual exercises (e.g.
"Exercise1" in Fig.   ??), categories of related exercises (e.g. "PlotUnit Exploration") and categories of related concepts that appear across multiple exercises
(e.g. "Intercept Exploration"). In this situation, the student has been presented
with two exercises: one where the student can explore a constant function and
another that provides the opportunity to explore a linear function.

Evidence is introduced into the network whenever the student experiments
with an element in the interface that the system considers to be a relevant
exploration case for that particular exercise. Nodes representing the relevant
exploration cases are labeled "ExerciseX CaseY" in Fig.   ?? (e.g. "Exercise1
Case1"). As an example of what it means to explore a relevant exploration case,
the system considers the student to have explored "Exercise1 Case1" when the
student drags the line to a position where the function has a positive y-intercept
(or edits function equation to produce the same result). Should this event occur,
the "Exercise 1 Case 1" node would be observed to be True.

3   Extensions to the Model

The model that currently exists within ACE is limited in two ways. (1) It is
not suciently detailed to allow the system to provide suggestions that are
tailored to the speci problems that cause the students ineective exploratory
behaviour. (2) It tracks eective exploratory behaviour through only interface
actions.

Modeling Causes of Poor Exploration.   The user's exploration process depends on a number of factors including knowledge of exploration strategies, domain knowledge, motivation, emotional states, and meta-cognitive skills, such as self-explanation and self-monitoring. We would need to investigate to use of alternative input devices, such as speech intonation recognition and aective computing devices, as a means of assessing emotional states and motivation levels.

Each factor, along with the probabilistic dependencies among factors, will be modeled in detail within the Bayesian Network. Querying variables in the model will allow the environment to sense when the student is not demonstrating effective exploratory behaviour. Sensing this, the model can obtain a probabilistic estimate of the specifi causes of the diculties (lack of motivation, lack of knowledge, etc) permitting the system to tailor its feedback to directly address the most likely causes. Alternatively, the environment could use the network's predictive inferences to adapt to the potential of poor exploratory behaviour should it observe the student to have, for example, poor knowledge of the domain.

Tracking Exploratory Behaviour.   Knowing where the user is focusing her attention would greatly increase the model's ability to interpret the user's actions as evidence of good exploratory behaviour. It may be possible that a student's interface actions indicate good exploration but that she is not paying attention to the results of that exploration. For example, in ACE's graph manipulation activity, the student may be actively manipulating the graph but not examining the function equation. In this case, the student would fail to gain an understanding of the relationship between a function graph and its equation. We plan to add to the model additional variables that model the user's attention pattern and use eye-tracking to update these variables.

References

1. A. Bunt, C. Conati, M. Huggett, and K. Muldner. On improving the eectiveness of open learning environments through tailored support for exploration. In   AIED 2001, to appear.

2. M. Njoo and T. de Jong. Exploratory learning with a computer simulation for control theory: Learning processes and instructional support.   Journal of Research in Science Teaching , 30(8):821–844, 1993.

3. V. Shute and R. Glaser. A large-scale evaluation of an intelligent discovery world: Smithtown. Interactive Learning Environments   , 1:55–77, 1990.

4. W. van Joolingen. Cognitive tools for discovery learning.   Journal of Artificial Intelligence and Education   , 10, 1999.

5. K. Veermans and W. van Joolingen. Using induction to generate feedback in simulation based discovery learning environments. In B. Goetl, H. M. Hal, C. Redeld, and V. Shute, editors,   Intelligent Tutoring Systems, 4th International Conference (ITS'98) , pages 196–205, Berlin, 1998. Springer.

Ascribing and Weighting Beliefs in Deceptive Information Exchanges

Valeria Carofiglio [1], Fiorella de Rosis [1], and Cristiano Castelfranchi [2]

[1] Department of Informatics, University of Bari
Bari, Italy
{carofiglio, derosis   }@di.uniba.it
http://aos2.uniba.it:8080/IntInt.html
[2] Department of Communication Sciences, University of Siena
Siena, Italy
castel@www.ip.rm.cnr.it

Abstract. Humans apply a large variety of deception forms in their communicative acts; they are not necessarily 'uncooperative' in doing so, as they may even deceive for the benefit of their interlocutors [2,3]. Deception may be active or passive, according to whether the Speaker does something or not, to achieve his goal. It may be applied directly to the deception object p or may indirectly influence it through some deception medium'q that may be a cause, an eect or a diverting cause or eect of p. In this short paper, we examine how deception may be simulated if mental states are represented as belief networks and various weights are attached to beliefs.

keywords   : belief ascription, belief networks, dialog simulation, deception.

1   A Deception Simulator: MOUTH OF TRUTH

MOUTH OF TRUTH enables simulating the way that a deceptive communicative act may be planned. The System plays the role of the Speaker S (the potential 'deceiver') and the User the role of the Addressee A. The problem considered may be stated as follows.

Given: (i) a domain; (ii) a mental state of S, as a set of beliefs about the domain represented in a bayesian network OWN-S;   (iii) a set T of domain facts that A is presumed to know and   (iv) a domain fact p that is taken as the 'deception object', plan a communicative act that involves a deception medium q and enables S to achieve a given goal about A's belief in p: G_S ($G_S B_A p$) or $G_S(\neg BW_A p)$.

The User interacts with the System through a Web interface; she may select a domain and declare what she knows about it; S builds a image of the mental state of A (IM-S-A), consistently with his own mental state. This image is an 'overlay model' of OWN-S with a reduced number of nodes. The two models are probabilistically compatible, as the prior probabilities of the nodes they share are the same. We assume that, to avoid arising suspicion, S is very prudent in evoking facts that are not 'in focus' in A's mind: his communicative acts then

M. Bauer, P.J. Gmytrasiewicz, and J. Vassileva (Eds.): UM 2001, LNAI 2109, pp. 222–224, 2001.
c Springer-Verlag Berlin Heidelberg 2001

possible to the beliefs that he considers as 'active', to A, in the given phase of interaction. Obviously, the set of active beliefs is inherently dynamic: some of them may become inactive after some time, other may activate as far as the dialog goes on. S keeps a memory of the facts that were active 'not too much long ago', in order to insure the safety of his communicative acts. Once IM-S-A has been built, the truth values of the facts in T are propagated and the System looks at the probability that A assigns to p, in her present state of knowledge. It then selects a candidate deception medium q, by considering the following factors:

a. ecacy   in achieving the goal G_S, as impact of the deception medium q on the deception object p; two dierent notions of impact are implemented:
   - degree of achievement of S's goal about A's belief in p, as a function of the dierence between the goal-value and the posterior probability of p, to A, after she comes to believe in q: $Imp^1(q,p) = 1 + G_S B_A P(p) - B_S B_A P(p|q)|$;
   - degree of change in A's belief about p that is induced by believing in q, as a function of the dierence between the prior and posterior probability of A's belief in p: $Imp^2(q,p) = B_S B_A P(p|q) - B_S B_A P(p)$;

b. plausibility of q to A, as a function of the likelihood that A will get convinced about q after S's communication. Again, we implemented two dierent notions of plausibility:
   - local plausibility , as a function of the dierence between what S presumes to be A's belief about q and the communication she receives from S: $Plau^1_{S,A}(q) = 1 + B_S B_A P(q) - B_S P(q)|$;
   - global plausibility, as a function of the same dierence, extended to all facts q_l that are 'connected to q', in the context of 'active beliefs': $Plau^2_{S,A}(q) = 1 - 1/w(\sum_{l=1,...w} |B_S B_A P(q_l) - B_S P(q_l)|)$. In this case, the plausibility of a fact is seen as the overall compatibility of new knowledge induced by q with the previous one, in the mentioned context.

c. safety of the communicative act: this is linked to the risk, to S, of being discovered, by A, in a deception attempt. This risk depends, in its turn, on various factors: (i) how plausible might be, to A, that S believes in what he says and (ii) whether A may come to understand that her believing in that fact is in S's interest and advantage;

d. reliability , to A, of the information source eventually evoked, by S, to support his statement. The credibility of a fact q referred by an information source IS may be defined, probabilistically, as: $Cred(q,IS) = P(q|Say(IS,q))$ (and alike for ¬q);it is a function of the reliability of IS: $Rel(IS,q) = P(Say(IS,q)|q)$ and of the prior probability of q (and alike for   ¬q). S may combine information sources in various ways to support his communication: he may cite several reliable sources or may combine reliable with unreliable ones, to try to confound A's ideas.

2 Related Work

dierent, the methods we apply have several analogies with those employed in other dialog systems (see [5,7]). Bayesian networks seem to us a very promising approach to deception modeling: from a logical viewpoint, the problem involves a very complex reasoning [1]: to Taylor and colleagues, modeling these dialogs would require reasoning at 'deeply-nested belief' level (higher that the third one) while, on the contrary, deeply-nested beliefs are known to be 'awkward and contrary to intuitions in human-human dialogs' [6]. The approach we are here describing enables avoiding deeply-nested belief reasoning through the following assumptions: (i) beyond intentionally insincere assertions, there is always some interest of the Speaker, the need to achieve some domain-goal; (ii) deception results from a conflict (between S and A) about this goal and (iii) S is interested to do his best to hide his deception attempts. From these assumptions comes that deceiving is not the same as lying, so that discovering contradictions in the interlocutor enlights only a subset of the large variety of deception attempts: this entails the need of tackling the problem from an 'uncertain' viewpoint and to attach, to beliefs, a system of weights formalizing the mentioned aspects. Besides representing the inherently uncertain process of suspicion, belief networks oer the possibility of applying various forms of reasoning (from causes to eects and vice-versa): this enables simulating the deception forms mentioned in the Abstract. The assumption of 'probabilistic compatibility' between OWN-S and IM-S-A reduces the range of deceptions we may simulate at present: S cannot exploit, in his deceptive attempts, dierences in the strength that A attaches to belief relations; this is one of the aspects we plan to investigate in the future. In general, we wish to assess whether our deception theory is eective in enabling the generation of the most common deception forms that we describe in [4]).

References

1. Ballim, A., Wilks, Y.: Beliefs, stereotypes ad dynamic agent modeling. User Modeling and User-Adapted Interaction, 1, 1, 1991.
2. Castelfranchi, C., Poggi, I.: Lying as pretending to give information. Pretending to Communicate, H. Parret (Ed), Springer Verlag, 1993.
3. Castelfranchi, C., de Rosis, F., Grasso, F.: Deception and suspicion in medical interactions; towards the simulation of believable dialogues. Machine Conversations, Y Wilks (Ed), Kluwer Series in Engineering and Computer Science,   511 , 1999.
4. de Rosis, F., Castelfranchi, C., Carofiglio, V.: Can computers deliberately deceive? A simulation attempt of Turing's Imitation Game. Sumbitted for publication.
5. Ndiaye, A. and Jameson, A.: Predictive role taking in dialog: global anticipation feedback based on transmutability. In Proc. 5th Int. Conf. on User Modeling, Kailua-Kona, Hawaii,137-144, 1996
6. Taylor, J.A., Carletta, J., Mellish, C.: Requirements for belief models in Cooperative dialogue. User Modeling and User-Adapted Interaction, 6, 1, 1996.
7. Zukerman, I., Jinath, N., McConachy, R., George, S.: Recognising intentions from rejoinders in a bayesian interactive argumentation system. In PRICAI 2000 Proceedings, Melbourne. 8.

Visual Search and Background Complexity:
Does the Forest Hide the Trees?

Martha E. Crosby, Marie K. Iding, and David N. Chin

Univ. of Hawaii, 1680 East West Rd POST 317, Honolulu, HI 96822, USA
phone:808-956-3493, fax:808-956-3548
crosby@hawaii.edu,

Abstract. This research addresses the issue of cognitive complexity or cognitive load in a visual search task. Eye tracking methodology was employed to track users' eye fixations and scan patterns while counting targets in a visual array. Background complexity and number of targets were varied. Results showed that there was a positive relationship between fixation duration and background complexity and between fixation duration and number of targets in the array. Fixation duration and saccade predicted background complexity and number of targets for simple and systematically varied arrays. These results indicate that eye-tracking data may contribute effectively to the development of user models in crisis management systems.

Key words : Eye-tracking. Cognitive-complexity

The issue of cognitive load has been explored in a variety of contexts, including students' working with examples in optics and kinematics [8] and peoples' work with textual and graphical displays for applications in electronics and biology [2]. Clearly, determining what information to present users is central to designing effective multi-user interfaces for crisis management. At what point does the level of detail increase cognitive complexity or cognitive load to the point where it interferes with performance or is detrimental? Here, it seems intuitive to predict that user characteristics (e.g., expertise within a profession, familiarity with the geographic region depicted, spatial ability, etc.), would interact with aspects of visual arrays, such as complexity, necessitating the development of effective user models. Hence, a central consideration in this research is determining how complexity of visual arrays affects user performance.

In order to reduce the users' information load by presenting only data that is relevant to the user's current task, more information is needed about how users' locate salient information in a multi-user interface. The focus of this study is visual search or the process of finding particular data within the visual field. Several studies have reported that search times are related to the density or complexity of the background [1;3;4;5;6]. Training improves performance when distractors and targets are switched between training sessions as reported by Rogers, Lee, and Fisk [7]. Williams studied the probability of fixating on objects of different size, shape and color [9]. He concluded that when two or more target characteristics were specified, fixations were generally based on a single characteristic. He proposed that the specification of a

M. Bauer, P.J. Gmytrasiewicz, and J. Vassileva (Eds.): UM 2001, LNAI 2109, pp. 225–227, 2001.
©Springer-Verl ag Berlin Heidelberg 2001

target creates perceptual structures that the searcher explores and the study of visual fixations is the study of the perceptual structures.

An experiment was performed using 31 undergraduates (27 male and 4 female) from the Department of Information and Computer Sciences at the University of Hawaii as participants. Each participant viewed 21 scenes (3 conditions of 7 arrays). The 3 conditions consisted of white vertical bars with black vertical and white horizontal bars as distractors (complex distractors), black vertical bars with black horizontal bars as distractors (simple distractors), and white vertical bars without distractors.) All scene conditions were intermixed. An Anova using the fixation times of correct searches as the dependent variable and the complexity factor as the independent variables found the fixation durations between the complexity groups to be statistically significant, $p < .0001$, $F(2, 476) = 23.75$, $MSE = 424,027$. For the condition without distractors, the mean fixation duration was 99.3 msec. For the condition with simple distractors (horizontal vs. vertical black bars), there was a mean fixation time of 154 msec and for the complex distractors, the mean fixation time was 204 msec. In addition, there were statistically different fixation times between searching for a small number of targets (1-3) M= 108ms and a large number of targets (4-7), M= 192ms, $F(1, 477) = 46.92$, $MSE = 837,154$, $p < .0001$. Error trials are excluded from both analyses. In addition, there appear to be predictable differences between the scan path and the fixations of the scenes with and without distractors. The nature of the fixation patterns that contribute to increases in processing time appears to vary with the spatial characteristics of the scenes and the complexity of the distractors. The difference in fixation patterns across scene types actually become greater as the number of target items increases. This research demonstrates that visual search is affected by complexity in several ways. First, increases in background complexity (i.e., presence of distractors) in visual arrays are associated with increases in processing time for simple visual search tasks where participants must count specified numbers of targets in arrays. Second, increases in number of targets are associated with increases in search time. Third, and most important for user modeling, fixation duration and saccade length appear to predict the background complexity as well as few (1-3) versus many (4-7) targets, at least for simple and systematically varied arrays like the ones in this experiment. Taken as a whole, these results provide an initial yet compelling indication that eye-tracking data may contribute effectively to the development of user models for incorporation into software systems. In addition to contributing to user modeling research, this research has theoretical implications that may be consistent with cognitive load theory. This suggests that effort expended in integrating among sources can have a deleterious effect upon cognitive processing, if the integration in itself is not meaningful [2]. In the case of developing an effective user models, future research should include an examination of the integration or visual search strategy among more complex arrays that are systematically varied as well as further determination of what integration is meaningful. This will depend not only on the specific task demands but also on the expertise of potential users.

This work was supported in part by IBM joint study agreement no. 3031, DARPA Space and Naval Warfare Systems ONR grant no. N660019818911, and ONR grant no. N00014970578.

References

1. J. Bloomfield. Visual search in complex fields: Size differences between target disc and surrounding discs. In Human Factors. 14 (2), pages139-148, 1972.
2. P. Chandler and J, Sweller. Cognitive load theory and the format of instruction.   In Cognition and Instruction. 8 (4), pages 293-332, 1991.
3. C. Drury, M. Clement and R. Clement. The effect of area, density, and number of background characters on visual search. In Human Factors. 20, pages 597-602, 1978.
4. C. Eriksen.   Object location in a complex perceptual field.   In Journal of Experimental Psychology. 45 (3) pages124-132, 1952.
5. D. Klahr.   Quantification processes.   In W. G. Chase (Ed.), Visual information processing, pages 3-34. New York, 1973. Academic Press.
6. T. Monk and B. Brown. The effect of target surround density on visual search performance. In Human Factors. 17(4). Pages 356-360, 1975.
7. W. A. Rogers, M. D. Lee, and A. D. Fisk. Contextual effects on general learning, feature learning, and attention strengthening in visual search. In Human Factors, 37 (1), pages 158-172, 1995.
8. M. Ward, M. and J. Sweller. Structuring effective worked examples. In Cognition and Instruction. 7 (1), pages 1-39, 1990.
9. L. Williams. The effect of target specification on objects fixated during visual search. In Perception and Psychophysics, 1, 1966.

Characterizing Sequences of User Actions for Access Logs Analysis

Thomas Draier and Patrick Gallinari

LIP6, Université Paris 6, 8 rue du Cap. Scott, 75015, Paris, Fr
Draier@poleia.lip6.fr, Patrick.Gallinari@lip6.fr

Abstract. The paper presents new measures for characterizing sequences of user actions. They are aimed at categorizing user behavior on intranet sites. Their relevance is evaluated using different encoding and clustering algorithms. New criteria are introduced for comparing clustering methods.

1   Introduction

The analysis of web access logs has motivated an important amount of research and development over the last years. It could be useful for a variety of applications such as web site analysis, interface adaptation, action prediction, etc. We focus here on the clustering of user behaviors for identifying typical profiles. The sequential nature of user accesses is essential for this characterization. Although this has been considered for e.g. predicting user behavior, only a few projects make use of sequences for finding groups of users from log files. One of the reasons for that is the high variability of user event sequences. We are looking here both for robust intranet user event sequence characteristics and robust clustering algorithms which are insensitive to the intrinsic noise of log patterns. We propose a series of sequence characteristics, evaluate them and compare the behavior and stability of two well known clustering algorithms using an information theoretic measure. We present results on intranet access logs gathered over several months.

2   Characteristics of User Sequences

User sessions are first identified and then segmented into a set of sequences (i.e. series of user requests with no backward reference) using the algorithm in [1]. For classifying web users, [2] show that the histogram of sequence lengths for each user is characteristic of the user category. We build on this idea and propose a series of event sequence characteristics. For each of them, we compute a histogram from the log files of each user, we encode this histogram into a concise description which is then used for categorizing the users. The characteristics we have considered are: (1) the number of events of each session, (2) the connection duration of sessions, (3) the number of sequences per session which indicates how the site is explored, (4) the sequence size, (5) the frequency - relative to the whole user panel - of the user sequences, which discriminates between standard and unusual users, (6) the time spent on the pages which gives an idea of the navigation speed, (7) the size of the documents retrieved for each request. Characteristics (4) and (5) are shown in fig. 1 for two users, they are clearly

M. Bauer, P.J. Gmytrasiewicz, and J. Vassileva (Eds.): UM 2001, LNAI 2109, pp. 228–230, 2001.

discriminative. Although only two users have been shown for clarity, the shapes are characteristic of the user type.

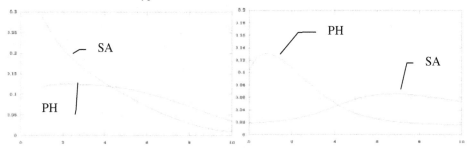

Fig. 1. : Smoothed histograms for feature 4 (left) and 5 (right) for two different users: a system administrator (SA) and a project head (PH). x axis indicates a normalized feature value and y axis its frequency.

We have considered three different condensed histogram representations for analyzing the user population: (1) Exponential regression model y = a*exp(b*x), a and b being used as features. (2) First four statistical moments of the distribution (mean, standard deviation, skewness and kurtosis). (3) Interpolation: each curve is represented by 15 regularly sampled values.

3   Data Clustering and Cluster Validity

We have evaluated these characteristics when using two popular clustering algorithms: Partitioning Around Medoïds (PAM) [3] which is an extension of k-means and Autoclass [4], a Bayesian model of mixture density. Determining the right number of clusters is a key issue which is still an open problem, and for real applications, we mainly rely on heuristics. Autoclass automatically selects the number of clusters via Bayesian learning. For PAM, this "optimal" number has been selected using the F-statistics.

For identifying user groups, we are looking for robust encoding and algorithms, so that similar groups are identified for different tests on the same site. Practically this is barely the case. In an attempt to explore the similarity between different classifications, and the robustness of each algorithm and feature representation, we propose to use an information based similarity measure between cluster distributions. Let C_A be a discrete random variable over the set of clusters for algorithm A (C_A identifies the clusters). For two algorithms A and B, the joint distribution $P(c_A, c_B)$ is the probability for any pattern x to be classified as (c_A, c_B) by A and B. Loosely speaking, if $P(c_A, c_B)$ is high for some couple of clusters, the two algorithms have identified similar structures in the population, otherwise clusters are independent. For comparing algorithms A and B, we use the mutual information (1) between distributions $P(C_A)$ and $P(C_B)$. Note that this measure allows us to compare two clusterings even when the number of clusters is different.

$$MI(C_A, C_B) = \sum_{c_A \ c_B} P(c_A, c_B) \log \frac{P(c_A, c_B)}{P(c_A)P(c_B)} \qquad (1)$$

4   Experiments

We have performed experiments using a software company intranet site which houses several applications in beta test. There are 253 users, 5 broad user categories (system administrators, project head, web and java developers, marketing people), about 300 pages and 120 K log events after removing irrelevant information from the access logs. For making easier the comparison between different experiments, we use a normalized MI measure MI_N, so that $MI_N (X,X) = 1$. These experiments allow analyzing the robustness of the algorithms, of features and encoding. Some results are shown below and are briefly discussed. Table 1 shows that PAM and Autoclass have a high degree of similarity at least for the moments and that the encoding heavily influences the clustering. In order to test individual feature robustness, we have divided each user log files into two parts and built two log sets using the 253 users. For each algorithm, the mutual information between the cluster distributions obtained for the two sets with each feature has been evaluated. Table 2 shows the relevance of features (4,5,6,7) according to MI_N for PAM, features (1,2,3) are below 0.1 and are not given. When using the former four features simultaneously with their best individual encoding, MI_N reaches 0.45 for PAM, which is better than any individual feature does. This shows that 4 among the 7 proposed sequence characteristics are relevant for classifying users and that the mutual information measure allows us to select the most relevant features, encoding and algorithm for a given data set.

Table 1. normalized mutual information between PAM and Autoclass for different encoding (2nd row) and normalized mutual information between the cluster distributions obtained with the different encoding for Autoclass (3rd and 4th rows). Note that $MI_N(X,X) = 1$

	Regression	Stat. moments	Interpolation
MI_N(PAM, Autoclass)	0.60	0.67	0.47
Regression	1	0.42	.32
Stat. moments		1	0.53

Table 3. normalized mutual information of each characteristic (4,5,6,7), for PAM (see text)

PAM	Regression	Stat. moments	Interpolation
Sequence size	0.30	0.14	0.17
Sequence frequency	0.08	0.12	0.37
Request time	0.16	0.05	0.17
Request size	0.24	0.04	0.04

References

1. Chen M., Park J., Yu P., Data mining for path traversal patterns in a web environment, 16th ICDCP, 1996.
2. Catledge L., Pitkow J.E.: Characterizing Browsing Strategies in the world wide web, Comp. Net. and ISDN systems, 27, 1995.
3. The comprehensive r archive network, www.r-project.org
4. Cheeseman P., Kelly J., Self M., Stutz J., Taylor W., Freeman D., Autoclass: a Bayesian classification system, Fifth ICML. Morgan Kaufmann, 1988.

Modeling Literary Style
for Semi-automatic Generation of Poetry

Pablo Gervá s

Departamento de Sistemas Informá ticos y Programació, Universidad Complutense de Madrid,
Ciudad Universitaria, 28040 Madrid, Spain. Tel.: (34) 91 3944293. Fax: (34) 91 3944602
pgervas@sip.ucm.es

Abstract. The generation of formal poetry involves both complex creativity - usually exercised by a human poet - and strict algorithmic restrictions regarding the metrical structure of the poem - determined by literary tradition. Starting from a generating system that enforces automatically the metrical restrictions, this paper presents a model for the literary style of a user based on four key features for user preferences - word selection, language structures, poem planning, and restrictions on realisation - governing the generation of poetry from input data provided by the user - a prose paraphrase of the intended message, a task specific vocabulary, and a corpus of construction patterns. The system exploits the CBR paradigm as a means to evolve a case base (a vocabulary / construction pattern grouping) that effectively models the style of a specific user as a result of multiple iterations through the CBR cycle.

Keywords: natural language generation, human-computer collaboration, task modeling

1 Introduction

Existing systems for the automatic generation of text have shown reasonable results in restricted domains [4,7]. The composition of poetry ranks among the most challenging problems of language generation, and is therefore a good test-bed for techniques designed to improve the quality of generated texts. There are currently at least two research efforts devoted to it, one in English [5,6] - dependent on having adequately rich lexicon, syntax and semantics for the language involved - and one in Spanish [2,3] - based on engineering solutions that achieve equivalent results without attempting to model the complexity of the human language.

These systems can automatically generate texts that conform to the rules of poetry, and they need to develop some way of modeling literary style, so that an automatic generation system can provide not only text that matches generic metrical rules for poetry, but that also presents a specified literary style.

To achieve this, an adequate set of parameters to characterise the elusive concept of literary style must be identified, and the process of poem generation must be adapted to take them into account.

M. Bauer, P.J. Gmytrasiewicz, and J. Vassileva (Eds.): UM 2001, LNAI 2109, pp. 231–233, 2001.
©Springer-Verlag Berlin Heidelberg 2001

2   Modeling Literary Style in Natural Language Generation

Statistic analysis of texts by computer is carried out in cases of disputed authorship [8,9], to identify the - unknown - author of a specific text by comparing it with texts known to have been written by specific authors. Frequency distribution of words of different lengths, sentence length, and combination of various mathematical analyses with word content analysis are generally regarded as having considerable validity in identifying differences between authors. This suggests such parameters may be acceptable as a trustworthy print of a specific style.

The process of generation of a natural language text can be divided in three different stages: gathering of the required data - identifying a specific message to be conveyed, the actual words that are going to be used, and the language structures that are going to be employed -, planning of the intended message over the text - splitting the message among the sentences in the text -, and realisation of the expression - building the final text from the data according to the planning.

A user model for the literary style of a particular poet, to be used in natural language generation, ought to include information about: word selection, language structures, poem planning, and restrictions on the realisation of the poem (including metric structure).

3   A CBR Approach to Modeling Literary Style

ASPERA [3] is a prose-to-poetry semiautomatic translator. The four aspects of a user model of literary style described in the previous section are covered by three kinds of input data provided to ASPERA by the user. The user is asked to provide a prose paraphrase of his intended message. The user must also provide a task specific vocabulary, a set of words to be used by the system. The system is provided with a corpus of construction patterns obtained from already validated verses (case-base). These last two kinds of data constitute a first approximation to the model of the literary style desired by the user. This is extended with explicit preferences represented in a user profile built beforehand by the user.

A Case Based Reasoning (CBR) approach [1] is applied to the input data together with the user profile to generate new verses. During a typical execution cycle, the ASPERA system performs the following sequence of operations: selects words and patterns useful for the poem from the task-specific vocabulary and corpus of verse patterns (CBR Retrieve step); generates each of the verses of the poem draft by mirroring the POS structure of the pattern of the retrieved verse pattern combined with the words in the selected vocabulary (CBR Reuse step); presents the draft to be validated or corrected by the user (CBR Revise step); and adds the corresponding information to its case-base for later use (CBR Retain step).

Word selection preferences are encoded in the user profile as a priority assignment to the three kinds of input data as preferred sources of vocabulary. Words to be added to the poem draft are initially looked for only among words with the highest priority, the search extending to words of lower priority only if none had been found earlier.

Language structure preferences are represented in the user profile in terms of restrictions that the elements in the corpus of construction patterns must satisfy. These construction patterns are vectors of part-of-speech (POS) tags corresponding to the words being used in the case base.

Poem planning preferences appear in the user profile in terms of constraints on the appearance of sentence breaks within a line, and maximum and minimum number of lines that a sentence can span. Additionally, where patterns are used to represent complete stanzas, they also encode the distribution of words over lines (number and type of words per line, type of word at the end of a line...).

Metric preferences are stored in the user profile as initial parameters for the construction algorithm (chosen stanza, chosen verse length, rhyme pattern...).

Word selection and language structure preferences affect the CBR retrieve step. Poem planning and metric preferences affect the CBR reuse step.

The CBR revise and retain steps allow progressive refinement of the approximation to the desired literary style represented by the accumulated system vocabulary and the corpus of construction patterns. The system is continuously feeding back into the system the results that are being validated. From the moment the case base holds more user generated poems than poems in the original corpus, the data available to the system can be considered to embody the literary style of the user that has been interacting with it. In the same way as a CBR system employed consistently to solve a particular type of problem acquires with normal use knowledge that its designers were unaware of, such a poem generator would develop with continuous use into a model of the literary style of its users.

References

1. Aamodt, A. & Plaza, E. (1994). Case-Based Reasoning: Foundational Issues, Methodological Variations, and System Approaches. AI Communications, 7(i), pp 39-59.
2. Gervá s, P., 'WASP: Evaluation of Different Strategies for the Automatic Generation of Spanish Verse', in: AISB-00 Symposium on Creative & Cultural Aspects and Applications of AI & Cognitive Science, 17th-18th April 2000, U. of Birmingham, England, pp 93-100.
3. Gervá s, P., 'An Expert System for the Composition of Formal Spanish Poetry', in: Macintosh, A., Moulton, M., and Coenen, F. (eds.), Applications and Innovations in Intelligent Systems VIII, Springer Verlag, London Berlin Heidelberg, 2001, pp 19-34.
4. Horacek, H. and Busemann, S., 'Towards a Methodology for Developing Application-Oriented Report Generation', in: Güter, A. and Herzog, O. (eds.), 22nd German Conference on Artificial Intelligence (KI-98), Proceedings, Bremen, Germany, 1998.
5. Manurung, H.M., Ritchie, G., and Thompson, H., 'Towards a computational model of poetry generation', in: AISB-00 Symposium on Creative & Cultural Aspects and Applications of AI & Cognitive Science, 17th-18th April 2000, U. of Birmingham, England.
6. Manurung, H.M., Ritchie, G., and Thompson, H., 'A Flexible Integrated Architecture for Generating Poetic Texts', Informatics Research Report, EDI-INF-RR-0016, Division of Informatics, U. of Edinburgh, May 2000.
7. Nederhof, M.-J., 'Efficient generation of random sentences', Encyclopaedia of Computer Science and Technology, Vol.41, Marcel Dekker, 1999, pp 45-65.
8. Stratil, M., and Oakley, R.J., 'A Disputed Authorship Study of Two Plays Attributed to Tirso de Molina', Literary and Linguistic Computing, Vol. 2, No. 3, 1987, pp 153-160.
9. Tankard, J., 'The Literary Detective', Byte, February 1986, pp 231-238.

Perceptual Considerations for Quality of Service Management: An Integrated Architecture

George Ghinea and George D. Magoulas

Department of Information Systems and Computing, Brunel University,
Uxbridge, UB8 3PH, United Kingdom
{George.Ghinea, George.Magoulas}@brunel.ac.uk

Abstract. In this paper, we suggest an integrated architecture that makes use of the objective-technical information provided by the designer and the subjective-perceptual information supplied by the user for intelligent decision making in the construction of communication protocols. Thus, this approach, based on the Analytic Hierarchy Process, incorporates not only classical Quality of Service (QoS) considerations, but, indeed, user preferences as well. Furthermore, in keeping with the task-dependent nature consistently identified in multimedia scenarios, the suggested communication protocols also take into account the type of multimedia application, which they are transporting. Lastly, our approach also opens the possibility for such protocols to dynamically adapt based on a changing operating environment.

1 Introduction

The focus of our research has been the enhancement of the traditional view of QoS with a user-level defined Quality of Perception (QoP). This is a measure which encompasses not only a user's satisfaction with multimedia clips, but also his/her ability to perceive, synthesise and analyse the informational content of such presentations. As such, we have investigated the interaction between QoP and QoS and its implications from both a user perspective [2] as well as a networking angle within the Dynamically Reconfigurable Stacks Project (DRoPS) [3]. In this work we address the problem of bridging the application-network gap from a multi-attribute decision making perspective. We have sought to use this approach to integrate results from our work on user-level Quality of Perception with the more technical characterisation of Quality of Service. Our ultimate aim is to provide a communications architecture which uses an adaptable communications protocol geared towards human requirements in the delivery of distributed multimedia.

2 User-Centred Design with Multi-criteria Constraints

In linking perceptual considerations with low-level technical parameters, the design process should take into account the subjective judgement of the end-user. To this end,

M. Bauer, P.J. Gmytrasiewicz, and J. Vassileva (Eds.): UM 2001, LNAI 2109, pp. 234–236, 2001.
© Springer-Verlag Berlin Heidelberg 2001

we have applied Saaty's AHP formalism [4] to obtain a method which, from combined user-, application- and network-level requirements, ultimately results in a protocol configuration specifically tailored for the respective user-needs. Thus, within the QoP framework, each multimedia application can be characterised by the relative importance of the video (V), audio (A) and textual (T) components as conveyors of information, as well as the dynamism (D) of the presentation. This agrees with the experimental QoP results obtained which emphasise that multimedia QoP varies with: the number of media flows, the type of medium, the type of application, and the relative importance of each medium in the context of the application. On the other hand, 5 network level QoS parameters have been considered: bit error (BER), segment loss (SL), segment order (SO), delay (DEL) and jitter (JIT). Together with the V, A, T and D parameters these constitute the criteria on the basis of which an appropriate tailored communication protocol is constructed. In DRoPS, the functionality of this protocol is realised through a number of 9 microprotocols, which perform arbitrary protocol processing operations, spanning 4 broad functionality classes [3].

By applying the AHP we obtain a total of 10 matrices. The decision-maker (both the designer and the user) has to express his/her opinion about the value of a single pairwise comparison at a time. 9 of these matrices give the relative importance of the various microprotocols (alternatives, in the AHP) with respect to the criteria identified in our model, while the last of these matrices details pairwise comparisons between the criteria themselves. Thus, the judgement "microprotocol A is equally important as microprotocol B with respect to BER" corresponds to an entry $a_{ij} = 1$ of a matrix, while the judgement "microprotocol A is absolutely more important than microprotocol B" would correspond to a value of $a_{ij} = 9$ [4]. Intermediate terms can also be assigned when compromise is needed between two adjacent characterisations. The tenth matrix, of each criterion with respect to all the other criteria, is the only one whose values may fluctuate as a result of changes in the operating environment, as well as a consequence of changes in user preferences and perceptions, and could conceptually be split-up into 4 sub-matrices (see Figure 1).

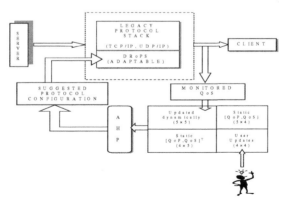

Fig. 1. AHP-based architecture for QoP management

Following the AHP, the weights w_i, i=1,...9 denoting the relative importance of each criterion i among the p criteria (p=9) are evaluated using the formula:

$$w_i = \frac{\left(\prod_{j=1}^{p} a_{ij}\right)^{1/p}}{\sum_{i=1}^{p}\left(\prod_{j=1}^{p} a_{ij}\right)^{1/p}} \quad i = 1,2,..., p \tag{1}$$

and a higher priority setting corresponds to a greater importance.

Pairs among alternatives are also compared with respect to the ith criterion and then a weight $w_{j,i}$, which denotes how preferable is the alternative j with respect to the criterion i, is derived. As previously, there is a total of p pairwise comparisons in the matrix and weights are calculated following Relation (1). The weighted product model, [1], is used to compare alternative v with alternative u. This can be done by multiplying a number of ratios, one for each criterion. Each ratio is raised to a power, which is equivalent to the relative weight of the corresponding criterion, i.e.

$$P_{v/u} = \prod_{i=1}^{p}\left(\frac{w_{v,i}}{w_{u,i}}\right)^{w_i} \tag{2}$$

If the ratio $P_{v/u}$ is greater or equal to one then the conclusion is that the alternative v is more preferable than alternative u. In the maximisation case, the best alternative is the one that possesses the highest value among all others.

The applicability of the proposed approach can be illustrated by means of a multimedia user scenario tested through simulation: a currently executing BER-sensitive application suddenly experiences deterioration in BER. Then this parameter becomes absolutely important with respect to the others i.e., a_{1j}=9 for j=2,...,5. This value is dynamically updated in the top-left 5×5 matrix (see Figure 1). The result of the AHP (calculations are omitted due to space limitation) then shows that the microprotocol that should preferentially be managed under the circumstances is the full Cyclic Redundancy Check - the strongest such microprotocol available to correct the quality loss in BER. This is in contrast to the scenario applicable just before the sudden surge in BER, which gave preference to an alternative microprotocol, the Strong Sequence Control.

References

1. Chen S.J. & Hwang C.L.: Fuzzy multiple decision making, Lecture Notes in Economics and Mathematical Sciences, Vol. 375, NY, Springer, 1992.
2. Ghinea G. & Thomas J.P.: QoS Impact on User Perception and Understanding of Multimedia Video Clips, Proc. of ACM Multimedia '98, Bristol, UK, 1998.
3. Ghinea G., Thomas J.P., Fish R.S.: Quality of Perception to Quality of Service Mapping Using a Dynamically Reconfigurable Communication System, Proc. of IEEE Globecom '99, Rio de Janeiro, Brazil
4. Saaty T.: The Analytic Hierarchy Process, McGraw-Hill, New York (1980).

Emotions and Personality in Agent Design and Modeling

Piotr J. Gmytrasiewicz[*] and Christine L. Lisetti[†]

[*] Computer Science and Engineering
University of Texas at Arlington
Arlington, TX 76019–0015
piotr@cse.uta.edu

[†] Information Systems and Decision Sciences
University of South Florida
Tampa, FL 33620-7800
lisetti@coba.usf.edu

Abstract. Our research combines the principled paradigm of rational agent design based on decision theory with formal definitions of the emotional states and personality of an artificial intelligent agent. We view the emotional states as the agent's decision-making modes, predisposing the agent to make its choices in a specific, yet rational, way. Change of the emotional state, say due to an external stimulus, invokes a transformation of the agent's decision-making behavior. We define personality as consisting of the agent's emotional states together with the specification of transitions taking place among the states. To model the personalities and emotional states of other agents and humans, we additionally provide a definition of a personality models of other agents. Our definition allows the personality models to be learned over the course of multiple interactions with the users and other agents.

1 Overview of the Approach

The objective of our research is to develop a fundamental understanding of the role and usefulness of the notions of emotions and personality in designing rational artificial agents. Our main hypothesis is that notions of personality and emotions are useful in designing competent artificial agents that are to operate within complex uncertain environments populated by other artificial and human agents. Our work draws on an emerging technology of rational agent design from artificial intelligence on the one hand [3, 7, 9], with research on human emotions in cognitive science and psychology on the other hand [2, 4–6, 8].

As research in cognitive science shows, some of the most important functions of emotions is to manage the individual's cognitive resources, allow him to understand the other agents' internal states, and to effectively communicate his internal state to others. The importance of managing the cognitive resources is clear when one considers the

[0] This work has been supported by the Office of Naval Research Artificial Intelligence Program under contract N00014 -95-1-0775, and by the National Science Foundation CAREER award IRI-9702132.

M. Bauer, P.J. Gmytrasiewicz, and J. Vassileva (Eds.): UM 2001, LNAI 2109, pp. 237–239, 2001.

cognitive limitations of animals, humans and machines on the one hand, and the computational demands imposed by complex dynamical environments on the other hand. Given these limitations, biological systems are equipped with simplified ways of arriving at the appropriate action to be executed. Lower-level mechanisms, such as instincts, are essentially condition-action rules. Higher-level mechanism is provided by emotions, which dictate not actions but action tendencies [5]. If an external event threatens the safety of an individual, the emotional state of fear restricts the alternative behaviors to a small repertoire of possible appropriate actions such as: interrupt current activity, monitor environment, flee, or fight. In this context, emotional states are modifying the parameters of deliberative rationality to control its complexity under time pressure.

Rational agents should be able to function efficiently under time and other environmental pressures, and be able to interact and communicate with other agents. This includes informing each other about details of the external environment and about the agents' own internal states, as well as the ability to model and predict the internal states of other agents. Apart from the area of multi-agent systems, our approach has applications in Human-Computer Interaction (HCI) that range from intelligent tutoring systems and distance learning support systems (with recognition of expressions signaling interest, boredom, confusion), to stress and lie detectors, to monitors of pilots' and drivers' state of alertness, to software product support systems (with recognition of users being dis/pleased with software products), to entertainment and computer games (enjoyment, confusion), and to ubiquitous computing and smart houses.

We use the decision-theoretic paradigm of rationality, according to which a rational agent should behave so as to maximize the expected utility of its actions (see [1, 3, 7] and references therein).

Definition 1: A decision-making situation of an agent is a quadruple:
$$, \text{where} \quad \text{is the set of possible environment states,}$$
is the probability distribution over   that describes the agent's state of knowledge about the state,   is the set of agent's alternative courses of action,
is a function describing the results of actions, and   is the agent's utility function.

Given its decision-making situation, a rational agent can compute its best action, as one that maximizes it's expected utility. It is clear that this computation can be fairly complex. In a multi-agent environment, for example, all of the information the agent has about the physical environment and about the other agents could be relevant and impact the expected utilities of alternative courses of action. Sometimes the agent may have information about the other agents' state of knowledge, which is also potentially relevant. Given these complexities it is clear that a mechanism for managing the agent's computational resources is needed. In our work, we exploit emotional states and personality as a tool providing for such ability.

We view emotional states as different modes of decision-making. The set of emotional states and transitions between them comprise the agent's personality.

Definition 2: An emotional state of an agent is associated with its decision-making situation   , defined above.

The above definition associates an emotional state with a decision-making situation, but it does not identify the two to be the same. The reason is that emotions, apart from being decision-making modes, may involve physical and other changes (say breathing rate, muscle tension, dilation of the pupil or rate of power consumption.)

Definition 3: An agent's personality is a finite state machine   ,
where D is a finite set of emotional states, IN is a set of environmental inputs,   is an emotional transformation function,   ,   is an initial (or neutral) emotional state.

The above definition specifies that the agent's emotional state can change due to a, possibly empty, sequence of environmental inputs. This means that emotions are passive - they happen to the agent without the agent's control. This definition formalizes personality from the individual agent's point of view, i.e., it describes the personality of the agent itself. To equip the agent with a tool with which to model emotional states of other agents we define a related notion of a personality model.

Definition 4: A personality model of agent   is a probabilistic finite state machine   , where D is a finite set of emotional states of agent   , IN is a set of environmental inputs,   is a probabilistic transformation function,   ,   is an initial (or neutral) emotional state of agent   .

In Figure 1 we present a very simple example of a personality model.

Fig. 1. Simple Personality Model of a Tit-for-Two-Tats Agent.

References

1. Craig Boutilier, Thomas Dean, and Steve Hanks. Decision-theoretic planning: Structural assumptions and computational leverage. Journal of Artificial intelligence Research, 11:1–94, 1999.
2. Antonio R. Dimasio. Descartes' Error. Grosset/Putnam, 1994.
3. Jon Doyle. Rationality and its role in reasoning. Computational Intelligence, 8:376–409, 1992.
4. N. H. Fridja. The Emotions. Cambridge University Press, 1986.
5. P. N. Johnson-Laird and K. Oatley. Basic Emotions, Rationality, and Folk Theory. Cognition and Emotion, 6(3/4):201–223, 1992.
6. Andrew Ortony, Gerald Clore, and Allen Collins. Cognitive Structure of Emotions. Cambridge University Press, 1988.
7. S. Russell and P. Norvig. Artificial Intelligence: A Modern Approach. Prentice Hall, 1995.
8. A. Sloman. Motives, Mechanisms, and Emotions. In M. Boden, editor, The Philosophy of Artificial Intelligence. Oxford: Oxford University Press, 1990.
9. Michael Wooldridge and Editors Anand Rao. Foundations of Rational Agency. Kluwer Academin Publishers, 1999.

Using Document Structures for Personal Ontologies and User Modeling *

Sanghee Kim[1], Wendy Hall[1], and Andy Keane[2]

[1]Intelligence, Agents, Multimedia Group, Department of Electronics and Computer Science, University of Southampton, U.K., Tel: 44-(0)23-80-59-3256, Fax: 44-(0)23-80-59-2865
{sk98r,wh}@ecs.soton.ac.uk
[2]Computational Engineering and Design Center, School of Engineering Science, University of Southampton, U.K., Tel: 44-(0)23-59-2944, Fax:44-(0)23-80-59-3220
ajk@soton.ac.uk

Abstract. We present a new approach that makes use of the embedded structural information of the documents which a user frequently refers to for deriving a personalized concept hierarchy and for identifying user preferences concerning document searching and browsing.

Keywords . Personal ontology, Supported browsing, Structured document

1 Introduction

As it has come to be harder for a user to locate relevant documents quickly, the intelligent document organization system that proactively retrieves, categorizes, and ranks searched documents has become an essential component of personal desktop applications. Not only does this system is required to model the salient characteristics of the user, but it also has to integrate heterogeneous document sources, each of which has its own structural elements and vocabularies. Reviews of current approaches show that the embedded structural elements of the documents are often ignored in building such systems even though these present semantic clues about the kind of underlying document handling that would provide relevant descriptions of the document.

2 Personal Ontology Building

Personal ontologies provide a uniform representation of a user's personally archived documents by explicitly specifying structural elements and their meanings. Initial information about the user is bootstrapped by making use of existing user defined categories, such as file directories, folder hierarchies of e-mail messages or a user's homepage. Not only does this initialization reduce the user's reliance on system interaction, but it also provides good training examples for profiling the user. The development of the personal ontologies involves three steps. First, it requires the definition of a hierarchy of structural elements and the extraction of the values of the specified tags from the documents. Given the structured documents, a set of top-level

---

* The work presented here has been supported by UTP (University Technology Partnership in Design) program sponsored by Rolls Royce Plc and BAE Systems.

M. Bauer, P.J. Gmytrasiewicz, and J. Vassileva (Eds.): UM 2001, LNAI 2109, pp. 240–242, 2001.
©Springer-Verlag Berlin Heidelberg 2001

concepts can then be derived from the user-defined categories through a two-step category clustering process. Finally, the explicit specification of relations among the concepts can be defined by using the technique of formal concept analysis.

Formal concept analysis (FCA) is based on an applied lattice theory and defines the formal context consisting of a set of concepts, each of which is specified as: (C,A_1), where C is the extent that holds all objects belonging to the concept, and A_1 is the intent that comprises all attributes valid for those objects [1]. In the personal ontology, the object corresponds to a document and the associated attributes are extracted features. A concept lattice is constructed through an attribute exploration process that extensively investigates the combinations of related attributes to define co-relationships among the concepts. A super or a sub-concept is defined as: (D,A_1) (C,A_2) D C (A_2 A_1) meaning that a concept C is a super-concept of D if and only if the attributes (A_2) of C are a subset of the attributes (A_1) of concept D.

3 Reinforcement Learning for Ranking Structured Documents

User preferences are modelled using two layers (i.e. global and local) in order to take into account semantic clues defined in the structural tags, so that terms can be differentiated which refer to different objects. The global profile represents overall user browsing preferences regarding the distribution of structural elements, each of which specifies its strength by a numeric weight. The local profile defines a set of features associated with importance weights for each element. Reinforcement learning is selected since its computation can be incrementally updated on-line and it directs a learner towards an optimal state in the future [3]. The feedback obtained from the user is through observation of whether or not the user clicks the specific document, and it is incorporated as the immediate reward which defines the effectiveness of ranking strategies. RLRSD (Reinforcement Learning for Ranking Structured Documents) ranks retrieved documents by their estimated relevance values to a user's query, so that the first placed document is presumably the most relevant. It also takes into account the feature differences of the ranked documents plus the previously learned user profiles in order to evaluate the value of next ranking strategy.

4 Evaluations

Two datasets were collected. One of the authors provided the first dataset which had a total of 1405 documents (1148 email messages, 166 bookmarked web pages, 88 texts in postscript format, and 3 web pages from a homepage) collected from 94 categories. 176 queries were simulated by assigning query terms from randomly selected document structures. The performance of RLRSD was compared to that of a flat vector model (FVM) which represents documents as an unstructured single layer. The approximately 37% higher precision of RLRSD shows the efficiency of using the structural information by assigning different weights to a feature that relates to different objects. We suggest that this is mostly due to a term confusion problem caused by the fact that no differences of structures are made in FVM. In other words, although it received feedback, it did not reflect the different contributions of a feature which relates to different objects; instead it assigned a uniform weight to a feature irrespective of its linked objects.

For the second experiment, we downloaded the publicly available cystic fibrosis (CF) dataset. It consists of 1239 XML documents indexed with the term 'cystic fibrosis' in the National Library of Medicine's MEDLINE database [2]. It gathered subjective relevance judgments (i.e., highly relevant, marginally relevant, or irrelevant) made by four users against the selected 100 queries. We created an individual relevance score file per user to compare the ranking results by using different structural elements, to which the user referred in deciding the scores. A user5 was artificially created by combining the relevance scores produced by the four users.

User4 shows a unique result in that no specific preferences concerning the document structures that the user made use of in deciding scores are observed. In fact, while the other three users are domain experts, user4 is a bibliographer who presumably has better knowledge of citation and reference elements. User4's relatively higher precision rate in terms of the use of the citation, the reference, and the source tag compared to those of the other three users confirms our finding that user4 uses bibliographic-related tags heavily.

The performance difference (11%) between RLRSD and FVM on the second experiment was not so significant compared to that (37%) of the first experiment. We base our conclusion on the following observation. Dataset2 shared the same structural specification, while dataset1 originated from heterogeneous sources and thus the variations in the distribution of the structural elements are wider than those in dataset2. As RLRSD utilizes both the distribution of structural elements and features, it is clear that RLRSD on dataset2 could not take full advantage of its global profile compared to dataset1. Moreover, while there were only three kinds of user feedback on dataset2, dataset1 used a minimum of one and a maximum of thirty kinds of feedback. The performance of user5 (who received nine kinds of feedback) showed higher precision values than those of the other three users. This proves that the ranking algorithms can improve ranking performance when feedback reflects more detailed user preferences.

5   Future Work

We have not yet fully investigated the impact caused by varying the number of retrieved documents on the performance results as our work assigned a fixed maximum number to all local profilers regardless of their different strengths. In addition, our assumption that user clicked documents are mostly useful in identifying user preferences needs to be further validated through a real-user interaction with our system.

References

1. Ganter, B., Wille, R.: Applied Lattice Theory: Formal Concept Analysis. Preprints, http://wwwbib.mathematik.tu-darmstadt.de/Math-Net/Preprints/Listen/pp97.html (1997)
2. Shaw, W., Wood, R., Tibbo, H.: The Cystic Fibrosis Database: Content and Research Opportunities. Int. J. Library and Information Science Research Vol. 13. (1991) 347-366
3. Sutton, R., Barto, A.: Reinforcement Learning: An Introduction. http://www-anw.cs.umass.edu/~rich/book/the-book.html (1998)

User-Tailored Plan Presentation

Detlef Küpper [1] and Alfred Kobsa[2]

[1] GMD FIT, German Nat'l Research Center for Information Technology,
D-53754 St. Augustin, Germany, kuepper@gmd.de
[2] Dept. of Information and Computer Science, University of California,
Irvine, CA 92697-3425, U.S.A., kobsa@ics.uci.edu

Abstract. This paper discusses plan presentation, the second phase in user-tailored advice giving. Its main task is to determine what knowledge must be provided to ascertain that the user comprehends the plan and is able to perform it, even if he detects unexpected obstacles. Plan presentation is guided by a model of the user's knowledge and of his capabilities to perform actions in the domain. Finally we describe how to bias the plan generation process to prefer plans that contain as little information unfamiliar to the user as possible.

1 Introduction

In [2] we introduced a plan generation algorithm for advice-giving systems that exploits a model of the user's capabilities (namely his physical abilities and his authorization to perform actions) to produce plans that are in principle executable by the user. In order to perform the plan, he may however still need additional information. This possibly missing knowledge – or in general the gap between a user's capabilities to perform plans and his knowledge how to do this – determines the scope of user-tailored advice. The main task of plan presentation is to identify and supply the knowledge that the user still needs to perform the plan.

We focus on two types of knowledge. Structural information of the plan is needed to comprehend the functionality of plan. Additionally it supports the user's replanning in case unexpected obstacles arise during plan execution. Furthermore, the user needs to know how to perform the steps of the plan. Such knowledge is however only useful if the user is able and authorized to carry them out. Thus the presentation process must consider both the user's knowledge and his capabilities.

2 Determining the Contents for Plan Presentation

A plan is an abstract object that usually needs further elaboration by the user who will execute it (cf. [4]). Often the user must decompose plan steps into substeps that he can execute directly, or has to modify the plan to remedy unexpected obstacles during plan execution. For both tasks, the user needs to comprehend the plan's functionality, i.e. he must know the role of each step in the plan. Our planning process represents this knowledge by causal links. Each of them links a step that satisfies a

M. Bauer, P.J. Gmytrasiewicz, and J. Vassileva (Eds.): UM 2001, LNAI 2109, pp. 243–246, 2001.
© Springer-Verlag Berlin Heidelberg 2001

condition with the plan's goal or with a step that requires this condition for its executability. Any further elaboration of the plan must not to destroy these links since this may jeopardize the plan's executability. If the user cannot execute a step of a plan directly, he must know how to decompose it into smaller sub-steps. The presentation process decides on the basis of the user model whether or not the user needs additional or correcting explanations. This user model extends the terminological representation of plan operators (so called plan concepts) described in [2] by decompositions that may be assigned to plan concepts. Similar to HTN-Planning (e.g. [1]), these decompositions are (simple) plans. Their steps are instantiated plan concepts like the steps of the generated plan. We assume that the generated plan considered all the conditions and dependencies that are relevant in the domain. Therefore we may ignore individual preconditions and effects of the steps in a decomposition and look at a decomposition as a recipe whose executability depends on the precondition of that plan concept only to which it belongs.

Whether or not the current user can execute at least one decomposition of a plan concept depends on his capabilities with regard to the steps of the decomposition. We call a decomposition usable (for the current user) if he is able to perform all its steps, and each step either is atomic or the system can provide a usable decomposition for it. Atomic means that the system assumes that the user has extensive competence in performing the plan concept (and its instantiations) or can execute it directly. A user has reliable knowledge of a plan concept if he does not know any false decomposition (compared to the system's knowledge) but at least one usable decomposition that contains atomic steps only, or steps only for which the user has reliable knowledge. The absence of wrong assumptions prevents the user from choosing an erroneous way to perform the plan concept. For all steps of the plan

---

present-plan (p:plan)
(p1) set effort initially to (| steps (p) | + 2 * | causal-links (p) |) * k_{pres}
(p2) set presentation initially to linearize(p)
(p3) for each s   steps (p) add the name of plan-concept(s) to s in presentation
(p4) for each pc   plan-concepts (p)
(p5)   add result of present-plan-concept(pc) to presentation, effort

present-plan-concept (pc:plan-concept)
(c1) initially set presentation to { } and effort to 0
(c2) if user doesn't know pc
(c3)   set presentation to descript(pc) and effort to effort(descript(pc))
(c4) if not (atomic(pc) or user has reliable knowledge of pc)
(c5)   add result of present-recipe-for-plan-concept(pc) to presentation, effort

present-recipe-for-plan-concept (pc:plan-concept)
(r1) let ec be the set of usable decompositions of pc acc. to system's knowledge
(r2) if ec = { }   set effort to   (plan presentation fails)
(r3) else set presentation, effort to results of present-plan (d) where
(r4)   d   ec   effort(present-plan (d)) = $\min_{(d'\ ec)}$ effort(present-plan (d'))

Fig. 1. Plan presentation algorithm

for which the user has reliable or atomic knowledge, he does not need any explanations. For all other steps, the presentation process of our system provides a usable decomposition.

The pseudo code of Fig. 1 summarizes the procedure for determining the knowledge that the user needs to successfully execute a plan p. Each function returns the values presentation (a data structure for the contents of the presentation) and effort (a numerical value for the amount of information that is unknown to the user). The algorithm starts by computing the effort for presenting all steps and causal links of the plan (p1). Since causal links are complex components, each contributes two basic effort units k_{pres} to this value. A linearization of the plan's data structure (p2) with a name for each plan step (p3) forms a basis for the presentation. For each plan concept that was used for the plan (p4), the user will obtain a canned description if he does not know it (c2,c3), and user specific information about how to perform it if he does not have reliable knowledge (c4,c5). This information is determined by selecting from the set of usable decompositions of the plan concept (r1) the decomposition with the minimal effort (r4). The presentations of these decompositions are computed by the function present-plan. The depth of these recursive calls is limited by the depth of the decomposition hierarchy of the plan concepts. Line (r2) handles the case in which the system cannot give a usable explanation. This possibility is a consequence of the incomplete knowledge of how to perform plan concepts. The subsequent enhanced plan generation process excludes such unexplainable plan concepts from further consideration.

Up to here our discussion separated the two phases of user-tailored advice. We can however identify two starting points for considering presentation aspects already during plan generation, to obtain plans that lead to better presentations. First, we exclude unexplainable non-atomic plan concepts from the planning process, because their presence in a plan always leads to a rejection of the presentation. Moreover, we influence the decisions of the planner so that it prefers plan concepts with low presentation effort for the current user. This effort may be computed by the function present-plan-concept (see above) before the planning process starts. As a result, plans with low presentation effort are preferred, but we do not loose any solution. Specifically, we do not loose the opportunity to give explanations to users. This technique of biasing the planning process can also be exploited for taking into account users' preferences for performing certain plan concepts, their practice in performing them, or the general probability of performing them successfully.

3   Summary and Further Development

We described the presentation of an already generated domain plan to a user. We claim that the user needs structural information to comprehend the plan's functionality and also knowledge of how to perform the plan steps. Although the user may already have such knowledge available, it might be wrong, incomplete or unusable, i.e. he cannot act along it. The presentation process exploits a model of the user's knowledge and capabilities to complement or correct the user's knowledge, in order to enable him to execute the plan. Finally we modified the plan generation process of our earlier work to prefer plans that lead to presentations with little unknown information for the user.

While the presentation process described so far considered the user's knowledge as well as his capabilities, it did not take the user's (likely) inferences into account, and thus may produce lengthy results. Our approach to tackle this problem is an improvement of Young's work [5]. It takes again a model of the user's planning knowledge and capabilities into account and is described in more detail in [3].

References

1. K. Erol, J. Hendler and D. Nau. Semantics for hierarchical task-network planning. Tech. Report CS-TR-3239, Computer Science Dept., Univ. of Maryland, 1994.
2. D. Küpper and A. Kobsa. User- tailored plan generation. In User Modeling: Proc. of the 7th International Conference, UM99, pages 45-54, Banff, Canada, 1999.
3. D. Küpper. Benutzermodellierung für benutzerspezifische Plangenerierung und - präsentation. Dissertation, Dept. Mathematics and Comp. Science, Univ. Essen, Germany, forthcoming.
4. B. Webber, N. Badler, B. DiEugenio, C. Geib, L. Levison and M. Moore. Instructions, Intentions and Expectations. Artificial Intelligence 73(1-2):253-269, 1995.
5. R. M. Young. Using Grice's maxim of quantity to select the content of plan descriptions. Artificial Intelligence 115(2):215-256, 1999.

Investigating Students' Self -Assessment Skills

Antonija Mitrovic

Intelligent Computer Tutoring Group
Computer Science Department, University of Canterbury
Private Bag 4800, Christchurch, New Zealand
Phone (64) 3 3642987 ext. 7771, fax (64) 3 3642569
tanja@cosc.canterbury.ac.nz

Abstract. Student modeling approaches predominantly focus on modeling student knowledge. For effective learning, however, it is necessary to teach students how to learn, as well as to provide support for learning domain knowledge. Recently, a number of projects focused on students' learning strategies, and initiated work on modeling students' metacognitive skills, such as self-explanation and reflection. This paper focuses on self-assessment as an important metacognitive skill. We present results of an initial study carried out in the context of SQL-Tutor, a system that helps students to learn a database language. We found that not all students are good at evaluating their own knowledge, and that their knowledge level is an important factor. The study is an initial step towards incorporating the meta-level into the existing student model in SQL-Tutor.

1 Introduction

In order to help students learn more effectively and efficiently, intelligent educational systems need to be able to monitor students' metacognitive skills, represent them in student models and provide support for further development. Studies show that improved metacognitive skills can be taught [3] and result in improved problem solving and better learning [2,5,8]. Self-explanation is a metacognitive skill that requires the student to explain a solution provided by the teacher/system, and has received the most attention so far [5]. A variant is explored in [2], when the student is asked to explain his/her own solution. In both cases, significant gains have been achieved by the students who explained the solutions. Knowing when a person needs help and what kind of help is appropriate has also been addressed in a recent project [1]. A study of how an inspectable student model encourages reflection on one's knowledge is presented in [4].

This paper focuses on self-assessment. If students are to learn, they also need to be able to critically assess their knowledge. This skill is important to identify topics that need attention, to assess the difficulty of the current problem, and to decide whether to abandon the problem or keep working on it. We report on a study of students' self-assessment skills in the context of SQL-Tutor, an intelligent educational system that teaches the SQL database language to university students. SQL-Tutor provides a facility for students to select problems on their own, which requires students to be able

M. Bauer, P.J. Gmytrasiewicz, and J. Vassileva (Eds.): UM 2001, LNAI 2109, pp. 247–250, 2001.
©Springer-Verlag Berlin Heidelberg 2001

to evaluate their own knowledge. For details of SQL-Tutor please see [6,7]. In the next section we describe our experiment, and the final section presents the results of the data analyses and conclusions.

2   The Experiment

Assessing one's own knowledge is a difficult task. Our hypothesis is that students are not generally good at evaluating their knowledge. We propose that there are several factors that influence this ability, and expect student's knowledge to be one of the main factors for being able to critically assess one's knowledge.

In order to evaluate our hypothesis, we performed an experiment on SQL-Tutor, which was modified slightly to allow for data collection. We focused on situations when students abandon the current problem, and ask for a new problem. In such situations, we asked for a reason for abandoning the problem. Three possible replies were offered: the current problem is too easy, or too difficult, or the student wants to work on a problem of a different nature. The student is then asked to specify the type of the next problem. For this purpose, there were seven groups of problems, one for each clause of the SELECT statement, plus the any clause option.

The participating students were enrolled in an introductory database course at the University of Canterbury. The usage of the system was voluntary. The system was demonstrated in a lecture at the beginning of September 2000. Prior to the experiment, all students listened to two lectures on SQL. During the experiment, there were five additional lectures and five labs on the Oracle DBMS. The experiment required the student to sit a pre-test consisting of three multi-choice questions, worth seven marks. All students' actions were recorded in logs. The post-test consisted of three questions similar to those in the pre-test, administered on paper seven weeks after the start of the experiment.

3   Results and Conclusions

Out of 142 students enrolled in the course, 79 logged on to SQL-Tutor and sat the pre-test. We excluded the logs of nine students who attempted no problems. The students had two sessions on average, with a total time on task of 95.6 minutes. The minimal number of problems attempted per session was just one, while the maximum was 30, with an average of 6.65. The students managed to solve 1.5 problems per session, or a total of 10.26 problems. The mean on the pre-test was 4.02 (SD=1.52), while the post-test results were better, with a mean of 5.01 (SD= 1.24). The difference between the pre- and post-test results is statistically significant (t=-4.49, p=1.63E-05).

Out of 70 students, 25 had not abandoned any problems. The remaining 45 students abandoned 3.87 problems on average. Most often (59.39%) the students abandoned problems without attempting them. In order to evaluate our hypothesis, we divided the students into two subgroups. Students who scored above average on the pre-test were put into the more able group (63.16%), and the rest into the less able group.

Table 1 presents statistics for the two subgroups. The mean of the post-test is lower than the mean of the pre-test for the more able students, although not significantly. However, the less able group benefited more from the system than their more able peers. More able students tended to work longer with the system and solve more problems. The number of problems abandoned after zero attempts is almost identical.

Table 1. Statistics for the two groups of students with different prior knowledge

Group	Pre-test	Post-test	Total time	0 attempts	Solved
More able	5.6 (0.75)	5.4 (0.94)	152.6	4 (2.3)	79%
Less able	2.91 (1.06)	4.86 (1.49)	115	3.95 (2.31)	68.75%

Next, we analysed the reason for abandoning problems. Out of 165 abandoned problems, 57 (34.54%) were the problems from the more able, and 108 (65.45%) were from the less able group. Therefore, less able students were much more likely to abandon a problem. The distribution of answers to this question is given in Figure 1. Less able students thought that the problem was too easy more often than more able students, although the inspection of the sessions very often contradicts the reason they specified. More able students asked for a different type of problems more frequently.

An analysis of the second question shows that more able students are better at identifying the types of problems they need to work on (Figure 2). As we hypothesized, less able students are not good at identifying the kind of problem to work on next, and therefore they specify any clause most often (in 69.44% of the cases). More able students ask for hard problems (group by and having) much more often than the other group (35.08% and 14.04% compared to 15.74% and 6.48%).

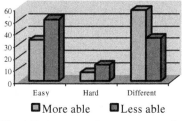

Fig. 1. Percentages of answers to question 1

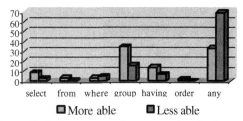

Fig. 2. Percentages of answers to question2

The results of data analyses justify our hypothesis. There are several ways to improve the SQL-Tutor system so that it may support students in acquiring self-assessment skills. The system may intervene in situations when a student keeps abandoning problems without trying to solve them, and encourage the student to solve the problem. Also, the system could intervene when the student does not have a preference about the type of the next problem. One way to help a student evaluate his/her own knowledge would be to visualize the student model. Since the student model in SQL-Tutor is quite complex, it could be summarized in a way similar to the answers offered for the second question. The student would then have a starting point from which to reason about their knowledge. Closer inspection of the student model may also have a positive effect on self-assessment skills. Future work on SQL-Tutor will develop the ideas presented in this paper further.

References

1. Aleven, V., Koedinger, K.: Limitations of Student Control: Do Students Know When They Need Help? In: Gauthier G., Frasson C., and VanLehn K. (eds): Proc. 5th Int. Conf. ITS'2000, Springer-Verlag, (2000) 292-303
2. Aleven, V., Koedinger, K., Cross, K.: Tutoring Answer Explanation Fosters Learning with Understanding. In: Lajoie, S.P., Vivet, M. (eds): Proc. Int. Conf. AIED (1999) 199-206
3. Bielaczyc, K., Pirolli, P., Brown, A.L.: Training in Self-Explanation and Self-Regulation Strategies: Investigating the Effects of Knowledge Acquisition Activities on Problem-solving. Cognition and Instruction, 13(2) (1993) 221-252
4. Bull, S. See Yourself Write: a Simple Student Model to Make Students Think. In: Jameson, A., Paris, C., Tasso, C. (eds): Proc. 6th Int. Conf. UM'97, Springer, (1997) 315-326.
5. Conati, C., VanLehn, K.: Further Results from the Evaluation of an Intelligent Computer Tutor to Coach Self-Explanation. In: Gauthier G., Frasson C., and VanLehn K. (eds): Proc. 5th Int. Conf. ITS'2000, Springer-Verlag, (2000) 304-313
6. Mitrovic, A., Hausler, K.: Porting SQL-Tutor to the Web. Proc. ITS'2000 workshop on Adaptive and Intelligent Web-based Education Systems, (2000) 37-44
7. Mitrovic, A., Ohlsson, S.: Evaluation of a Constraint-based Tutor for a Database Language. Int. J. on Artificial Intelligence in Education, 10(3-4), (1999) 238-256
8. Swanson, H.L.: Influence of Metacognitive Knowledge and Aptitude on Problem Solving. J. Educational Psychology, 82 (1990) 306-314

Generating Personal Travel Guides –
And Who Wants Them?

Cé cile Paris, Stephen Wan, Ross Wilkinson, and Mingfang Wu

CSIRO, Division of Mathematical and Information Sciences, Australia
{Cecile.Paris,Stephen.Wan,Ross.Wilkinson,Mingfang.Wu}@cmis.csiro.au

Abstract. In this paper we describe a system that generates synthesized web pages as a travel guide through integrating a discourse planner with a document retrieval system. We then present our investigation on whether the guide generated by such a system is actually preferred by users over a more general guide.

1 Introduction

Information retrieval is a proven technology for searching large document collections. However, the search result is usually a list of discrete units that are not easy for users to assimilate. In contrast, the discourse-oriented technologies aim at ensuring that the result is coherent and appropriate through explicit text planning. In our work, we have been designing a new approach to the tailored information delivery by combining both technologies. This approach assumes a user profile, a discourse model, and a set of web data sources, and delivers information from those sources in a coherent form to a variety of media including paper, hand-held devices, and the web. Embodying this new approach, we have developed a prototype system for generating tailored travel guides in the tourism domain. In this paper, we first describe our approach and then present one of our experiments to test the value of tailored travel information delivery.

2 Tailored Information Delivery Using the Tiddler System

The architecture of Tiddler is shown in Figure 1. The core elements include a discourse planner, a presentation planner, and a surface generator. A user dialogue system is also needed to capture the user model and to deliver the information.

The discourse planner takes the user model and discourse plans to create a discourse tree that represents the rough content of the guide and specifies which information is to be included in the text, and its organisation. The discourse planner, modeled on the one described by Moore and Paris [1], uses a library of discourse plans, which indicate how a discourse goal can be achieved. Mann and Thompson's Rhetorical Structure Theory (RST) [2] is used here to represent coherency.

M. Bauer, P.J. Gmytrasiewicz, and J. Vassileva (Eds.): UM 2001, LNAI 2109, pp. 251–253, 2001.
©Springer-Verlag Berlin Heidelberg 2001

The discourse plans were designed based on a corpus analysis and represent the prototypical structure of a travel guide. In our application, we studied and analyzed a variety of travel guides. The resulting overall structure of the guide consists of a general introduction, and, depending on the user model, the information about accommodation, restaurants, special events when available, and activities. The user model contains the characteristics about the user that can affect the production of a personalized travel guide, namely: the type of accommodation required, the interests in terms of activities, the location and date of the trip, whether or not to show restaurant information, and the medium in which to present the guide.

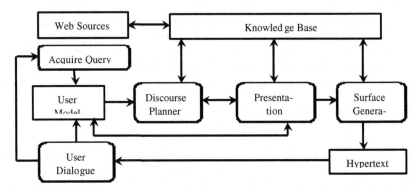

Fig. 1. Tiddler System Architecture

The presentation planner   decides how best to express the intermediate discourse tree resulting from the discourse planner, such as the amount and conciseness of the information to be included in each page and the navigation needed. Our presentation plans are based on both goal decomposition, which expands the tree, and pattern matching, which manipulates and transforms the discourse tree. The presentation planner populates the discourse tree with a series of queries against web sources. The Norfolk system [3] is used to create a set of virtual web pages by evaluating queries lying in the nodes of the discourse tree structure. Norfolk also synthesizes the results of these queries synthesized into a set of XML answer fragments. Exploiting this document and information retrieval technology allows Tiddler to query all available information (as if using information retrieval by itself), without having to first produce the knowledge sources appropriate for language generation (the main limitation of that technology), while still preserving coherence a discourse planning approach provides.

In addition to the constraints of the data itself, the presentation planner also considers the constraints of the delivery channel. For example, a hand-held device can present much less information on one screen than a standard web page. Its presentation should thus have a lot of navigation but very concise information on each particular page, whereas the Web form will use less navigation but more layouts.

Finally the surface generator   traverses the generated discourse tree. At each node, the surface generator maps the RST relationship to its final presentation form as defined by a lexicon dependent on medium chosen by the user. Leaf nodes may also contain text retrieved by the search engine that is also appended to the document. Both the textual realization of the RST, which may be in the form of XML markup, and the text retrieved by the search engine are appended to the final document during the traversal to produce a linearization of the discourse tree.

3 Evaluation

An experiment was conducted to examine whether a group of users preferred a tailored guide to a generic guide. We wished to explore how useful two guides were for people planning a short holiday on the coast in South-Eastern Australia. One guide was generic for the selected location(s), and the other guide was tailored to the user's particular information needs or preferences around the type of accommodation and activities. Both guides were delivered in the paper format. Our null hypothesis, therefore, was that there is no preference difference between two guides.

Of the 19 participants, 11 people preferred the tailored guide, 4 people preferred the generic guide, and the remaining 4 people had no preference. The preference difference between two guides is only significant at the level 0.059 (sign test). Although this difference is not significant enough to reject the null hypothesis, we see a promising tendency of preference to tailored delivery that could prove statistically significant with an experiment of greater power.

4 Discussion

We have described a system that delivers travel guides tailored to individual needs. By basing this system around a series of transformations of a basic discourse plan, different applications, different user models, and different delivery platforms can be supported by just changing the data and the transforms. There is no need to change the software. While engineering benefits accrue from this approach, we also believe that the key issue is the level of benefit of a discourse approach to tailored information delivery, which ensures a coherent presentation no matter what the circumstances are. Our key observation from an initial evaluation showed that users have a strong tendency to prefer tailored documents as a whole.

References

1. Moore, J.D. & Paris, C.L. (1993). Planning Text for Advisory Dialogues: Capturing Intentional and Rhetorical Information. In Computational Linguistics, Cambridge, MA. Vol 19(4), pp. 651- 694.
2. Mann, W.C., & Thompson, S.A. (1988). Rhetorical structure theory: Towards a functional theory of text organization. In TEXT, 8(3), pp. 243- 281.
3. Paradis, F., Vercoustre, A.M., and Hills, B. (1998). A Virtual Document Interpreter for Reuse of Information. In Lecture Notes in Computer Science 1375, Proc of Electronic Publishing, Saint-Malo, France. pp. 487-498.

Inspectability and User Controlled Revision on Long Term User Models

Antóio Silva [1], Zita A. Vale[2], and Carlos Ramos[3]

[1] Polytechnic Institute of Porto (IPP)/Institute of Engineering/Computer Engineering Dept.
Rua de S. Tomé -4200 Porto – Portugal / Fax: 351-22-8321159 / Phone: 351-22-8340500
asilva@dei.isep.ipp.pt

[2] Polytechnic Institute of Porto (IPP)/Institute of Engineering/Electrical Engineering Dept.
Rua de S. Tomé -4200 Porto – Portugal / Fax: 351-22-8321159 / Phone: 351-22-8340500
zav@dee.isep.ipp.pt

[3] Polytechnic Institute of Porto (IPP)/Institute of Engineering/Computer Engineering Dept.
Rua de S. Tomé -4200 Porto – Portugal / Fax: 351-22-8321159 / Phone: 351-22-8340500
csr@ dei.isep.ipp.pt

Abstract. Typically, the user models used in Intelligent Tutors tend to be tightly controlled by the system, due to the constraints imposed by the specific nature of the tutoring process. Therefore, no control by the user himself is usually allowed over his/her model's contents. In order to make the evaluation of the tutoring process a cooperative task adequate techniques should be devised. This paper describes early attempts to build a user model module for an Intelligent Tutor to be used in the training of electrical network Control Center operators. It also attempts to address the different requirements of the distinct phases of this tutoring environment.

1 Introduction

This paper tries to address the issues raised by the building of a User Model component for a Intelligent Tutor (IT) aimed at the training of electrical networks Control Center (C.C.) operators. These operators' tasks are very demanding especially when an incident involving several plants occurs, in which case, the huge quantity of information suddenly arriving to the C.C. can easily overwhelm the operators, affecting their decision-making capability. Current electrical networks are generally very reliable and serious incidents seldom occur. But the sheer fact of those incidents being so rare does not allow for an efficient training of the very same operators whose expertise is essential for facing those crises. This training not being possible in real time, alternative ways must and have been devised.

The introduction of Artificial Intelligence techniques in this area made possible applications like ITs being conceived to specifically address the training needs of these operators. One of these tutors, SPARSE-IT was developed by the authors to be used as a training tool for the C.C. operators at REN (Rede Elé ctrica Nacional), the Portuguese electrical transmission utility. It worked closely with the expert system SPARSE, a fault diagnostic and decision support tool to help C.C. operators [1]. This

M. Bauer, P.J. Gmytrasiewicz, and J. Vassileva (Eds.): UM 2001, LNAI 2109, pp. 254–256, 2001.
©Springer-Verlag Berlin Heidelberg 2001

tutor used a User Model module to keep track of the trainees' evolution and to adapt methods and contents of the tutoring process to the trainee knowledge and expertise level. It was a simple linear model covering parameters like the number and complexity level of the problems solved and the time trainees took to solve those problems. This simple model couldn't cope with the complexity of the domain knowledge needed to become a proficient operator.

The acknowledgement of these limitations rendered clear that if a IT was to be a real tool in helping trainees to become full C.C. operators, it would benefit from the modelling of the skills and knowledge of an experienced operator. It had already been stated that the expert knowledge might be seen as a paradigm for the knowledge that the trainee should possess [2]. A detailed study has been therefore undertaken to try and establish the characteristics that may describe the "perfect" C.C. operator. By that, we mean aspects like the conceptual and procedural knowledge he uses in the diagnostic and the service restoration processes, as well as the operational skills that enable him to perform quick, reliable and consistent analysis of serious incidents. This later skill represents the operator's ability in using those concepts and procedures in a fast and reliable manner, as well as his ability in dealing with dynamic problem solving, often involving multiple activities and differentiated goals.

2   Operator and Trainee Models

Our work identified so far the following parameters as the most relevant for the modelling of electrical network C.C. operators:

1. Knowledge about the network structure and behaviour, its topology and the different types of equipment connected.

2. Experience in network control under normal conditions.

3. Experience in diagnosing the different types of incident that can occur in the electrical network as well as the knowledge about the service restoration techniques, based on traits such as diagnosis validity and reliability, speed, autonomous decision capacity and variety of the problems solved.

4. Capability to perform post-mortem analysis, in order to extract information about how to prevent or circumvent future occurrences of the same type.

We decided to use a flexible approach to the problem of extracting this kind of data from direct interaction between system and user: to use a supervisor to gather this data during a long interaction with the different operators and to build a simple tool to help him to organise, display and edit this data. We expect to be able to accurately model the typical experienced operator, after a process that will include the gauging of the different parameters' relative weight and the inclusion of parameters not foreseen in our initial analysis.

As the characteristics of a good C.C. operator lay under three different types, we must devise different methods and tutoring strategies to train operators in those areas. The development of the operational skills must take into account the fact that the aim of this tutoring phase is the automation of processes, the speed of execution and the accuracy of the work. This can only be achieved by repeated drilling of the procedures and techniques learnt during the previous phases. In studies carried out in somehow related performance-based tasks, it has been acknowledged that improvements in performing these tasks come only after long periods of training [3].

We intend to reflect in the trainee's model structure the conclusions to be issued by the Operator's Model validation process. For the representation of the trainee's model (viewed as a would-be expert operator) we'll use a mixed approach. For the conceptual knowledge area, we decided to use a knowledge tree, reminiscent of the task hierarchies concept as described in [4] and [5. For the procedural knowledge area, we planned to use a plain task hierarchy, describing all the steps that must be performed to warrant a correct diagnostic. For the operational skills area, a linear model covering all the different parameters is being used, due to the non-discrete nature of the parameters involved.

In order to offer full inspectability, we decided to allow the user not only to consult his own model, but to also make an auto-evaluation of his work so far, changing the model accordingly. If the trainee feels that the evaluation made by the system is not correct, he can request that a change be made. If he thinks that the evaluation is optimistic, then his request is mandatory. In the opposite case, his request will trigger a specific test, prior to acceptance. A prototype tool for testing trainee's model data acquisition and maintenance has been built. We figured that the system would not need to make any a priori assumptions concerning trainee's prior expertise, due to the long period of interaction between user and system to be expected. In tutoring systems it is common to privilege the accuracy of the model over its immediate availability. The system will then assume that any new user will be a novice and treat him like that until further notice.

References

1. Vale. Z. 1994: Intelligent Tutoring Systems for Power System Control Centers, 1994 IEEE Intern. Conf. on Systems, Man and Cybernetics, San Antonio, USA, (1994) 1832-1837
2. Kass, Robert: Student Modelling in Intelligent Tutoring Systems – Implications for User Modeling. User Models in Dialog Systems. Springer-Verlag (1996)
3. Gentner, Donald: Expertise in typewriting, in The Nature of Expertise. Ed. Michelene Chi. L. Erlbaum Associates (1988)
4. Collins, Jason 1997: Inspectable User Models for Just-in-time Workplace Training. User Modeling: Proceedings of the Sixth International Conference (1997)
5. Vassileva, Julita: A Task-Centered Approach for User Modeling in a Hypermedia Office Documentation System. User Modeling and User-Adapted Interaction (1996)

Getting the Right Information to the Right Person

Gloria Teo

German National Research Center for Information Technology, Schloss Birlinghoven,
D-53754 St. Augustin, Germany, gloriateo@netscape.net

Abstract. Classical personalization methods require prior knowledge of
user in order to adapt to user's needs. This paper presents an algorithm
that generates an initial personal profile for new user with no prior
knowledge of user's interest.

1   Introduction

Personalizing information access and delivery is a solution to bridge the gap of broad
coverage and focused interests by providing users with a wide range of information
space with adapted content, structure and/or presentation formats based on users'
background, interest, behaviour and task environment [1]. One such system is the
ELectronic Funding Information Service, ELFI [4]. ELFI provides over 2000
registered users on funding opportunities over 600 German and European funding
sources.

The system was reviewed to enhance easier usage. The results of log file analysis
had shown that more support is needed for new users in the selection of an initial
personal profile. Classical personalization methods were explored and examined.
However, ELFI has no prior knowledge of new user's research interest. Thus, the
solution is to exploit other sources to gain this background knowledge of user [5].

2   ELFI System and Usage Data

Universities and research institutions are increasingly dependant on outside funding to
finance their research work. ELFI presents this information in a unified form [4]. In
ELFI, funding programmes are categorized in four hierarchies, namely the research
topic hierarchy, the sponsor's hierarchy, the funding types hierarchy and the cross-
domain hierarchy.

A log file analysis was conducted in a period of three months each in two
subsequent years. It was found that new users spent most of their time selecting and
deselecting the topics in the hierarchy, especially the research topic hierarchy, and
session length is short. This is not the case with experienced users. Hence, generating
an automatic personal profile could be a solution but where do we get research
interest information about users, as it is not available in the system?

M. Bauer, P.J. Gmytrasiewicz, and J. Vassileva (Eds.): UM 2001, LNAI 2109, pp. 257–259, 2001.
©Springer-Verlag Berlin Heidelberg 2001

3   Personalization Algorithm

There are three classical personalization concepts. (1) Adaptation of content, where different users are presented with different content [3]. (2) Adaptation of presentation, where that the layout or format of the system changes while keeping the informational content the same [2]. (3) Adaptation of Structure, where navigation and/or orientation support is available, such as an adaptive guidance, links sorting and so on.

These classical personalization concepts could not solve our problem of acquiring users' background information, as classical personalization methods require user knowledge in advance, in a form of stereotypes or a history of user interaction behaviour with a system. Thus, other sources have to be exploited.

With this notion of exploring other sources, an algorithm was designed (see Fig. 1), implemented and evaluated.

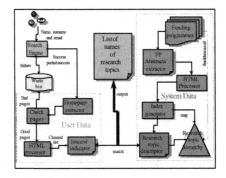

Fig. 1. The Algorithm

This algorithm comprises two main acquisition parts, the acquisition of user data and the acquisition of system data. (1) The name, surname and email address of user were extracted, at log in. (2) These three information were then fed to the search machine – AHOY the Homepage Finder. (3) The acquisition of user data. (a) The search result was parsed and the relevant links were traced and the homepages extracted. (b) These pages were checked. Good pages were kept and bad pages were thrown away. Good pages are pages that could give indication of a research interest. (c) The good pages were then converted to a readable form and syntaxically tagged. Nouns and compound nouns were extracted giving a list of words that described the user's homepage – interest indicator . (4) The acquisition of system data. The funding programmes abstracts were extracted and processed likewise to step 3c, giving a list of words that describe the funding programme – research topic descriptor . (5) The words in the interest indicator were then matched against the words in the research topics descriptor. It was then traced which field of research this funding programme belongs, giving a list of names of research topics that could be of interest to the user.

4   Evaluation

To measure the performance of the algorithm a baseline was constructed based on two experts' binary rating of the homepages with respect to the topics in the research topic hierarchy as relevant or not relevant to user's interest. The reliability of the baseline was also measured. A total of 809 funding programmes were taken arbitrarily from the ELFI System. 94 of the users' homepage were used. After discarding useless homepages, 75 user samples were left for further evaluation.

The three parameters that could affect the output of the algorithm were varied. They are the sources of the system data, the depth of the hierarchy and the art of counting the threshold, giving 12 variations. The results were evaluated and the precision and recall of the 12 variations were then measured against the baseline. The method using both sources, the second last depth of the hierarchy and the ranked threshold produced the best result with 85% of precision at about 30% of recall.

5   Conclusion

We have a situation where users patronize the ELFI system occasionally, the count of new users are increasing daily, sessions of users are short and most of their interaction time were spent on selecting and deselecting topics in the research topic hierarchy. The solution presented is to automatically generate a personal profile with a pre-selection of relevant research topics. To achieve this pre-selection of research topics, more user (background) data of users were required, but such information were not available in our system. Thus, other sources were exploited. The precision and recall of the best case was presented.

References

1. Ardissono, L., Goy, A., Petrone, G., Segnan, M.: Adaptive user interfaces for on-line shopping. AAAI Spring Symposium on Adaptive User Interface. Stanford University, CA (2000) 13-18
2. Brusilovsky, P., Specht, M., Weber, G.: Towards Adaptive Learning Environments. GISI 95, Herausforderungen eines globalen Informationsverbundes füdie Informatik, Springer Verlag, Berlin (1995) 322-329
3. Fink, J., Kobsa A., Nill, A.: Adaptable and Adaptive Information Provision for All Users, Including Disabled and Elderly People. The New Review of Hypermedia and Multimedia 4 (1998) 163-188
4. Nick, A., Koenemann, J., Schalük, E.: ELFI: information brokering for the domain of research funding. Computer Networks and ISDN Systems, Vol. 30 (1998) 1491-1500
5. Teo, G., Koenemann, J.: Personalising ELFI: user data as a source for adaptation. In Proc. of the 7th GI – ABIS99, LWA99, Sammelband, Magdeburg (1999) 273-282

Goals, Tasks and Application Domains as the Guidelines for Defining a Framework for User Modelling

Ilaria Torre

Dipartimento di Informatica - Universitàdi Torino
Corso Svizzera 185 - 10149 Torino (Italy)
Tel. +39.335.5994323   Fax. +39.011.8122173
ila.torre@di.unito.it

Abstract. The exponential increase of adaptive systems and the difficulty of identifying the relevant dimensions for the construction of user models, are the bases of the choice of building a framework for user modelling. The goal is that of defining a method for identifying such dimensions and moreover creating a taxonomy of goals, features and dimension for different application domains.

Keywords. Framework and dimensions for user modelling, ontology for adaptation features, reusable user modelling components, adaptive hypermedia.

1 Principles for the Construction of the Framework

Systems are progressively substituting humans in many activities, and the request of interactivity is growing. As personal assistants, systems are asked to provide users with information and services fitting them, at the right time and in the right way. However, defining what right means is a difficult task, which implies knowing the user (his goals, interests, believes, etc.) and the context around him. An adaptive agent must be supplied with an adequate knowledge base and the first problem related to that is the ability of building reliable and predictive models of the users.

Many systems lack a deep study about this problem, in particular because of its interdisciplinary nature. The efforts of my research work are directed toward the definition of a framework for user modelling with the following goals:
- creating some guidelines to simplify the analysis that has to be performed when designing new adaptive applications,
- building user modelling components to be reused across different applications.

The construction of the framework is based on the hypothesis that the features of the user that must be considered, in order to personalize the interaction, depend on - and can be deduced from - the intersection of i) the goals and sub-goals of the system ii) the tasks performed to obtain such goals and iii) the features of the application domain. A second hypothesis is the possibility of abstracting such essential components from specific adaptive systems, to finally obtain a taxonomy of the possible goals, tasks, domains and of the conceptual dimensions of user modelling relevant for them [5]. The work started with the analysis of several adaptive systems, both designed by my group and taken from projects described in the literature and

M. Bauer, P.J. Gmytrasiewicz, and J. Vassileva (Eds.): UM 2001, LNAI 2109, pp. 260–262, 2001.

operating on the field. The scheme below summarizes the steps of the methodology, dividing a phase of analysis from a subsequent phase of abstraction.

Analysis phase

1°Identification of a set of representative types of applications (starting from the taxonomies in the literature [2,3,4], I produced a new classification, fitting my method of analysis: e-commerce applications; information services; education systems; decision support systems; applications for co-operative work).

2°Analysis of a set of instances of each application type, (e.g. news server and collaborative filtering systems, that are instances of the application type "information services"). The analysis is performed through a decomposition process:
- decomposition of the adaptation goals, sub-goals and tasks of the system,
- decomposition of the domain features.

The result is the creation of a matrix (see Fig. 1) with the adaptation goals and tasks on the x-axis and with the domain features on the y-axis: this matrix represents the basic tool for the identification of the user modelling dimensions that are relevant in the specific application instance. Briefly, the dimensions are extracted analysing each intersection point that describes the application and answering the question: "what features of the user do I (and the system) have (has) to consider to achieve that one goal which has that one sub-goal(s) and is related to that one domain context?".

3°Definition of the general characteristics of each application type by means of a join operation between the matrices. The resulting matrix becomes an instrument (guideline) for analysing and describing every specific application of that type.

Abstraction phase

1°Abstraction of the goals, sub-goals and tasks from the matrices above, to obtain an taxonomy of goals, independent of the specific systems and, in a similar way, abstraction of the domain features and of the conceptual dimensions. This means extracting, for each type of element, the features at the highest level of generality.

2°Join of all the taxonomies to obtain an ontology of user modelling dimensions with a semantic-net-like structure.

3°Building of a library of modules which represent the user modelling dimensions.

2   Results

According to the work I made up to now, the approach seems to be quite effective as regards the analysis phase. The idea of decomposing goals and domain features exploits the established principles of task and functional analyses and the method introduced for extracting the user modelling dimensions is a valid mean to activate all the links that allow one to discover the relevant dimensions: it is a systematic approach to a process that is usually carried out in an ad hoc way for each application. The matrices method has been, and is currently being, employed in some projects of my research group. Two of them belong to the application type information services.

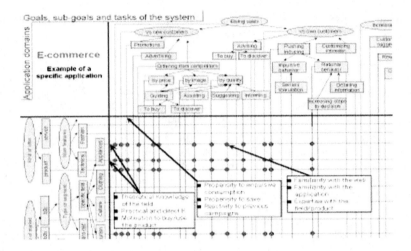

Fig. 1. Part of a matrix representing an example of an e-commerce system

The first one is an adaptive newspaper [1] and the second is a tourist information service implemented in an automotive context. Other two projects belong respectively to e-commerce applications and to decision support systems.

As regards the abstraction phase, the initial study seems to confirm the hypothesis that the components of specific adaptive systems can be generalized to obtain the taxonomies described in the methodology. It emerges, in fact, that while the high-level goals of a system are related to the application context, the sub-goals and the tasks are often common to many applications (the opposite happens for the y-axis features) and thus the dimensions for user modelling related to these sub-goals (and features) can be re-used for different applications. In this way the taxonomy could become a guideline for new projects but also a library of modular knowledge sources. Anyway, more work is needed to produce a complete and reliable (strong) ontology.

References

1. Ardissono, L., Console, L., Torre, I.: On the application of personalization techniques to news servers on the WWW. In Lamma, Mello. (eds.): Advances in Artificial Intelligence. lncs, Vol. 1792. Springer Verlag, Berlin Heidelberg New York, (2000) 261–271.
2. Brusilovsky, P.L.: Methods and Techniques of Adaptive Hypermedia. User Modelling and User-Adapted Interaction 6 (1996) 87–129.
3. Kass, R., Finin, T.: Modelling the User in Natural Language Systems. Special Issue on User Modelling. In Computational Linguistics, Vol. 14, N. 3, (1988) 5–22.
4. McTear, M.F.: User modelling for adaptive computer systems: a survey of recent developments. Artificial Intelligence Review 7 (1993) 157–184.
5. Torre, I.: A Modular Approach for User Modelling. In Brusilovsky, P., Stock, O., Strapparava, C. (eds.): Adaptive Hypermedia and Adaptive Web-Based Systems. lncs, Vol. 1892. Springer Verlag, Berlin Heidelberg New York (2000) 415–420.

Doctoral Consortium

Improving Student Models by Reasoning about Cognitive Ability, Emotions and Gender

Ivon Arroyo [1,2] and Beverly Park Woolf [1,2]

[1] Department of Computer Science, University of Massachusetts, Amherst
[2] School of Education, University of Massachusetts, Amherst
{Ivon, Bev }@cs.umass.edu

Abstract.   We explore how cognitive, socio-biological and emotional conditions of the student help predict behavior within an ITS, and how instruction should be adapted depending on these variables to improve educational outcomes. Cognitive, social and emotional factors tend to be more permanent in nature than student's knowledge. Our approach is to diagnose them with pre-tests before the user starts using the system.

1 Introduction

While trying to improve the eectiveness of intelligent tutoring systems (ITS), the researcher can focus on: 1) representing the student more accurately, 2) improving the quality and amount of teaching elements available, 3) improving the adaptive mechanisms of the tutoring system (i.e. the pedagogical reasoning). Our research is a contribution to all of the mentioned areas, as we explore how the cognitive and socio-emotional conditions of the student help predict their behavior within an ITS, and how help provision mechanisms can be varied depending on these variables. This research work is peformed on a mathematics tutoring system for 8-11 year old children called Animalwatch. This ITS has been tested in schools and has been highly rated both by students and teachers [3].

We have analyzed students' cognitive development [6]. It is known that students at this age range can handle most concrete operations (the ability to manipulate ideas over concrete objects). Some students are transitioning to being able to handle formal operations (the ability to manipulate abstract ideas). Although students are expected to develop specific cognitive abilities at a certain age, not all children develop at the same time. This makes cognitive development an interesting variable to focus on while looking for individual dierences among student-users.

Gender is an interesting variable to analyze. It is an easy variable to measure, allowing to enrich the predictability of the student model at a low cost. More importantly, recent research suggests that girls and boys have dierent approaches to mathematics problem solving [5]. Also, prior research makes us believe that emotional factors can contribute to gender dierences in learning: it has been shown that in early adolescence, gender dierences exist in math self-concept and math utility; girls have negative emotions and self derogating

M. Bauer, P.J. Gmytrasiewicz, and J. Vassileva (Eds.): UM 2001, LNAI 2109, pp. 265–267, 2001.

attributions about their math performance [7]. These varying emotions about the subject being taught should produce dierent student behaviors within the tutoring system, both for boys and girls. Incorporating them into the student model should provide for the possibility to take some positive action.

The first research question in this doctoral thesis work is to what extent these variables, which cover dierent dimensions of a human being, can enhance the prediction of student behavior in the context of a one-to-one tutoring system. If higher accuracy is achieved in the student model, then the following question is how this information should be used to improve adaptivity in systems that support human learning. Are there some teaching strategies that are better for a student who fits some stereotype? This will involve finding interactions between student stereotypes and the available educational treatments.

2   Summary of Completed Work

Diagnosis of cognitive abilities . We have produced a computer-based pre-test to measure children's cognitive ability [2]. The test consists of ten highly interactive tasks that students are asked to solve. An adaptive version of this test can reduce significantly the number of questions while maintaining high accuracy. Students of this age should have abilities in the range from concrete to formal thinking. We designed tasks that measured abilities within these two stages of development. All these tasks are adapted from descriptions in [8]. The result of this test is a score that reflects students' logico-mathematical ability. This cognitive development test has been used with hundreds of 8-11 year-old students before and after using Animalwatch. The test outcomes make us believe that it is accurately measuring cognitive ability. The test produced reasonable measures of reliability, predictive validity and face validity.

Diagnosis of socio-emotional variables . We have pre and post-tested students with an instrument that measures math self-concept (the belief students have about their ability to learn math), math utility (the student's belief that mathematics is important and valuable to learn) and math liking [4]. We are building regression models from the collected student data that depend on these emotional attitudes for predicting number of mistakes and time spent solving a problem.

Design of pedagogical interventions. Adaptivity . Having accurate student models is useful if we can identify what teaching methods work for the student we are representing with accuracy. We look for kinds of pedagogical interactions that work better for students falling into some stereotype (aptitude-treatment interactions). We built alternative help provision systems: when a student makes a mistake, dierent types of hints could be presented to the student depending on amount of information, hint interactivity, concreteness and structure. We are looking for new descriptors of the hints we already have, and we are building new dierent types of hints. We gave dierent versions of the tutoring system to students, with dierent remediation mechanisms. We are building models that predict changes in emotional attitudes depending on the remediation mechanism of the ITS. We have evidence to think that low cognitive ability students work better with highly interactive and concrete explanations, while high cognitive ability students work better with more symbolic explanations [1]. We also have evidence for girls working better with hints that are more structured, while boys do better with hints that demand less interaction.

3   Future Work

The immediate future work will be to build a population model that integrates all these variables together in predicting performance along several measures: time to solve a problem, number of mistakes, generation of positive attitudes towards math, etc. We have built statistical linear regression models for this purpose, but we will also experiment with tools that produce non-linear models, always with the objective of accounting for more variance. It will be interesting then to see to what extent the model built from one population of students generalizes to a new population, and also what variables are more relevant than others. The following step will be to decide what other variables could characterize the student and the hints, and how they can be measured. Last, we plan to reason from this information, using the rules derived from the interactions in the models. We intend to put the derived teaching strategies into practice, by testing a version of an ITS which incorporates this reasoning compared to another one which does not take these variables into account. The hypothesis is that the system which reasons about the cognitive, gender and emotional characteristics of the student will be more eective than the control one.

References

1. Arroyo, I.; Beck, J.; Beal, C.; Woolf, B.; Schultz, K.: Macroadapting Animalwatch to gender and cognitive dierences with respect to hint interactivity and symbolism. Proceedings of Intelligent Tutoring Systems (2000)
2. Arroyo, I.; Conejo, R.; Guzman, E.; Woolf, B.P.: An Adaptive Web-based Component for Cognitive Ability Estimation. Proceedings of Artificial Intelligence in Education (2001)
3. Beal, C. R, Woolf, B. P., Beck, J. E., Arroyo, I., Schultz, K., Hart, D. M.: Gaining Confidence in Mathematics: Instructional Technology for Girls. Proceedings of Mathematics/Science Education and Technology (2000) pp. 57-64.
4. Eccles, J.S., Wigfild, A., Harold, R.D., Blumenfeld, P.: Age and gender dierences in children's self and task perceptions during elementary school. Child development, 64, (1993) pp. 830-847.
5. Fennema, E., Carpenter, T. P., Jacobs, V. R., Franke, M. L., Levi, L. W. (1998, June-July). A longitudinal study of gender dierences in young children's mathematical thinking. Educational Researcher, 27, 6-11.
6. Piaget, J. How Children Form Mathematical Concepts. 1953. In Scientific American.
7. Stipek, D. J., Gralinkski, J. H.: Gender dierences in children's achievement. Related beliefs and emotional responses to success and failure in mathematics. Journal of Educational Psychology (1991), 83, 361-371.
8. Voyat, G. E.: Piaget Systematized (1982). Lawrence Erlbawm.

Integrating Multilingual Text Classification Tasks and User Modeling in Personalized Newspaper Services

Alberto Díz Esteban

Departamento de Inteligencia Artificial, Universidad Europea – CEES, 28670 Villaviciosa de Odó, Madrid, S pain. Tel.: (34) 91 6647800 ext. 671. Fax: (34) 91 6168265
alberto@dinar.esi.uem.es

Abstract. In this paper a methodology designed to improve the intelligent personalization of newspaper services is presented. The methodology integrates textual content analysis tasks to achieve an elaborate user model, which represents separately short-term needs and long-term multi-topic interests. The characterization of user's interests includes his preferences about structure, content and information delivery. A wide coverage and non-specific-domain classification of topics and a personal set of keywords allow the user to define his preferences about content. The application of implicit feedback allows a proper and dynamic personalization. Another topic that have been addressed in the thesis is the evaluation of systems offering to send users a selection of the daily news by electronic mail. Finally, the extensions to a multilingual framework are studied.

Keywords. Short/long-term models, multi-topic user profile, adaptive user model, evaluation, multilingual text classification tasks

1 Introduction

In recent years, innumerable providers are making their presence in Internet a main strategic goal. The providers must help the customers to find the desired products, which are frequently supplemented with text descriptions in different languages, that help the customers to find interesting items in web sites with search functions.

Simple user models usually result in the introduction of irrelevant information. The integration of textual content analysis tasks can be used to achieve a more elaborate user model, to obtain a suitable representation of document contents, and to evaluate the similarity between user's interests and information. Representative examples of information access systems that integrate this kind of techniques are WebMate [3], News Dude [2] and SIFT [8].

The aims of this thesis are:
1) To present a methodology to improve the personalization of information access services and to describe can be applied to the electronic newspaper domain.
2) The evaluation of systems offering to send users a selection of the daily news by electronic mail.

M. Bauer, P.J. Gmytrasiewicz, and J. Vassileva (Eds.): UM 2001, LNAI 2109, pp. 268–270, 2001.
©Springer- Verlag Berlin Heidelberg 2001

2   The Monolingual User Model

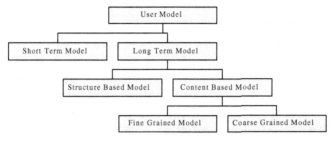

Fig. 1. User Model

The user model proposed (Figure 1) represents separately short-term needs and long-term multiple interests. Users can express, in addition to personal information and format information [1], their preferences both in terms of structural and content based information. The sections of the newspaper acts as structural information. A wide coverage classification of topics non-specific for the newspaper domain, the first level of categories of Yahoo! Spain (coarse grained interest), together with a set of keywords (fine grained interest), is used to characterize the content based interest of a user. Users can show their preferences giving their degrees of importance on each on: without interest, of some interest, interesting, very interesting. The personalization architecture allows an extra level of user specification. Each of the three features (sections, categories and keywords) has a weight that represents its importance for the user interests.

The kind of necessity determines the news access method. Short-term needs are handled by the ad hoc retrieval subsystem, whereas long-term needs are managed by the dissemination information subsystem, which selects relevant news according to user's models and sends an e-mail message to the readers containing them.

The representation of the documents is obtained applying the Vector Space Model to their texts [6]. A representation for each category can be obtained by applying text categorization techniques [7] and using a set of training documents, in this case, the web pages indexed by the Spanish version of Yahoo!. The keywords also are represented with VSM, using the weight assigned for each word in the model. To perform the selection we applied category-pivoted categorization [7] with the categories and information retrieval with all the keywords. Also all the news are processed to check if they belong to one of the sections selected in the user model.

The monolingual part has been developed in the Mercurio system [4] and the evaluation of the results has shown, in a first instance, a better personalization through a more complete user model. The study of the different behaviors [5] of the three methods used to specify user interests (sections, categories and keywords) has shown how delicate the interaction is between the complete set of parameters involved: news item per section, maximum number of news item per message, etc.

To achieve a long-term dynamic model that evolves together with user's interest, it is necessary to apply feedback techniques that provide information about this evolution. However, in practice, many users are unwilling to provide relevance judgments on retrieved documents. An alternative is to use implicit feedback, i.e. to inference document relevance from user's behavior. Then, we use the documents read by the user as feedback. The system provides numerous context elements, including a user-adapted summary that can assist users to decide about document relevance without inspecting the full text.

3   The Multilingual Extension

The multilingual approach proposes the same user model in a single language but with documents to be filtered in different languages, e.g. one Spanish newspaper and one English newspaper. There is a Yahoo version for the most important languages (with the same categories for every language). These versions are used to construct the representation of the categories that are used in the categorization process. The idea is to categorize with the version of the Yahoo that corresponds to each language and to translate the keywords of the model (instead of translating the news), thereby performing cross-language information retrieval.

The problem with the translation of the keywords is the polisemy. The solution performs a word sense disambiguation process with each word to obtain the correct sense before to make the translation. To make the disambiguation one need information about the different senses (obtained from EuroWordNet) and information that allows deciding on the correct sense of the keyword (obtained from the User Model). EuroWordNer is also used to make the translation.

References

1. Amato, G., Straccia, U.: User Profile Modeling and Applications to Digital Libraries. In: Abiteboul, S., Vercoustre, A.M. (eds.), Proceedings of the Third European Conference on Research and Advanced Technology for Digital Libraries, Lecture Notes in Computer Science 1696 (1999) 184-197, Springer-Verlag
2. Billsus, D., Pazzani, M.J.: A Hybrid User Model for News Story Classification. In: Proceedings of the Seventh International Conference on User Modeling, Banff, Canada (1999)
3. Chen, L., Sycara, K.P.: WebMate: A Personal Agent for Browsing and Searching. In: Proceedings of the Second International Conference on Autonomous Agents, Minneapolis, (1998)
4. Díaz, A., Gervá s, P., Garcá, A.: Evaluating a User-Model Based Personalisation Architecture for Digital News Services. In: Proceedings of the Fourth European Conference on Research and Advanced Technology for Digital Libraries, Lisbon, Portugal (2000).
5. Díaz, A., Gervá s, P., Garcá, A., Chacó, I.: Sections, categories and keywords as interest specification tools for personalised news services. Online Information Review, OIR 2001, no 3. (in press)
6. Salton, G., McGill, M.J.: Introduction to Modern Information Retrieval. McGraw Hill, New York (1983)
7. Sebastiani, F. (1999) A Tutorial on Automated Text Categorisation. In Proceedings of the First Argentinean Symposium on Artificial Intelligence (ASAI-99).
8. Yan, T.W., Garcia-Molina, H.: SIFT – A Tool for Wide-Area Information Dissemination. In: Proceedings of the USENIX Technical Conference, (1995)

Enhancing Embodied Intelligent Agents with Affective User Modelling

Patrick Gebhard

German Research Center for Artificial Intelligence, Saarbrüken, Germany

gebhard@dfki.de

Abstract. The objective of this research is the exploration how affective knowledge used in global controlling mechanisms for public information systems with lifelike presentation agents will increase the effectiveness of such systems in terms of information presentation, but also help the user to better explain his/her needs by adopting a more natural conversational style through interactive dialogue.

1 Background

Conventional public information systems are static in nature, forcing a user to navigate his/her way through a series of multiple-choice options before the required information is obtained. Despite the fact that the information is then well presented, the acceptance level of these systems remains quite low [7].

Recent research has shown that the acceptance level can be significantly improved if a lifelike presentation agent is utilised as a conversational dialogue partner in much the same way as a real human would act [3]. Unfortunately, these systems have so far only been able to create believability through a carefully choreographed presentation of hand-coded dialogue scripts. This approach is obviously very labour intensive, and the breadth of the lifelike character's persona can quickly become exhausted after very few interactions. Unlike chat bots, information systems are primarily geared to impart information, and so cannot simply rely on the "Eliza" effect of making the user feel good about him/herself.

The main challenge of this work will be the combination of the different approaches in dialogue modelling and information presentation. This Ph.D. work uses results and methods from the following research areas: user stereotypes, inference techniques of affective user modelling, adaptive natural language systems, and human-human communication strategies (e.g. sales strategies).

2 Goals

This research will address the problem of user fatigue by explicitly modelling both the user's, and lifelike character's, personality and affective state, and then using these dynamic components to guide the conversational dialogue. This process will be

M. Bauer, P.J. Gmytrasiewicz, and J. Vassileva (Eds.): UM 2001, LNAI 2109, pp. 271–273, 2001.
ⓒSpringer-Verlag Berlin Heidelberg 2001

achieved by the following iterative steps:Adaptation of communication strategies for the use in the affective presentation and dialogue planning mechanisms.

- Development of an affective reasoning component for the dynamic modelling of the user's and agent's affective model with the required inference methods. The reasoning process appraises events, actions, and objects in the light of the user's and the agent's goals, standards and attitudes. The result will be used to: a) provide a more natural conversation style, and b) provide affective feedback by expressing the emotional state in its gestures and utterances, allowing the agent to adapt better to the needs of the user.

- Evaluation of the effectiveness of affective user/agent models and explicit dialogue strategies in achieving the research objective of increasing information acceptance. The results from these trials will be used to improve the communication strategies and affective model.

3 Issues and Status

This Ph.D. thesis integrates work done in the area of user modelling with research on affective reasoning. In particular, I will enhance a user modelling component with affective information on stereotypes. This knowledge will be used by an affective reasoner component, which includes a reactive primary input appraisal component [6] and a hierarchical presentation planning mechanism [1], [2]. Especially this knowledge will be used to control the selection of dialogue and presentation strategies.

The basic flow of information within this system starts with the analysis of the user's verbal input by the speech component. The speech component attempts to map the input to a specific speech act, and also identify the emotional value. Currently this is done by spotting emotionally loaded words and phrases. Both, speech act and emotional value will be directly appraised with respect to the agent's emotional status. This might then trigger a reactive behaviour, which is immediately shown by the agent. In parallel the agent's deliberative behaviour will be shaped. The affective user-model component is the first step in this process line. It is used to draw inferences from the user's input in relation to specific affective stereotypes. The result will be a goal objective according to the current user's affective state. Based on the user's goal and the system's goal, the affective state of the system will be computed. This has a direct effect on the output strategy selection and on the generation of the following presentation. The affective state of the system is also reflected in the gestures the agent uses and affective speech output.

The building of a complete "affective" lifelike presentation agent system is well beyond the resources of a single Ph.D. research project. Fortunately, I am able to adapt a number of components from projects within the DFKI for my purposes. The EU-funded SAFIRA project, in which a toolkit for supporting affective interactions for real-time applications will be developed, gives me the possibility to implement the affective speech generation software component.

Currently, the following modules are implemented:

- A template based speech interpreter (combined with a primary input appraisal) with a rudimentary dialogue history support. This module is further developed in the SMARTKOM project.
- An Affective Reasoner, based on the Five-Factor model for personality and the Ortony, Clore and Collins (OCC) model for emotions [4], [5].
- The presentation-planning component, based on the PREPLAN engine [1].
- An output rendering module for translating the output of the planning process to commands for the presentation agent, the browser, and the speech output engine.
- A user interface applet, which controls the presentation agent engine and the speech input and output facilities. Currently, the instructions for the rendering components do not yet contain any detailed affective information.

In addition, we have collected information about the first example domain, in which the agent plays the role of a virtual receptionist. Currently visitors can obtain information about people working in the DFKI. In the future, it will answer questions on wider range of dialogue topics covering news, projects, and people within the DFKI.

References

1. André , E. (1995). Ein planbasierter Ansatz zur Generierung multimedialer Präsentationen, DISKI 108, infix.
2. André , E. (1997). WIP and PPP: A Comparison of two Multimedia Presentation Systems in Terms of the Standard Reference Model, in: Computer Standards and Interfaces, Volume 18, No: 6-7, pp. 555-564.
3. Lester, J. C., S. A. Converse, S. E. Kahler, S. T. Barlow, B. A. Stone, and R. S. Bhogal. 1997. The persona effect: Affective impact of animated pedagogical agents. In S. Pemberton, ed., Human factors in computing systems, CHI'97 conference proceedings, 359–366. New York: ACM Press.
4. Ortony, A., Clore, G. L., and Collins, A. (1988). The Cognitive Structure of Emotions. Cambridge: Cambridge University Press.
5. McCrae, R. R., and John, O. P. (1992). An introduction to the five-factor model and its applications. Special Issue: The five-factor model: Issues and applications. Journal of Personality 60: 175-215, 1992.
6. Sloman, A. (1999). Architectural Requirements for Human-like Agents Both Natural and Artificial. (What sorts of machines can love?). To appear in K. Dautenhahn (Ed.) Human Cognition And Social Agent Technology, John Benjamins Publishing.
7. Van Mulken, S., André , E., and Müler, J. (1998). The Persona Effect: How Substantial Is It? In: Hilary Johnson, Laurence Nigay, and Chris Roast (Eds.) People and Computers XIII, Proceedings of HCI-98. Berlin: Springer. pp. 53--66.

Designing TV Viewer Stereotypes
for an Electronic Program Guide

Cristina Gena

Dipartimento di Informatica, Universitàdi Torino
Corso Svizzera 185; I-10149 Torino, Italy
{cgena@di.unito.it}

Abstract . This paper describes how a user modeling knowledge base for personalized TV servers can be generated starting from an analysis of lifestyles surveys. The aim of the research is the construction of well-designed stereotypes for generating adaptive electronic program guides (EPGs) which filter the information about TV events depending on the user's interests.

1 Introduction

With satellite and cable TV, the convergence of TV and Internet and the advent of digital networks, the offer of TV channels will increase in the near future. Consequently, it will be very difficult for the users to find quickly their favorite programs. In such a scenario, personalized filtering techniques will become fundamental to reduce the huge amount of broadcasted programs. Therefore, it will be necessary the presence of an intermediary between the TV broadcasters and the viewers, such as a personalized electronic programs guide (EPG), in order to recommend in a timely fashion the programs which best match the individual viewing preferences. In the area of personalized services for TV programs, several tools exploit collaborative and content-based filtering techniques for user profiling and recommending the appropriate programs. For example, PTV [1], a Web-based personalized television listings service, learns the individual user's viewing preferences on the basis of explicit program ratings and then generates personalized TV guides by applying hybrid collaborative and case-based filtering techniques. As far as the application of stereotypes-based user modeling techniques to TV services is concerned, not many examples are available. In the FACTS project, Bellifemine et al [2] classify viewers into three featured groups on the basis of their watching behavior: common user group, special user group, and collective user group.

This paper describes how a knowledge base for user modeling techniques adopted in the generation of personalized TV program guides can be designed starting from an analysis of lifestyles surveys. This work is part of a more extensive research for the development of a system which generates adaptive EPGs [3]. The system includes a user modeling component which exploits stereotypical information. We decided to use a stereotype-based user-modeling system in order to personalize and adapt the interaction with the user since the first time he logs into the system. The stereotypes enable the system to make default inferences starting from a small amount of

M. Bauer, P.J. Gmytrasiewicz, and J. Vassileva (Eds.): UM 2001, LNAI 2109, pp. 274–276, 2001.

information about the user [4]. This generic user model can be revised after monitoring the user's behavior.

2 Stereotypical Knowledge

The exploitation of sociological stereotypes seems to be usual in the mass-media world. Thus, we decided to generate our user modeling knowledge base starting from an analysis of existing surveys about TV viewers. Particularly, we examined the lifestyles surveys which cluster the population into groups according to consumers' preferences, socio-cultural trends, homogeneous behaviors. Especially, we concentrated on a lifestyles' study, Sinottica, conducted by Eurisko data analyzers [5]. Given the completeness of the considered viewpoints and the reliability of collected data, we decided to build the stereotypes knowledge base starting from the Eurisko lifestyles. However, the information regarding the lifestyles is not defined in a formalized way. Thus, we exploited a formalism to structure the information characterizing each user class in order to represent in a formalized way the lifestyles descriptions [6]. Moreover, we structured the stereotypes in two main parts, assuming a plausible correlation among homogeneous user groups and their preferences: a profile, containing the classification data of individuals belonging to the represented stereotype; a prediction part , containing the preferences typical of such individuals. A similar approach has been adopted in SETA, a prototype toolkit for the construction of adaptive Web stores [7]. While the classification data are used to evaluate how close the individual viewer using the EPG matches a stereotypical description, the preferences are used to enable the user modeling system to make initial predictions by exploiting stereotypical information. The Eurisko lifestyles description has been used for the profile of the stereotypes, which has been further split into two main parts: personal data (age, gender, education level, type of job, geographic zone); interests.

Regarding the prediction part of stereotypes, we initially analyzed a survey on the exposure to the TV, made by Eurisko in collaboration with Auditel, the "super partes" company which daily picks up information about TV audience [8]. We analyzed these information items considering the average audience reception rating (number of average viewers in every minute of a program) and the share (percentage of viewers of a program compared to the overall audience in the same time slot)[9]. To obtain more detailed information, we decided to merge the Eurisko/Auditel audience data and the information about interests. We assumed an existing correlation between the user's interests and the programs concerning his interests. Moreover, we refined such collected data by comparing it with the audience data of Eurisko Big Map [9], a sociographic analysis of Italian society. Finally, we included in the prediction part two temporal dimensions: the watching frequency and the viewing time.

3 Conclusion

The stereotype knowledge base which we described bas been used within the user modeling component of a system for the generation of personalized EPGs [3]. After having gathered real people descriptions, we tested the effectiveness of the system as regards the classification of people in stereotypical descriptions and the predictions. The initial results showed the fact that stereotypical knowledge is meaningful for users clearly fitting a lifestyle, but does not make good predictions in the cases where users match different lifestyles in different aspects of their behavior. In particular, the system fails when the user's interests are different from those evaluated according his socio-demographic data. However this situation is not unusual, so we have to solve these contrasts to improve the system's recommendations. Thus, we designed the User Modeling Component of the system as structured into different user modeling modules, which exploit alternative sources of information about users. In addition to the Stereotypical Module, an Explicit Preferences Module manages the user's declared preferences and the User Modeling Component is in charge of solving the possible conflicts in the predictions of the two modules.

We believe that the exploitation of stereotypes during the initial interaction with the user gives good results. Moreover, the existence of stereotypical behaviors in watching TV is also supported by empirical studies. At the moment, we are testing new solutions starting from information about different types of people, to simulate the real behavior of the system. During with this second test phase, we will also concentrate on: refining the prediction part of the stereotypes by analysing new audience data; reclassifying user in more suitable stereotypes, after monitoring the real user's choices; exploiting personalization strategies to adapt the content and layout of the TV guide to the user model.

References

1.   Cotter P., Smyth B. (2000): A Personalized Television Listing Service. Communications of the ACM 43 (8).
2.   Bellifemine F. et al. (1999): Deliverable A12D1 "Agent-system software for the AVEB Phase 1 Demonstrator". http://sharon.cselt.it/projects/facts-a1/.
3.   Ardissono L., Portis F., Torasso P., Bellifemine F., Chiarotto A., Difino A. (2001): Architecture of a system for the generation of personalized Electronic Program Guides. Submitted.
4.   Rich E. (1989): Stereotypes and User Modeling. In A. Kobsa and W. Wahlster, editors, User Models in Dialog Systems, pages 31-51. Springer Verlag, Berlin.
5.   Calvi G. (1986): Indagine sociale italiana. Rapporto Eurisko 1986. FrancoAngeli
6.   Torasso P., Console L.(1989): Diagnostic Problem Solving. North Oxford Academic.
7.   Ardissono L., Goy A. (2000): Tailoring the Interaction With Users in Web stores. To appear on User Modeling and User-Adapted Interaction. Kluwer Academic Publishers.
8.   Auditel (2000): http://www.auditel.it
9.   Casetti F., Di Chio F. (1998): Analisi della televisione. Strumenti Bompiani.

AGENDA CULTUREL
An Adaptive Cultural Information Service

Jessica Givone

Equipe Syst`emes Communicants - Universit´ e de Savoie
http://www.univ-savoie.fr/labos/syscom
jessica.givone@univ-savoie.fr

Abstract.   In the context of   Cartable Electronic   project we developed
a cultural information diusion service. We describe the knowledge to
define and exploit the user model. Then we propose a multi-agent architecture and we describe the system implementation.

1   Introduction

The aim of the Agenda Culturel project is the development and evaluation of an
adaptive cultural diary service for pupils and teachers that provides hypermedia
information about cultural events, in the context of the   Cartable Electronique
project [6]. This project is funded by the Rh^ one Alpes regional council and Savoie
Council (France).

The existing systems for cultural diusion do not adapt to the user and
usually provide static information. Our goal is to propose an architecture to
provide a dynamic adaptive system behaviour. The system interface has to be
able to adapt itself according to user preferences, to dierent contexts of use
and, particularly, to user characteristics that change during time.

With respect to the classification of adaptive systems given by P. Brusilovsky
[1] and P. de Bra [3], the system described in this paper can be classified as
adaptable and dynamic.

Several questions were identified during the design of   Agenda Culturel . Which
kind of user knowledge do we have to acquire? How do we split up a cultural
event description into fragments? Which knowledge do we need about description
fragments to successfully personalize the presentation? What do we have to
know about the presentation structure with respect to dierent users? Which
kind of architecture is better to use? How can the service be integrated into
the Cartable Electronique   portal? In order to solve these problems we studied
similar systems described in the literature, and we defined an architecture and
developed a prototype to test our model. In the prototype the whole domain-
depending information (concerning users and the cultural events) is represented
by exploiting XML [9].

2   User Model

In order to provide user-oriented adaptivity, the system maintains a user model.
Since studies about French cultural habits are too macroscopics, we identified

M. Bauer, P.J. Gmytrasiewicz, and J. Vassileva (Eds.): UM 2001, LNAI 2109, pp. 277–279, 2001.

the data for configuring the user model by interviewing teachers and cultural partners who brought their experience in the domain.

The system keeps two user models. The user can look for information for his/her own interest. However he/she can also look for information for others, e.g. for his/her classmates. From these two models, we distinguish a lot of information: we are interested to acquire user personal knowledge, institutional knowledge and knowledge about the groups to which the user participate.

The user model for a specific user is filled in a semi-automatic way. The user profile is stored in the Cartable Electronique portal (user personal information includes age, gender, cultural interests, address, profession; institutional information includes school address, class projects, attending school year and number of children in the classroom). Other specific information can be obtained compiling a form.

To exploit the user model we decided to use stereotypes, as suggested in [8]. In particular, we have defined two types of stereotypes, in order to distinguish information necessary to a user who is querying the system for him/herself from information he/she is looking for other people. To each stereotype we also add knowledge about the presentation style for the corresponding answer. For instance, if the user is a 5 year-old child, the final form privileges images and sounds to help the child to understand.

3   The Architecture

In according to the AEIO methodology for multi-agent-oriented analysis and design defined by Y. Demazeau [4], we designed our system based on a multi-agent architecture composed of various modules corresponding to functionalities involved in the adaptation process.

We propose to associate to each user an interface agent who can assist him and manage his profile. We introduce a matching agent whose activity is to adapt the system and supply it with the right knowledge about the information to acquire and the final presentation. We also introduce an agent to manage the information search in the database.

To acquire the cultural oer, we fist proposed a centralized cultural server. Cultural partners are provided with an interface that allow them to put information about cultural events on the server.

When the user opens a new session, the system presents her an adapted event list in order to let her to select one of interest. When the user selects an event from the event list the system shows her the adapted details about it.

4   Implementation Details

The system has to create dynamically the cultural event presentation, so it is useful to reuse the same information and adapt it to the user profile [7]. For this reason we decided to implement our system using the XML paradigm and the XSL standard. The system is developed using a Client/Server architecture, and

Servlets are used to implement the agents, that communicate (through HTTP) using the XML language.

The user profile and the stereotypes are built using the XML paradigm, according to a predefined schema. We made this choice in order to make our model independent from any system implementation in which the cultural diary could be integrated. We defined two schemas [9] to specify the profile and stereotype form. In particular, we can apply the DOM [9] functionality for the matching operation.

The personal knowledge of the various users is implemented with Zope objects [10], transformed in XML objects according to the defined schema. The presentation knowledge is implemented using the XSL standard. The information are shown in plain HTML format, that is supported by every browser. The LotusXSL [5] parser is used for the translation into HTML.

The cultural server is a relational database. The management agent queries are performed using db2xml [2].

5   Open Issues

Many things can be done to improve our system. The system behaviour can become adaptive, not only adaptable. Indeed, some user behaviour observations could be used to improve the user model, leaving to the user the control of the information stored about him/her. The role of each agent can be enriched in order to improve the interaction with the user and the adaption process.

References

1. Brusilovsky, P.: Methods and techniques of Adaptive Hypermedia. User Modeling and Use-Adapted Interaction, Vol. 6, 2-3 (1996), 87-129
2. http://www.informatik.fh-wiesbaden.de/ turau/DB2XML/index.html
3. De Bra, P.: Design Issues in Adaptive Web-Site Development. Proc. of the 2nd Workshop on Adaptive Systems and User Modeling on the WWW, (Ban, 1999)
4. Demazeau, Y.: Step toward Multi-Agent Oriented Programming. 1st International Workshop on Multi Agent Systems, IWMAS (Boston, 1997)
5. http://www.alphaworks.ibm.com/tech/LotusXSL
6. Martel, C., Vignollet, L.: Educational Web Portal on Personalized and Collaborative Services. submitted to IEEE International Conference on Advanced Learning Technologies (2001)
7. Moulin, C., Pazzaglia, J.C.: Documents p´ edagogiques adaptatifs dans un environment d'apprentissage distribu´ e. Atelier A2, 11ème conférence francophone Interaction Homme Machine IHM '99 L'interaction pour tous, (Montpellier, 1999)
8. Rich, E. (eds.): User Modeling via Stereotypes. Cognitive Science 3 (1979), 329-354
9. W3C http://www.w3.org/
10. Z Object Publishing Environment (Zope) http://www.zope.org

Ubiquitous User Modeling
for Situated Interaction

Dominik Heckmann

European Post-Graduate College "Language Technology and Cognitive Systems"
Saarland University, Department of Computer Science,
D-66123 Saarbr¨ucken, Germany,
dominik@cs.uni-sb.de ,
http://www.dfki.de/   heckmann

Abstract.   The main contribution of my doctoral proposal will be the
design of a standardized and expandable XML-based User Modeling
Ontology Language, which enables ubiquitous systems to communicate
about user models. The second contribution will be the investigation
of combining simple partial user models from the point of view of the
user modeling ontology language, as well as the specific example domain
of speech and manual input, which will be realized by object-oriented
dynamic Bayesian networks.

1   The Questions That I Am Addressing

Increasing mobility of interactive systems like portable and wearable computers,
as well as embedded small computing devices in objects of daily life give increasing importance on context-aware, situation-aware and ubiquitous computing.
Most currently implemented systems however that employ a user model work
with an isolated model. The intrusive idea of my doctoral proposal is to let different systems, possibly very small units, communicate about their user-models.
This idea is similar to parts of Orwant's Doppelg¨ anger project, which is a generalized tool for gathering, processing, and providing information about users in
a distributed architecture, while making the resulting information available to
applications (see, e.g., [1]). The approach, described here, has a dierent focus:
the main challenge to enable such communication would be the development of
a representation language for user models in intelligent environments. Such a
User-Modeling-Ontology-Language, which could be abbreviated 'UMOL', would
enable communication about partial user models. Thus the first question that I
am addressing is,

1. How can a user modeling ontology language be designed, in order to enable
the communication with dierent user modeling applications ubiquitously?

A second issue that arises, when the first question has been answered, concerns the combination of partial models into one multi-purpose, conglomerated
user model, which could be handled by a newly introduced personal ubiquitous

M. Bauer, P.J. Gmytrasiewicz, and J. Vassileva (Eds.): UM 2001, LNAI 2109, pp. 280–282, 2001.
c Springer-Verlag Berlin Heidelberg 2001

user-modeling agent. Let us assume people carry a personalized user-modeling agent within a PDA and transmit their long-term properties anonymously to human-computer interaction systems. This could enable user-adaption from the beginning of using a new interaction system. After the interaction session, the system could transmit the partial user model of this session back to the personal agent within the PDA and also use the enriched data anonymously for collaborative filtering for example, but the following question arises,

2. How can the combination and integration of simple instantiated partial user models be realized within a ubiquitous user modeling agent?

The answer of this second question could be applied to this specific example domain, in which I am currently working. In [4], we analyzed the symptomatic behaviors of time pressure and high cognitive load while using a manual input device. We generalized the symptoms into a Bayesian network model from low-level observable behaviors to the resource limitations of a user.

2 The Methods That I Am Addressing

2.1 XML-Based Ontologies

An ontology names and describes the entities that may exist in that domain and the relationships among those entities. It therefore provides a vocabulary for representing and communicating knowledge about the domain. Ontologies also enable knowledge-level inter-operation of agents, since meaningful interaction among agents can occur only when they share a common interpretation of the vocabulary used in their communications. Finally, ontologies provide the foundation for the dialog between the user and the system.

Ontological Extensions of XML like OML, XOL, or OIL oer the semantical foundation for Agent systems to communicate via Internet. The preferred implementation language is OIL (Ontology Inference Layer). OIL is properly grounded in W3C standards such as RDF/RDF-schema and XML/XML-schema (see, e.g., [6]). OIL is a web-based representation and inference layer for ontologies, which combines the widely used modeling primitives from frame-based languages with the formal semantics and reasoning services provided by description logics. Fink's generic architecture for the user modeling shell system BGP-MS (see, e.g., [2]) proposes an object-oriented approach to realize a network-oriented user modeling shell system. It allows a distributed use of a central user model. Billsus and Pazzani's Adaptive Information Server, (see, e.g., [3]), is based on a client/server architecture and oers a framework for adaptive news access. These two approaches are dierent from the ontology one, but I will investigate their architectures and look for similarities. Acquisition, processing, and storage of personal data ubiquitously requires an intensified consideration of user demands to security, privacy, and anonymity (see, e.g., [7]). Access control and cryptographic techniques enable secure communication free from interception and modification. I have to take them into account while constructing the ontology.

2.2   Object-Oriented Dynamic Bayesian Networks

Much of the evidence that a system can obtain about the situation or the physiological state of a user is unreliable and uncertain. Bayesian networks create a
very ecient language for building models of domains with inherent uncertainty.
Implementation of the Bayesian networks is realized with the 'Hugin Expert system' API for C/C++ or Java. Ralph Sch¨   afer has shown in his dissertation (see,
[8]), that dynamic Bayesian networks are suitable as an inference mechanism for
user modeling components of adaptive dialog systems. This inference mechanism
oers the ability to deal with uncertainty about many properties of the user and
in particular make it possible to model properties that change over time. For
ubiquitous user modeling with the focus of communication about and combining partial models the formalism will be extended to object-oriented dynamic
Bayesian networks.

3   The Tentative Plan for Future Work

I will gradually develop the User Modeling Ontology Language in OIL, and
start with simple communications for example about users' interests in specific
domains. Furthermore a profound investigation of the research fields of user
modeling and ontologies has to be carried out. Then, question two, the combination and integration of simple instantiated partial user model is addressed.
And finally, a small system will be embedded into an intelligent environment.

References

1. Jon Orwant: Heterogeneous Learning in the Doppelg¨   anger User Modeling System.
   User Modeling and User-Adapted Interaction   4 (1995) 107-130
2. Josef Fink: "A Flexible and Open Architecture for the User Modeling schee System
   BGP-MS", German National Research Center for Information technology, Human-
   Computer Interaction Research Division (HCI)
3. Daniel Billsus and Michael J. Pazzani: User Modeling for Adaptive News Access.
   User Modeling and User-Adapted Interaction   10 (2000) 147-180
4. Kristin Lindmark, Dominik Heckmann: Interpreting Symptoms of Cognitive Load
   and Time Pressure in Manual Input. In M. M¨   uller (Ed.), Adaptivit¨ at und Benutzer-
   modelierung in interaktiven Softwaresystemen (2000) 93-101
5. Anthony Jameson: "Modeling Both the Context and the User", Personal Technologies, 5 (2001)
6. Dieter Fensel et al: "OIL in a nutshell" In: Knowledge Acquisition, Modeling, and
   Management, Proceedings of the European Knowledge Acquisition Conference), R.
   Dieng et al. (eds.) (2000)
7. J¨org Schreck: "Security and Privacy Issues in User Modeling" User Modeling Conference, Doctoral Consortium (1997) 453-454
8. Ralph Sch¨ afer: "Benutzermodellierung mit dynamischen Bayes'schen Netzen als
   Grundlage adaptiver Dialogsysteme" Dissertation, University of Saarbr¨   ucken (1998)

An Intelligent Pedagogical Agent in CALL

Ognian Kalaydjiev

Bulgarian Academy of Sciences, CLPP, Linguistic Modeling Dept.,
25A Acad. G. Bonchev Str., 1113 Sofia, Bulgaria,   ogi@lml.bas.bg

Abstract.   The contribution presents a planning agent in an adaptive Web-environment for second language terminology learning. This pedagogical agent provides active or passive sequencing and suggests system-learner dialogue by open learner model. It performs as well task-specific personalized information retrieval of relevant readings.

Thesis synopsis.   Thesis topic is "Intelligent Agents in Natural Language Processing Applications". The idea is to design and implement agents in information extraction, retrieval and filtering, and to apply them in a number of projects dealing with language technologies.

1   Completed Work

The reported work in the area of intelligent tutoring and student modeling is completed after the first year of the PhD study, in the context of a CALL project. The research includes issues of both designing eective tutorial strategies and planning the content to be tailored to the individual user. It includes as well the choice of relevant texts to be displayed to the learner at a particular learning situation, as personalized information retrieval and filtering. The work done so far is related to the joint R&D project LARFLAST (Learning Foreign Language Scientific Terminology), funded by EC Copernicus programme [1].

LARFLAST paradigm.   Larflast aims at the development of an intelligent, knowledge-based, adaptive www-learning environment for computer-aided learning of foreign language terminology. The prototype operates with about 200 terms and is tuned to the domain of financial English. The target users are adults non-native English speakers. The prototype integrates complex components like: Open Learner Model   (OLM, developed by CBLU, Leeds), the natural language understanding system   Parasite   (developed by the Manchester team, UMIST) and   Web-agents - spiders   for searching texts in Internet, developed in Montpellier (LIRMM). In this way the planning agent is supposed to balance and integrate the modules dealing with intelligent tutoring, student modeling, and web-based text retrieval in the context of language learning.

Domain knowledge is kept as a KB of conceptual graphs. The Learner Model (LM) stores clauses reflecting the learner moves and her performance in drills. Drills are especially designed to test domain concepts and KB facts and the drills' goal is explicitly recorded in drill annotation. Thus the LM records can be directly targeted to KB units (not to linguistic ones). LM contains four kinds of clauses: (i) know - the learner knows a domain concept (fact);   (ii) not _know

M. Bauer, P.J. Gmytrasiewicz, and J. Vassileva (Eds.): UM 2001, LNAI 2109, pp. 283–285, 2001.

- the learner doesn't know a domain concept (fact);   (iii) self _not _know - the learner has registered himself that he doesn't know a domain concept (fact); (iv) know _wrongly   - the learner has built knowledge (concept/fact) that is considered as wrong by the system (eventually, might need to be corrected). Adaptivity of the presentation (next drills and tutoring materials) is provided by a pedagogical agent (PA), implemented by the author (see [1]).

The planning agent.   PA plans future learner's moves between   (i) performing drills (active sequencing),   (ii) suggestion of readings (passive sequencing) and (iii) suggestion of dialogue by OLM. At present the planning is reactive and local [2]. Since considerations concern presentational as well as educational issues, according to the terminology in [3] we would classify the planner as performing some aspects of instructional as well as content planning. PA has two main strategies for active sequencing -   local and global. The local strategy plans moves between drills testing dierent characteristics of one concept. Its main goal is to create a complete view about learner's knowledge about this concept. This strategy chooses drills with increasing complexity when the learner answers correctly and gives again previously completed drills if the student has performed poorly. The global strategy plans movements between drills testing dierent concepts, according to their place in the fiancial ontology. PA chooses next learner's movement depending on: (i) the predefined drill's goals,   (ii) KB items, (iii) concept weights defined in the drills' annotations and   (iv) current learner's score.

Below we focus on the recently implemented modules providing personalized information retrieval and information filtering in Larflast. This task is not considered in detail in [1] and therefore represents an original contribution.

The overview [4] states that the currently available www-ITS systems are most often sets of static, hyperlinked html-pages. Larflast aims at a more elaborated, intelligent decision concerning personalized presentation of tutoring materials. The idea is inspired by the Web-context, where many financial sites expose and frequently update texts. To show to our learner readings containing most relevant information, we have to support and contiguously update a database of documents. (The collection itself is performed by Web-agents). Our planer thus operates with: (i) a data base, containing financial texts collected from Internet and (ii) a relevance measure, showing for each text the percentage of its relevance to the domain terms T_1, T_2, ..., T_k. These terms are juxtaposed to KB concepts. The relevance measure is associated automatically to each text by a LSA-module [5] (an original implementation of Sofia team).

The goal of PA is to select which text is most relevant to be displayed as a tutoring material (reading) at the particular learning situation. At each situation, LM keeps track of the terms which are unknown or wrongly known to the learner. The text with higher relevance to all these terms has to be selected. Most generally, this is done as follows: The learning situation is estimated with respect to the terms T_{n1}, T_{n2}, ..., T_{nm} which appear in not _know , self _not _know and know _wrongly   LM clauses. Actually we operate with the KB concepts, juxtaposed to these terms. The estimation is unique for the current learning situation, it is calculated for each term T_{ni} from T_{n1}, T_{n2}, ..., T_{nm} and represents the sum of: (i) the predefined weight of the corresponding concept in the KB hierarchy, an integer between 1 and 10; and (ii) closeness of the focused concept T_{ni} to the concepts T_{n1}, ..., T_{ni-1}, T_{ni+1}, ..., T_{nm}. All pairs (T_{ni}, T_{n1}), ..., (T_{ni}, T_{ni-1}), (T_{ni}, T_{ni+1}), ..., (T_{ni}, T_{nm}) are considered and the values "close-distant" (respectively "1-0") are summed. Two concepts are close if they are either linked as child-parent in the KB hierarchy, or they are sisters according to the same partitioning perspective. Otherwise the concepts are considered as distant ones.

After calculating the sums S_1, S_2, ..., S_m for the terms T_{n1}, T_{n2}, ..., T_{nm}, the integers S_1, S_2, ..., S_m are sorted in decreasing order. In a sense, the terms in question are "sorted" in decreasing order according to their relevance to the particular learning situation. Let T_{r1}, T_{r2}, .., T_{rm} be the new order (by relevance). For each term T_{r1}, T_{r2}, .., T_{rm} the planner finds the set of relevant texts, available at the moment in the text data base. Starting from T_{r1} to T_{rm}, the planner looks for texts maximally relevant to all terms. In this way PA proposes readings that provide "maximal relevance" to the unknown terms, taking into consideration the estimation of terms' weights. In other words, the idea is to select readings giving preference to: (i) term importance in the domain and (ii) term closeness (in order to explain in one document as many terms as possible). Since Larflast project is entering the final evaluation phase, the planner and its strategy for choosing relevant text will be soon evaluated too. Therefore small modifications of the above-described heuristics might be expected.

2   Future Work

Currently Larflast KB encodes 200 terms. Experiments in personalized text retrieval include more than 300 texts. The future work concerns the elaboration and mainly assessment of the intelligent planning agent, with focus on the evaluation of the user-tailored presentation.

References

1. Sv. Boytcheva, O. Kalaydjiev, A. Nenkova and G. Angelova. Integration of Resources and Components in a Knowledge-Based Web-Environment for Terminology Learning. In Proc. AIMSA-2000, Springer, LNAI 1904, pp. 210 - 220.
2. McCalla, G. The Fragmentation of Culture, Learning, Teaching and Technology: Implications for the AI in Education Research Agenda in 2010. In IJAIE (2000), 11, pp. 177-196.
3. Vassileva, J. and B. Wasson. Instructional Planning Approaches: from Tutoring towards Free Learning. In Proc. EuroAIED'96, Lisbon, Portugal, 1996, pp. 1-8.
4. Brusilovsky, P. Adaptive and Intelligent Technologies for Web-based Education. In: C. Rollinger and C. Peylo (eds.) KI 1999 (4), pp. 19-25.
5. Deerwester S., Dumais S., Furnas G., Laundauer, T. and Harshman R.: Indexing by Latent Semantic Analysis. JASIS 41(1990), pp. 391-475. LSA URL: http://lsa.colorado.edu (1990-99).

How to Learn More about Users
from Implicit Observations [1]

Ingo Schwab

humanIT Human Information Technologies
D-53757 Sankt Augustin, Germany
Ingo.Schwab@humanIT.de

Abstract. In this paper, an approach to learning user interests is presented. It relies on positive evidences only, in consideration of the fact that users rarely supply the ratings needed by traditional learning algorithms, specifically not negative examples. Learning results are explicitly represented to account for the fact that in the area of user modeling explicit representations are known to be considerably more useful than purely implicit representations. A content-based recommendation approach is presented. The described framework has been extensively tested in an information system.

1 Introduction

Our modern society is confronted with an exploding information increase via electronic media like the World Wide Web, digital library systems and e-commerce sites. To cope with this huge amount of information as effectively as possible, users need guidance through this information space considering their personal interests.

In many systems, users must provide explicit ratings to express their interests and non-interests. But computer users are known to only provide little feedback when they are supposed to rate the quality of items recommended to them, and specifically to hardly ever give negative ratings. Traditional learning algorithms however rely mostly on explicit positive and negative examples. We therefore focused on algorithms that would operate in the presence of implicit positive examples only. That means that they have to be able to learn from a single learning class only.

2 Definition of the Problem

The main topic to be addressed in this research is to develop methods which are able to learn user interests by just observing the user. Users may select from a set of objects that have features and attributes. The features and attributes of objects define an n-dimensional information space. Different users select objects from this information space and - based on an individual user's selections - the features the user

---

[1] I would like to thank my advisor Alfred Kobsa for his inspiring discussions and comments about this work.

M. Bauer, P.J. Gmytrasiewicz, and J. Vassileva (Eds.): UM 2001, LNAI 2109, pp. 286–288, 2001.
©Springer-Verlag Berlin Heidelberg 2001

is interested in become extracted. These preferences are stored in an explicit user model and can be used to recommend new or overseen objects to the user.

The quality of the developed algorithms was determined by a post-hoc logfile analysis [4]. To show that the proposed algorithms are not restricted to one domain or one user interface only, we will test them with two different user interfaces and two different databases. Then we independently evaluate the accuracy of prediction for the four possible configurations.

3 Proposed Methodology

A straightforward way of using machine learning for acquiring interest profiles is to assume that the set of information objects can be divided into classes (e.g., "interesting" and "not interesting"). Then, content-based filtering can be achieved by letting the user classify given objects, thus providing examples for both classes (see e.g., [3]), and by applying an inductive classification algorithm to these examples. For new objects, this algorithm can then determine whether they belong to the "interesting" or to the "not interesting" class.

As discussed above, supplying an appropriate set of negative examples (i.e., examples of the "not interesting" class) is problematic. If we do not require users to rate objects explicitly, the central source of information about the user is the sequence of selected objects. Selections are made from the current information subspace, that is a set of available objects with common properties. There are some systems, which use unselected objects as negative examples in such a situation (e.g. [1] and [2]). However, we claim that unselected objects may exist that are interesting to the user (they may just have been overlooked by the user or will perhaps be visited later). Classifying them as negative examples is a dangerous assumption. Many of these classifications may become erroneous and cause too much noise in the training data. Instead, it is more suitable to only take those objects that the user selected as examples for the "interesting" class. However, in this case standard classification methods are not applicable. Thus, for learning interest profiles, new learning methods had to be developed or existing ones had to be modified.

An instance-based approach was developed that can be applied to learn a general characterization of objects that are relevant to the user [4]. This method deals with the positive example problem by employing the notion of object similarity or distance.

4 Clickstream Analysis

In the work done so far we described an algorithm to learn information interests from positive evidence. It has been shown that it is possible to learn user interests and disinterest implicitly. To learn even more about the user and to still improve the performance of the system, other implicit information sources can be fruitfully used.

The additional evidence types, and sources of information, could be:
- the path to the observed objects
- excluded attributes (values)
- saved bookmarks

- operations at the interface (e.g., scrolling a slider)
- mouse movements
- timestamps, etc.

This "Clickstream Analysis" follows the idea that it is important how the user interacts with the system and that this additional information will improve the recommendation accuracy. It was not given (and used) in the environment so far. Therefore we chose InfoZoom [6], an explorative visual data mining tool that provides intelligent access to data sets. It can supply evidences for many different types of user interaction.

Our goal is to incorporate the different evidence types into a single learning algorithm. Some evidences are stronger indicators for an interest or disinterest than others. They are more important and should enter the learning algorithms with larger weights. Our idea is to learn these weights automatically. In terms of machine learning, this means that a set of observed user interactions (evidences) is given. A model m is needed which integrates all evidences in the given learning algorithms and maximizes the recommendation accuracy. In this way, the whole problem can be reduced to an optimization task [5] of the function:

$$f = \text{performance}\,(m(w(e1),\,w(e2),\,\ldots\,,w(en))) \to \max$$

The goal is to find the best evidence weights for the different evidences e1,..., en and the given learning algorithms to maximize the prediction quality.

References

1. Lieberman H. (1995). Letizia: An Agent That Assists Web Browsing. International Joint Conference on Artificial Intelligence, Montreal.
2. Mladenic D. (1996). Personal WebWatcher: Implementation and Design. Technical Report IJS-DP-7472, Department of Intelligent Systems, J. Stefan Institute, Slovenia.
3. Resnick P. and Varian H. R. Recommender Systems. Communications of the ACM, 40, 3, 56-58, 1997.
4. Schwab I., Pohl W. and Koychev, I. (2000). Learning to Recommend from Positive Evidence, Proceedings of Intelligent User Interfaces 2000, ACM Press, pp. 241-247.
5. Schwefel H.-P. Evolution And Optimum Seeking. John Wiley & Sons, Inc. 1995.
6. Michael S., Beilken Ch.: Visual, Interactive Data Minung with InfoZoom - the Financial Data Set. In: Workshop Notes on Discovery Challenge. Proceedings of the 3rd European Conference on Principles and Practice of Knowledge Discovery in Databases, PKDD '99, September 15-18, 1999, Prague, Czech Republic, page 33-38. http://fit.gmd.de/~cici/InfoZoom/DiscoveryChallenge/Financial.ps

Student Modelling f or CALL
Based on Pedagogical Standards

Monika Tarantowicz-Gasiewicz

ul. Na Polance 12B/2, 51-109 Wroclaw, Poland
monika@irga.wroc.pl

Abstract. The doctoral dissertation summarised in this paper contains a proposal of pedagogical standards for the design and evaluation of a student model in a CALL system, and of such a system itself. The standards were derived from the Theory of Versatile Education. Upon these standards, a theoretical design of a student model in a CALL system was proposed. It was demonstrated how the potential of educational tradition and SLA research can be applied to CALL software for the sake of its pedagogical quality.

1 Goals

From the analysis of pedagogy-related literature devoted to Computer-Assisted Instruction (CAI) and Computer-Assisted Language Learning (CALL) it appears that pedagogical standards for both, systems and their student models are missing [2], [3]. In this situation, a primary goal of research was to formulate such pedagogical standards, helpful in the design or the evaluation of a student model (SM) in a CALL system. Another purpose was to develop an outline of a SM based on the earlier proposed standards.

2 Methodology

In order to achieve the main purpose of the dissertation - to outline a SM based on pedagogical standards - it was necessary to make the following steps:

1. work out a framework for construing pedagogical standards for a CAI system in general,
2. choose a particular pedagogical theory to underlie the system,
3. based on the general framework (step 1), formulate a set of CAI standards rooted in the chosen theory, and in didactic principles agreeable with this theory
4. from this set of CAI standards derive a set of standards for a SM,
5. relying on CAI standards and on a self-chosen approach to foreign language teaching, outline a CALL system as an environment for a SM,
6. with the pedagogical standards for a SM (step 4) and the outline of CAL system (step 5) as the foundation, work out the design of a SM for this CALL system.

Below, the crucial steps: 2, 4, and 6 are described.

M. Bauer, P.J. Gmytrasiewicz, and J. Vassileva (Eds.): UM 2001, LNAI 2109, pp. 289–291, 2001.

As for the choice of a pedagogical theory to underlie the standards (step 2), one possibility is Wincenty Okon's Theory of Versatile Education (TVE) [4], [5], [7]. It is consistent with the humanistic trend in pedagogy [6]. The main assertion of TVE is that if students are to comprehend the complexity of reality, they must be exposed to it through four categories of resources: receptive, explorative, emotional and practical. The use of resources is regulated by respective four types of didactic methods, and these are related to the analogous four categories of activities, called "routes of learning." The four-fold structure of TVE makes it possible to prepare schemes and algorithms easily applicable to CALL.

The final set of standards for a SM in CAI system (step 4), based on TVE and didactic principles consistent with TVE, includes the following items:

- A student model should record the learner's routes of learning based on the four categories of resources and methods.
- A student model should model facts and processes that are important from the point of view of the methodology of the teaching of a given school subject.
- A student model should record the learning process in all its stages.
- A student model should collect personal factors influencing the learning effects.
- A student model should collect personal factors influencing the reception of the program's content.
- A student model should monitor the processes of the learner's individualised and socialised development.
- A student model should monitor the learner's approaching the didactic purposes of the program.

As was argued earlier, the choice of data to be gathered by the SM is not dictated by some accidental factors, but results form theoretical assumptions made in advance. This feature is deemed to be the main advantage of the design.

3 Research Results

The result of research undertaken in the dissertation is a description of the SM operation during a lesson with an ICALL system (relying on the communicative approach to language learning.). In the introductory part of the lesson, the SM procures data about the student's linguistic and educational background and learning needs. In subsequent stages, the SM monitors: developing motivation, learning facts, making generalisations, formulating rules, consolidating knowledge and applying it into practice. In ensuing lessons, the SM performs long-term monitoring of learning: it analyses communicative competence development, searches for sources of persistent learning problems, and scrutinises the development of the learner's autonomy and certain other personality features [1], [8]. Two types of modelling techniques were developed: behavioural and cognitive-collaborative. The earlier method is aimed at describing the "visible" side of the learning process, like the amount of time spent on tasks, number and types of errors, etc. The latter technique is expected to inform the SM about the "invisible" aspects of learning, e.g.: motivation, reflection, mental learning strategies, etc. These are elicited from the so called "emotional task" and student-completed checklists.

After the description of the SM, it was demonstrated that all the pedagogical parameters are respected in the actual design of the SM.

4 Summary

Thanks to pedagogical parameters prepared in advance, it was possible to begin the design of the SM based on a well-established theoretical foundation. This seems to be an infrequent approach, though justified from the methodological perspective. After completing the design, it was possible to check whether the SM is still consistent with the initial assumptions, which turned out to be the case. Another asset is, presumably, a considerable degree of interdisciplinary work at the interface of linguistics, pedagogy, methodology, psychology and artificial intelligence. Such work is necessary, as it appears that technology without humanism may not give fully successful educational software. Hopefully, research results can be useful for future applications. At present at least some fragments of the SM design could be incorporated into commercial software.

References

1. Brown, Douglas, H., 1994. Principles of Language Learning and Teaching. San Francisco: Prentice Hall Regents
2. Ephratt, Michal, 1992. "Developing and Evaluating Language Courseware." Computers and the Humanities 26: 249-259
3. Manning, Patricia, 1990. "Methodological Considerations in the Design of CALL Programs." CITE Report No. 131. Milton Keynes: Open University
4. Okon, Wincenty, 1967. Podstawy wyksztalcenia ogólnego. Warszawa: WSiP
5. Okon, Wincenty, 1995. Wprowadzenie do dydaktyki ogólnej. Warszawa: Wydawnictwo Zak
6. Rogers, Carl, 1983. Freedom to Learn for the 80's. Ohio: Bell and Howell
7. Tanas, Maciej, 1997. Edukacyjne zastosowania komputerów. Warszawa: Wydawnictwo Zak
8. Tarone, Elaine, and George Yule, 1991. Focus on the Language Learner. Oxford: Oxford University Press

Evaluation of Adaptive Systems

Stephan Weibelzahl

Pedagogical University Freiburg, Germany
weibelza@ph-freiburg.de

Abstract.   Unambiguously, adaptive systems have to be evaluated empirically to guarantee that the adaptivity really works. Nevertheless, only
few of the existing adaptive systems have been evaluated. One of the most
important reasons for this lack is, that measures for adaptivity success
have not been investigated systematically up to now.
The aim of this PhD thesis is to explore a methodology for the empirical
evaluation of adaptive systems, including validated criteria, experimental designs and procedures. It will be demonstrated that cognitive and
behavioral factors provide important evidence for adaptivity success.

1   Introduction

Empirical evaluations of adaptive systems are hard to find. Several reasons have
been identified to be responsible for this lack (e.g., H¨oök [1]). Besides some
structural problems (e.g., short development cycle) one of the major issues is
methodological: What has to be done to guarantee the success of adaptation?
Straightforward approaches (e.g., asking the users whether they enjoyed the
interaction) frequently fail to proof an advantage of adaptive systems or suer
from low test quality.

2   Aim

The aim of this PhD thesis is to explore a methodology for the empirical evaluation of adaptive systems. Such a methodology consists of at least two components: First, a bunch of criteria that are proofed to be reliable and valid to
measure adaptivity success. Probably, only a combination of several criteria will
be adequately meaningful. Secondly, a specification of experimental designs and
procedures is needed to apply those criteria.

Both, criteria and experimental designs, should be independent of the domain
and the inference mechanism, because this would allow for a comparison of
dierent approaches. We certainly do not ignore the fact, that there are domain
specifi dierences between systems.

That is, there are criteria that evaluate system specific goals. However, our
approach explores those goals that all (or most) adaptive systems have in common: to improve and to simplify interaction.

We claim that such a general approach yields a methodology that is trans-
ferable to many systems and would enable researchers to

M. Bauer, P.J. Gmytrasiewicz, and J. Vassileva (Eds.): UM 2001, LNAI 2109, pp. 292–294, 2001.
ⓒ Springer-Verlag Berlin Heidelberg 2001

- find system deficits and failures
- show that adaptivity in their system is useful and successful
- justify the enormous eorts spent on making systems adaptive
- point out deficits of non-adaptive systems.

3   Approach

A synopsis on published evaluations (http://www.softwareevaluation.de) armed our claim that only few studies are based on proper experimental designs and statistical methods. We found that evaluation issues can be categorized in accordance with an information processing model of adaptive systems. This model serves as evaluation framework for further considerations.

3.1   Model of Adaptivity

The basic principle of adaptive systems is, that they acquire data about the user, which are used to infer abstract characteristics. Based on these characteristics (sometimes called user properties) the system decides how to adapt, which has impact on both the system behavior and the user behavior [2]. Thus, we distinguish six evaluation steps [6]:

1. Evaluation of reliability and external validity of input data acquisition
2. Evaluation of the inference mechanism and accuracy of user properties
3. Appropriateness of adaptation decisions
4. Change of system behavior when the system adapts
5. Change of user behavior when system adapts
6. Change and quality of total interaction

The point is that this last evaluation step can only be interpreted correctly if all the previous steps have been completed. Especially in the case of finding no dierence between an adaptive and a non-adaptive system the previous steps provide hints at shortcomings. The results of such a layered evaluation [3] are much better to interpret and give more exact hints for failures and false inferences than a simple global evaluation of the usability.

3.2   New Criterion: Behavioral Complexity

An evaluation methodology also requires criteria for adaptation success, however, our systematic overview made obvious that most current criteria are either not reliable (or at least not tested to be reliable) or are low in external validity (e.g, duration of interaction as a criterion for satisfaction with a learning environment).

Our approach is based on the assumption that adaptivity aims at reducing the complexity of interaction. E.g., an adaptive help system infers the user's current goals and selects adequate help texts. Thus, the user does not need an overview of all possibly presented themes and then to select the most suitable section. The same argumentation holds for other adaptive systems, e.g., product presentation systems or learning environments.

According to Kieras and Polson [4] the concrete behavior of a user can be described as a state transition network. According to this idea, a system is defined by disjoint states and the transitions between these states. A user's input equals a transition to an other state.

A single network is derived for each user. The complexity of these networks can be computed in several ways. In a series of laboratory experiments Weibelzahl, Klein, and Weber [5] compared four measures of complexity in two dierent systems (which implemented dierent inference mechanisms in dierent domains). Users that had been supported by an adaptive system produced behavior of reduced complexity compared to users that completed the same task ("Find a suitable vacation home in this electronic catalog"; "Complete this chapter in the online-learning-course") with a non-adaptive version.

4   Future Perspectives

As the experimental results with behavioral complexity are very encouraging, a more detailed evaluation of an adaptive learning environment was designed to validate this criterion.

The online-course HTML-Tutor will be tested both in laboratory and in the field which will explore the external validity of behavioral complexity and the scope of our framework.

References

1. K. H¨o¨ok. Steps to take before intelligent user interfaces become real.   Interacting With Computers , 12(4):409–426, 2000.
2. A. Jameson.   Systems That Adapt to Their Users: An Integrative Perspective   . Saarland University, Saarbr¨ ucken, 2001.
3. C. Karagiannidis and D. G. Sampson. Layered evaluation of adaptive applications and services. In P. Brusilovsky and C. S. Oliviero Stock, editors,   Proceedings on International Conference on Adaptive Hypermedia and Adaptive Web-Based Systems, AH2000, Trento, Italy   , pages 343–346, Berlin, 2000. Springer.
4. D. E. Kieras and P. Polson. An approach to the formal analysis of user complexity. International Journal of Human-Computer Studies   , 51(2):405–434, 1999.
5. S. Weibelzahl, B. Klein, and G. Weber. Criteria for the evaluation of adaptive systems. User Modeling and User Adapted Interaction   , submitted.
6. S. Weibelzahl and C. U. Lauer. Framework for the evaluation of adaptive CBR-systems. In I. Vollrath, S. Schmitt, and U. Reimer, editors,   Experience Management as Reuse of Knowledge. Proceedings of the 9th German Workshop on Case Based Reasoning, GWCBR2001   , pages 254–263, Baden-Baden, Germany, 2001.

Supporting Negotiated Assessment
Using Open Student Models

Juan-Diego Zapata-Rivera

ARIES Laboratory, Department of Computer Science, University of Saskatchewan,
Engineering Building, 1C101 57 Campus Drive, Saskatoon, SK, S7N 5A9, Canada
Diego.Zapata@usask.ca

Abstract. During the last two years our research on open student models
have led us to experiment with visualization and inspection of Bayesian student
models – ViSMod, and employing conceptual maps as a representation of the
student through ConceptLab, a knowledge construction and navigation system.
Although previous work have given us interesting results, several questions
remain to be solved, such as: How open should be the student model to better
enhance the learning process?; How should students and teachers interact
with the model?; Are students and teachers willing to interact with the model
or it should be done as part of a supervised learning activity?

In order to solve some of these questions, this thesis explores different scenarios in which open student modelling can be used as means of supporting reflection, negotiated assessment, and enhance the learning process.

Keywords : Open Student Modelling, Visualizing and Inspecting Bayesian Student Models, Conceptual Maps, and Negotiated Assessment.

1   Introduction

Student models can not be considered anymore as hidden components used within an
ITS. Several authors in the area of open student modelling have demonstrated that
students and teachers can use the student model as a means of supporting reflection
and knowledge awareness. Within open student modelling there are still some research directions that remain unexplored, such as: How open should be the student
model to optimise the learning process?; How should students and teachers interact
with the model?; Are students and teachers willing to interact with the model or it
should be done as part of a supervised learning activity?; How does the student
model information support students' reflection?; Is it possible to use student feedback to build more accurate models?

This thesis focuses in solving some of the questions presented above. In particular,
how different degrees of student modelling openness, different kinds of models (i.e.
Bayesian student models, conceptual maps), the role of students and teachers, and the
learning activity affect the learning process. Some initial hypotheses for this project
are:

- The student model should be open according to the degree of knowledge of the
  student making sure that the ontology employed is the same as that used by the

M. Bauer, P.J. Gmytrasiewicz, and J. Vassileva (Eds.): UM 2001, LNAI 2109, pp. 295–297, 2001.

student. Too much information or too little will negatively influence the learning process.

- Students won't be willing to interact with the model without a directed activity that makes it clear what to do. Students working in groups or with a teacher will get better results from the activity than those who work individually.
- A planned activity in which the student interacts with the teacher using the model as a tool will give better learning gains than a group of students working together or an individual student working alone on the same activity.
- Student models partly created and inspected by students will have an important positive effect on the learning process.

During the last two years several software tools have been developed in order to attack small parts of the problem. Previous work on visualization and inspection of Bayesian student models - ViSMod [3] showed that students and teachers can easily visualize the student model using different visualization techniques, such as: colour, size, proximity (closeness), link thickness, and animation. Using ViSMod it is possible to inspect the model of a single student, and compare several students by comparing their models, navigate throughout the model changing focus according to students' and teachers' interests, and use several sources of evidence to animate the evolution of a new model. By allowing inspection of student models and the creation of what-if scenarios, ViSMod supports students' reflection, knowledge awareness, and refining of student models.

Considering the student as a part of a learning community in which situational factors play an important role on the learning process, we have developed a knowledge construction and navigation system called ConceptLab [2]. ConceptLab allows collaborative construction of XML-based conceptual maps. ConceptLab provides the possibility to link different kinds of resources to specific nodes. Students can create their own knowledge structure using a set of predefined concepts (common vocabulary given by the teacher) and use their own map to access class resources. These resources are suggested by the teacher (initial links) or by his/her classmates during the creation of their maps (collaborative browsing). As it is done with some constructivist tools, ConceptLab considers the object resulting from the student's work as his/her representation.

The Learner module in ConceptLab maintains basic student information as well as their XML-maps (map structure, links, and preferences). In addition, students can use an existing map as a guide to study the content, or use this system as a learning tool to facilitate remembering, create maps collaboratively, share their maps, and engage in interesting discussions about a particular topic. Teachers can use XML-maps to assess the student's knowledge. This can be done by comparing different maps (visually or through queries) to determine problems in the learning process for a particular student or groups of them. Finally, teachers can use this system as an adequate environment to promote reflection among students on a specific topic.

ViSMod provides a way for students and teachers to interact through the creation of different views of a Bayesian student model. Each view could have different nodes and evidence. Students and teachers experiment with their views in order to create a model that reflects their own perception of their learning process with high fidelity. Student modelling views in the case of ViSMod and ConceptLab maps in the case of ConceptLab become key elements to engage students and teachers in discussions that support knowledge reflection. Assessment in these contexts is a negotiation process that we called negotiated assessment. Negotiated assessment [1] allows the student and the teacher (or an agent acting on the teacher's behalf) to dialogue about the model asking to each other and providing additional information that will result in a more accurate assessment and an optimised student model.

Four different scenarios have been defined in order to create a full set of settings in which experiments can be done to answer the questions arising from the hypothesis. Each scenario offers different characteristics such as different activities, different roles for student and the teacher, different tools with different level of functionality, individual and collaborative activities, and directed and undirected activities. Table 1. summarises the scenarios.

Table 1. Open student modelling scenarios.

Scenarios	Student Model	Tool	Description
1	Predefined Bayesian student model including content and social aspects of the learner.	ViSMod	Students reflect upon the model both without any guide and solving a questionnaire.
2	Predefined Bayesian student model including content and social aspects of the learner.	ViSMod	Dialogue between the student and the teacher based on the model.
3	Individually built Concept map overlaid with information from the BSM.	Concept Lab	The student creates the model as part of a guided activity and negotiates the model with the teacher.
4	Collaboratively built Concept map overlaid with information from the BSM.	Concept Lab	Students create the model as part of a guided activity and negotiate the model with the teacher.

The next stage of this project will be focused on designing and running some experiments. It will be necessary first to define tasks, subjects, and measurements for each of these scenarios. It is hopped to get enough evidence to validate or refuse our initial hypothesis. Resulting data will provide important insight to improve the development of new systems in this area.

References

1. Brna, P., Self, J., Bull, S., and Pain, H. (1999) Negotiated Collaborative Assessment through Collaborative Student Modelling. Proceedings of the workshop 'Open, Interactive, and other Overt Approaches to Learner Modelling' at AIED'99. Le Mans, France. 35-44.
2. Zapata-Rivera, J.D., Greer, J.E., & Cooke, J. (2000) An XML-Based Tool for Building and Using Conceptual Maps in Education and Training Environments. Proceedings of the 8th International Conference on Computers in Education, ICCE 2000. 755-762.
3. Zapata-Rivera, J.D. & Greer, J. (2000) Inspecting and Visualizing Distributed Bayesian Student Models. Proceedings of the 5th International Conference on Intelligent Tutoring Systems, ITS 2000. 544-553.

Using Markov Chains for Structural Link Prediction in Adaptive Web Sites

Jianhan Zhu[1]

School of Information and Software Engineering, University of Ulster at Jordanstown
Newtownabbey, Co. Antrim BT37 0QB, United Kingdom
Phone: +44 (0)28 9036 8197 Fax: +44 (0)28 9036 6859
jh.zhu@ulst.ac.uk

Abstract. My research investigates into using Markov chains to make link prediction and the transition matrix derived from Markov chains to acquire structural knowledge about Web sites. The structural knowledge is acquired in the form of three types of clusters: hierarchical clusters, reference clusters, and grid clusters. The predicted Web pages and acquired Web structures are further integrated to assist Web users in their navigation in the Web site.

Keywords. Markov chains, grid clusters, hierarchical clusters, reference clusters

1 Introduction

Learning about Web users from Web usage data for designing an Adaptive Web site has been proposed as an AI challenge by Perkowitz and Etzioni [3]. Web log files, which record Web users' accesses to the documents on a Web site, are the major sources of Web usage data for machine learning.

My research aims to integrate link prediction with structure discovery to facilitate Web users' navigation. I want to develop an Online Recommendation Explorer (ORE) which presents a hierarchy of clusters of Web pages with relevant clusters expanded, predicted pages highlighted, and different states of clusters and pages displayed. The ORE works along the existing Web site, and, like the windows explorer, allows the user to activate pages, expand clusters and browse the hierarchy. Each cluster or page is given a description (topic) by concept learning. The ORE provides the user with structured, informative and focused recommendations and the flexibility of being able to move around within the hierarchy of relevant clusters and pages.

Web link prediction is the process to predict the Web pages to be visited by a user based on the Web pages previously visited by him/her. Web structure discovery is to identify different structures among the Web pages. Albrecht et. al. [1] proposed to build three types of Markov models from Web log files for pre-sending Web documents. Sarukkai [5] also discussed about link prediction based on Markov

---

[1] A second year PhD student supervised by Dr. Jun Hong (University of Ulster at Jordanstown)

M. Bauer, P.J. Gmytrasiewicz, and J. Vassileva (Eds.): UM 2001, LNAI 2109, pp. 298–300, 2001.
© Springer-Verlag Berlin Heidelberg 2001

models. In my research, I want to develop a Markov model from Web log files to predict the Web pages to be visited by a user based on the Web pages previously visited by him/her.

Inspired by Spears' work on transition matrix compression [6], I have tried to extend cluster analysis to the transition matrix [7] to identify structures among the Web pages, i.e., hierarchical clusters, reference clusters, and grid clusters.

2 Proposed Approach and Relevant Issues

The ECLF (Extended Common Log File), which contains URIs of requested pages and referrers, is used as the data source to build the Markov model. Due to the influence of page caching, proxy servers etc., the directed weighted graph extracted from the log file is further processed to conform to flow equation and make the Markov chain irreducible, i.e., every two pages are connected.

When the current state of a Web page in the chain (visited or not visited) is given, the probability of visiting any other Web page in the next m steps can be calculated. If n previously visited Web pages are given, the n corresponding probabilities of visiting any other Web page in the next m steps can be summed up to estimate the overall probability of visiting the page in the next m steps.

A combination of the original organization of the Web pages on a Web site and the organization perceived by the Web users are reflected in the Web log files. Visualization of the transition matrix clearly shows that Web pages are organized in hierarchical structures. This reflects the fact that Web pages are conceptually hierarchical, i.e., topics presented in Web pages are generally at different conceptual levels, from the homepage to general topics, followed by less general topics, more specific topics, and so on. Inspired by Spears' transition matrix compression algorithm [6], we have used link similarities between Web pages to find three types of clusters defined below.

Grid cluster (GC): is a set of Web pages having both similar incoming links and outgoing links, which generally describe the same concept (topic). This concept is generally a sub-concept of concepts in higher-level Web pages, which have significant links to the GC.

Hierarchical cluster (HC): is a set of Web pages having similar incoming links, which generally describe closely related concepts (topics). These concepts are generally sub-concepts of concepts in higher-level Web pages, which have significant links to the HC.

Reference cluster (RC): is a set of Web pages having similar outgoing links, which generally serve as references to the same Web pages.

Our approach looks for grid clusters first. This also serves as a matrix compression process to speed up later probability calculation, since pages in the same grid clusters have similar or closely related contents. The approach then tries to find hierarchical clusters. Finally it looks for reference clusters. Hierarchical clusters provide the framework into which reference and grid clusters can be embedded. A link between two clusters is built when the overall transition probability, which is also the weight on the link, from one cluster to the other cluster is significant enough. Links are generally from higher to lower conceptual level hierarchical clusters, or from reference clusters to hierarchical clusters or grid clusters. In the end, all the Web pages are put into a hierarchy of linked clusters and pages. The hierarchy starts with the home page as the root, moves down to hierarchical clusters at the general conceptual level covering general topics, further to hierarchical clusters at less general level covering less general topics, and finally to individual Web pages at the lowest conceptual level covering the most specific topics. Grid and reference clusters are the "fruits" on this hierarchy of clusters and pages.

3   System Overview

Currently a prototype system has been developed to present structural recommendations as Web users' navigation aids. Starting from the homepage, followed by multiple levels of hierarchical clusters, reference clusters, and grid clusters, all the Web pages are put into a hierarchy of clusters with the home page as the root in the Online Recommendation Explorer (ORE) window. Each cluster is given a description about the pages in the cluster by conceptual text learning. Each time when a user requests a new page, probabilities of visiting any other Web pages or grid clusters within the next m steps are calculated. Then the Web pages and grid clusters with the highest probabilities are highlighted and the clusters containing the pages and grid clusters are expanded in the ORE window. The user can also browse the clusters and pages like in the Windows Explorer. Icons are used to represent different states of pages and clusters.

4   Future Work

Future work includes improving the accuracy of link prediction by identifying users' goal in each visit [2]. The threshold for clustering decides the size and quality of the clusters. Further study will explore the appropriate threshold values for Web sites of different scales and types.

References

1.   Albrecht, D., Zukerman, I., and Nicholson, A.: Pre-sending Documents on the WWW: A Comparative Study. In Proc. of the Sixteenth International Joint Conference on Artificial Intelligence, 1274-1279 (1999).
2.   Hong, J.: Graph Construction and Analysis as a Paradigm for Plan Recognition. In Proc. of the Seventeenth National Conference on Artificial Intelligence, 774-779 (2000).
3.   Perkowitz, M., Etzioni, O.: Adaptive Web Sites: an AI challenge. In Proc. of the Fifteenth International Joint Conference on Artificial Intelligence (1997).
4.   Sarukkai, R.:Link prediction and path analysis using Markov chains. In Proc. 9th WWW (2000).
5.   Spears, W.: A compression algorithm for probability transition matrices. In SIAM Matrix Analysis and Applications, Vol. 20, No. 1, 60-77 (1998).
6.   Wishart, D.: Efficient Hierarchical Analysis for Data Mining and Knowledge Discovery. Computing Science and Statistics, 30, 257-263 (1998).

Invited Talks

Tailoring Privacy to Users' Needs [1]

Alfred Kobsa

Department of Information and Computer Science
University of California, Irvine, CA 92697-3425, U.S.A.
kobsa@uci.edu

Abstract. This article discusses how the deployment of personalized systems is affected by users' privacy concerns and by privacy legislation. It shows that these impacts are substantial and will require a significant enhancement of current systems. Basic requirements can already be met with existing technology. Most privacy laws however also impose demands that call for new technologies that still need to be researched. A central conclusion of the paper is that a uniform solution for privacy demands does not exist since both user preferences and legal stipulations are too heterogeneous. Instead, privacy will have to be dynamically tailored to each individual user's needs, and to the jurisdiction at both the location of the personalized system and that of the user.

1 Personalization in Online Systems Is Beneficial for both Internet Users and Internet   Sites

Computer systems that take individual characteristics of their current users into account and adapt their behavior accordingly have been empirically shown to benefit users in many domains. Examples for successful application areas of these recently so-called personalized systems include education and training (e.g., [1]), online help for complex PC software (e.g., [2, 3]), dynamic information delivery (e.g., [4]), provision of computer access to people with disabilities (e.g., [5]), and to some extent information retrieval systems (e.g., [6]).

Recently, personalized systems have also started to conquer the World Wide Web. Personalization thereby is mostly used for purposes of Customer Relationship Management [7]. The single most important way to provide value to customers is to know them and serve them as individuals. The terms micro marketing and one-to-one marketing are being used to describe this business model [8, 9]. Customers need to feel they have a unique personal relationship with the business.

Current adaptation to the user is still relatively simple. Examples include customized content (e.g., personalized finance pages or news collections), customized recommendations or advertisements based on past purchase behavior, customized

[1] This research has been supported by grants from NSF to the Center for Research on Information Technology and Organizations (CRITO) at the University of California, Irvine. I would like to thank Josef Fink, Judy Kay and Jörg Schreck for their comments on an earlier version of this paper.

M. Bauer, P.J. Gmytrasiewicz, and J. Vassileva (Eds.): UM 2001, LNAI 2109, pp. 303–313, 2001.
©Springer-Verlag Berlin Heidelberg 2001

(preferred) pricing, tailored email alerts, express transactions, etc. [10]. Personalization that is likely to be found on the web in the future includes, e.g.,

- user-tailored text whose level of difficulty is geared towards the presumed level of user expertise;
- tailored presentations that take users' preferences concerning advertisement style and modalities (text, graphics, video) into account;
- personalized tutoring that takes the user's prior knowledge as well as the learning progress into account;
- recommendations that are based on recognized interests and goals of the user; and
- information and recommendations by portable devices that take the user's location and habits into account.

It is very likely that the benefits for users that were found in other application areas of personalized systems will also carry over to web-based systems. The first limited findings that show this is indeed the case were made by Jupiter Communications who report that personalization at 25 reviewed consumer E-commerce sites boosted the number of new customers by 47% [11]. Nielsen NetRatings reports that registered visitors to portal sites (who obtain the privilege to cater the displayed information to their interests) spend over three times longer at their home portals than other users and view 3-4 times more pages [12]. In a recent poll of the Personalization Consortium (an industry advocacy organization), 73% found it helpful and convenient when a web site remembered basic information about them (e.g., their names and addresses), and 50% found it helpful and convenient when a web site remembered more personal information about them (e.g., their preferred colors, music or delivery options) [13].

Personalization not only benefits users but clearly also online vendors. Benefits occur throughout the customer life cycle and include drawing new visitors, turning visitors into buyers, increasing revenues, increasing advertising efficiency, and improving customer retention rate and brand loyalty [11, 14-17]. Nielsen NetRatings [18] report that e-commerce sites offering personalized services convert significantly more visitors into buyers than e-commerce sites that do not offer personalized services. According to [8] and [19], improving customer retention and brand loyalty directly leads to increased profits since it is much cheaper to sell to existing customers than to acquire new ones (the costs of selling to existing customers decrease over time and the spending of loyal customers tends to accelerate and increase over time). Consequently, businesses focus today on retaining those customers with the highest customer life time value, on developing those customers with the most unrealized strategic life time value, and on realizing these profits with each customer individually [15, 20].

Appian [21] estimates that the revenues made by the online personalization industry, including custom development and independent consulting, will reach $1.3 billion in 2000, and $5.3 billion by 2003. Gartner predicts that "by 2003, nearly 85 percent of global 1,000 Web sites will use some form of personalization (0.7 probability)" [22].

2 Benefits Are Currently Offset by Privacy Concerns

At first sight, personalization on the web looks like a win-win technology for both Internet users and Internet sites. However, this optimistic outlook is very likely to be marred by serious privacy concerns of Internet users. Also, it completely ignores the existence of privacy laws that regulate the collection, processing and transfer of personal data.

2.1 Web Users Are Concerned about Privacy on the Web

According to recent polls, web users reported

- being extremely or very concerned about divulging personal information online: 67% [10], 74% [23], and
- being (extremely) concerned about being tracked online: 54% [24], 77% [23].
- Web users are not only concerned but already counteract. They reported
- leaving web sites that required registration information: 41% [25],
- having entered fake registration information: 40% [26], 27% [25], 32% [10], 24% [24], and
- having refrained from shopping online due to privacy concerns, or having bought less: 32% [10]; U.S. 54%[2], Great Britain 32%, Germany 35% [28]; 24% [23].

Internet users who are concerned about privacy are thereby not naïve isolationists, but have very pragmatic demands. They

- want Internet sites to ask for permission to use personal data: 81% [24], and
- are willing to give out personal data for getting something valuable in return: 31% [26], 30% [10], 51% [13].

Traditional websites already collect large amounts of personal data about web visitors[3], and personalized systems even more so since they generally adapt to users the better the more data they have about them. Personalized systems therefore tend to collect as much personal data as possible about users, and "lay them in stock" for possible future usage. This is however incongruent with basic principles of privacy that call for parsimony when collecting personal data. Moreover, personalized systems seek to use personal data originally collected for some purpose, for other purposes as well. This is inconsistent with the principle of purpose-specificity of personal data collection and exploitation.

---

[2] Jupiter estimates that the lost online sales due to privacy concerns amounted to 2.9 billion U.S.$ in 1999, and will be 18 billion U.S.$ in 2002 (which corresponds to a 31% loss in the projected online sales). These figures (among others) recently prompted the U.S. Federal Trade Commission to reverse its previous position and to recommend to Congress the introduction of privacy legislation [27].

[3] Of 1400 random websites reviewed by the Federal Trade Commission in 1998, 92% collected "great amounts of personal data" [27].

2.2. Personalized Websites Must Abide to   Privacy Laws

Most industrial countries have national privacy laws, in some cases already since more than 20 years. In the U.S., privacy legislation is currently restricted to very few types of data (e.g., credit data) and user subgroups (particularly children). However, one can expect that restrictions in the U.S. on the processing of personal data will be tightened in the future, both through self-regulatory contracts of relevant industries mediated by the Federal Trade Commission (e.g. the self-regulatory principles of the online marketing industry [29]) and possibly even through federal privacy laws [30].

Since personalized websites collect personal data, they have to abide to relevant privacy laws. As long as websites are physically located and registered in a single country only, and only serve clients in this country, they are merely subject to the privacy law of their own country (and/or state if a state law exists). If they serve clients abroad, they are often also subject to restrictions imposed by the country or state where the clients reside since data collection about the clients legally takes place at the client's side.[4]

Following the OECD Privacy Guidelines [31], many countries that enacted privacy laws restrict transborder flow of personal data into other countries that do not provide adequate levels of protection or where the re-export would circumvent its domestic privacy legislation.[5] Such provisions exist, e.g., in the European Data Protection Directive [32] that sets minimum standards for the national privacy laws of the European member states. Other countries that have adopted export restrictions for data include Argentina [33], Hong Kong [34], Hungary [35], and Taiwan [36]. In some cases, this prohibition can be overridden by the user consenting to the transborder data transfer, and in a few cases an automatic exception is made if the data is necessary for the fulfillment of a contract.

Rather than regulating the transborder flow of personal data, New Zealand [37] instead subjects foreign agencies who process data that were collected in New Zealand to some articles of its national privacy act, and Australia [38] to nearly its complete national privacy act if the data concern, e.g., Australian citizens and permanent residents.

In the case of the European Union, organizations abroad who collect information from residents of a member state are additionally obliged to appoint a representative for enforcement purposes in one of the European member states.

While enforcement is still of course a very open issue, it should be noted that national Internet service providers in Germany and France have been required to bar domestic web users from foreign material that violates national laws [39]. One can speculate that foreign sites that have been found to violate a national privacy law could be subject to the same fate. Arguments of the foreign site that it is not possible

---

[4] If a site chooses to perform part of the processing in a third country (like storing user data in a user model server abroad), privacy laws of this third country must also be respected.

[5] With regard to adequate protection in the foreign country, the Hong Kong Privacy Ordinance requires that there "is in force in that place any law which is substantially similar to, or serves the same purposes as, this Ordinance." The European Data Protection Directive [32] specifies more vaguely that "the adequacy of the level of protection afforded by a third country must be assessed in the light of all the circumstances surrounding the transfer operation or set of transfer operations".

for them to identify clients from a specific country will not be able to be upheld in the future due to the recent advent of geolocation software based on geographic mapping of IP addresses [40, 41].

3   Impacts of Privacy Laws and Privacy Concerns on Personalized Systems

Privacy laws regulate the kinds of protection that personal data must receive, and the rights that subjects enjoy with regard to personal data about them. Data may usually be collected for specific purposes only, and only those personal data may be collected that are necessary for the indicated purposes (principle of parsimony). They may not be stored longer than is necessary for these purposes, and not further processed or given to third parties in a way incompatible with those purposes. An agency that processes personal data must usually implement appropriate technical and organizational measures to protect these data against accidental or unlawful destruction or accidental loss, alteration, unauthorized disclosure or access. Additional restrictions sometimes exist for very sensitive data (e.g., racial or ethnic origin, political opinions, religious or philosophical beliefs, trade-union membership, and data concerning health or sex life). Except for very sensitive data, most protection requirements can usually be waived with the consent of the user.

The rights that privacy laws give to data subjects are in contrast mostly inalienable and include, e.g., the following ones:

- to receive notice about the purposes of the processing for which the data are intended (as soon as data are collected), and
- to inspect data about themselves, and request blocking, rectification and erasure in case they are incorrect or obsolete, or processed in violation of a privacy law.

The mentioned stipulations of privacy laws already have far-reaching impacts on personalized systems. In most cases they imply that users must be notified about and consent to personalization, and that their user model must be made accessible to them (see Section 4 for a more detailed discussion).

In addition, both users' privacy preferences as well as some privacy laws also have impacts on the personalization methods that may be applied, and consequently on the components that embed such methods. We will illustrate this point in the following, using the Privacy Preferences Protocol P3P as an example for the former, and the recent privacy agreement of the U.S. online marketing industry, the European Data Protection Directive and the German Teleservices Data Privacy Act as examples for the latter.

P3P [42, 43] is currently in the process of being adopted by major manufacturers of web browers [44]. It will allow websites to express their privacy policies and users to express privacy preferences. Customers will be alerted when the proposed privacy policy does not meet their requirements, and they can thereupon grant exceptions or leave the site.[6] With regard to the concerns of personalization, two types of privacy policies can be specified in P3P:

- data-oriented policies: these concern particularly the access to, and recipients and retention of, personal data;
- method-oriented policies: these concern methods used by the site, like automatic personalization without user control in the current session only ("on-time tailoring"), manual tailoring of content and design by the user ("affirmative customization"), and arbitrary analyses and decisions in combination with personally identifiable information ("individual-analysis", "individual-decision") or with pseudonyms only ("pseudo-analysis", "pseudo-decision"). Users can indicate whether or not they consent to the use of these personalization methods.

User's choice with regard to permissible methods for processing personal information is also part of recent self-regulatory principles of the U.S. online marketing industry [29]. According to these principles, users will e.g. be given a choice regarding a merger of personally identifiable information (PII) with non-personally identifiable information, and of PII collected online with PII collected offline. In this way, users can directly control methods that are being used, e.g., for personalized ad targeting or promotional offers on websites.

According to the European Data Protection Directive [32], no fully automated individual decisions are allowed that produce legal effects concerning the data subject or significantly affect him and which are based solely on automated processing of data intended to evaluate certain personal aspects relating to him, such as his or her performance at work, creditworthiness, reliability, conduct, etc. Educational sites located in the EU (e.g., learner-adaptive web-based tutoring systems) that assess learners' proficiency and issue some sort of transcript therefore need to ascertain that students can appeal to a human decision-maker who is able to override decisions of the computer system.[7]

The German Teleservices Data Privacy Act [45], which is widely regarded as being the most stringent world-wide with regard to consumer protection, requires explicit user consent before usage logs of a session may be stored beyond the duration of the session, usage profiles of different services combined, and user profiles constructed in a non-pseudonymous manner. Websites also may not decline service if customers decline to grant approval, but have to abandon these methods or use other methods that are legitimate. All these restrictions can severely impact the permissible methods in personalized systems that are located in Germany.

---

[6]   Note that this "take-it-or-leave-it" approach does not seem to constitute a request for the user's permission, as is required in many privacy laws. The German Dataservice Privacy Protection Law [45] even explicitly prohibits the denial of service if the user declines approval.

[7] This provision has not been included in the Safe Harbor Privacy Principles [46] that were negotiated between the U.S. and the European Commission. Hence U.S. sites that declare themselves as adhering to these principles currently do not have to observe this provision, even when they have students residing in Europe.

4 Catering to Privacy Concerns and Privacy Legislation

Privacy laws differ from country to country, and privacy preferences presumably vary considerably across users. It is therefore not possible to provide general design specifications for personalized systems that ensure that all possible privacy requirements are being met. Instead, privacy will have to be tailored to each user, taking the user's preferences into account as well as the national laws that govern privacy at the location of the personalized system and the location of the user.

However, some architectural and organizational requirements can be identified as required by most privacy laws:
1. Inform the user explicitly about the fact that personalization is taking place, and describe the data that are being collected and inferred for this purpose as well as the adaptations that take place[8].
2. Solicit the user's consent to personalization. An opt-in mechanism, or a conclusive action of the user (like setting his or her own profile), is a minimum requirement for this consent. Some privacy laws require a "written consent" though.
3. If technically possible with reasonable efforts, provide a non-personalized version of the system for users who do not consent to personalization.
4. Provide state of the art security mechanisms that give protection commensurate with the sensitivity of the stored user data (see [47] for an overview).

As an alternative to (1)-(4), anonymous or pseudonymous access to a personalized site can be provided since such a site is then not subject to privacy laws any more as long as individual users cannot be identified. An architecture that supports full personalization while maintaining an arbitrarily high degree of anonymity is described in [47]. The German Teleservices Data Privacy Act [45] even requires the provision of anonymous or pseudonymous access if this is technically possible with reasonable efforts.

The above-mentioned technical and organizational mechanisms can be implemented with existing technology. It should be noted, however, that they constitute minimal answers only to the stipulations of privacy legislation. Several privacy laws may impose far more severe requirements, which in some cases can probably not be met with current technology. In the following, we discuss a few of these provisions and regard them as challenges for future research in the field of user modeling and personalization.

- Support of P3P
  User-adaptive system should support P3P [42, 43], to allow user clients to express their privacy preferences. It is true that in its current form, P3P falls far short of being able to express all privacy preferences regarding personalized systems, and carry out the communication required by privacy laws [48]. It also cannot substitute baseline privacy legislation, as is rightly pointed out in [49]. It is however currently a first interesting start and can probably be extended so that it would allow true communication between the user and a personalized system about privacy options and their advantages and disadvantages. Finding the right extensions to the P3P protocol will open a fruitful field of research.

---

[8] It may also be worthwhile to declare personalization as an explicit purpose of the system.

- Intelligible Disclosure of Data
  The EU Privacy Directive [32] requires the "communication [to the user] in an intelligible form of the data undergoing processing and of any available information as to their source" (emphasis A.K.). Simply displaying the internal representation structures to the user will in most cases probably not qualify as intelligible communication. The communication of user model contents becomes specifically difficult when non-conceptual and implicit representations of user model contents are being used (e.g., connectionist networks, parameter distributions, decision networks, user clusters, etc.).
  Natural language generation techniques, and in some cases visualization techniques, will probably have to be employed to meet these requirements. Summarization (with details on request) and highlighting important data as well as data that deviates from the average will help users understand the system assumptions about them better. Such summarization and verbalization techniques would also be able to be used for reporting purposes, for generating transcripts, etc.
- Disclosure of Methods
  The EU Privacy Directive [32] gives data subjects the right to obtain "knowledge of the logic involved in any automatic processing of data concerning [the user] (at least in the case of fully automated individual decisions)". This requirement can be relatively easily fulfilled in systems that use a static decision logic (e.g. by a canned description of the general program logic with reference to the individual data of the user). It is much harder to meet for several methods that are frequently used in personalized systems, particularly machine learning techniques where the "decision rules" are not explicitly represented .
- Provision of organizational/technical means for users to rectify user model entries
  Virtually all privacy laws require the implementation of organizational and technical means that enable data subjects to inspect and possibly rectify personal data about them. While online inspection and rectification is not specifically required, this is probably the best realization for web-based services. Caution must however be exercjsed to distinguish between data that the user may change at any time (like personal preferences), data that the user should not change without special care (like system assumptions about what the user does not know), and data whose incorrectness the user may first have to prove (like his or her social security number).
- User model servers that support a number of anonymization methods
  The reference architecture for secure and anonymous personalized systems proposed in [47] requires users to employ a specific anonymization method. Users may however wish to use competing methods. User model servers should accommodate such preferences.
- Tailoring of user modeling methods to privacy preferences and legislation
  As discussed above, users' privacy preferences and the privacy laws that apply to the interaction with them may have an impact on the permissible user modeling and user modeling methods. Architectures for user modeling servers will have to be developed that allow for the configuration of methods (or more precisely, of components implementing these methods) dependent upon the current privacy constraints. The reconfiguration must be able to be performed dynamically at runtime. The architecture should also allow for a graceful degradation of the degree of personalization if user preferences or privacy legislation prohibit the application of

certain methods. Alternative methods that are permissible should be used in such situations, if available.

5   Conclusion

This paper discussed the impacts of privacy concerns and privacy legislation on the deployment of personalized systems. It demonstrated that these impacts are far-reaching: privacy concerns of Internet users are likely to be an impediment to the acceptance of personalized systems, and recent privacy legislation in many countries has serious consequences for the legitimacy of quite a few methods that are used in personalized systems. While this has already been suspected more than a decade ago [50, 51], it can now be substantiated with data from opinion polls and on the basis of modern privacy laws that have since stepped out of the datafile and batch processing paradigms.

A number of recommendations were given how personalized systems can cater better to privacy concerns and stipulations from privacy legislation. Common requirements can be fulfilled with traditional technology already. Most privacy laws however also contain requirements whose fulfillment requires technology that still needs to be researched. Methods that need to be looked into range from natural-language generation to dynamic configuration management at runtime.

An important consideration was that a single solution for all privacy issues does not exist. Privacy preferences and privacy stipulations differ from user to user and from country to country. They therefore need to be catered dynamically to each individual user, taking his or her preferences and the jurisdiction at both the system's as well as the user's location into account.

References

1. Corbett, A., McLaughlin, M., and Scarpinatto, K. C.: Modeling Student Knowledge: Cognitive Tutors in High School and College. User Modeling and User-Adapted Interaction 10 (2000) 81-108.
2. Strachan, L., Anderson, J., Sneesby, M., and Evans, M.: Minimalist User Modelling in a Complex Commercial Software System. User Modeling and User-Adapted Interaction 10 (2000) 109-146.
3. Linton, F. and Schaefer, H.-P.: Recommender Systems for Learning: Building User and Expert Models through Long-Term Observation of Application Use. User Modeling and User-Adapted Interaction 10 (2000) 181-208.
4. Billsus, D. and Pazzani, M. J.: User Modeling for Adaptive News Access. User Modeling and User-Adapted Interaction 10 (2000) 147-180.
5. Kobsa, A.: Adapting Web Information to Disabled and Elderly Users (invited paper). WebNet-99, Honolulu, HI, (1999).
6. Shapira, B., Shoval, P., and Hanani, U.: Information Filtering: Overview of Issues, Research and Systems. User Modeling and User-Adapted Interaction (forthcoming).
7. Kobsa, A., Koenemann, J., and Pohl, W.: Personalized Hypermedia Presentation Techniques for Improving Customer Relationships. The Knowledge Engineering Review (forthcoming), http://www.ics.uci.edu/~kobsa/papers/2001-KER-kobsa.pdf

8. Peppers, D. and Rogers, M.: The One to One Future: Building Relationships One Customer at a Time. New York, N.Y.: Currency Doubleday, (1993).
9. Peppers, D. and Rogers, M.: Enterprise One to One: Tools for Competing in the Interactive Age. New York, N.Y.: Currency Doubleday, (1997).
10. The Privacy Best Practise. Forrester Research, Cambridge, MA (1999).
11. Hof, R., Green, H., and Himmelstein, L.: Now it's YOUR WEB. Business Week, October 5, (1998) 68-75.
12. Thompson, M.: Registered Visitors Are a Portal's Best Friend. The Industry Standard, June 7, 1999, http://www.thestandard.net
13. Personalization & Privacy Survey. Personalization Consortium, Edgewater Place, MA (2000), http://www.personalization.org/SurveyResults.pdf
14. Bachem, C.: Profilgesttiztes Online Marketing. Personalisierung im E- Commerce, Hamburg, Germany, (1999).
15. Cooperstein, D., Delhagen, K., Aber, A., and Levin, K.: Making Net Shoppers Loyal. Forrester Research, Cambridge, MA June 1999.
16. Hagen, P. R., Manning, H., and Souza, R.: Smart Personalization. Forrester Research, Cambridge, MA (1999).
17. Schafer, J. B., Konstan, J., and Riedl, J.: Recommender Systems in E-Commerce. ACM Conference on Electronic Commerce (EC99), Denver, CO, (1999) 158-166.
18. More Concentrated than the Leading Brand. ICONOCAST, 1999, http://www.iconocast.com/icono-archive/icono.102199.html
19. Reichheld, F.: The Loyalty Effect. Boston, MA: Harvard Business School Press (1996).
20. Peppers, D., Rogers, M., and Dorf, B.: The One to One Fieldbook. New York, NY: Currency Doubleday (1999).
21. Appian Web Personalization Report. Appian, 2000, http://www.appiancorp.com/ awpr.asp
22. Abrams, C., Bernstein, M., deSisto, R., Drobik, A., and Herschel, G.: E-Business: The Business Tsunami. Gartner Group Symposium/ITxpo, Cannes, France (1999).
23. DePallo, M.: AARP National Survey on Consumer Preparedness and E-Commerce: A Survey of Computer Users Age 45 and Older. AARP, Washington, D.C. March 2000.
24. Fox, S., Rainie, L., Horrigan, J., Lenhart, A., Spooner, T., and Carter, C.: Trust and Privacy Online: Why Americans Want to Rewrite the Rules. The Pew Internet & American Life Project, Washington, DC (2000).
25. eTRUST Internet Privacy Study: Summary of Market Survey Results. Boston Consulting Group, 1997,
26. GVU's 10th WWW User Survey. Graphics, Visualization and Usability Lab, Georgia Tech, 1998, http://www.cc.gatech.edu/gvu/user_surveys/survey-1998-10/
27. Privacy Online: Fair Information Practices in the Electronic Marketplace. A Report to Congress. Federal Trade Commission, Washington, D.C. May 2000, http://www.ftc.gov/ reports/privacy2000/privacy2000.pdf.
28. IBM Multi-National Consumer Privacy Survey. IBM Oct. 1999. http://www.ibm.com/ services/files/privacy_survey_oct991.pdf
29. Self-Regulatory Principles for Online Preference Marketing by Network Advisers. Network Advertising Initiative, 2000, http://www.ftc.gov/os/2000/07/NAI7-10Final.pdf
30. U.S. Lawmakers Examine Pros, Cons of Privacy Law. SiliconValley.com, 1 March 2001, http://www.siliconvalley.com/docs/news/tech/039799.htm
31. Recommendation of the Council Concerning Guidelines Governing the Protection of Privacy and Transborder Flows of Personal Data., OECD, 1980, http://www.oecd.org//dsti/sti/ it/secur/prod/PRIV-EN.HTM
32. Directive 95/46/EC of the European Parliament and of the Council of 24 October 1995 on the Protection of Individuals with Regard to the Processing of Personal Data and on the Free Movement of such Data. Official Journal of the European Communities (1995), p. 31. http://158.169.50.95:10080/legal/en/dataprot/directiv/directiv.html
33. Argentinia Personal Data Protection Act., 2000, http://www.privacyinternational. org/countries/argentina/argentine-dpa.html

34. Hong Kong Personal Data (Privacy) Ordinance, 1995, http://www.privacy.com.hk/contents.html
35. Hungary Act LXIII of 1992 on the Protection of Personal Data and the Puclicity of Data of Public Interest., 1992, http://www.privacy.org/pi/countries/hungary/hungary_privacy_law_1992.html
36. Taiwan Computer-Processed Personal Data Protection Law., 1995, http://virtualtaiwan.com/members/guide/legal/cpdpl.htm
37. New Zealand Privacy Act., 1993, http://www.knowledge-basket.co.nz/privacy/recept/rectop.html
38. Australian Privacy Act., 2000 http://www.privacy.gov.au/publications/privacy88.pdf
39. NYT: Welcome to the Web. Passport, Please? New York Times, March 15, 2001.
40. GeoPoint., 2001, http://www.quova.com/service.htm
41. GeoGrid., 2001, http://www.ingeodesy.com/
42. Reagle, J. and Cranor, L.: The Platform for Privacy Preferences. Communications of the ACM 42 (1999) 48-55.
43. The Platform for Privacy Preferences 1.0 (P3P1.0) Specification., 2000, http://www.w3.org/TR/2000/WD-P3P-20001018/
44. Microsoft Announces Privacy Enhancements for Windows, Internet Explorer. Microsoft Corporation, 2000, http://www.microsoft.com/PressPass/press/2000/ jun00/p3ppr.asp
45. German Teleservices Data Protection Act., 1997, http://www.datenschutz-berlin.de/recht/de/rv/tk_med/iukdg_en.htm#a2
46. The Seven Safe Harbor Principles. Federal Trade Commission, 2000, http://europa.eu.int/comm/internal_market/en/media/dataprot/news/shprinciples.pdf
47. Schreck, J.: Security and Privacy in User Models. Dept. of Mathematics and Computer Science, Univ. of Essen, Germany (2000) http://www.ics.uci.edu/~kobsa/phds/schreck.pdf
48. Grimm, R. and Rossnagel, A.: Can P3P Help to Protect Privacy Worldwide? ACM Multimedia 2000 Workshops, Los Angeles, CA (2000) 157-160.
49. Pretty Poor Privacy: An Assessment of P3P and Internet Privacy. Electronic Privacy Information Center and Junkbusters (2000), http://www.epic.org/reports/prettypoorprivacy.html
50. Kobsa, A.: User Modeling in Dialog Systems: Potentials and Hazards. AI and Society 4 (1990) 214-240.
51. Herrmann, T.: Benutzermodellierung und Datenschutz (User Modeling and Data Protection). Datenschutz und Datensicherheit 14 (1990) 352-359.

Heavyweight Applications of Lightweight User Models: A Look at Collaborative Filtering, Recommender Systems, and Real-Time Personalization

Joseph A. Konstan

University of Minnesota

Real-time personalization is one of the goals behind building eective and accurate user models. A wide variety of applications, from graphical user interfaces to information filtering and retrieval systems to electronic commerce displays, can better serve users if they adapt to user wants and needs. Many personalization systems take a heavyweight approach to personalization–extensive modeling of the problem domain, user tasks, and user preferences. While these heavyweight models can be very successful, they can be extremely challenging to build and adapt, and the eort involved can lead system designers to ďut corners"and reduce their fielity and eectiveness.

A dierent approach, and one that is used in a wide variety of commercial recommender systems, is to build lightweight models that are almost entirely generic, and to rely on the presence of large amounts of data to overcome the reduced "intelligence" of the model. Collaborative filtering, the technology behind many of these recommenders, is often implemented using only minimal assumptions (i.e., that user preferences are relatively consistent) and highly generic data (i.e., preference or purchase data).

This talk explores recommender systems, focusing on their strengths and limitations when used to achieve real-time personalization, and comparing them with richer, knowledge-based models. This exploration includes a tour of deployed research and commercial applications, viewed from both the developer's and the user's perspective.

M. Bauer, P.J. Gmytrasiewicz, and J. Vassileva (Eds.): UM 2001, LNAI 2109, p. 314, 2001.

Eye Tracking:
A Rich Source of Information for User Modeling

Sandra P. Marshall

Department of Psychology
San Diego State University

This presentation focuses on two aspects of eye-tracking research: using point-of-gaze information to look at shifts in attention and using changes in pupil diameter to know when cognitive demands occur. Both aspects are immediately important in cognitive modeling because as modelers, we want to understand as much as we can about individuals' underlying cognitive processes. Eye tracking yields very precise behavioral and physiological data that contribute to our understanding.

The presentation describes several research examples in which eye-tracking data have been incorporated into basic cognitive models. Video clips illustrate the basic tasks and the ways that individuals' eyes respond when they attempt to complete the tasks. Graphic representations highlight and quantify the eye movements, providing colorful traces that show the position of the point-of-gaze every 4 msec. And, plots of pupil change over time show the correlation between effortful cognitive processing and stimulus difficulty.

Research examples range from simple arithmetic calculations to complex military situations. The emphasis is on the ways that eye-tracking information can facilitate the modeling process, and the strengths and weakness of eye tracking methodologies are examined.

Finally, the presentation showcases a few commercial applications in which eye-tracking analyses have yielded important insights into human behavior. These examples show a vital connection between theoretical development of cognitive models and practical adoption of their results.

M. Bauer, P.J. Gmytrasiewicz, and J. Vassileva (Eds.): UM 2001, LNAI 2109, p. 315, 2001.
© Springer-Verlag Berlin Heidelberg 2001

Author Index

Lecture Notes in Artificial Intelligence (LNAI)

Lecture Notes in Computer Science